D0875318

"Focusing on process in addition to results differentiates lean thinking from conventional thinkers' 'metrics'-driven sole focus on results. Schonberger reinforces the distinction, emphasizing process data, senior leaders' presence at the point of execution, and asking those performing the process to help set goals for improving it."

—David Mann
  Manager Lean Management and O.D.
  Steelcase, Inc.
  Author of *Creating a Lean Culture*

"Schonberger has hit the nail on the head—clear, concise, to-the-point—just what a book on Lean Best Practices should be. Reading Best Practices will result in lots of 'that's exactly what I see at work!' moments."

—Bob Miller
  Director of Advanced Factory Management, Advanced Bionics Corp

"One of the world's foremost authorities on leading-edge management practices, Dick Schonberger once more sheds new light on the practices of best-performing companies. This time focusing on process improvement, his *Best Practices in Lean Six Sigma Process Improvement* gives readers a wholly new understanding of the promises and pitfalls of lean and six sigma."

—H. Thomas Johnson
  Professor of Operations Management
  Portland State University
  2001 & 2007 Shingo Research Prize Laureate
  Coauthor of *Profit Beyond Measure*

"Over the decades there has been a constancy and a depth in Schonberger's work. This book has lessons that take us right back to the fundamentals of involving everyone in improving our processes so that we increase our ability to meet our Universal Customer Wants."

—Carla Geddes
  Founder, High Performance Consortium, Australia

"This is a remarkable book. It should be required reading for every executive struggling to make his company successful in the global economy—both today and tomorrow. Richard tells us (and shows us based upon extensive research not suppositions) that Lean is a journey not a destination. The journey is long with extensive rewards to those whose are not distracted and persevere. Richard provides ample recommendations to make that long journey a successful one."

—Michael Paris
  President, Paris: Consultants, Inc.

BEST PRACTICES IN LEAN SIX SIGMA PROCESS IMPROVEMENT

A Deeper Look

RICHARD SCHONBERGER

John Wiley & Sons, Inc.

Library of Congress Cataloging-in-Publication Data:

Schonberger, Richard.
    Best practices in lean six sigma process improvement/Richard Schonberger.
        p. cm.
    Includes index.
    ISBN 978-0-470-16886-8 (cloth)
    1. Six sigma (Quality control standard) 2. Total quality management. 3. Production management. I. Title.
    HD62.15.S365 2008
    658.4′013—dc22   2007022155

Printed in the United States of America
10 9 8 7 6 5 4 3 2 1

Contents

PART VI

WHY INDUSTRIES RANK WHERE THEY DO   **213**

Epilogue   **273**

Index   **275**

Preface

Like many who are veterans of some sort of crusade, my latter-day role includes trying to make sense out of the confused state of process improvement. The easy way would be just to rely on my experience, and, on that, to offer up opinions on what is going well and what is not. Nobody would be interested. For anyone to want to look over *Best Practices*, strong research and teased-out facts would have to form the basis. I am talking about direct research: carefully referenced data about best practices in process improvement.

The main sources must be the originators. They include individuals who have developed and articulated the ideas, people such as W. Edwards Deming, Kaoru Ishikawa, and Shigeo Shingo. But much of development of best practices comes from companies, not individuals. Thus, the companies themselves must be primary sources. Direct research relies mostly on these two sources, and not lofty, unsubstantiated claims, theories, opinions, and assumptions.

Direct research runs into obstacles, because some of the manufacturers, wholesalers, distributors, and retailers that this book studies have become cautious about revealing much of anything. But for the 1,400 publicly held, global companies in my main research database, public records are available, including audited data required by regulatory agencies. I've found a lot in such records, and the book is peppered with findings there from.

Direct research includes going to present and former company executives and managers, including at least a few in privately held companies. Comparing and contrasting these people's spoken or printed statements about what went right or wrong over time provides further enlightenment.

As for the book's content, it presents things about process improvement that you (your company, your business unit) didn't know—or know but simply do not practice, or once practiced but let go. I didn't know these things either, until all that research revealed unexpected tendencies and truths, and until probing unearthed reasons why. I didn't know until I did and redid the math, and added up the data, the expert explanations, and the trend lines to expose the bigger picture.

In the summer of 2006, the title of a new book caught my eye: *Hard Facts, Dangerous Half-Truths and Total Nonsense: Profiting from Evidence-Based Management*, by respected author Jeffrey Pfeffer and co-author Robert Sutton.[1] Since I've tried to underpin the message in *Best Practices* with hard data—lots of it—I thought I might find kinship in the Pfeffer/Sutton work.

Big disappointment—right off the bat in a segment called "Casual Benchmarking," pages 6 through 8. The authors take United Airlines to task for trying to compete in California by imitating Southwest Airlines, including "copying Southwest's legendary quick turnarounds." United Shuttle was a failure, they say, because

"Southwest's success is based on its culture and management philosophy. . . ." Culture maybe; but philosophy? I thought the book was to be about facts and evidence. Citing philosophy as the reason for a business phenomenon is rather like saying it stems from alignment of the planets.

Yes, I know it is not uncommon to find the philosophy label attached to management practices. In the early 1980s, the West discovered *just-in-time* and *total quality control*, which consisted of lengthy lists of operating practices. Consultants and book authors became so enamored of the power of these practices to uplift sick manufacturers that by the middle of that decade some started making the philosophy assertion. The *APICS Dictionary* chiseled the idea not in stone but into several editions of itself. No one has bothered to change the definition, which in the 2005 edition begins: "Just-in-Time (JIT)—A philosophy of manufacturing based on . . . ."[2]

No one calls JIT a *philosophy* any more. That word has re-attached itself to a preferred term, the *Toyota production system (TPS)*. Pfeffer and Sutton follow their discussion of United Airlines' failure with one about wrong-headed attempts by U.S. automakers to compete. The automakers' emulation of Toyota's practices was inadequate because "the secret to Toyota's success is not a set of techniques but its *philosophy*. . . ."[3] There is good stuff in the Pfeffer/Sutton book. But management philosophy claims are a poor substitute for hard facts.

Best Practices does a lot of ranking. It rank-orders the regions of the world, and also the dominant industrial sectors, in long-term *leanness*, which you may think cannot be done reliably. It can. Very good data are available on the most visible, fungible, and encompassing measure of leanness, namely absence of inventory. Data go back tens of years for hundreds of companies in many countries, so that the rankings detect not just who has become lean lately, but the *elite*—those that have sustained improvement for many years.

The book names the companies with the world's longest, steepest rates of improvement in leanness, then attempts to examine how they got that way. The expectation was that a lot of them would have discovered and exploited somewhat the same set of best practices. That turns out to have been incorrect. The deeper the investigation, the clearer it became: There are many ways to become lean.

In this book, when I say "lean" I mean *Lean* with a capital *L*. It has to be lean *with total quality*. They go together like Fred and Ginger, or pencil and paper, or rhythm and blues. Lean won't work without quality. Quality in turn runs into blind alleys in an unlean, batch-and-queue environment. Poor quality produces scrap and rework and injects extra flow-time loops to fix problems that never should have occurred in the first place.

As for terminology, lean is so well named that it has built-in endurance.[4] Six sigma, on the other hand, is likely before long to go up on the easel to be painted over—with a new name and gussied up with new trappings. Even *lean* will get renamed sooner or later. Whatever the names, there will always be flaws and faults needing to see the light of day and to be amended and corrected. A good deal of that is included in some of the chapters herein.

The best-known set of practices out there today I'll call the *lean core*. Their main elements are cells, kanban/pull system, quick setup, small lots, supplier partnership, total productive maintenance, and so on—practices that originated in Japan, mostly at Toyota. The research shows that some companies are doing very well with the lean core. Most are not. Anyway, the lean core is mostly inward looking—at things operational.

Some of the world's leanest have found other ways to maintain a long, steeply inclined improvement trend. There is compelling evidence that lean's highest-potential gains are not in operations but external to the company. By *external*, I mean the pipelines, a hot potato for which neither supplier nor customer wants to be responsible. Through accounting games the huge problem-filled pipelines are made to disappear—from your books, anyway. Dealing with this issue requires a blend of close collaboration and tough love among suppliers and customers. A few companies, mainly retailers, not manufacturers, are the pacesetters here.

In some companies, the most effective route to leanness is through product design: standardized parts, modular assemblies, and so on. Simplifying the design has leanness effects that snowball through process after successive process. A whole industrial sector, electronics, has elevated itself on the leanness scale through outsourcing, creating, in the bargain, a large new sector—electronic manufacturing services. Other companies have improved their leanness for years through astute acquisitions, mergers, and divestitures. This book identifies some acquirers that have developed best practices by mining the expertise and competencies of the acquired. It names others prone to squandering the opportunity.

The lean core seems to have everything going for it: simplicity, low cost, common sense, and relatively quick payoff. Yet it tends to fade, chiefly for lack of an overriding Big Idea that companies, executives, marketers, suppliers, customers, the work force, and other stakeholders can rally around. It is too easy for companies to cherry-pick from the lean core, and to neglect the difficult but more beneficial elements of the core. The book elaborates on this issue, and gives examples of companies that rely on a truly Big Idea as still another way—and an especially effective one—of achieving a continuing, high rate of process improvement.

The book also plunges into *metrics madness*. The topic includes the aforementioned accounting sleight-of-hand that removes pipeline inventories from the collective consciousness. The topic includes, as well, worthy metrics that, when pushed, inevitably have backlash effects. The discussions go on to show how unwise uses of management metrics tend to drive out attention to process data, which is the real key to process improvement.

Best Practices has no single, dominant theme. It is just the topic itself, best practices in process improvement, and a wide variety of findings about that topic that have been unearthed through research. The following is a listing of companies discussed in this book as examples and sources of the research findings. Many more companies get briefly mentioned.

NOTES

1. Jeffrey Pfeffer and Robert I. Sutton, *Hard Facts, Dangerous Half-Truths and Total Nonsense: Profiting from Evidence-Based Management* (Cambridge: Harvard Business School Press, 2006), p. x. In a pro–con dialogue, *Academy of Management Review*, 31, no. 4 (October 2006), a con view, has it that evidence-based management (EBM) is a sham because proofs are weak—as compared with medicine where EBM is well established; see Mark Learmonth, "Is There Such a Thing as 'Evidence-Based Management'?," pp. 1089–1090. Disputing Learmonth's opinion is Denise M. Rousseau, "Keeping an Open Mind about Evidence-Based Management," pp. 1091–1093.

2. John H. Blackstone Jr. and James F. Cox III, eds., *APICS Dictionary*, 11th ed. (Alexandria, VA: American Production and Inventory Control Society, 2005), p. 58.

3. Pfeffer and Sutton, op. cit., p. 7.

4. The term *lean* production or lean manufacturing apparently had its origin, at least its published one, in John F. Krafcik, "Triumph of the Lean Production System," *Sloan Management Review*, vol. 30, no. 1 (1988), pp. 41–52.

Adam Opel (Germany)

Advanced Bionics

Alaris Medical

Alvis (U.K.)

American Standard

Amer Group (Finland)

Amore Pacific (Korea)

Apple

Atlas Copco (Sweden)

Auto Nation

Avnet

BAE Systems (U.K.)

Barilla (Italy)

Batesville Casket Co.

Bausch & Lomb

Baxter International

Benetton (Italy)

Boeing

Bombardier

Bridgestone/Firestone
(Japan/U.S.)

Brush Engineered Materials

Buick

Cardinal Health

Caterpillar

Champion Enterprises

Church & Dwight

Control Data

Costco

Cryovac, Div. of Sealed Air

Cutler-Hammer

Dana

Danaher

Dassault (France)

Deere & Co.

Dell Inc.

Delphi

Daihatsu (Japan)

DJO, Inc.

Dorbyl (South Africa)

Eastman Kodak

Eaton

Emerson Electric

Ericsson (Sweden)

Excel Pacific Diecasting (Australia)

Flextronics

Fluke Division, Danaher

Ford

Freudenberg/NOK (German-Japanese joint venture)

Fuji Heavy Industries (Japan)

Gamma Holding (Netherlands)

General Dynamics

General Electric

General Motors

Genie Industries

Genlyte

Genuine Parts

Gerber Scientific

Gillette

GKN (U.K.)

Global Engine Manufacturing Alliance (GEMA)

Goodrich

Gorman-Rupp

Graco Inc.

Hach, Div. of Danaher

Harley-Davidson

Haworth

Heineken (Netherlands)

Hero AG (Switzerland)

Hewlett-Packard

Hindustan Motors (India)

Honda (Japan)

Hon Industries (HNI)

Honeywell

Hormel

HUI Manufacturing

Hutchinson Technology

IBM

Illinois Tool Works

Imperial Oil (Canada)

Intel

International Game Technology

Ishikawajima-Harima Heavy (Japan)

Isuzu (Japan)

Italcementi (Italy)

ITT Industries

JLG

John Lewis Partnerships (U.K.)

Kawasaki (Japan)

Kenworth

Kinnevik (Sweden)

Kubota (Japan)

Lam Research

Lear

Legrand (France)

Lockheed Martin

Loral

Magna International (Canada)

Mars

Mattel

MeadWestVaco (Canada)

Medtronic

Metaldyne

Milliken

Milton Plastics (India)

Mine Safety Appliances

Mitsubishi Electric (Japan)

Nacco

Nampak (South Africa)

NEC (Japan)

Nihon Radiator (Japan)

Nippon Sheet Glass (Japan)

Nissan (Japan)

Nokia (Finland)

Nordson

Nordstrom

Northrop-Grumman

Nypro

O.C. Tanner

Office Depot

Paccar

Pacifica (Australia)

Pacific Scientific

Parker Hannifin

Pepsico

Petro-Canada (Canada)

Peugeot-Citroën (France)

Phillips NV

Phillips Plastics

Pick 'N Pay (South Africa)

Pier One Imports

Pilkington (U.K.)

Plamex (Mexico)

Powerware (Mexico)

Porsche (Germany)

Precor

Procter & Gamble

Prolec (Mexico)

Queen City Steel Treating Co.

Raytheon

Renault (France)

Renold (U.K.)

Rheinmetall (Germany)

Rohm & Haas

R.W. Lyall

Saint-Gobain (France)

Scania (Sweden)

Schlumberger (Netherlands Antilles)

Schweitzer Engineering Laboratories

Sealed Air

Shell Canada (Canada)

Siemens Energy & Automation (Germany)

Skandinavisk Tobakskompagni (Denmark)

Simpson Lumber

SKF (Sweden)

Smart Car (France)

Smurfit-Stone Container

Sony (Japan)

Starrett, L.S.

Steelcase

SWEP (Sweden)

Takata Seat Belts (Mexico)

Takata Seat Belts (Japan)

Talles (France)

Tecumseh

Terex

Tesco (U.K.)

Textron

Thomas & Betts

Thor

3Com

3M Corp.

Tiffany

Toro

Toyota Motor (Japan)

Upright-Ireland (Ireland)

Volkswagen (Germany)

Volvo (Sweden)

Wal-Mart

Warner Robbins Air Logistics Center

Webster Plastics

Western Digital

Westinghouse

Wiremold

Woolworths (Australia)

Xerox

Yazaki (Japan)

Zara, Div. of Inditex (Spain)

Part I
Hyper-competition

Four decades ago, Japanese manufacturers in many industries were embroiled in Darwinist battles. The conquering few emerged supremely toughened, primed for turning their attack forces toward the world's only (at that time) mass market: the United States.

Lucky for the U.S., as intensive competition had created the greats of Japan (Sony, Mitsubishi Electric, Honda, Canon, etc.) so would it harden the likes of Johnson Controls and Hewlett-Packard, 3M and Emerson Electric, Costco and 7-Eleven. The word (about quality-at-the-source and quick-response operations) spread fast among targeted industries, preparing them for the emerging globalization of competition.

Later, across the ocean, when the Margaret Thatcher regime pried open Britain's trade barriers, leading Japanese automakers settled into the U.K.'s industrial heartland. Nissan was first, opening an assembly plant in Sunderland on the northeast coast.[1] Meanwhile, esteemed Japanese and newly rejuvenated American electronics companies were moving in large numbers into southern Scotland to form Silicon Glen. Lucky for the U.K., which, from the Japanese and American transplants, learned its lessons in world-class manufacturing ahead of challengers on the European continent. Lucky also for Canada, Ireland, South Africa, and Australia. Those English-speaking countries quickly gathered in and began applying the outpouring of English-language lore on the new best practices in manufacturing management.

The 1980s were the heady days of just-in-time (JIT) and total quality control (TQC). But just as what goes up must come down, what's hot eventually cools off. By the late 1980s and into the 1990s, industry was tiring of JIT/TQC. A ready solution was to change the names. JIT was rejuvenated under the new name, *lean*. TQC, based on the quality sciences, was retitled, and gradually watered down, as total quality management (TQM), then re-juiced in the 1990s by black-belt/green-belt pizzazz under the six sigma banner. Whatever the names, several whole industries never did seriously subscribe to the large set of practices making up the continuous-process-improvement regime.

Backtracking a bit, continental Europe, well aware of what was going on in the United States and then the U.K., was nevertheless falling behind. This happened for a couple of reasons: one was retention of barriers to foreign producers. Europe did not want to tangle with Japanese automakers and their triple-threat capability: better quality, quicker throughput, and lower cost. While the U.K. was offering investment opportunities to bring Nissan in, "the French and Germans huffed and puffed about Britain becoming a 'Japanese aircraft carrier anchored off Europe.' "[2] The other reason was denial, especially by Germany and Sweden. Their attitude was, "Our manufacturing is world renowned; the Japanese system is not for us." So the Continent continued to drown itself in inventory as its manufacturers clung to long-reigning batch-and-queue methods and inspected-in quality. Those practices never were sound (we just didn't know any better) and now were competitively untenable.

By 2005, all had changed. Sweden and its Nordic neighbors, Denmark, Finland, and Norway, had become the world's grand champions of lean. Denial was long gone throughout Europe, and batch-and-queue management was widely disparaged, at least in the more globally competitive industrial sectors.

The turn toward lean, in Scandinavia and beyond, was to be expected; global competition favors what works. The great surprises are these:

- Japan, crucible of JIT/lean and total quality, has sunk to the bottom of all regions in ability of its companies to sustain a lean trend.

- Toyota, the origin of most of the elements of lean, and still regarded as lean's platinum standard, has a 13-year record of greatly fattening up on inventory.

- Confounding expectations of progress, relatively few companies in the world are able to mount and sustain a long-range leanness trend.

- Retailing, distribution, and logistics have emerged as founts of innovation in lean management. Manufacturers, who once prodded retailers and distributors, now should be, and increasingly are, taking lean lessons from them.

- Lean's common core practices, developed and honed in Japan, especially at Toyota, are one way to achieve sustained lean. But there are a variety of other unsung ways that are producing excellent results in certain companies and industries.

These five points, along with most of what has been said in this introduction, are backed up with concrete data. The four chapters in Part I provide initial information, with emphasis on broad-swath trends and emergent high standards of excellence. More detailed data support discussions of finer-grained issues in later sections and chapters.

NOTES

1. Thatcher, Prime Minister from 1979 to 1990, participated in the opening of the U.K.'s first Japanese auto assembly plant, Nissan in Sunderland in northeast England, in September 1986 (www.sunderland.gov.uk). The first such plant in the United States was Honda, in Marysville, Ohio, in 1979 (ohio.honda.com).
2. "Fight for the Nissan Micra" (no author), www.thisisthenortheast.co.uk, January 26, 2001.

Chapter 1

Magnitude Advances in Competitive Standards and Technologies

In the healing trades, blood-letting is *out*. Leeching has gone much the same way. But putting leeches on wounds has been found to draw extra supplies of blood to the wound, thereby healing it faster. Leeching works, though the practice has limited application.

In getting work done, batch-and-queue management is going the way of blood-letting. Lean in all things is taking over. As for process quality, the inspection-based mode, once the norm, is like leeching: by no means the preferred way, but there if needed. Modern practices in lean and quality are, like those in medicine, a mixed bag. Some treatments have broad curing powers, others are weak or limited, still others are dubious, and a few that have fallen into neglect deserve resurrection. A central aim in *Best Practices* is to critically sort out these treatments. This initial chapter provides a bit of historical perspective.

HOW ARE WE DOING?

Are management practices any better today than 30, 60, 90, 120 years ago? The answer is *much better*, as applied to both people and processes.

First, let's look at people. In about 1975, in an earlier life as a university professor (after a still earlier one as a practicing industrial engineer), I frequently took students on plant tours. One was to a Goodyear plant that made rubber drive belts and hoses. At about 1:30 in the afternoon we walked down a corridor past the plant's cafeteria. Tables were filled with production employees playing cards; yet the day shift wasn't over until 3:30. What were they doing there? Our guide explained: They had met their quota. They couldn't go home until 3:30 and wouldn't do any other work but their designated job. Moreover, as was the norm back then, the company was disinclined to spend money to train employees to do other work, much less endow them with responsibilities beyond their narrow tasks.

Fifteen years later, broadened responsibilities were all the rage in industry. I was an invited speaker at a 1990 conference of human-resource directors for the Pharmaceutical Manufacturers Association. Moderator Jonathan Griggs, HR director for Park Davis, told the audience how HR had changed: In the 1960s, he said, it was "beat 'em and cheat 'em." In the 1970s, it was "cheat 'em but make 'em feel good." In the 1980s, it was "allow them

3

a voice but retain control." Finally, in the 1990s, it would be "employee ownership." The other HR directors gave him a rousing hand. I did too, because though ownership still had a long way to go in most companies, employee ownership had never even been a popular notion. That changed with discovery of employee involvement's contributory role in Japan's ascension as industrial powerhouse.

How were companies to carry out the notion? Three prominent initiatives, quality circles, total quality control (later changed to total quality management), and total productive maintenance (TPM), would provide platforms for employee ownership—otherwise called *empowerment*. The *total* in such terms meant *all employees* and *all processes*.[1] Quality would no longer be the purview of the quality department; rather, first responsibility shifts to the operators. The quality department was not demoted, but elevated: to teacher, facilitator, and auditor. Similarly, maintenance would no longer be owned by the maintenance department. Under TPM, operators take primary ownership of their equipment. Maintenance retains responsibility for plant-wide facilities management; also, with operator help, installs, retrofits, upgrades, and overhauls equipment; and serves as facilitator, trainer, and monitor. It is sad but true (based on telling evidence sprinkled throughout this book) that many companies once pursuing these concepts have backslid. That, I suppose, is to be expected: the two-steps-forward, one-step-back phenomenon.

Let's go back 120 years, or to almost anywhere in the nineteenth or eighteenth centuries. Here are two reports from that era, not about people-management practices but inability to do much of anything through people:[2]

> All hands drunk; Jacob Ventling hunting; molders all agree to quit work and went to the beach. Peter Cox very drunk and gone to bed.

> Men worked no more than two or three hours a day; spent the remainder in the beer saloon playing pinochle.

But we needn't go back a century or more to see profound improvements in the management of people. Exhibit 1.1 shows this from the perspective of the employee. The data come from identical surveys of a cross-section of U.S. employees in 1977 and 2002.[3] Aside from the one about taking breaks, the questions are substantive. They relate closely to what best practices in process improvement call for from the work force: making decisions, learning, responsibility, the job, creativity, meaning, and use of skills and abilities.

Turning from people to *processes* brings into play a large set of concepts and tools of lean and its aliases (just-in-time, flow), close partners (quality), and extensions (e.g., world-class excellence). It is a well-known list that needs no detailing here (but see Chapter 10). It is sufficient for now to draw broad contrasts with discredited practices of long ago.

We need not go back far. Prior to about 120 years ago, codified management did not exist. Outstanding process management happened, then died out. Consider the Arsenal of Venice in the fifteenth century. Ten ships per day were sequentially outfitted, just in time, as they floated along a canal past loading stations on the loop,

Exhibit 1.1   Survey of U.S. Employees on Degree of Autonomy

Percent of employees responding "strongly agree"	1977	2002
I have the freedom to decide what I do on my job.	18.1	24.1
My job requires that I keep learning new things.	45.4	62.3
It is basically my responsibility to decide how my job gets done.	32.3	54.6
I have a lot of say about what happens on my job.	20.8	31.9
I decide when I take breaks.	22.6	53.1
My job requires that I be creative.	20.4	45.2
The work I do is meaningful to me.	26.9	66.0
My job lets me use my skills and abilities.	27.8	68.5

with crew and marines jumping on board last, at canal's end.[4] But that and other impressive case examples now heralded in management history books were one-off— not taught, copied, or enhanced.

FLAWED AMERICAN SYSTEM

That state of affairs changed in the early 1900s, when Frederick W. Taylor, Frank and Lillian Gilbreth, and others ushered in *scientific management*. They were highly successful in proselytizing their methods of work study. Scientific management, along with Eli Whitney's interchangeable parts and Ford's assembly lines, came to be known (more or less) as the American System. It was effective—among reasons why, in the first half of the twentieth century, the United States overtook Europe and the rest of the world as an economic force.

Still, by today's standards, the system was badly flawed—in four main, closely related ways:

1. Its management concepts were founded on research, but a reductionist brand of it: Analyze the small pieces, down to Gilbreth's therbligs and the Hawthorne Studies' effects of light on labor productivity. Integrative research was missing. (Matthew Stuart's article, "The Management Myth," scorns the kinds of research and conclusions emerging from both the works of Taylor and the Hawthorne Studies.[5]) See the box, "Blaming Taylor."
2. Partly because of piecemeal analysis, the system contributed to the raising of ever-higher walls around each piece or function of the business: the silo syndrome.
3. The production operative was, in a way, siloed, too. A 1932 report reads, "I always think about a visit ... to one of Ford's assembling plants. ... Every employee seemed to be restricted to a well-defined jerk, twist, spasm, or quiver resulting in a fliver. ... I failed to discover how motive power is transmitted to these people and as it don't seem reasonable that human beings would willingly consent to being simplified into jerks."[6]

4. In production, logistics, and administration, silo-centered analysis discouraged close linkages from process to process, shop to shop, office to office, plant to plant, and even company to customer. Each entity would be independently scheduled and managed. The result was large-batch processing and large queues of inventory-at-rest (including documents in in-baskets) between each step of the long flow path. There were few mechanisms for attacking the costly, time-wasting disconnects among the processes.

Blaming Taylor

For his advocacy of expertise carved up by functions, Frederick Taylor has served as the management field's favorite whipping boy. But the bulk of management studies have been similarly reductionist and silo-separatist. When I began my graduate studies, business schools included a discipline called *human relations*, linked to industrial psychology. Later, in the late 1970s, that title was superseded by the broader-sounding title, *organizational behavior*. But the dominant focus of org behavior has remained on individuals and small groups, and little on compounding effects in whole organizations, whose complexity overwhelms the dominant research methodology, which itself is reductionist.

MUTUALLY BENEFICIAL PRACTICES

Rectification arrived in the early 1980s. Several sets of best practices largely new to Western industry came together: one set for fixing the broken quality system; another, just-in-time/lean, to tightly time-link the processes; still another to make the workplace a continuous-improvement laboratory staffed by an empowered, multi-skilled work force; and more. None were in conflict. Rather each nurtured the others with high synergies:

- The quality practices make JIT/lean workable. Without quality improvement, defects, scrap, rework, and process variation wreck notions of tightly linked process flows.

- JIT makes the quality system effective. In stamping out process delays, JIT keeps trails of causes fresh; and it ensures that the inevitable defects do not move through the processes in large batches. This JIT–quality connection is illustrated by the case study at the end of the chapter, "JIT Falls Flat at Firestone: Impact on Quality."

- Work forces at their worksite laboratories apply improvement techniques on the spot. Main improvements are corrective actions to improve quality and tighten just-in-time linkages.

There are still more mutually beneficial components of process improvement: design for manufacture and assembly slashes part counts. That allows quality, JIT, and empowerment to beam in on small numbers of parts, rather than being nickeled-and-dimed by large numbers of them.

Total productive maintenance empowers the operators as facilities caretakers. Their mandate includes keeping equipment from being the cause of quality failures, and preventing stoppages ruinous to tight JIT processing.

Among still more components of process improvement are, prominently, visual control, supply-chain compression, target costing, lean machines, and lean accounting. The benefits crisscross among all of these in too many ways to count. The point is simply that the interacting components of process improvement have the effect of breaching the silos. Solutions traverse the functions of the enterprise. Global hypercompetition dictates that, to stay in business, companies need to understand all this, and put that understanding to intensive use.

But do they? Chapters 2, 3, and 4 help answer the question with data. All the other chapters probe selected lean/quality practices with a critical eye.

Case Study: JIT Falls Flat at Firestone: Impact on Quality

In 2000, there were many reports making headlines about rollover deaths, tire recalls, lawsuits, and recriminations involving Ford Explorers equipped with Firestone tires. It brought to mind an experience of mine with Firestone manufacturing years earlier.[7] I could not help but think that *lean/JIT practices*, especially cellular manufacturing, might, possibly, have saved the day.

The year was 1984. The site was a Firestone radial-tire plant in Albany, Georgia. It was a typical batch-and-queue factory, in which quality problems are mostly invisible to the work force. I had been invited to conduct a one-day JIT seminar for 56 managers and engineers on a Saturday in June.

I arrived midday Friday in time for a thorough factory tour. I learned that the plant built tires in four steps, each a "department" (or shop): first-stage, third-stage, press-cure, and final finish. (A second stage had been eliminated when the plant converted from bias-ply to radial tires. The rubber itself was mixed and processed in stages at the other end of the plant.) About 20 first-stage machines produced carcasses that went into racks holding, typically, 12,000 units. From there, 40 third-stage machines converted carcasses to "green" tires, which filled racks awaiting the next processing in 200 press-cure machines. Those racks held 10,000 to 12,000 green tires.

I had learned enough to devise, that evening, a plan to reorganize the plant for cellular tire-making with small-lot flows. My Saturday presentation included sketches on acetate of conversion to multiple cells. For good balance each cell would have two first-stage machines feeding one second-stage machine, feeding four press-cure machines, feeding one final-finish station. Plant manager Dick Clarke and his staff were enthused and bent on doing the conversion.

Later, in mail and phone consultations with Clarke, the plan was refined. (It became part of a case study published in a casebook on implementation of JIT and TQC.[8]

(Continued)

The instructor's manual for the casebook includes a sketch of the cells, with estimates of benefits.) Did it actually get implemented? It did not. Contrary to Clarke's wishes, Firestone headquarters opted for automation, some $20 million worth. That was no surprise: GM, and later even Toyota, had romanced with automation, which can conflict with simplicity precepts native to lean manufacturing. That spending was for naught: A year after my visit the company shuttered the plant, idling around two thousand people.

Whether the cellular plan would have saved the plant from extinction is not the reason for this discussion. Rather it is this: Tightly linked work cells give operators, supervisors, technicians, and engineers whole-process visibility. Defects come to light without getting lost among large volumes of in-process and finished materials and before causal evidence is lost in time. By rejecting the cellular formula, this and many other plants in the industry seem to have set themselves up for a quality debacle—maybe even one of the extreme kind that Bridgestone/Firestone experienced with its radial tires on Ford's Explorers.

In late 2005, Bridgestone was reported to have spent $440 million (not including legal costs) for recalling 6.5 million tires. Ford had demanded additional recalls; when Bridgestone refused, Ford recalled the tires on its own. Ford is still embroiled in many lawsuits. And "Bridgestone still faces hundreds of lawsuits on similar tires built at the same plants as the recalled ones."[9]

Yet, the tide is turning in this new century. Most tire-makers have been experimenting with small plant designs made up of compact cells, plus new process-linking equipment that largely avoids fork-trucking in and out of storage racks.[10]

NOTES

1. In Nakajima's milestone TPM book, the T means "total participation of all employees," and "total maintenance system," which would include all processes; Nakajima includes "total effectiveness" as a third T: Seiichi Nakajima, TPM: *Introduction to Total Productive Maintenance* (Cambridge, MA: Productivity Press, 1988), p. 11.

2. Shoshana Zuboff, *In the Age of the Smart Machine* (New York: Basic Books, 1988), p. 32.

3. Cited in James O'Toole and Edward E. Lawler III, *The New American Workplace* (New York: Palgrave Macmillan, 2006), p. 55.

4. Pero Tafur, *Travels and Adventures* (London: G. Routledge & Sons, 1926), p. 1435; cited in R. Burlingame, *Backgrounds of Power* (New York: Charles Scribner's Sons, 1949).

5. Matthew Stuart, "The Management Myth," *Atlantic Monthly* (June 2006), pp. 80–87.

6. The words of an unnamed production employee, quoted in *Tri-City Labor Review*, Rock Island, Illinois, 1932; cited in David A. Hounshell, *From the American System to Mass Production, 1800–1932: The Development of Manufacturing Technology in the United States* (Baltimore: Johns Hopkins University Press, 1984), p. 321. A "flivver" (fliver is not the usual spelling) is an old, uncomplimentary slang term for an automobile.

7. This Firestone case study is adapted from Richard J. Schonberger, *Let's Fix It! Overcoming the Crisis in Manufacturing—How the World's Leading Manufacturers Were Seduced by*

Prosperity and Lost Their Way: Paying the Price of Stock Hyping and Management Fads (New York: Free Press/Simon & Schuster, 2001), Chapter 9, "Focus Within," pp. 143–144.

8. Richard J. Schonberger, *World Class Manufacturing Casebook: Implementing JIT and TQC* (New York: Free Press/Simon & Schuster), 1987, pp. 165–172.

9. Timothy Aeppel, "Mounting Pressure: Under Glare of Recall, Tire Makers Are Giving New Technology a Spin," *Wall Street Journal* (March 23, 2001), pp. A1 and A8.

10. Karen Lundegaard and Timothy Aeppel, "Bridgestone, Ford Reach Recall Deal," *Wall Street Journal* (October 13, 2005), p. A3.

Chapter 2

Global Leanness: An Unstable Phenomenon

In 1994, we began collecting inventory-turnover data in a long-range study of how companies are progressing with the lean/process-improvement agenda. By the turn of the century, the sample size had enlarged enough to tell about the state of manufacturing globally. My 2001 book, *Let's Fix It! How the World's Leading Manufacturers Were Seduced by Prosperity and Lost Their Way*,[1] set the tone of problems in lean-land. (Herbold echoes that theme in his 2007 work, *Seduced by Success*.[2])

The database now is made up of more than 1,400 manufacturers, retailers, and distributors in 36 countries.[3] In this chapter, we plumb that database in order to shed light on two primary questions: (1) Are these companies, on average, improving? (2) Are they, on average, maintaining an improving trend for a period long enough to include changing conditions? The second question is more significant than the first and requires more penetrating data analysis. Before pressing on with the two questions, a few comments about the inventory metric are in order.

INVENTORY: A TELLING METRIC

Lack of inventory is a convenient, close proxy for lean. Anyone looking around a facility and spotting goodly amounts of materials correctly sees the facility as fat, not lean. When a close check turns up very little inventory, we conclude the opposite.

Inventory is visible, countable, and objectively researchable. It is on the books and readily comparable from company to company as well as over time within a company. The most common metric for keeping tabs is *inventory turnover*. By the accountant's definition, this is cost of sales (also called cost of goods sold) from the income statement divided by value of inventory from the balance sheet.[4] In some countries, cost of sales is not normally included in the income statement. In that case, we use the alternative formula, sales revenue divided by value of inventory. That works, because *improvement trend*, not absolute value, is the point of the research. Before proceeding, we note these qualifications:

Inventory is an echo. Its reduction is not a primary objective of continuous improvement, which must be in the eyes of the customer. Those eyes seek ever-better quality, quicker response, greater flexibility, and higher value. In this book, we shall call those four the *golden goals*. Inventory reduction does not rank with those goals, but is a valued by-product and measuring stick in achieving the goals.

Inventory is to lean/TPS/JIT as fever is to health (TPS stands for Toyota production system). As fever is a catchall symptom of many illnesses, so inventory is a catch basin for a multitude of business ills needing correction in order to improve in the eyes of the customer.

ARE COMPANIES IMPROVING?

Turning to the first question, the answer is clearly the affirmative: Companies are improving. On what basis? Take a look at Exhibit 2.1. For the global database of publicly traded companies, median inventory turnovers got worse until 1970. (Note: All data come from companies' audited financial statements.) From then on, the trend line vectors upward. That trend is for a mix of inventory-intensive industry sectors, mostly manufacturers but also retailers, wholesalers, and distributors.

Separate trend lines in Exhibit 2.1 are for the United States, U.K., and Japan, which contribute more companies to the research than other countries. Retailers and distributors are unequally represented among the three countries. So, to forestall country-to-country bias, only manufacturers make up the trend lines for the three countries. By the simple measure, median inventory turnover, the average manufacturer is improving in all three. (Calculated but not shown are trends for six other countries or regions. Their trend lines

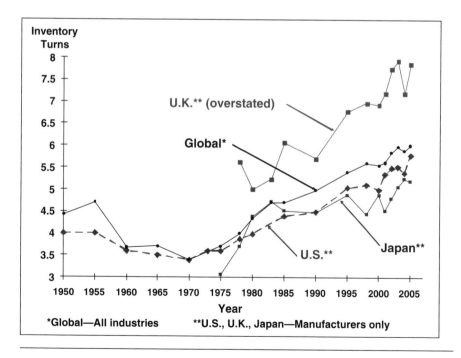

Exhibit 2.1 Median Inventory Turnovers

are more erratic but similar to the patterns in Exhibit 2.1: sharply upward since 1975 or 1980.) And why not? Process-improvement initiatives have become commonplace, especially in these large, publicly traded companies.

Nor is it any surprise that turns were worsening from 1950 to 1970. That was before the outside world (meaning outside of Japan) knew anything about JIT and total quality control. In those years, nearly all western companies were enamored of large lot sizes and long production runs. And they lived with high rates of scrap and rework for lack of effective quality management. It is unexpected that the upturn began in 1970, about 10 years before the West had begun its JIT/TQC lessons. Though lacking the tools and understanding, the motivation to change was there: Companies in key industries, especially in the United States, were engaged in devastating competition with Japan's best.

Among the three countries, the U.K. exhibits the most rapid rate of improvement (steepest upward trend). The higher absolute values along the U.K. trend line are not significant, because most U.K. companies' inventory turns are based on sales, their financial statements usually not providing cost of sales. The steady upward trends for the U.K. and United States contrast with the trend line for Japan, which is sharply upward until 1983, and upward again since 2003, but nearly flat for about 20 years toward the middle of the 30-year period. That Japan, birthplace of lean, failed to improve for so many years suggests that lean is not easy to sustain.

The median, though, is a simple statistic that does not reveal much. That makes the trend lines in Exhibit 2.1 a poor indicator of sustained improvement. By analogy, say that for young people the median speed in the 100-meter dash increases steadily from age 8 to 18. But does that statistic come from continuous improvement in speed in each of the 10 years for the typical youth? That is unlikely. Instead, a few youths may actually lose running speed as they age. Most probably have their ups and downs in running speed. Short-term gains may be explained by a physical growth spurt coupled with good diet and conditioning. Then in other years, bad habits set in, leading to no improvement, or even loss of speed. The median tells nothing about these factors and within-group patterns. It is simply an average for the group as a whole.

Process improvement in business is the same: many different up, down, and flat patterns for different subgroups. In some companies, good conditioning may yield flashes of lean that later fade. A few other companies may, through retention of good habits, achieve long-term sustained lean. The next section employs stronger measures than the simple median. It sheds good light on companies unable to move lean off the mark, others in the flashes-of-lean category, and still others that are able to keep lean's benefits coming over the long term.

NO LEAN, FLASHES OF LEAN, SUSTAINED LEAN

James Womack (who may be considered today's "Mr. Lean") is concerned. His organization does an annual survey of its lean-inclined constituency. They say that a leading problem with "their improvement efforts is 'backsliding to old ways of working' after initial progress."[5]

Gaining a clearer picture of this "sustainability" issue requires refined analysis of our leanness data: looking at companies' inventory performance over long time spans. The leanness research uses 15 years as a minimum span,[6] with close analysis of the most recent ten years. That rules out about 200 companies for which we have data but for fewer years. It still leaves more than 1,200 companies meeting the 15-year minimum. Companies in economically developed countries are over-represented, because they have longer traditions of making their public companies' financial reports publicly available.

Fifteen years, with close analysis of the past 10, should be enough to include changes in the senior executive team, markets, supply bases, technologies, competitive threats, and other disruptions. Process improvement that can weather these storms would appear to be strong, somewhat entrenched, and maybe even continuous—as in *continuous improvement.*

For assessing a company's performance, we graphically plot its inventory turnovers, year by year. A scoring system reduces visual assessment of trends to numbers, which point to how lean is faring long term. The scoring is as follows:

- Two points for a clearly improving trend of at least 10 years.
- One point for the same (10 years of improvement), but followed by 5, 6, or 7 years of no improvement or decline.
- Half a point for 5 to 9 years of steady improvement (jerky improvement does not count here).
- Zero points for no clear trend at all—just up and down, irregularly.
- Minus ½ point for at least 10 years of decline.

Why penalize by a maximum of one-half point while rewarding by as much as two points? Because with all the changes that companies experience in 10 years, it is hard to keep improving and easy to experience downturns. This is a conservative scoring scale that gives plenty of credit for good results and not a lot of penalty for marginal or poor ones.

Exhibit 2.2 shows four examples of scoring. Mattel, the U.S.-based toy company, gets two points. Its uptrend in inventory turns spans 24 years from a clear low point in 1982. Looking at the plotted points year by year, the company would have first been eligible for two points in 1992 and 1993. In the late 1990s, its points would have fallen to zero because of a flattening of the trend line since the late 1980s. Elevated turns since 2002 draw the eye away from the flattened area and to the upward, longer trend since 1982, justifying its current two points.

Heineken, the Netherlands brewer, warranted two points from 1992 to 2004. Throughout those years it had maintained an improving trend of at least 10 years. In 2005, the company's score fell to one point owing to 5 years of decline following its 20-year improvement trend.

Saint-Gobain, the French glass-producing giant, has no clear trend up or down over the past 17 years: zero points. If the company's turnover had improved between

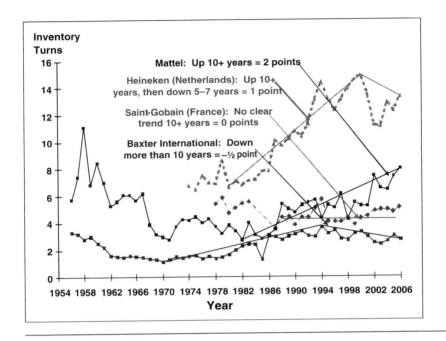

Exhibit 2.2   Points for Inventory Turnover Trends

2004 and 2005, it would have had a clear uptrend of 6 years, which would have met the criterion for one-half point.

Baxter International, producer of medical devices and supplies, had improved its turns for 24 years, 1970 to 1994, which would have made it a two-point company. Its turns for the past 12 years, though, have trended downward: minus half a point.

A caveat: The inventory trend for a single company is indicative but sometimes not a fair and accurate gauge of process-management excellence. Companies may shift product lines, acquire and divest, move offshore, and so forth. Those and other changes can abnormally affect inventory performance for a few years. Heineken, Saint-Gobain, or Baxter, for example, may have been expanding globally at a fast pace in recent years. Though that usually means growth of pipeline inventories, that penalty could be justified by overall long-term strengthening of competitive position in the world. (But Chapter 12 will cast some doubt on practices that sacrifice leanness for such outcomes as growth.) The possibly unfair grading for a single company washes out for groupings of them, especially larger, more stable groups.

That brings us back to the investigation at hand: isolating patterns of long-term performance for companies in the database. Exhibit 2.3 shows aggregate scores on sustaining a long-term trend for the growing global database. It displays separate trend lines for two large subgroups, U.S. and non-U.S. companies. In numbers, U.S. companies dominate, constituting about two-thirds of database companies since 1995. That is the case because U.S. data are readily available in libraries dating back to

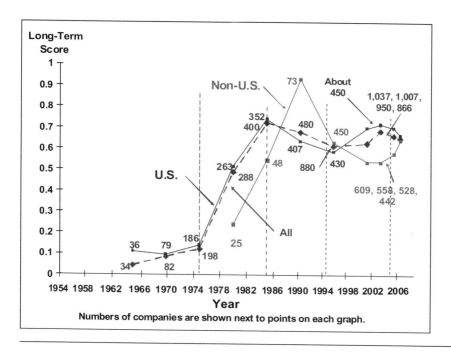

Exhibit 2.3   Long-Term Improvement

the early 1900s, whereas public access to financial data for other regions is more recent, and limited as to back-years. Compilations for the 1960s through 1990s are at five-year intervals, which is sufficient to show overall trend.

For all companies, the long-term leanness trend was sharply upward in the 1970s and 1980s. That came to a halt in the 1990s. Since then, the pattern has been generally flat with a slight downward tilt.

The U.S. and non-U.S. trend lines are similar in shape. Notably, however, directional changes for the non-U.S. group lag those for the United States: The U.S. score peaked in 1985, and for the rest of the world in 1990. The U.S. score rose again in 2000 and 2002; the rest of the world followed suit in 2002 and 2004. There is a reasonable explanation: The large U.S. market was the first target of Japan's premier companies. U.S. companies most affected (the survivors anyway) reacted to the onslaught by learning Japanese methods and putting them to use. Japan's best turned next to smaller markets elsewhere in the world, and the reaction was the same—with a lag of about five years at first, narrowed to only about two years recently.

The non-U.S. data cover the main industrial regions of the world, each with some of its own special conditions: regulations, infrastructures, openness to trade, and so on. Do the separate regions follow the same pattern as for the global total? Exhibit 2.4 provides a partial answer, showing trends in five regions: United States, Japan, U.K., Nordic, and Germany/Austria. Sufficient data for these five reaches back to at least

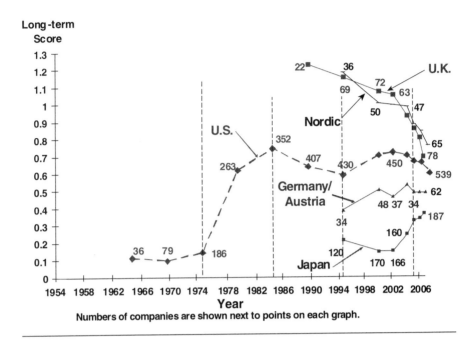

Exhibit 2.4   Long-Term Inventory Turnover Performance

1995, but fewer years for other regions and countries. For most companies, 2007 financial data on the graphs come from 2006 annual reports.

What Exhibit 2.4 shows most notably is that the gap among the five regions, once wide, has narrowed a great deal. Perhaps this is one more indicator that, as Thomas Friedman's book declares, *The World Is Flat.*[7]

The U.K. and Nordic regions, by their sharply plunging trends, have contributed the most to the convergence. U.S. scores have been falling as well since 2002, but less sharply than for the U.K. and Nordic regions. Overall, the worsening scores say that fewer companies are able to become and stay lean.

The low score for Germany/Austria, and an even lower score for Japan, indicate still weaker performance in leanness over the long term. The upward climb in Japan's numbers from 2004 to 2007 reduces but does not erase the gap with the four other regions. Why Japan's long-term score should be rising in the 2000s after falling in the 1990s is a matter that deserves further consideration.

CYCLICITY

The data for Japan in Exhibit 2.4 show a high–low–high cycle from 1995 to 2006. The much longer U.S. trend line shows a similar cycle but stretching over 17 years from

1985 to 2002. While Japan was the origin of TPS/JIT and the West the follower in the early years, these more recent cyclic patterns suggest a switch: the United States leading with Japan following. There may be some logic to that idea.

From a peak in 1985, the U.S. score headed downward for 10 years. Why? Call it JIT fatigue—like TQM fatigue and reengineering fatigue in earlier years. When intensity of effort on one of these hot management initiatives fades, it is probably not because it didn't work. More likely it just got pushed lower on companies' priority ladders. Senior executives thought JIT was going well enough to give less time to it and more to new products, acquisitions, off-shore expansion, and so on. With executives less involved, others in the companies follow suit and scores fall.

There is no reason to think that the same would not happen in Japan. The Japanese portion of the database does not reliably show long-term leanness scores for years prior to 1995. (A long-term score for 1990 would require company data for the prior 15 years—back to 1975. But the database includes only 13 Japanese companies whose financial data reach back that far.) It seems likely, though, that sustainable lean scores in Japan would have been rising through the 1970s and into the 1980s. TPS was fully developed and in place by about 1970 at Toyota and its main suppliers. Other Japanese companies should have been doing well with TPS by a decade later. Offering partial confirmation is Exhibit 2.1, showing sharp improvement in median inventory turnovers for Japan from 1975 to 1983. Later, the fatigue factor may have set in, which would help explain Japan's very low long-term scores (Exhibit 2.4) since 1995, as well as its flat median turns (Exhibit 2.1) from 1983 to the early 1990s.

Exhibit 2.5 captures these points. In the United States in the 1980s, the dominant term was *JIT*, not *TPS*, and not yet *lean*. As fatigue drove long-term scores downward,

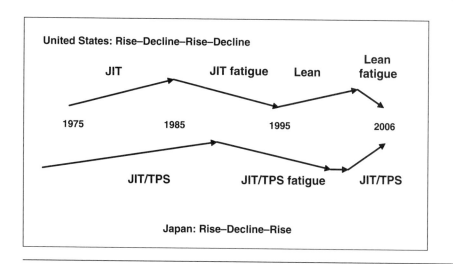

Exhibit 2.5 Rise–Decline Cycles in the United States and Japan

the term of choice shifted from JIT to lean, and hubbub over lean re-energized the movement and raised the scores again. Finally, from 2002 to 2006, U.S. scores again worsened, possibly suggesting lean fatigue. Or was it anxieties related to the 1991 World Trade Center tragedy and its aftermath?

Japan's simpler pattern began as a lengthy incline in scores well into the 1980s. Then, JIT/TPS fatigue developed. (In Japan, most companies called it JIT, though they recognized Toyota and its production system as the origin.) A long decline in scores followed until JIT/TPS reasserted itself and, since 2002, raised the scores again in belated reaction to Japan's "lost decade" of economic malaise. (Usage in Japan still favors the JIT label rather than lean—perhaps because lean was coined in the United States, not Japan.)

So far, this discussion of findings has been limited to five countries/regions, those for which we have the largest number of years of inventory-turnover data. Exhibit 2.6 brings in the remaining regions, placing them in rank order by latest average score on long-term leanness. The United States, Japan, and U.K. provide enough companies to treat as separate regions. Southern Europe includes France, Greece, Italy, Portugal, Spain, Switzerland, and Turkey. Denmark, Finland, Norway, and Sweden are the Nordic region. Benelux (Belgium, Netherlands, and Luxembourg) plus Ireland is the smallest region. Israel, not fitting naturally into any region, is arbitrarily added to Brazil, Canada, and Mexico as an ersatz-region. Germany and Austria go together reasonably well. Asiana/South Africa is made up of quite a few Australian and South African companies plus a small number from each of 10 more countries: Hong Kong/

Sectors	Score	Sample Size	Recent Trend
1 Southern Europe	.83	68	↗
2 Nordic countries	.76	65	↘
3 Brazil/Canada/Mexico/Israel	.67	88	↘
4 United Kingdom	.66	78	↘
5 Benelux/Ireland	.61	33	→
6 United States	.59	539	↘
Global Average	*.58*	*1,219*	↘
7 Asiana/So. Africa	.53	101	↘
8 Germany/Austria	.48	62	→
9 Japan	.37	187	↗

#Positive 10-to-50 year trend, 2 points; same but lapse last 5-7 years, 1 point; 5 to 9 years of steady improvement, plus ½ point; negative 10-or-more year trend, minus ½ point

Exhibit 2.6   Long-Term Leanness Scores and Trends

PRC, India, Indonesia, Korea, New Zealand, Pakistan, Philippines, Singapore, Taiwan, and Thailand.

As has been noted, the dominant recent-year trend in the world is one of faltering. The arrows in the rightmost column show this to be the case in all regions except Southern Europe and Japan, which have improved, and Benelux/Ireland and Germany/Austria, which exhibit little clear change. (Southern Europe's rise drops the Nordic to second place.) Though still a lot worse than the rest, Japan's score rose fairly steadily from 2003, when it was 0.28 to the current 0.37.

WHY DOESN'T LEAN LAST?

We posited fatigue plus changing executive priorities and interests to explain why long-term lean scores fade. But wait a minute. Lean and its close partner, total quality, should not give ground so easily. Consider what they are based on and what they entail: simplicity, reduction of resources, low implementation costs (mostly for training), broad application, and customer-focused synergies (quality, quick response, flexibility, and value—a mutual-improvement society, no trade-offs). Making lean/ TQ a permanent fixture almost seems to be, as they say, a no-brainer.

Surely there are other factors, maybe different from one country or region to another. For example, could Japan's reversal—up in the 1970s, down in the 1990s— be explained in part by the bursting of the Japanese economic bubble and following long years of economic malaise?[8] That may be so. The crash of Japanese real estate, bad loans, and so on, began in about 1990, which looks to be around the time that Japan's long-term leanness scores were worsening. That suggests that Japanese companies reacted in a contrary manner, turning off some of the features of JIT/ TPS/lean and allowing inventories to grow.

In other countries, when times are tough, industry's natural reaction is to shrink: Reduce production, shutter plants, cut the work force, seek lower costs offshore, and so forth. In Japan, such actions are socially difficult, owing to traditions of lifetime employment (which is fading) coupled with lack of a well-developed social-welfare system.[9] (Japan has, nevertheless, considerably lowered its labor costs. Thanks to deregulation it has greatly shifted the labor mix from full-timers to lower-paid temporary employees.[10]) Nor is money-saving retrenchment a natural business decision in Japan. From the 1960s through the 1980s, as noted by Robinson and Shimizu, Japanese companies tended to focus "on sales, growth, and market share, with less regard for profitability."[11] For all those reasons, as compared with other countries, Japan was:[12]

- Late to restructure.[13]
- Late to outsource offshore.
- Late to learn and implement design for manufacture and assembly.
- Late to employ modular deliveries from suppliers.

If those points help explain Japan's low scores, they are of no help in answering why western countries have tended to lose their leanness. Other chapters will delve into that matter while proceeding with the main purpose of this book, which is to sort out best practices in process improvement. This chapter has set the stage with a researcher's examination of the effects of best practices, the large majority of which entail inventory reduction as a salutary by-product.

We are not done with the inventory-turnover database. Findings from it are scattered throughout remaining chapters. Moreover, the book's final section, Part VI, begins with another full chapter, Chapter 18, on the leanness-study findings. You'll want to study it, because it features a ranking of 33 industrial sectors according to short-term and long-term effectiveness in becoming and staying lean. For example, petroleum and distribution/wholesale share the number-one ranking—leanest of the lean—and pharmaceuticals ranks as fattest.

But does lean or fat really matter? To clarify, does it matter financially? Financial relevance is the main reason for running a business. This financial impact is the subject of Chapter 3, which firmly answers this question.

NOTES

1. Richard J. Schonberger, *Let's Fix It! How the World's Leading Manufacturers were Seduced by Prosperity and Lost Their Way* (Free Press/Simon & Schuster, 2001).

2. Robert J. Herbold, *Seduced by Success: How the Best Companies Survive the 9 Traps of Winning* (New York: McGraw-Hill, 2007).

3. The database grew over time as more companies in more countries had their annual reports and other audited financial records published on the Internet and/or in standard library reference publications. For the year 1965, the sources provided 227 companies, largely from the United States, the UK, and Canada, plus one company each from Italy, Japan, Netherlands, and Sweden. For 1970, 1975, and 1980 respectively, companies were added from France, Germany, and Mexico; then Israel and Spain; and then Australia, Austria, Belgium, Denmark, Finland, India, Hong Kong/PRC, Norway, Pakistan, Philippines, Portugal, Singapore, South Africa, Switzerland, and Taiwan. Finally, in 1985, 1990, 1995, and 2000, additional data came, respectively, from companies in Ireland, Korea, Luxembourg, and New Zealand; Brazil, Greece, and Indonesia; Thailand; and Turkey. Attrition—mergers, acquisitions, bankruptcies, and privatizations—has countered some of that growth. In addition, some of the reduced number of companies in 2005 is owing to delayed filings of financial data, especially in less-developed countries. (Financials are now available for hundreds more companies globally, but as yet for too few years to be worth adding to the database.)

4. Ray H. Garrison, *Managerial Accounting*, 6th ed. (Homewood, IL: Richard D. Irwin, 1981), p. 783. The precise definition has *average* value of inventory in the denominator, which could be based on quarterly financial statements. But the research herein need not be that refined, since the matter of interest is in long-term trend, not absolute value of inventory turnover; therefore, this research simply uses end-of-year inventory value.

5. Jim Womack, "The Problem of Sustainability," e-mail to a mailing list, May 30, 2007.

6. Fifteen years happens also to be the minimum required for entry into Jim Collins's database, which he carved out of the *Fortune* 500 largest U.S. companies. His analysis of that database resulted in his mega-selling book, *Good to Great: Why Some Companies Make the Leap—and Others Don't* (New York: HarperBusiness, 2001).

7. Thomas L. Friedman, *The World Is Flat: A Brief History of the Twentieth Century* (New York: Farrar, Straus and Giroux, 2005).

8. Joseph Stieglitz, "Lessons from Japan's Economic Malaise," Project Syndicate, www .project-syndicate.org/commentaries/commentary_text.php4?id=1140&lang=1&m=con-tributor.

9. Layoffs are more difficult in Japan because "unemployment insurance covers no more than a year." See footnote 15, p. 57, in Patricia Robinson and Norihiko Shimizu, "Japanese Corporate Restructuring: CEO Priorities as a Window on Environmental and Organizational Change," *Academy of Management Perspectives*, 20, no. 3 (August, 2006), pp. 44–75.

10. In 2007 one in three Japanese employees was a temp, versus one in five 10 years earlier. That has contributed to a lowering of Japan's overall wage rates by 7.3 percent in the decade ending with 2005: Juka Hayashi, "Japan Adds Factories at Home," *Wall Street Journal* (June 12, 2007), p. A8.

11. Robinson and Shimizu, ibid., p. 61.

12. Richard J. Schonberger, "Japanese Production Management: An Evolution—with Mixed Successes," *Journal of Operations Management*, 25, no. 2 (March 2007), pp. 403–419.

13. Finally, late in the decade, Japanese companies reacted. In 1999, Sony announced that it would slash 17,000 jobs; Mitsubishi Electric would trim 10 percent of its 146,000 global employees; Nissan would close three assembly plants and two engine facilities, and reduce employment by 21,000. These three companies "barely represent the tip of the iceberg of major Japanese companies that have announced restructuring plans." D. Ostram, "Corporate Japan's Restructuring Efforts: A Progress Report," *Japan Economic Institute Report*, 20 (May 19, 2000).

Chapter 3

Big Question: Does Lean Beget Financial Success?

Cliff Ransom, vice president, State Street Research in Boston, "is one of two or three stock analysts whose understanding of lean manufacturing gives them an edge analyzing manufacturing companies. Now and then Cliff participates in a shop floor kaizen event himself." With that introduction, *Target* magazine reported on an interview with Ransom, asking what he looks for in a manufacturing company. Ransom replied, "Investors prefer to see rising returns on their money. While there are various ways to measure that, I look for cash flow. Next to inventory measures, cash doesn't lie."[1]

There's one in almost every audience: the wise one who wants to know, and may finally call the question. It may be phrased something like this: "All well and good. But what is the financial impact of lean [or JIT, or world-class manufacturing, or process improvement]? Is there research, are there studies to prove bottom-line benefits?"

The question is exasperating to the presenter. Why don't they get it? Lean is common sense. It's continuous improvement. There's no big capital investment involved. It can be done piecemeal, in any order. It embraces the best instincts of the work force. It melds beneficially with a flock of other improvement campaigns from total quality to six sigma to plant maintenance to supplier partnership.

Still, the almighty dollar (pound, yen, mark) rules, especially among chief decision makers. So we see where the question is coming from.

MOOT MATTER

Doing leanness studies by the inventory-turnover yardstick is time consuming but straightforward. Tying those results to financial indicators is daunting in comparison. There are a lot of ways to measure financial results, and each one comes with complex factors to beware of or adjust for. Everyone likes profits (earnings). But profits are not a good measure of success or failure of an improvement campaign. To foil the taxman, companies seek ways to hide profits; for example, shift sales or costs to another period, an untaxed application, or an offshore tax haven. Other financial measures—such as return on investment, earnings per share, and economic value added—are similarly problematic. Companies like to report cash but not profits.

Professor friends at two universities[2] and I have mulled over these issues. We've made stabs at correlating lean indicators with some of the main financial measures, and mostly ended up with confused results. (The matter has foiled other researchers as well.[3]) We gravitated away from measures such as profit and return on investment. The last sentence in the previous paragraph, plus the chapter opening comments of Cliff Ransom, made more sense: In business, cash is king. And companies' annual reports readily yield cash flow.

So the analysis shifted to one of correlating inventory turnovers with cash flows. But that study soon came to a halt, because it became clear that the conclusion is foregone! The analysis is redundant, tautological, moot! Here's why.

Shrinking inventories puts cash in the bank—automatically. It does so, that is, if the shrinking derives from a process-improvement campaign, which is what lean, total quality, and six sigma are. If a company cuts inventories without the process improvement, shortages and lost customers are likely to outweigh the cash-flow benefits.

Hovering over all attempts at correlating lean with bottom-line performance is this: Many companies undertake lean first and foremost to survive, and secondarily to flourish. In some whole industries, such as consumer electronics and grocery retailing, profit margins are thinner today than before the lean era. In these and other industries, many competitors have not survived. Therefore, if a research project were to prove that most companies are less profitable despite impressive lean accomplishments, there might not be a single sad face among those companies—for two reasons:

1. They are the survivors.
2. They have learned how to keep improving, which they did not know before.

In light of these points, studying how lean affects the bottom line did not seem likely to be enlightening. Banked cash is by no means the sole financial effect. Any process improvement yields multiple benefits that enlarge the top line and the bottom line, and lines in between.

MULTIPLE EFFECTS, COMPOUNDED OVER TIME

The direct aim and effect of lean is quicker, more flexible response through all processes up and down the value chain. Final paying customers get faster, better-targeted services. Present customers are more likely to stay and increase their business, and new customers to come out of the woodwork, both enhancing the top line.

The quick/flex side of process improvement is inseparable from other aspects, especially (1) higher quality and value, and (2) reduced overhead activities and costs. Consider the big three of lean manufacturing: work cells, kanban, and quick setup (each furthering the move toward one-piece flow).

Cells are best known for their operational impacts:

- A cell eliminates inventory, freeing cash for income-producing earnings.
- Cells draw the processes close together in time and distance. Defectives show up quickly while colleagues at an earlier cell station often can still see and correct the

cause forthwith. If they are not fixed right away, problem solvers, blessed with a warm trail of clues, have good chances of finding and rooting out the causes. Costs of scrap and rework fall or are avoided, yielding savings that directly improve the bottom line. With consecutive processes at close quarters, non-value-adding costs of handling and transport plunge—also to the bottom line.

- A cell eliminates many overhead costs. If five processes formerly in separate shops come together as a cell, there is only one rather than five scheduling transactions, labor transactions, material-handling transactions, and cost reports. As the overhead transactions shrink, so do related overhead staffing and payrolls. (Advanced lean and lean accounting eliminate most remaining scheduling, labor, and handling transactions, and the cost report.)

A high-level effect of cells is altering the usual financial mismanagement of the business. A cell is a cost-containment center. It contains direct and overhead costs that formerly, confusedly, and inaccurately were allocated to criss-crossing component parts and products. Newly reliable product cost information translates into sharpened pricing and bidding. Marketing's thrust changes from more sales to more profitable sales.

Kanban is the visual partner of cells. It further quickens response to quality issues, cuts inventories, and eliminates transactions, all freeing cash.

Quick setup and changeover cut lot-size inventories, thereby quickening response to problems and freeing cash.

We need not go on. The point of the chapter, that financial benefits of lean/TQ are a sure thing, has been made.

Further discussion of the benefits continues in following chapters. That discussion blends with more detailed examples, case studies, and evidence of what is going right—and wrong—with best practices in process management. Next chapter reviews a few of the leanest companies in the global database—based on inventory performance (the metric favored by analyst Cliff Ransom, as noted in this chapter's opening paragraph). As we shall see, though, inventory is very much an imperfect measure when applied to a single company.

NOTES

1. Robert Hall, "Lean Manufacturing: Fat Cash Flow," interview with Clifford F. Ransom II, *Target* (August 2004), pp. 6–7. Along the same lines is the following: "The value of any stock, bond, or business today is determined by the cash inflows and outflows—discounted at an appropriate interest rate—that can be expected to occur during the remaining life of the asset": Berkshire Hathaway Annual Report, 1992.

2. Professor Thomas G. Schmitt, University of Washington, teaching lean-oriented operations management (and with an undergraduate degree in finance), was an advocate (in about 1998) of using cash flow as the most promising way to investigate the financial benefits of lean. Professor Eric O. Olsen, California Polytechnic University, formerly worldwide education manager for Hewlett-Packard, explored the complexities of lean practices and

financial results in *Lean Manufacturing Management: The Relationship between Practice and Firm-Level Financial Performance*, doctoral dissertation (Columbus, OH: Ohio State University, 2004).

3. For example, Roger C. Vergin, "An Examination of Inventory Turnover in the Fortune 500 Industrial Companies," *Production and Inventory Management Journal*, 1st quarter, 1998, pp. 51–56.

Chapter 4

Ultimate Trend: Improving the *Rate* of Improvement

This chapter zeroes in on eight companies whose inventory graphs seem to justify calling them "the leanest of the lean." As has been stated, though, the inventory-turnover evidence, reliable for groups, is less so for individual companies. Findings throughout the book, and this chapter as well, reinforce that caution. What can be said about single companies is limited, as follows:

- A multi-year *decline* in inventory turnover is strong—though imperfect—evidence of insufficient or weak commitment to and application of the full lean set.
- Impressive *improvement* in inventory turnover is a good preliminary indicator of a truly lean company. But further evidence is required on whether there is high commitment and application to the full lean set.

For ranking groups by leanness, Chapter 2 employed a scoring scheme. For sizing up individual companies, in this and later chapters, scores convert to *A-B-C-D-F* letter-grades, which are easier to comprehend. The grades (mirroring the point system) are:

- *A* (superior): A clearly improving trend of at least 10 years.
- *B* (good): The same (10 years of improvement), but followed by 5, 6, or 7 years of no improvement or decline.
- *C* (mediocre): No clear trend at all—just up and down, irregularly.
- *D* (poor): Years of improvement followed by at least 10 years of decline.
- *F* (failing): A many-year declining trend.
- *B+, C+, D+,* or *F+* (clear improvement): 5 to 9 years of steady upward trend (jerky improvement does not count).

CONCAVE UPWARD TREND

Can companies get too lean? Barry Lynn, author of *End of the Line*, thinks so. He cites a 1999 earthquake in Taiwan that, because of tight JIT linkages, "shut down electronics factories around the world."[1]

Well, that is hardly convincing. Chapter 2 provided substantial data showing the opposite: leanness being insufficient and temporal. Anyway, better to have Lynn's kind of rare, short-lived disasters than the constant disruptions of the old days. Before JIT/lean, plants and supply lines were choked with inventories—of wrong quantities and wrong stuff. Companies bought, produced, and shipped in outsized batches triggered by chronically inaccurate item-demand forecasts. Today, best practices aim at bringing users and producers into some semblance of synchronization: As we use, you make and ship. Where this is done well, there is little need for item forecasts, though aggregate demand forecasts, for planning capacity, will always be necessary. (Lynn has other, valid concerns about highly concentrated mega-corporations whose power can transcend governments.)

EIGHT STANDOUT COMPANIES

Such synchronization requires fixes in hundreds of problem-laden processes, a never-ending battle. Multi-year tightening of inventory works well as a measure of gains. In this chapter, the analysis singles out eight companies of the 1,200 in the long-term database. They are special because they appear to be doubly lean. First, they have sharply improved their inventory turns for at least 10 years and receive a grade of *A*. The names of the eight, along with their average per-year improvement rates and years of improvement, are shown in Exhibit 4.1.

Second, what makes them rare is they have also exhibited an extended *accelerating rate* of improving inventory turns, which shows up as a long, upward-arcing trend line. The chapter discussion of each company includes a graph showing those concave-upward patterns.

My early thought about these companies was that perhaps they are examples of *learning organizations*.[2] To be sure, accelerating inventory turnover is an imperfect measure of learning, because a terrific or appalling trend can result in part from such factors as lucky or unlucky timing. For example, at just the right time an unlean company jumps on a long, blissfully rising wave of consumer demand for a product line that otherwise would have fallen flat. The high demand eats excessive inventories

Exhibit 4.1 Eight Companies Exhibiting Accelerating Rates of Improvement in Inventory Turnover

Dell	Up 5.8% per year for 17 years since 1987
Wal-Mart	Up 2.8% per year for 16 years since 1990
HP	Up 3.2% per year for 22 years since 1984
NEC	Up 3.2% per year for 20 years since 1985
Eastman Kodak	Up 3.7% per year for 18 years since 1988
Lam Research	Up 3.5% per year for 19 years since 1987
Gerber Scientific	Up 3.9% per year for 20 years since 1986
Sony	Up 3.6% per year for 17 years since 1989

faster than the company's unlean systems can keep up. Though inventory turnover rises at an increasing rate, learning has not taken place.

Acquiring lean companies is another way to look good on lean. This chapter includes examples of that. If the acquisitions possess large amounts of lean expertise, the acquirer may gain both immediate and long-term learning benefits. If the acquired companies have no particular lean expertise—they just happen to be in an industry inherently less inventory-dependent—the advantages are likely to be short-lived.

So, regarding our eight companies, their eye-popping improvement graphs are not sufficient evidence that each is among the world's elite in application of best practices in process improvement. Better evidence requires deeper research, which has been undertaken—with mixed results. Plentiful information has been obtained for just a few of the eight companies.

THE FINDINGS IN GENERAL

As we shall see, all the companies except NEC have had interruptions in their uptrends in the past two to four years. (Some may have been left with excess inventories in the aftermath of the 9/11 Twin Towers disaster.) That is not enough to discount their prior strong trends, which are worthy of keen investigation.

Of all companies in the database, Dell's 2006 turnover of 79 is highest, though its turns have fallen from more than 100 in 2003. In the volatile electronics industry, ups and downs in performance metrics are commonplace. Wal-Mart's inventory turns in the past three years continue upward, but as a straight line off its prior accelerating curve. Inasmuch as Dell and Wal-Mart are widely recognized for their innovative advances in lean customer and supply chains, those achievements neutralize their falloff from concavity in the last two or three years.

Besides the eight featured companies, five others merit honorable mention based on lesser improvement rates over fewer years or with less concavity. They are Bausch & Lomb, Nordson, Thomas & Betts, and Switzerland's Hero AG (producer of jams and other foods). Bausch & Lomb is revisited in Chapter 22.

A few petroleum companies, notably Imperial Oil of Canada, also have steeply concave-upward inventory-turnover trends. However, Imperial's rising pattern is jagged, and its ups and downs correspond well with those of other oil companies (e.g., ExxonMobil, ConocoPhillips, Murphy Oil, Amerada Hess, Giant Industries, Shell Canada, and Petro-Canada). It looks as though the accelerating rate of improvement for these oil companies is an artifact of supply and demand in the industry. High demand and pinched supply, though, could be generating innovative practices for becoming lean. More on this in Chapter 22.

In the following discussion, four of the eight companies are referred to as *strongly lean*. The other four are labeled *equivocal*, meaning the investigation raised doubts, qualifications, or uncertainties about the underpinnings of their outstanding trend lines. The strongly lean do not necessarily have long track records in applying the lean core: such practices as kanban, quick setup, cellular organization, TPM, visual management, and six sigma. There is some of that. But these are not the companies frequently found making presentations at lean and six sigma conferences. How else can a company get lean? In general, the interface with customers and suppliers is where the greatest lean benefits lie. The analysis shows that to be a main strength for some of the strongly lean. Another common factor propelling accelerating inventory trends is a fortuitous blend of acquisitions and divestitures. That pays most of the same big dividends as getting lean in other ways, and in some cases yields sufficient learning to keep the benefits flowing.

STRONGLY LEAN

Dell heads the global list of the strongly lean. The others are Wal-Mart, the only retailer; Hewlett-Packard; and NEC. Separate study of each brings up some evidence of organizations that have learned how to learn. That is, it retains good practices of prior years while coming up with new innovations for more ways to simplify and improve processes. (The opposite tendency—the forgetting organization—may be the norm.) Discussion of Dell and Wal-Mart is rather brief here, because their special stories fit well into later chapter topics.

DELL

Dell ($56 billion in sales) is an open book. It makes the news nearly every day. Dell's steeply upward inventory-turnover trend line, Exhibit 4.2, is unmatched in the world. Coupled with that hard evidence, Dell is a famed example of mass customization,[3] the ultimate stage in flexible response to the customer. These and related attributes earn it the title of global grand champion of lean. (Note: The very high peak turnover for Dell necessitates a soaring vertical scale on its graph. The other eight companies' graphs have a flatter scale, from zero to 10 inventory turns.)

Of late, Dell has been experiencing competitive problems that may or may not be easily fixed.[4] This book, though, is not about who is doing what right now. Our aim is to try to squeeze out a few lessons in how Dell and the other companies highlighted were able to achieve accelerating long-term leanness.

Dell appears to have command of some of the basics of lean as applied to production and production support. Far more importantly, Dell is a master of tight synchronization of its own operations with customer demand and with the supply system. Innovative uses of information technology deserve much of the credit for that. But IT is more an enabler than the main reason for Dell's extraordinary record of driving out delays and inventories. Why did excellence in IT develop? I believe the answer lies in Dell's unique business model, called "Dell-direct." We revisit Dell in Chapter 11 for a close look at the power of Dell-direct.

WAL-MART

The king of retailers ($316 billion in annual sales) shrouds itself in secrecy. Suppliers tell of their dealings with Wal-Mart at their own peril. Nevertheless, plenty is known

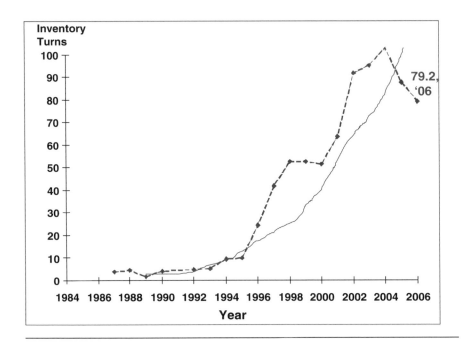

Exhibit 4.2   Dell's Accelerating Rate of Improvement

about how Wal-Mart operates and how it has managed to slough off large amounts of inventory, and at an accelerating rate (see Exhibit 4.3), even in the midst of rapid global growth. The main upward curvature occurs between 1990 and 1999. In the 2000s, Wal-Mart's trend is more of a straight line. Still, among retailers, Wal-Mart's nine years out of 16 are unmatched. (Staples, the office-supplies retailer, has a mostly concave-upward trend line but its total years of improvement span 12 years versus Wal-Mart's 16.)

Like Dell, Wal-Mart employs advanced IT to synchronize supply with its retail sales. Wal-Mart's innovations do not stop with IT. Equally impressive are its continuing efforts to streamline logistics (through cross-docking, direct shipment, and more). Many of the innovations get worked out or refined through intensive, face-to-face dealings with suppliers, freight handlers, and other stakeholders. Those collaborations pave the way for effective IT. Underpinning all this is, as with Dell, a unique business model. In the trade it is called EDLP, everyday low prices, and on Wal-Mart's shopping bags it reads, "Always low prices. *Always.*"[5] Wal-Mart's business model gets closely inspected in Chapter 11, along with that of Dell.

HEWLETT-PACKARD

HP ($87 billion in sales) is largely a make-to-stock company. HP and its contract manufacturers produce to refill their own and their distributors' and retailers'

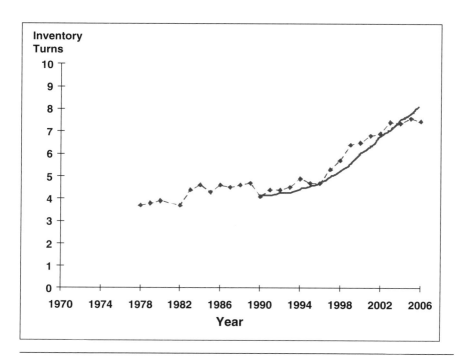

Exhibit 4.3   Improving Rate of Improvement at Wal-Mart

inventories. HP may have led all Western companies in early learning and application of JIT/TQC.[6] Its annual reports for 1982, 1984, 1985, and 1989 articulate the company's JIT/TQC emphasis and successes. Evidence of the successes should show up as rising inventory turns from the mid-1980s into the 1990s. The evidence is missing. As Exhibit 4.4 shows, HP's turns were at 2.1 in 1984, then got stuck at an average of about 2.3 until finally starting to climb in 1992. The rapid, accelerating improvement since then bears further discussion.

Exhibit 4.4 shows two sharply upward spikes in HP's trend line. The first follows the March 1999 spin-off of Agilent Technologies. Amounting to about 15 percent of HP's prior-year sales, Agilent included HP's original test and measurement business, plus semiconductors, healthcare, and chemical analysis. As revealed by subsequent annual reports, Agilent had better annual inventory turns (5.1 in 2000) than its former parent. Yet, HP saw its own turns rise from 3.9 in 1998 to 5.2 in 1999 and 2000. Why? Maybe losing Agilent freed HP to pursue its budding plans for improved supply-chain management, which is mentioned in HP's 1999 annual report (though not in relation to the Agilent spin-off).

The second sharp rise in HP's turns occurred in 2002, the first full year following the 2001 acquisition of Compaq Computer. There is no doubt that HP benefited hugely in the inventory arena. Exhibit 4.5 includes Compaq's inventory turns along with HP's. It shows that Compaq, before being acquired, had been graded *A* for its

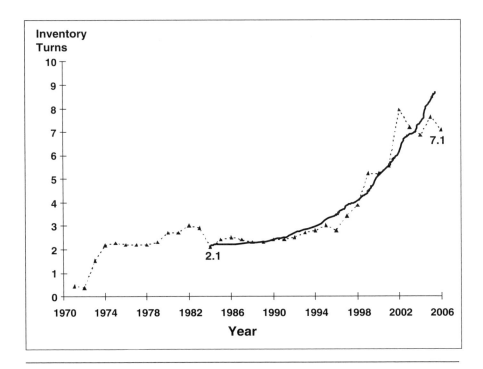

Exhibit 4.4   Improving Rate of Improvement at Hewlett-Packard

spectacular 12-year, 6.7 percent average annual rate of improvement. When HP made the purchase at the end of 2001, its turns were 5.6 versus Compaq's 15.4. Study of Compaq's annual reports from 1999 through 2002 suggest that HP may have bought itself not just a major computer manufacturer but also a lot of advanced lean-management expertise.

Compaq's 1999 annual report includes a sentence about moving from a build-to-stock to a build-to-order/configure-to-order model. Its 2000 annual report gives the same concept a paragraph. It explains how the new model allows catering to two different kinds of customers, and that both BTO and CTO generate efficiencies related to advanced JIT manufacturing, inventory, and distribution practices. HP's 2005 annual report includes a paragraph using similar words. HP appears to have learned lessons from Compaq, a shining star among electronics companies as judged by its steep rate of improvement in inventory turns.

For some years, HP's advances in supply-chain management have been the subject of numerous academic and trade articles.[7] According to one report, HP "has spawned any number of unique and innovative purchasing and procurement practices ... credited as being a strategic part of HP's success as it manages the largest portion of the company's expenses."[8] Whether HP developed those practices or learned them from Compaq doesn't matter. The acquisition that led to the HP board's ouster of

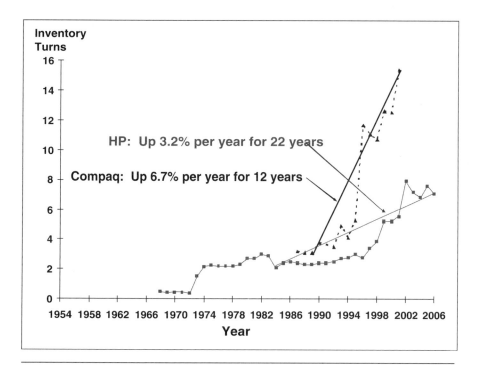

Exhibit 4.5 Annual Rates of Improvement for Hewlett-Packard and Compaq Computer

William Hewlett, son of the company's co-founder, and had stock analysts shaking their heads, has pushed total shareholder returns up 46 percent in five years.[9] HP's chief financial officer, Bob Wayman, notes that following the merger "free cash flow soared from $1.5 billion in 2001 to $6.6 billion in 2005." Of course; inventory reduction automatically generates cash flow, which can rank in importance with the broad array of benefits accruing in the chain of customers.

NEC

Japan's NEC, the world's forty-fifth-largest manufacturer ($46 billion in sales),[10] produces a broad line of electronics, from semiconductors to networking equipment to personal and high-end computers and peripherals. NEC's story is one of continually repairing a leaking boat to avoid floundering.

NEC lost money in 1993, 1999, 2002, and 2003.[11] Most companies in a bad year end up with excessive unsold inventories. Not NEC. Inspection of its trend line, in Exhibit 4.6, shows inventory turns improving in each of the red-ink years—and in all but one year since 1996. What can we make of that? From Chapter 3 on financial impacts: NEC would have been in much deeper trouble had its accelerated leanness

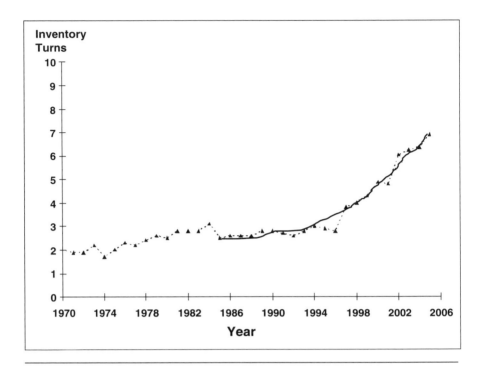

Exhibit 4.6   Improving Rate of Improvement at NEC

not spun off gobs of cash during those tough years. (The naïve view that NEC was starving itself of inventory, thereby losing sales and customers and profits, is roundly rejected.)

That point is strengthened by information from NEC's annual reports since 1997 (prior reports not available). Whereas annual reports typically gloss over details about manufacturing, inventory, and related matters, NEC's say quite a lot. Its 1997 report states that NEC's semiconductor group was awarded the first Japan Quality Award. Years leading up to that should, by 1999, have reduced inventories in the form of scrap, rework, and customer returns—along with costly scheduling and planning disruptions. The lean core gets directly mentioned in 1998 ("innovative manufacturing techniques, such as lean production") and 1999 (an inventory-reduction goal employing build-to-order production for corporate customers, and increased JIT procurement). Annual reports from 1999 through 2005 talk about NEC's outsourcing of production, mainly to China, tightening of supply chains, and inventory issues. Several reports cite plant closures, work-force reductions, restructurings, and joint ventures. Simplifications of product offerings and improved product designs were mentioned in 1998 (concurrent engineering) and 1999 (PBX platforms common to all customers). The $456 million acquisition of Packard Bell NEC Europe (formerly a separate business that NEC had a stake in) near the end of FY1999 might also have benefited NEC's inventory turns.

For all its capacity downsizing, NEC's sales have held up well: 2004 was NEC's second-best sales year and 2005 their third-best. Long-term leanness should have that result, because its compounding, quick-response effects have high customer appeal.

Of the four strongly lean companies that have been reviewed, NEC emerges as perhaps the most impressive. Its upward-arcing trend line is still intact (through 2005; 2006 data are not available at this writing). It stands tall among companies in a nation that has been especially weak for some 15 years on the leanness scale. All the information about NEC, however, is secondary, from annual reports. Inability to visit NEC facilities and to conduct interviews with NEC people (our attempts to do so were not successful) clouds the picture somewhat. That limitation carries over to the four companies labeled *equivocal*, discussed next.

EQUIVOCAL

Owing to difficulties in obtaining information, the "lean" stories of Eastman Kodak, Gerber Scientific, Lam Research, and Sony are incomplete or ambiguous. Their inventory graphs are impressive, but available information does not clearly or completely show why. None of their records of improvement appear to be based on broad-ranging, systematized excellence in lean management.

Nevertheless, all four would have gained a lot from their lengthy upward trend. When inventory turns keep improving for many years, manifold benefits accrue and compound themselves. A large question remains. In upcoming years will those benefits tail off because of failure to have acquired and deeply implanted the necessary process-improvement learning? Discussion follows.

EASTMAN KODAK

Kodak ($14 billion), like Hewlett-Packard, is a make-to-stock company producing for its own and its distributors' and retailers' inventories. Also, like HP, Kodak was among the western world's leaders in learning about JIT/TQC in the early and mid-1980s. Inspection of Kodak's trend chart (Exhibit 4.7) seems to indicate that all that learning paid off handsomely. A closer look does not fully support that conjecture.

The year 1988 looks to be the start of its accelerating leanness pattern, with an average rate of improvement of 3.7 percent per year for 18 years. (The 19 prior years show good but generally linear improvement, muddied with large up–down swings in the 1980s.) The information search for Kodak focused on two questions: (1) Why do Kodak's considerable JIT/TQ efforts in the 1980s show up as mostly worsening inventory turns? (2) What was happening in the 1990s and 2000s to cause the huge up–down spikes in the midst of Kodak's excellent long-term trend?

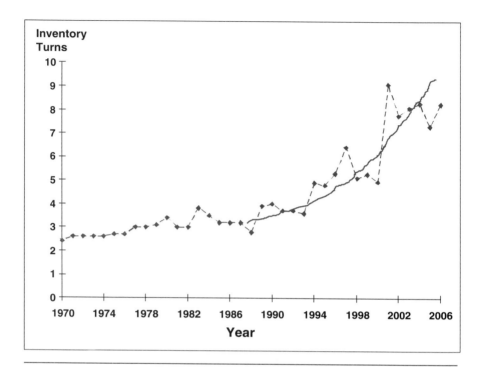

Exhibit 4.7   Improving Rate of Improvement at Eastman Kodak

Kodak's annual reports do not mention just-in-time or lean. However, my own bulging file on the company details extensive 1980s-era just-in-time and total-quality activities. Besides unpublished and published materials, they include my notes from a few personal visits to Kodak in the decade.[12] Both Kodak and Kodak's home city, Rochester, New York, were hotbeds of JIT/TQ training through the 1980s.[13]

Countering all that activity was another, perhaps stronger movement in the company: MRP advocacy. Material requirements planning (MRP) is still alive and co-existing with lean/JIT in many companies today, but usually in simplified, reduced forms. In the 1980s, a Class-A MRP facility had to track every move of materials, including in and out of locked work-in-process (WIP) stockrooms. JIT/lean does away with most of the transactions, and the WIP stockrooms as well. MRP formally scheduled every operation, whereas JIT/lean employs visual kanban to direct the flow. At Kodak, the MRP faction was in league with the large information-systems function. Both were in favor of JIT but their complex, costly systems stood in the way of one-piece flow, pull systems, and inventory reduction.

The JIT people were frustrated enough that on May 3, 1988, they scheduled me for a sort of showdown meeting with then–vice chairman J. Phillip Samper. They hoped that I could relate to Mr. Samper why the company should mount an effort to turn off some of the complex, JIT-retarding features of MRP, including halting the proliferation of tracking terminals on the factory floor. The meeting did not accomplish anything. Samper was sympathetic, but the Kodak hierarchy at that time had him too many levels above the fray to do anything; his role was to rely on the chain of command, in which the upstart JIT people lacked numbers and clout.

Those points may help explain why, for all the JIT, Kodak's inventory turns fell rather than rose from 1983 to 1988. Besides that, Kodak was and is largely a consumer-goods business in which marketing is the principal power. Marketing and sales want more, not less inventory. Thus, much of Kodak's worsening turnover may have been marketing-induced growth of finished goods in the pipelines.

Public records cast some light on Kodak's highly erratic upward trend in the 1990s and 2000s. The company was shrinking,[14] as electronics were replacing chemistry-based photography. While shuttering plants and shedding employees by the thousands, Kodak made many acquisitions and a few divestitures. Those efforts, aimed at shifting its line of products and services toward digital photography and electronics, may have been instrumental in Kodak's improving inventory turns. Electronics is inherently far leaner than chemistry. For example, the sharp rise in turns in 1997 may have had a lot to do with the $688 million sale of Kodak's money-losing Office Imaging business, which may have been burdened with large inventories. The giant leap from less than 5 turns in 2000 to more than 9 in 2001, then down to about 8 in 2002, is harder to explain. Records show just two acquisitions made early enough in 2001 to have had an impact: Bell & Howell's imaging business for $141 million and Ofoto's online digital photography business for $58 million. The two were privately held, so no inventory turnover data are available to verify whether they had exceptionally high turns, giving Kodak's turns an upward jolt.

Whatever the explanation, Kodak's accelerating rate of casting off inventory ranks among the world's most impressive. Time will tell whether the improvement is mostly an artifact of acquisitions and divestitures, or whether in-depth process-improvement expertise resides in the company.

LAM RESEARCH

Silicon Valley's Lam Research ($1.6 billion sales) produces semiconductor processing equipment, mainly for etching and cleaning wafers. Lam's web site includes a long list of awards it has received from customers such as Samsung, Motorola, Analog Devices, Toshiba, and NEC. Eighty-six percent of its 2006 sales were to non-U.S. customers, a percentage that has been rising over the years. Thus, like Wal-Mart, its gains in inventory turnover have come even as it has been lengthening its supply lines to customers.

Public records give no hints that Lam has employed any of the common-core aspects of process improvement: JIT, TQ, lean, TPM, 5S, and so on. (Attempts to interview Lam people were unsuccessful.) Yet its inventory turns have risen sharply and at an accelerating rate since 1991; see Exhibit 4.8 (which also includes the graph for Gerber Scientific, our next company). The rise in turns starts slowly in 1991, then

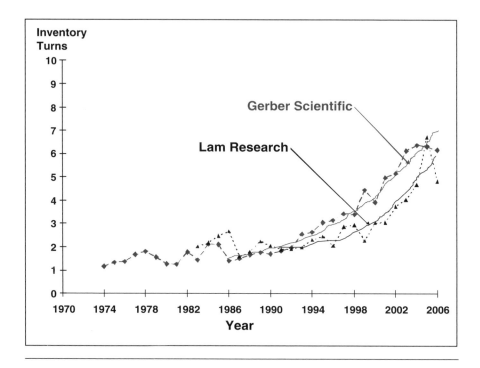

Exhibit 4.8   Improving Rate of Improvement at Lam Research and Gerber Scientific

jumps a bit in 1994–1995 and a lot in 1996–1997. Because Lam made acquisitions in 1993 and 1997, high inventory turns of the acquired companies may partly explain those jumps. The small company acquired in 1993 was privately held, so its turns are unknown. The 1997 acquisition, OnTrak, was much larger and publicly held, and its 3.8 inventory turns were high compared with Lam's 2.1 in that year. Lam's turns would have been pumped somewhat by OnTrak's numbers, which were folded in for the past 10 months of FY97 and continuing into FY98.

Reading any more into the ups and downs of Lam's turnover pattern for 1991 through 2001 is hazardous, because Lam is in an extremely cyclical industry. Its sales revenue went from $140 million in 1991 to $1.3 billion in 1996, down to $650 million in 1999, up to $1.52 billion in 2001—and so on for another such cycle to the present. But here is a bit of speculation on the decade starting with 1991. Lam could have gained nearly all of its leanness in that period simply by better designs of its etching and cleaning equipment: standardized parts, modular components, and the other aspects of design for manufacturing and assembly. If design for manufacture and assembly (DFMA) were at work at Lam, it should show up quickly as improved turnover of work-in-process inventories. Lam's WIP turns soared from 1994 through 2000.

In addition, here and there Lam may have been employing various JIT and total-quality methods. They were well known and in wide use in nearly all of Lam's OEM (original equipment manufacturer) electronics customers since the mid-1980s. Plenty of Lam people should have been aware, which would be likely to have triggered some JIT/TQ activity.

Beginning in 2002 Lam began aggressively to outsource elements of its manufacturing, production, warehousing, and logistics, and also to end up with fewer, larger suppliers.[15] Lam's stated purpose of the outsourcing is to enable it "to focus on new and existing product development, sales and marketing, and customer support."[16] Such outsourcing is what most western electronics OEMs had been doing for some years. As detailed in Chapter 17, it has restructured the industry, creating the now-huge electronic manufacturing services subsector. For the large majority of electronics OEMs, the outsourcing has paid off handsomely in most of the usual financial measures, including inventory turnover. The effects at Lam: Its inventory turns more than doubled in just four years, from 3.1 in 2001 to 3.7 in 2002—and kept going to 4.0 in 2003, 4.7 in 2004, and 6.7 in 2005. As expected, during those years Lam's raw-material turns shot upward.

This outsourcing in the electronics sector is a valued form of process improvement and becoming lean, though one that has finite limits. And at Lam the good trend did not continue in 2006. Though it was a good year for Lam's sales and earnings, inventories surged and turns fell sharply, to 4.8. The reasons are unclear. It may be just a temporary blip. However, perhaps lack of a full-fledged process-improvement commitment has caught up with the company.[17]

These points raise the question: Is getting lean by outsourcing fools-gold lean? Is it just shifting the inventory from your books to those of your suppliers? As a way to pump your company's short-term numbers, it is a weak practice. The best way to obviate the phoniness is through use of a metric devised at IBM many years ago, called "joint inventory." More on that in Chapter 17.

GERBER SCIENTIFIC

This $530 million company produces industrial equipment for sign-making and specialty graphics, fabric cutting and cleaning, and ophthalmic lens processing. (Gerber baby food comes from a different, unrelated company.) Gerber's accelerating upward trend in inventory turnover extends from 1986 to 2006 and averages 3.9 percent improvement per year. The trend includes only a single large up–down–up spike—between 1998 and 2001; see Exhibit 4.8. From public records,[18] the causes seem clear: Gerber made two large acquisitions and a large divestiture late in FY98. The turmoil appears to have dragged down Gerber's turns slightly in that year. (Being private, the three acquired companies' inventory records are not available for confirmation.) The full effects would be felt in FY99, a year in which inventory turns rose sharply from 3.4 to 4.9. The main causal factor appears to be by far the largest of the two acquisitions, Spandex plc. This U.K.-based producer of sign-making and graphics equipment became the source of 38 percent of Gerber's revenue in 1999. If Spandex had comparatively high inventory turns that would have raised Gerber's turns in that fiscal year. Gerber's turns fell to 3.9 in 2000 (five more acquisitions in FY2000 were all small), but recovery was quick: Turns shot back up to 5.0 in 2001.

In 2005, Gerber completed its "three-year business re-engineering plan, which included consolidation of production and warehouse facilities; centralization of supply chain, customer service, information technology, and accounting," plus implementation of its SAP ERP system in most operating locations.[19] Contrarily, Gerber's inventory turns fell in 2005 and 2006, the only two-year decline in 20 years. Moreover, the company's raw-material turns plunged in 2004 through 2006, after improving greatly between 1996 and 2001. (Gerber's financial reports divide its total inventories into two components, raw and WIP/FG.) In the years between 1996 and 2001, raw-material turns had greatly improved.

The reengineering so far seems to have had mostly negative consequences. That is not a surprise. ERP systems and traditional accounting usually require a heavy diet of transactions and complexity, which is counter to the simple, visual management that is elemental in lean. Consolidation of production can be beneficial. But if it brings dissimilar product lines into a single, outsized building, growing complexities, lengthened material handling distances, and losses in focus can offset the benefits. (Chapter 16 expands on the contrary effects of large, unfocused manufacturing buildings.)

In short, study of limited information about Gerber does not reveal expertise in the lean core, astute pipeline management, or external collaborations. Still, shrinking its inventories from 1986 through 2003 would have brought many of Gerber's processes closer together, generating multiple benefits that go to both the top and bottom lines.

SONY

Sony ($67 billion sales), though now prominent in entertainment businesses (movies, TV, music), still gets 64 percent of its sales from electronics and another 12 percent from electronic games. Factors contributing to its 27-year up-swooping trend (see Exhibit 4.9) are the subject of this discussion. Prior to 1998, Sony's annual reports were devoid of comments pertaining to the lean core, supply chains, restructuring, outsourcing, or standardized parts or platforms. From then on, the reports have given plentiful attention to those kinds of topics.

Generally, the comments convey deep concern about Sony's difficulties in the marketplace. The reports from 1998 through 2005 refer many times to a variety of measures that would reduce inventories and improve cash flows: restructurings, plant closures and consolidations, outsourcings, head-count reductions, strengthening supply chains, integration of the functions, and localizing procurement.

Those reports also refer to *"cell production method"* (in quotation marks), *lean*, *six sigma*, *lead-time reduction*, *continuous improvement*, and *economic value added*. Each is mentioned just once with no accompanying discussion. One gets the impression that Sony saw those terms as management fads in the United States, to be inserted to indulge enthusiasts from Sony's large U.S. operations.

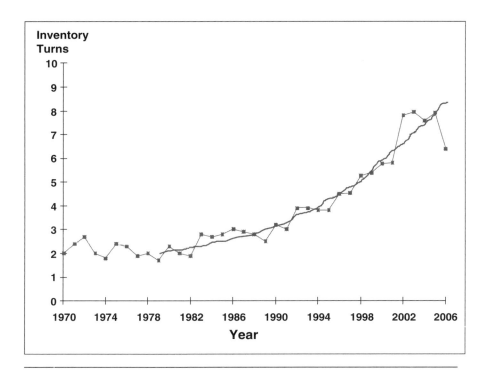

Exhibit 4.9   Improving Rate of Improvement at Sony

By 2006, it must have seemed clear to Sony executives that its efforts to slim down and change had not been sufficient. For four years, Sony's total sales and electronics sales, earnings, and margins had stagnated and its share price had deteriorated. Inventory turns had plunged from 7.9 in 2005 to 6.4 in 2006. The 2006 annual report ceased all talk about inventories, supply chains, and functional integration. Instead, it simply declared there will be 200 billion yen in cost reductions, 80 percent by end of FY07 and the rest by end of FY08, as follows: 11 of 65 manufacturing sites closed or consolidated; 20 percent reduction in product model count; and 10,000-person head-count reduction. The stated reason was the massive shift in consumer demand to plasma and LCD TV technologies, and away from Sony's huge CRT-based manufacturing.

The steep rise in Sony's inventory turns between 2001 and 2002, from 5.8 to 7.8, may be related to a large joint venture and a sizeable acquisition. The joint venture in mid-FY01, with Sweden's Ericsson, established Sony Ericsson Mobile Communications for manufacturing and marketing mobile phones. It appears that Ericsson's mobile phone business was sufficiently lean to bump Sony's 2002 inventory turns upward. Then, in mid-FY02 Sony parlayed a minority interest in Aiwa, an audio products manufacturer, into a wholly owned subsidiary. Aiwa's inventory turns at the time were at 5.0 versus Sony's 5.8—no apparent help. Confirming this conjecture, Exhibit 4.9 shows Sony's turns rising only a bit in 2003, and then beginning to sink.

Not mentioned in the annual reports is product simplification via design for manufacture and assembly. Sony appears to have been late to see the importance of this, maybe because DFMA's development took place not in Japan but in the United States.[20] Attesting to this, a 2003 story says Sony "will seek to reduce the number of parts to 100,000 from 840,000 [and include] in a database 20,000 'Sony-defined standard parts.'" The same story says it will attempt to "trim the number of its parts suppliers to about 1,000 from 4,700."[21] In this, Sony is not alone among Japanese manufacturers. Others late to adopt these high-impact process-improvement practices are noted in Chapters 19 and 20.

Until the 2000s, Sony's electronics business was widely admired for its string of innovative, highly popular consumer products. During that stretch, Sony was successful as well in accelerating its inventory turns. Since the late 1990s and to the present, product-line difficulties have impelled Sony to adopt tough coping practices, though mostly not in the lean core. In the near future, as it adjusts its product line and focuses more on wide-ranging process-improvement practices, Sony may again become one of the world's most admired companies. (On the other hand, a hot-selling Japanese book suggests that Sony and the other major Japanese electronics companies must massively merge, or expire.[22])

This chapter, with its examples of exceptional trends in sustained leanness, brings Part I to a close. The three chapters in Part II target certain features of lean management that are popular, but not altogether sensible and sound. If they look to you like unsupported opinions, you may change your mind after reading subsequent chapters in Parts III through VI that weave in many examples of how companies excel or fail to excel in the excellence quest.

NOTES

1. Cited in Paul Magnusson, "Too Lean a Machine?," book review of Barry C. Lynn, *End of the Line: The Rise and Coming Fall of the Global Corporation* (New York: Doubleday, 2005).

2. Peter M. Senge, *The Fifth Discipline: The Art and Practice of the Learning Organization* (New York: Doubleday/Currency, 1990).

3. Frank Piller and Ashok Kumar, "For Each, Their Own: The Strategic Imperative of Mass Customization," *Industrial Engineer* (September 2006), pp. 40–45.

4. Having reinstalled himself as CEO, Michael Dell has hinted at transitioning to a "light touch" model, meaning less internal manufacturing: Christopher Lawton, "Dell Gives Job to Cannon of Solectron," *Wall Street Journal* (February 15, 2007), p. B6.

5. Charles Fishman, "The Wal-Mart Effect and a Decent Society: Who Knew Shopping Was So Important?" *Academy of Management Perspectives*, 20, no. 3 (August 2006), pp. 6–25.

6. A sample of publications about HP's implementations includes: Richard C. Walleigh, "What's Your Excuse for Not Using JIT?" *Harvard Business Review* (March–April 1986), pp. 38–54; and Richard J. Schonberger, *World Class Manufacturing Casebook:*

Implementing JIT and TQC (New York: Free Press/Simon & Schuster, 1987), in which 6 of 26 cases are on HP implementations including one with the disguised name, Ultrix Corp.

7. For example: Edward Feitzinger and Hau L. Lee, "Mass Customization at Hewlett-Packard: The Power of Postponement," *Harvard Business Review* (January 1997), pp. 116–122; and Hau L. Lee, Corey Billington, and Brent Carter, "Hewlett-Packard Gains Control of Inventory and Service through Design for Localization," *Interfaces*, 23, no. 4 (July–August 1993), pp. 1–11.

8. Institute of Management and Administration, "Procurement Head Reveals Keys to Achieve World-Class Status," *Supplier Selection & Management Report*, Issue 05–02 (February 2005), pp. 1ff.

9. Roy Harris, "Rush to Judgment," *CFO* (October 2006), pp. 31–32.

10. "IW 1000: World's Largest Manufacturers," *Industry Week* (June 2005), pp. 39–62.

11. Source: Annual reports found on NEC's web site.

12. One 26-page Kodak document dated 1983 (Edward Ehlers, "JIT: Just-in-Time," Eastman Kodak Corp., unpublished) includes 16 pages of achievements. One page, regarding Kodak's X-Omatic Department, cites reduction of cassettes from a supplier: cassette inventory cut from 63 to 10 days' worth. Another for the same department is on the results of moving machines close together: inventory cut from 2 months' supply to zero, and scrap from 20% to 0.5%; and in circuit-board assembly, lot size was reduced from 500 to 40. In Opaque Plastics Molding, finished goods in front of the customer were down from $8 million to $1.4 million. Edward Ehlers, one of Kodak's full-time providers of JIT-oriented activities, edited a series of JIT news updates distributed to like-minded people in the company. My files include a few of them, the latest being issue number 39.

13. Richard Schonberger was one of the various JIT/TQ presenters conducting Kodak in-house seminars and public ones co-sponsored by Kodak. Those seminars took place in Rochester on December 7, 1984; November 10–11, 1987; May 5–6, 1988; and November 1–2, 1988. Tom Billesbach was brought in to run two JIT simulation training programs at Kodak on May 10 and May 12, 1988.

14. Kodak's sales hit a peak in 1992 of $20.2 billion, fell to $10.6 billion in 1985, and have ranged up and down from $12.8 to $16.0 billion ever since. Sources: Kodak's annual reports and Value Line Stock Reports.

15. Lam Research, 10-K report (June 27, 2004), p. 17.

16. Lam Research, 10-K report (June 27, 2006), p. 20.

17. Executives at Lam Research chose not to comment on what has been written about the company in these paragraphs.

18. Gerber Scientific, 10-K reports for 1999, 2000, and 2001.

19. Gerber Scientific, 10-K report (April 30, 2005), p. 46.

20. DFMA's principal developers were Professors Geoffrey Boothroyd and Peter Dewhurst at the University of Rhode Island from the beginning of the 1980s. One of their publications is *Product Design for Assembly* (Kingston, RI: Department of Industrial and Manufacturing Engineering, University of Rhode Island, 1987).

21. Kanji Ishibashi, "Sony Will Slash Parts List, in Bid to Boost Margins," *Wall Street Journal* (October 7, 2003), p. B5.

22. Fumiaki Sato, *A Scenario for the Realignment of Japan's Electronics Industry,* 2007.

Improvement Gone Wrong—and Made Right

O.C. Tanner in Salt Lake City, 1999 recipient of a Shingo Prize,[1] does not have something called the Tanner Production System. The word *production* would not be helpful in drawing in people from functions such as sales, accounts receivable, and purchasing. Instead, it is the Tanner Improvement System.

Perhaps Tanner got the idea from Milliken and Co., which in 1985 tossed out its *suggestion system* in favor of initiating its *opportunity-for-improvement (OFI)* system. OFI thrives at Milliken today.[2] Word choices make a difference.

Effective improvement systems are uncommon. In a typical facility with two, three, or four hundred people, ten people are improvement-adding, the rest non-improvement-adding. How to harness people's talents and experience to achieve high rates of process improvement remains, largely, a riddle. Managers and professionals see part of their role as generating improvements. Others—the bulk of employees—do not, mostly because of management-system obstacles and neglect.

Getting back to the point of the two opening paragraphs, word choices make a difference. Each chapter in this second section probes improvement methodologies with familiar names, each one generally admired. They include waste elimination, kaizen, continuous improvement, goals, metrics, dashboards, scorecards, lean accounting, overall equipment effectiveness (OEE), zero-defects six sigma, and *gemba*. In all of these we look for, and find, flaws and faults that help explain weaknesses in our improvement systems, some minor and others major.

NOTES

1. Dustin Ott, "Getting to Continuous Flow in a Make-to-Order Environment," Lean Practitioner presentation, *Proceedings, 1999 Annual Shingo Prize Conference and Awards Ceremony*, pp. 609–625.

2. More on the development of Milliken's OFI system in Alan G. Robinson and Dean M. Schroeder, *Ideas are Free: How the Idea Revolution Is Liberating People and Transforming Organizations* (San Francisco: Berrett-Koehler, 2004), pp. 212–213.

Chapter 5

Waste Elimination, Kaizen, and Continuous Improvement: Misdefined, Misunderstood

Among the best-accepted concepts in the pursuit of process improvement are: (1) *lean*, defined as elimination of wastes, and (2) *kaizen events* as the dominant way to achieve lean and continuous improvement. This chapter takes a close, critical look and finds flaws in those viewpoints. It finds them deficient as to definition and also in comprehension. The discussion begins with lean/waste elimination and follows with kaizen events and *true* continuous improvement.

CUSTOMERS TO THE FORE: WASTE ELIMINATION AS AN ENABLER

Current definitions of lean/TPS are oddly slanted toward one of the enabling tool sets rather than focused on more clearly competitive factors. *Wikipedia* leads off its definition as: "*Lean manufacturing* is a management philosophy focusing on reduction of the seven wastes ...."[1] Is losing weight the definition of a good diet? No; it is better health, increased capabilities, longer life. So it must be for lean.

More fittingly, lean employs a large set of concepts and tools to reduce delays and quicken response in all processes. That is fundamental lean, with time compression as its main focus.[2] The time-compression viewpoint does not lack for its adherents, past and present. Lean's predecessor, just in time, had the same primary focus (still, its definitions also sometimes deviated.[3]) When the textile-clothing-retail triumvirate took its remarkably successful JIT-lean–supply chain plunge, it named it *quick response—QR*. (More on that in Chapter 13.) Professor Rajan Suri directs the Center for Quick Response Manufacturing at the University of Wisconsin—Madison.[4] Stalk's milestone article, "Time—The Next Source of Competitive Advantage," provides strategic grounding for the primary focus of lean and JIT.[5] Time compression squares directly with what the customer cares about. As Bicheno puts it, "Stand back and look at the customer as the 'object' of one-piece flow."[6]

Lean does not stand alone. It links easily and naturally with process improvement as a whole. What is important in that broadened linkage, with quality as a co-equal, is ensuring that the *purposes* are foremost in people's understanding. With that in mind, continuous improvement directs itself to the goals/wants/needs of all customers, internal and external, and in every process. They are the *golden goals*: ever-better quality, quicker response, greater flexibility, and higher value.

To be sure, reducing the seven wastes is a worthy pathway in furthering the golden goals. The five *why*s are good, too. So are TPM, SPC (statistical process control), and 5S, and supplier partnership and collaborations with customers. Why, then, do lean definitions wrap themselves around the seven wastes?

There are some fairly good reasons. The seven wastes (or *seven cardinal sins*, as one wag put it in an executive session at Cardinal Health) capture a lot of common process woes in just a few common words. They are easily taught, and outfitted with a helpful mnemonic:

- Seven wastes: *D*efects *T*ransport *M*otion *I*nventory *P*rocessing *O*ver-production *W*aiting
- Mnemonic: *D*on't *T*ell *M*e *I*'m *P*utting *O*n *W*eight

McManus, in arguing that lean is all about "customer pull," offers a reason for the common focus on waste reduction: it "does not involve as much human interaction and is easier to measure" than customer pull.[7]

So what's the rub? It is that the seven wastes are production/operations oriented. They do not resonate much with customers, marketers, upper managers, senior executives, stock analysts, and investors. Defined as waste elimination or reduction, lean doesn't even register with some of the leading authors of business books; more on that later.

The golden goals do. Even analysts and investors place high value on companies known for quality; quick, flexible response; and value. Moreover, well-known close-to-the-action performance metrics attach well to each of the golden goals. For example, defects, nonconformities, rework, and process capability are among the many ways of tracking process quality. Flow time, cash-to-cash time, percent value added, and on-time rate are measures of quick response. Setup and changeover time and number of skills mastered per associate are good determinants of flexibility. Value, too, has its measures, a lot of them technology-specific: price per pound, per megawatt, per lineal meter, and so on. Not only are these metrics close to the processes and the process teams, most are also what customers care about.

Nor are the seven wastes comprehensive. Here are eight more, which have been labeled *nonobvious* wastes:[8]

1. *Promotional waste (negative selling):* Getting customers to buy what they don't want or need.

2. *Order tracking waste:* Performing a tracking transaction for every move of an order through offices, plants, and transport.

3. *Automating the waste:* Spanning process-to-process space with powered conveyors rather than shortening the flow.

4. *Container-to-container waste:* Taking an item out of one container and putting it into another, which is elemental in the kitting process. This actually is covered by the seven wastes because it adds unnecessary inventory, transport, motion, and processing. Nevertheless, kitting is apparently nonobvious as waste since many companies still treat kitting as a valued practice. (Kitting between geographically separate facilities is valued, but within a facility it is a workaround solution that does not get at the root cause. In other words, transport kits, yes; material-handling kits, no.)

5. *Analyzing the waste:* Not content with just attacking waste, many companies expend resources and time studying it, costing it, and labeling it as non-value-adding.

6. *Costing the cost reductions:* Not content with just reducing non-value-adding activities, many companies, especially larger ones, waste resources toting up how much money the reductions have saved.

7. *Costing the bad quality:* Not content with just attacking the causes of bad quality, some companies continue expending resources estimating the costs of the bad quality or the money saved by reducing it.

8. *Reporting the utilization and efficiency:* Not content with just fixing causes of poor utilization and efficiency, many companies maintain administrative systems for tracking and reporting the resulting improvements in utilization and efficiency.

The seven wastes make up a strong set of lean enablers. They ought to be widely taught and widely used. Attacking the seven wastes bears good fruit, though not enough of it. Eight more enablers, the nonobvious wastes, deserve attention, too, especially as companies extend their lean efforts into administrative and support functions. The enablers, though, should be far less prominent—in training, problem-solving, and celebration—than the four customer-centered golden goals of lean/TQ.

Redefining lean/TQ can help clear away some of the obstacles to sustained, high-energy process improvement. There are, however, many more hurdles in the way. More than just lean/TQ, the whole matter of best practices in process improvement is scarcely recognized among some leading writers of business books. The two giant sellers by Jim Collins—*Built to Last* and *Good to Great* [9]—do not mention lean or TPS—or, for that matter, JIT or TQ, or process improvement. And except for two pages on total quality management, the same goes for O'Toole and Lawler's 2006 book, *The New American Workplace*.[10] Intended as a sequel to the influential 1973 book, *Work in America*,[11] the O'Toole and Lawler volume shows no recognition that process improvement is a vital, meaningful part of the work lives of employees in well-run companies. The remainder of this chapter, and all remaining chapters, too, bring out the obstacles and ways of dealing with them.

THE KAIZEN TRAP: *DIS-CONTINUOUS* IMPROVEMENT

For many companies the practice of lean includes a process-improvement methodology called *kaizen events* (or sometimes *kaizen blitzes*).[12] Commonly, *kaizen*, from the Japanese, is translated as "continuous improvement." However, in no small irony, a kaizen event is a project, and projects are, by definition, discontinuous. Projects are essential but only half the battle. In this chapter we reprise the lore, distressingly forgotten, minimized, or set aside, that constitutes the continuous side of process improvement.

Maasaki Imai, author of a 1986 U.S.-published book on kaizen, may have introduced the word to the West.[13] (A search of many earlier English-language books and articles, including those about the Toyota system, failed to turn up any reference to *kaizen*). Imai's book was not about kaizen events. Rather it included a variety of improvement methods including TQC, QC circles, employee suggestions, and others.

A kaizen project is an intensive, quick-hit, at-the-site method of achieving improvement in a targeted area. Some companies rely heavily on this kind of short-duration project, usually of about two to five days. A limitation is that kaizen projects tend to be dominated by salaried experts with only sporadic contributions from the bulk of the work force. Exception: In very small companies kaizen projects are likely to include nearly everybody, benefit from less complex conditions, and get done quickly, often in one day instead of two to five.

Companies also engage their people in projects that require more time and deliberation, such as six sigma projects, designed experiments, and failure mode and effects analysis (FMEA). These projects rely on special kinds of expertise and are less likely than kaizen events to involve front-line associates.

INTENSIVE OBSERVATION AT THE *GEMBA*—BUT WHO ARE THE OBSERVERS?

Still another kind of kaizen, if you will, is improvement arising from intensive observation. The Japanese word *gemba* refers to the action zone, spot, or place, where the observer stands to intensively observe. (*Gemba* and several other Japanese words that had enjoyed brief western popularity in the 1980s have been resurrected and inserted into the global lexicon on process improvement. A few of those words, such as *kanban* and *kaizen*, have been internationalized. Many others, perhaps including *gemba*, seem likely to be replaced by western-language equivalents.)

My first exposure to the intensive-observation mode of process-improvement was during visits to the Kawasaki motorcycle plant in Lincoln, Nebraska, from 1980 to 1983. In some of the visits I was struck by seeing the plant manager, Mr. Saeki, standing in the same spot in the factory for the duration of my tour. I was inclined to offer a greeting, but was warned not to interrupt his concentration.

Two decades later I was on the phone with one of the Kawasaki managers I had known best. I mentioned Mr. Saeki's unusual practice. That drew a wry chuckle from my friend, who said that back then everyone joked about the boss's lone-wolf approach to process analysis. (Since Mr. Saeki left the plant many years ago, there seems to be no need for a disguised name or location.) Mr. Saeki, my friend said, did not believe in employee involvement. Some years later, when a sister plant for motorcycle engines opened in Marysville, Missouri, the management there did believe in employee involvement, and put it into force.

The message here is not that intensive observation is a bankrupt idea. To the contrary. In my own plant visits, there to learn, my strongest inclination, always foiled, is to stand somewhere and watch and take notes for a long time. Mr. Saeki had the right idea but, like many of us, was a micro-manager, and probably very good at it. But the large potential benefits of the method are squandered when restricted to a single person or to salaried observers only. Intensive observation is not for the limited few but for the work force as a whole. What plant manager, accountant or trainer, or industrial engineer with stop watch, can see and observe with as much perspicacity as those who do the work? At Kawasaki I would have been amazed and delighted had I seen production associates here and there in ones and twos, intensively observing, with clipboard and pencil in hand, for long stretches of time. That is what was missing then, and it is still missing today. In the many companies that are taken with the idea of "going to the *gemba*," the wrong people, and too few of them, are involved.

THE CONTINUOUS SIDE OF IMPROVEMENT: FULL ENGAGEMENT

It is time to rejuvenate continuous, data-driven improvement with full engagement of the work force.[14] Intensive observation can be no more than a small part of it. The bulk of it has all employees, in their jobs, all day long recording every process glitch, hiccup, mishap, and frustration. Dr. W. Edwards Deming and Dr. Kaoru Ishikawa showed the way and got Big Industry going on this in the previous century, first in Japan, and then everywhere. A competitive edge goes to companies with an equitable mix of project and continuous improvement.

Just as there are several standard kinds of improvement projects, so there are several continuous improvement (CI) modes. Suggestion forms and boxes can be made to work, but need a lot of enlightened care and feeding. Otherwise they yield but a trickle of ideas, often of small or dubious value.

High-intensity CI, producing a flood of valued solutions, requires a flood of data. The recording media must be readily available and easy-to-use. Flipcharts and dry-erase boards, in every work center, usually will do. The data, or their first derivative, need to emerge formatted so as to make sense out of the jumble. Doing just that are Ishikawa's seven tools: flowchart, check sheet, Pareto chart, fishbone diagram, histogram, scatter diagram, and process control chart. These are well known and need not be detailed in this book. What is necessary is that companies train everyone—not just those who are to become black belts—in their use. That includes the janitor and the security force. Everyone experiences plentiful mishaps, frustrations, and fears that need to be addressed, for the betterment of their work lives plus the competitive strengthening of their company.

COMPETITIVENESS TRAINING

The work force needs not only to learn the tools of process improvement. Like managers and professionals, the associates will use them only half-heartedly if they do not fully understand the benefits if they do, and the consequences if they don't. The way to impart that understanding is through *competitiveness training*. Learning the tools and techniques captures the details; competitiveness training brings in the big picture. That training could include elements such as the following, backed up with plentiful case examples:

- We are in a new, globally hyper-competitive era. Besides our traditional competitors, we need to watch out for many new ones from anywhere on the globe.

- The new competitors can steal our customers in different ways. One from a developing country will go for our price-sensitive customers. A rival that focuses on quality will take our exacting customers. Any that master the simplifying practices called lean will mop up more of our business by beating us on lead times and flexibility. And a competitor good on the full set of best practices in process improvement will eat all our lunch—the full plate. That is because each of the best practices meshes with the others to improve quality and customer response. And it does so by simplifying processes rather than spending itself out of business.

- Once it was enough to produce a static product line well, with slow change and slow improvement. The edge today goes to companies that have mastered rapid, continuous improvement. (For many years, A-graded office-furniture maker Hon Industries has called its effort just that, rapid continuous improvement, and has long had a full-time RCI manager—Danny Jones.[15])

- Don't confine learning to the home base. Seeing is believing, and you, the work force, need to visit some local-area, high-performance companies to see what is possible and hear how many jobs they saved by improving their processes.

- If you think your company is different, is strong enough to hang on, you need to consider the facts: that 40 U.S. steel companies went bankrupt between 1997 and 2004;[16] that in the past few years each of the following famous companies have laid off at least 5,000 (most at least 10,000) employees:[17] Kodak, Ford, Motorola, Delphi, Intel, Textron, Xerox, Consolidated Freightways, General Motors, EDS, Sun Microsystems, DuPont, Schwab, VF Corp., BellSouth, Solectron, Delta

Airlines, American Airlines, Hewlett-Packard, Lucent, Kmart, WorldCom, Coca Cola, Avaya, Alcoa, Winn-Dixie, Sony, Hitachi, Toshiba, Honda, Kyocera, Nissan, Sanyo, Oji Paper, Matsushita Electric, Japan Tobacco, Fiat, Rolls-Royce, Marconi, Siemens, Deutsche Telecom, Philips, Daimler-Chrysler, Volkswagen, Ericsson, Alcatel, Peugeot-Citroën, Telefonica de España, Santander Central Hispano Bank, Air Canada, Nortel, Celestica, Petroleos de Venezuela, and many more.

- Best protection from getting downsized or shut down is to elevate our company in the eyes of the customer through better quality, quicker response, greater flexibility, and higher value. These are the main objectives of process improvement through lean and total quality.

CIRCLES REDUX

Ishikawa, famous for developing the fishbone chart and advocating the seven tools of process improvement, also gave us quality-control circles. The three words became two, *quality circles (QCs)*, when the West dropped the word *control*. It was a good move, because quality, not control, is the object.[18] (It may not signal another name change, but Ron Crabtree, columnist for *APICS* magazine, has done a series on what he calls "circle teams."[19]) Process data usually arise from people as individuals. Problem solving, presentation, approval, implementation, and celebration must be with and for small groups, such as cell teams or quality circles. QCs blend continuous data collection with frequent, though non-continuous, attacks on problems revealed by the data.

After having gained a high head of steam in the 1980s, quality circles faded fast in the 1990s. At least they did in the West. Their popularity remains strong in Singapore and a few other Asian countries. Singapore's high standing among global industrial powers may be owing in part to early development and continuing application of process improvement in the QC-circle mode.

Though down, QC circles still are alive and well in a few western locales, especially in Japanese-owned companies. In 2005, a quality-control circle team at a Yazaki plant in Griffin, Georgia, won the company's QC-circle award.[20] (Yazaki, with numerous automotive electrical power-distribution plants in North America, had previously limited the award to Japan.) After many years of use, the QC-circle process at Yazaki is in a high state of maturity. Among its worthy features are the following four: (1) Circle members vote to prioritize the top five issues revealed by process data. They vote on importance, urgency, solvability, and controllability. (2) At least some of the circle members learn PowerPoint or other presentation skills so that they are able to efficiently explain what they come up with. (3) Circle teams must determine whether their solution can be standardized for other groups in the same plant and other facilities. (4) In celebration of results, Yazaki employs plenty of hoopla: visits to customer plants, award luncheons and dinners, and distribution of press releases to local news media and trade publications. Also, winners receive a "best of the best" trophy and bragging rights for the next year, plus an all-expenses-paid trip to Japan to compete in international competition there.

To sum up the main points of the chapter, the ideal approach to process improvement is a combination: kaizen and other projects for jolts, and empowered teams of associates continuously collecting and reflecting on process data for continuity.

NOTES

1. *Wikipedia* definitions change along with the court of expert opinion; this definition was as of September 2006.

2. Masaaki Imai, who is rightfully respected for his many contributions to process improvement (but like all of us does not always say what is wise), has expressed a contrary view in an interview. He states, "In the United States JIT is primarily viewed as a tool to reduce lead time. In my view, JIT is a strategy to continuously remove waste from a system and drive down inventory." Laura Smith, "Profiles in Quality with Masaaki Imai, *Quality Digest* (October 2005), pp. 54–55.

3. *Wikipedia* (as of September 2006) limits its definition of JIT to inventory reduction. The *APICS Dictionary* (Alexandria, VA: American Production & Inventory Control Society, 11th ed., 2005, p. 58) gives JIT the same central aim as it does for lean, that of "elimination of all waste"; APICS adds to that "continuous improvement of productivity." Since there are endless management programs that profess to improve productivity, saying that of JIT is not illuminating.

4. www.engr.wisc.edu/centers/cqrm.

5. George Stalk, Jr., "Time—The Next Source of Competitive Advantage," *Harvard Business Review*, July–August 1998, pp. 41–51; George Stalk, Jr. and Thomas M. Hout, *Competing Against Time: How Time-Based Competitive Is Reshaping Global Markets* (New York: Collier McMillan, 1990); Joseph D. Blackburn, *Time-Based Competition: The Next Battle Ground in American Manufacturing* (Homewood, IL: Business One Irwin, 1991).

6. "The Lean Route," interview with John Bicheno, director of the MSc program in lead operations at Cardiff Business School, in white paper: "The Road to World Class Manufacturing," *The Manufacturer* (2002), pp. 22–25.

7. Kevin McManus, "The Pull of Lean," *Industrial Engineer*, April, 2007, p. 20.

8. The eight *nonobvious* wastes were the topic of a chapter in Richard J. Schonberger, *Building a Chain of Customers: Linking Business Functions to Create the World Class Company* (New York: Free Press/Simon & Schuster, 1990), Chapter 7.

9. James C. Collins and Jerry I. Porras, *Built to Last: Successful Habits of Visionary Companies* (New York: HarperBusiness, 1994); James C. Collins, *Good to Great: Why Some Companies Make the Leap . . . and Others Don't* (New York: HarperBusiness, 2001).

10. James O'Toole and Edward E. Lawler III, *The New American Workplace* (New York: Palgrave Macmillan, 2006).

11. U.S. Department of Health, Education, and Welfare, *Work in America* (Cambridge, MA: MIT Press, 1973).

12. *Kaizen blitz* is a term coined and promulgated by the Association for Manufacturing Excellence: Anthony C. Laraia, Patricia E. Moody, and Robert W. Hall, *The Kaizen Blitz: Accelerating Breakthroughs in Productivity and Performance* (New York: Wiley, 1999).

13. Maasaki Imai, *Kaizen: The Key to Japan's Competitive Success* (New York: McGraw-Hill, 1986).

14. Donald L. Lowman, managing director of HR services firm, Towers Perrin, was asked, "What's the single most important issue, or investment, HR executives should be considering in the year 2005?" His answer was "reengaging employees . . .": "My Take," *Human Resource Executive* (November 17, 2004), p . 4.

15. Danny Jones and James McKnight, "Kaizen at the Hon Company: A Decade of Lean," Lean Practitioner session at 16th Annual Shingo Prize Conference and Awards Ceremony, Lexington, KY (May 20, 2004).

16. These data on steel company bankruptcies were found in James O'Toole and Edward E. Lawler III, *The New American Workplace* (New York: Palgrave Macmillan, 2006), p. 236.

17. Many of these layoffs are reported in www.timesizing.com.

18. With the same thought in mind, the membership of the American Society for Quality Control voted, in 1997, to change the society's name to American Society for Quality.

19. Ron Crabtree, for example, "Organizing Circle Teams," second in a series on circle teams, *APICS* (September 2006), p. 18.

20. Marc A. Gattoni, "Quality Circles Work," *Quality Digest* (August 2006), p. 81

Chapter 6

The Metrics Trap

When JIT and TQC first lapped up on western shores, it quickly became clear: Our management accounting systems were wrong—three times wrong.

1. *Wrong costs.* The system spread overhead costs evenly among easy work (high-volume standard products) and taxing stuff (low-volume specials), warping pricing, resource allocation, and profit determinations.
2. *Wrong motivation.* Fed by wrong cost data, the cost-variance system drove work centers to produce in excess of and oblivious to usage at the next process, also to neglect training, maintenance, and safety in order to produce more and avoid negative cost variances.
3. *Wrong locus of control.* Centers of control were remote, in place and time, from where the work was done: Control was in the hands of accountants and other distant staff, and relied on well-after-the-fact reporting. (The accounting data is the batch-and-queue information equivalent to batch-and-queue production.) Problem signals were outdated by a week or a month, so that symptoms of problems could not be tied to specific causes.

Lean accounting aims at righting those wrongs. Those prominent in lean accounting see process improvement as the driver of cost reduction, rather than the other way around. Lean accounting's early (1980s) innovation was activity-based costing, which greatly improves cost accuracy and precision. But does that accuracy serve any valid purpose, given the common misuses of cost information? There is just one purpose that scarcely anyone would argue against: improving competitive decisions of an *infrequent* nature, such as pricing, go/no-go, and make-or-buy.

Now, in lean accounting's second generation (see the box, "The Rise, Fall, and Rise of Lean Accounting"), all aspects of accounting for management decision making are under the microscope.[1] (Financial accounting, for regulatory reporting, is getting its own close scrutiny, resulting in stiff new authentication requirements such as those of Sarbanes-Oxley in the United States.) Sweeping changes in management accounting are being proposed and tested. The most profound have to do with management's cherished system of managing by metrics—the main topic of this chapter.

The Rise, Fall, and Rise of Lean Accounting

Lean accounting is still in its formative stages. An early innovation, activity-based costing,[2] played to packed houses in the late 1980s and into the 1990s. Then, for a decade, it was quiet time for the movement. Those involved (myself included[3]) continued to think and write about how to fix the dysfunctions in management accounting, but they were mostly their own audience. Now, with interests piqued by its engaging new name, *lean accounting*,[4] conferences and educational events on the matter are again drawing full houses. A main idea is for management accounting to be reorganized the same way as most other resources, that is, around value streams. Thus far, though, implementations, applied research, case studies, and company examples are in short supply.

Where is all this heading? The opening section, referring to *ultra*-lean accounting, offers a few answers. Remaining sections provide examples of what is wrong with our metrics; process data as a proven alternative; frustration-relieving data as the driving force for high work-force involvement; and finally a critical appraisal of three widely used performance measures.

FROM UNLEAN TO ULTRA-LEAN ACCOUNTING

Some best practices in management accounting do not stand up to close scrutiny. Over-arching guidance follows the economy-of-control principle: *The best control requires the fewest controls—and controllers.*[5] The lean/TQ and the lean-accounting communities provide this common belief as a guide: *Process improvement drives cost reduction*, not the reverse.

Under high-energy process improvement, powered by lean/TQ, costs fall of their own accord. The ultimate goal, as Jim Huntzinger puts it, "is when all component parts cost the same at all volumes."[6] To approach that ideal, all parts are made and consumed one at a time. Operators move flexibly to where the demand moves. When demand is very low, they work on process improvements, the payroll costs of which are offset by resulting lowering of component parts costs. Costs of idle equipment are minimized through "right-sizing": no monuments to the false god of scale economies.

Cost-management practices, such as the following, become seen as cost-consuming, non-value-adding excess: monthly cost reporting, standard costs, cost variances,[7] monetary goal-setting, and cost as a carrot-and-stick motivator. Inaccuracy and wasteful ineffectiveness plagues all of these. Stew Witkov, CFO at Ariens, the mower and snowblower manufacturer, offers his take on the plague of standard costs and cost variances. "Your setup [cost] is an estimate, your budgeted hours are an estimate, your materials are based on a quote, your lot size is based on a guess, and the budgeted hours you are going to manufacture is a forecast. So you have an estimate, an estimate, a quote, a guess, and a forecast—how accurate is that going to be?"[8] There's more. Once upon a time, labor, a variable cost, was more than 50 percent of production cost. Now it's under 15 percent, and most of the cost is fixed. When most costs are fixed, calculating unit costs becomes almost pointless.[9]

Under ultra-lean, process improvement provides a more effective, achievement-based source of motivation. The work force gets further pumped by visual, public plotting of the results on trend charts—in natural, not monetary units. The trends praise their achievements and scold their laxities. The many components of visual management accomplish directly and simply what cost-denominated devices do indirectly and ineffectively.

In general, ultra-lean's target is excesses related to management's misbegotten metrics. Our discussion points even to flaws in such respected metrics as on-time, six sigma, and OEE. In this chapter, data supersede metrics, and goal-setting gets de-emphasized, generalized, and moved low in the organization. Low-level process data and primary results, visually displayed, supplant management dashboards. That addresses the fallacy of drilling down from high-level (dashboard) metrics, such as OEE, to low-level zones of action. Popular performance metrics, on-time and zero defects, retain their importance but not their prominence as metrics to be managed, because managing the processes takes precedence. We take up these topics one by one. But first, to properly set the stage, we further examine *unlean* accounting and the ultra-lean alternative.

FEWEST CONTROLS AND CONTROLLERS

Lean means less. Thus, lean accounting means less accounting. The following five accounting practices therefore must be considered unlean:

1. Using cost (even enhanced-validity activity-based cost) to drive process improvement.
2. Using cost (even enhanced-validity) to motivate and manage performance.
3. Replacing the conventional cost-accounting system with an activity-based *system*, or maintaining both systems.
4. Frequent feeding of cost reports to the work force in order to raise their business literacy and concern for financial results.
5. Replacing conventional profit-and-loss (P&L) reporting with lean, activity-based P&L reports for improved executive-level planning and control.

All of these are fat because they require retention of sizeable accounting and IT staffs who do not add value. Each, as well, is deficient and unlean for its own reasons, taken up briefly next and in more depth in later sections of the chapter.

DRIVING PROCESS IMPROVEMENT

There is no point in doing cost studies to pinpoint and prioritize processes to improve. Lean/TQ offers a better way: visual process data. Flowcharts, check sheets, run diagrams, control charts, and other visual devices are excellent for collecting and arranging data about process problems. They are simple, low-cost aids in process improvement.

Cost-driven process improvement, in contrast, is redundant as well as high in non-value-adding costs. More to the point, cost is usually a by-product rather than the main reason for improving a process. Primary aims of lean/TQ are quicker, more flexible response with better quality.

MOTIVATING AND MANAGING PERFORMANCE

Cost is a weak motivator of process improvement and manager of employee performance. Cost has only an abstract and indirect connection with processes, and cost-driven performance management requires a costly staff.

Lean/TQ offers a better way: empowered cell-teams/operators setting their own goals and visually plotting process (non-monetary) results.

INSTALLING ACTIVITY-BASED COSTING

Activity-based costing (ABC) as a cost-reporting *system*—collect costs on every job or operation, report those costs every month—is unlean. To be sure, all organizations need to know their costs, with reasonable accuracy, but not for driving process improvement, and not for motivating and managing performance. Rather, costs are needed for competitive decisions, the kind that arise infrequently, much less often than monthly. Companies typically revise prices only about yearly. Make-or-buy decisions are similarly seldom. A third type of infrequent decision is go/no-go, as applied to products, suppliers, customers, facilities, and technologies. For example, shall we shutter a certain plant? cease doing business with a difficult customer? develop a new product line with advanced materials?

RAISING COST CONSCIOUSNESS

It helps to have a financially wise work force, the better to help the company find ways to cut costs besides reducing head-count. Feeding them a steady diet of the company's cost and financial reports is a poor way to gain that support.[10] The associate confronted with frequent cost reports (whether ABC-improved or not) soon comes to react more to the abstraction of cost than to its direct causes. When costs go up, usual reactions are to take anti-lean, bad-for-the-company shortcuts, such as deferring maintenance and training or lengthening production runs.

Better ways to instill cost consciousness are: (1) training the work force in budgeting and (2) putting cost labels on expensive parts, consumables, utilities, and in some cases tools. The work force takes over part of the job of budget-watching. It does so in a direct way through careful use of costly resources. (The budget may be the only business numbers that bear scrutiny at all levels, from the chief financial officer to the janitor.) The work force does need to know how the company is doing, financially and otherwise, but that should be done one to four times a year in state-of-the-company presentations delivered by executives and managers.

MORE RELEVANT P&L REPORTING

The mechanisms that produce profit-and-loss reports are elaborate, costly, and unlean. So, it occurs to some, why not a lean P&L? P&L reports, though, are for external reporting to regulatory agencies and investors. Every country has its reporting standards that must be adhered to. P&L reporting must, in the United States, abide by generally accepted accounting principles (GAAP), and, in every country, governmental regulations. The lean P&L may be a good idea, but only if the powers that be were to fold it into GAAP and governing regulations.

Is the idea, then, to continue with conventional external P&L, but also produce a lean P&L for internal decision making? A lean P&L could organize financial information by value streams. Still, the P&L would remain a highly aggregated set of measures of company performance made up of thousands of variables. The causes of good or bad P&L numbers would remain a blur, of dubious help in decision making and open to manipulations harmful to the company as a whole (including trying to influence share prices).

PRICING FOR SPEED

Most companies use erroneous cost data in arriving at price points for their goods and services. Some simply set prices by adding a markup percentage to those faulty costs. There is a better way, and it perfectly fits the lean ideal of simplicity. Here is how it works.

Your best products are the leanest products. They are the ones that zip through pre-production, production, and shipping in no time flat—in one day or less. They pause hardly at all to collect overhead charges, so the cost to make them is rock-bottom low. There is no point in doing a cost study to prove it. It's clear and obvious.

Time to reprice. The new price structure for your zippy products also must be rock-bottom low. The results: Competitors, still taking 20 days (19 of them accumulating overhead costs), blink and falter. Your sales and market share surge, scale economies push product costs down even further, and gross and net margins soar. It's a virtual linkage—from lean-speed to pricing to volume to profit.

DATA SUPERSEDING METRICS

The managerial class clothes itself in measures of performance. The new, shortened term, as of 10 or 15 years ago, is *metrics*. In that 10 or 15 years, managers have grown increasingly dependent on their metrics. At the same time they have become less interested in process *data*, including ensuring that data are regularly collected. That is short-sighted, because process data are only once removed from the reality of what goes wrong with the processes. Metrics are twice, three times, or even more removed from that reality. Metrics distant by two or more orders of magnitude from root processes absorb large aggregations of variables. Sight lines to causes of process failures and weaknesses become dim and confounded.

Michael Hammer, in "The Seven Deadly Sins of Performance Management," gives an example. A fashion retailer's high-level metrics (e.g., percentage of customers who buy something) were "desirable goals but not ones that can be achieved directly." Advertising revenue seemed, to the chief operating officer, a better aimed metric. It wasn't. The root causes were inadequate on-shelf availability and customer coverage. Those two factors become key metrics. The improvement of each metric "is to be accomplished through process management."[11]

DATA-DRIVEN SOLUTIONS

In manufacturing, managers' favorite mid-range metrics include labor productivity, unit cost, output, on-schedule, yield, inventory turns, and utilization. Though worthy as outcomes, they are unfair to the work force whose productivity, output, and so on are being measured. The causes of process shortcomings reside in management systems. Typical failures of the management system include late or misfit parts, faulty tools or equipment, missing or wrong specs, impossibly tight or jerky schedules, and inadequate training. (Dr. Deming is famous for attributing 85 percent of process failings to the management system.[12]) Those are the main reasons for low productivity and output, high cost and cost variance, poor yield and utilization, defects, low turns, and lateness. Yet management posts its metrics in the work centers with the astonishing presumption that the work force is responsible.

Management by metrics has other faults. The common metrics are remote from the associates' main concerns, which revolve around conditions, frustrations, and fears. Employees everywhere want conditions that allow the work to be done well and safely. Frustrations and negative behaviors mount when those conditions are not met. Unfair metrics intensify the negatives. (Frustrations have mostly to do with hundreds of detailed aspects of the job and the process. Fears have more to do with big issues that might lead to loss of life, loss of a customer, loss of a major capacity unit, and so on. Fears, and how to capture "fear data," get further attention in Chapter 17 in connection with large external impacts.)

Course correction requires favoring data over metrics. In that environment the negatives may be turned into positives. It is a simple three-part formula:

1. Process data reveal true causes.
2. Causes lead to solutions.
3. Solutions relieve job and employment frustrations, and the metrics, unmanaged, take care of themselves.

SIX SIGMA, KAIZEN EVENTS, OTHER IMPROVEMENT PROJECTS

When concern for metrics debases collection of process data, the whole process-improvement regime stumbles. Consider the project mode of improvement. An early step is to define the project and its expectations. In the formal six sigma procedure this is the D—Define—step of DMAIC: Define, Measure, Analyze, Improve, Control. Next comes data collection: M—Measure.

But stop right there. If all employees' jobs entail continual collection of process data, recording everything that goes wrong, it is a gift for the six sigma team. They have a great head start. With much less additional data to unearth, their project is into the Analyze stage quickly. Moreover, the data will be in the form of trends, not single points in time. Trend data are far more revealing.

Now back up once more to Define. With the work force continually plotting process failures and concerns, the six sigma or kaizen team may tap those data at the outset. The project definition becomes precision targeted, focusing on known specifics (severe, frequent current fluctuations; chronic tool breakage) rather than assumptions (poor equipment) or generalities (poor on-time performance). Lacking such advance, already-on-display process data, the team may set off at a gallop in an obtuse direction.

INSTEAD OF METRICS

This brings up two concerns. First, without metrics to authenticate progress, how do you get management buy-in? Second, if managers are not to manage by metrics, what do they manage with?

Both questions have about the same answer. If managers do what they should be doing, they gain confidence and gratification from data-driven (not metrics-driven) process improvement. Instead of looking through the telescope the wrong way, managers keep busy "being there." They are visible, listening, clearing out obstacles, providing resources, doing train-the-trainer, coaching, coordinating, and mediating. A critical responsibility is ensuring knowledge transfer. That comes largely through presentation events in which low-level improvement teams present their success stories to peers, other teams, and sometimes sister plants. Those events usually double as recognition and celebratory occasions.

For lack of up-to-date process knowledge and experience, managers and executives up two or three levels may feel awkward being there, because they lack up-to-date process knowledge and experience. That obstacle goes away if they are invited and go, often, to improvement-teams' presentations. Besides providing visible support for the improvement effort, the presence of senior managers yields two valuable by-products. One is they gain process knowledge—vital because senior managers' jobs involve major decisions about processes. The other is they are personally auditing the improvement effort rather than just hearing consultants and their own staff rave about how great it is. It is rarely that great, and executives need to know about it and to involve themselves in making it better.

There are still other ways for managers and executives to effectively become engaged in process improvement. Management by walking around (MBWA)[13] can be a step in the right direction (but also, as Deming once said, can be a waste of time[14]). Three examples of improvement aided by MBWA follow.

FRUSTRATION RELIEF

M, the general manager, believes in management by walking around. M does so, accompanied by the appropriate department head or production manager, every day. In every office or work center these walkers ask employees how they would improve their operations. Good ideas trickle in. After a time the frequency of the walks is reduced, first to twice weekly, and later to once a week. Enough good ideas still come in to make the exercise worthwhile.[15]

O, general manager at another company, takes her frequent walks, too. Except O and her co-walker always ask, "What have you changed since I was here last?" This is a call for action, and for the employee to take that action. A high rate of *implemented* changes ensues.

T, another general manager at still another company, takes a different approach. T and co-walkers ask employees about the frustrations of their employment. One operator, whose job entails turning down hundreds of machine bolts every day with a hydraulic tool, had a ready answer. "The worst for me, and it happens too often, is when the bolt gets in there cross-threaded. I back it out and try again. But quite often the threads are stripped and the bolt has to be tossed. It may seem like a small thing, but it grinds on me. I suppose it's my fault, but I don't think the others do the job any better."

Of the three examples, the first, M asking for ideas, is somewhat common but not very effective. At least in this case M and area managers are visibly involved and are fairly systematic (regular walk-around schedules) in seeking ideas. As they cut back or cease walking around, or a new general manager doesn't follow that practice at all, the ideas melt away.

The second approach, O asking "what have you changed lately," seems very effective. It is limited, however, to simpler, less costly changes. Maybe that is why I've heard of only one example of a manager actually doing this.[16]

That brings us to work-life frustrations. In the third example, what chronically spoiled the operator's work day were frequent cross-threading occurrences. T's question, in bringing forth the operator's worst frustration, at the same time reveals a clear source of defects, scrap, rework, delays, potential customer returns, and cost. There is high synergy here. What is bad for the operator is doubly bad for the company. Anything the company can do to eliminate the causes of cross-threading has the full support and gratification of the operator. If the work force is fully empowered, it's the reverse: Operators' efforts to collect data on cross-threading, analyze it to discover causes, and take the initiative to solve problems has the full support and gratification of the company.

The following points emerge from the three examples.

1. Frustration relief is a potent avenue for process improvement. If you think about it, on-the-job frustrations are likely also to be serious performance shortcomings for the company. Even those that are personal, such as frustration at not being able to care for a family member in trouble, are serious for the company. Such

frustrations add up and sink morale and dedication. A work-center team's priority-ordered list of frustrations tends also to be a rather sound priority list of opportunities for improvement for the company. The following real example from a Chicago-area plant of Sealed Air Corporation illustrates.

At this plant, producing bubble mailers and packaging, stock pickers had a seething frustration. Their difficulties in finding items on pick lists meant that outbound trucks were stalled on the docks, sometimes blocking incoming trucks. The pickers (actually picker-loaders) were smack in the middle of the crossfire, from drivers, supervisors, and schedulers. It got bad enough that sometimes a picker would go to one of the co-extrusion lines and implore the operators to stop their current job and re-setup to run off a few units of a missing pick item—and get the driver on the road. An interview with one picker, call him Reggie, disclosed items high on his frustration list. They included trucks leaving late, drivers yelling, interrupting a co-extruder job (obviously a costly, dumb thing to do) and taking the static from the involved operators, and catching flack from the supervisor. Reggie didn't mention other lesser frustrations. If he had, one of them might be taking out his frustrations on family members at home. Still lower on the frustration scale would be small things such as a teammate who comes late, and lack of a decent place for coffee and lunch breaks. If teammates coming late were a dominant reason for late truck departures, that would rise to a high position on Reggie's list. Though all the frustrations deserve attention, a high-to-low rank-order for Reggie fits well with high-to-low for the company.

2. Expressing frustration does not solve problems, though it will spur action under the right conditions. The missing ingredient between frustration and early solution is process data. For Reggie, the mere act of recording the reasons for things going wrong provides a large measure of frustration relief. Likely causes are: pick item found in wrong storage location, pick item not in any location, pick item found but damaged, pick list illegible so had to run off duplicate, cube does not fit in trailer, pallet jack "borrowed" by someone, and so on. All Reggie needs is a large poster board, whiteboard, or flipchart headed in large letters, FRUS-TRATIONS. A check sheet goes below the heading. (The check sheet is one of Ishikawa's seven tools.[17]) He records each incidence and type of the common failures by a tally mark on the check sheet. Other nonrepetitive reasons he writes down rather than tallies. With all that data marking the *real* causes, no one barks at Reggie anymore. The quest is on to fix the causes, for example, by purifying the storage locations and the cubing data and algorithm.[18]

Would you prefer, instead of frustrations, that the check sheet be labeled *problems*, *defects*, *causes*, *flaws*, *bugs*, or *OFIs* (opportunities for improvement)?[19] The *frustrations* label has the advantage. The daily and one-off frustrations are what weigh heavily on Reggie's consciousness. They are frustrations for management, too. So why not call them that?

3. General manager M combines a good practice, MBWA, with a weak one, open-ended questions on ideas for improvement. Both the number and the quality of ideas will be disappointing. When managers say all it takes to get good ideas is to

listen to their employees, they are wrong. Without process data to direct people's minds toward causes, good ideas will be uncommon. That applies as well to engineers and scientists. They are unlikely to do well in innovating and solving problems without good data (which is what data-driven six sigma is all about). A new, effective scenario for M's plant would feature recording frustration data everywhere. In walking around, M would not be asking for ideas but rather gathering large amounts of information on the state of process data collection, analysis, and improvement—and determining how he may be of greatest help in moving the effort forward.

4. O's approach, "what have you changed lately," might be very effective in an organization committed to constant data collection. With the work force plotting everything that goes wrong, especially in the frustration mode, high-value problem solving and implemented changes should be plentiful. In that case, O might develop a sharper understanding of what it is that the business should be improving—our next topic.

THREE MISUNDERSTOOD MEASURES OF PERFORMANCE

We wind up this chapter with a close look at three respected targets of improvement. The first, on-time delivery, is deserving. The second, six sigma (the metric, not the process), is respectable but in a limited way. The third, overall equipment effectiveness (OEE), is non-value-adding and unlean—with a small exception.

ON TIME, YES, BUT...

The esteemed performance target, *on-time delivery*, gets plentiful attention because of its high degree of customer sensitivity. Yet, on-time does not rank as one of the *golden goals*—ever-better quality, quicker response, greater flexibility, and higher value. Like on time, they, too, are highly customer salient. On-time is not the golden fifth simply because it *derives from* the other four, as portrayed in Exhibit 6.1.

Moreover, we don't even have consistent ways to measure on-time. A survey of customers in the shipping business comes up with *on-time* defined in "at least six different ways."[20] In manufacturing, on-time is sort of a nudge-nudge, wink-wink metric. On-time to one's own shipping schedule may be far from on-time as the customer sees it.

We know a lot about how to improve quality, quick response, flexibility, and value. The lean and total-quality methodologies work to improve each of the four in any kind of manufacturing and in most kinds of service work. There is no such established set of management tools that direct themselves squarely at on-time performance. Instead, on-time becomes easy to achieve, close to being automatic, if the quality is good, the response times quick and flexible, and activities are of high value (non-value-adding elements excised).

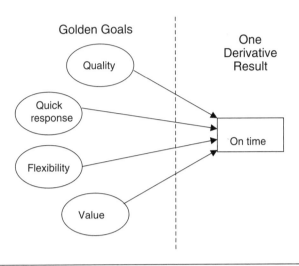

Exhibit 6.1 Golden Goals

SIX SIGMA (ZERO DEFECTS, TOO): NOT GOOD ENOUGH

Our second, misunderstood improvement target is *six sigma*, which refers to a statistically tiny allowable number of defectives. Though good, six sigma is not good enough. For the same reason, neither is zero defects. The deficiency is that both are measures of attainment against specifications, which are set subjectively. Design engineering may do it, specifying, for example, that a box of raisin bran breakfast cereal is correct if it contains no fewer than 47 and no more than 53 raisins. Or the same may be set forth by a weights-and-measures regulatory agency. Or marketing sets those spec limits based on what marketing thinks customers generally will accept. Sometimes the spec limits are built into a contract with the customer, such as between a cereal manufacturer and a grocery chain. Anthony Burns offers this critique: "It's easy for consultants to claim they'll halve defects. They simply change the specification."[21] Being within the spec limits, though, is a worthy achievement, especially if those limits have been agreed upon by, or otherwise represent, the tolerance levels of the customer. Then, to be out of spec incurs various costly penalties.

The endless road toward perfect quality is continuous reduction of process variation. That challenge represents a more stringent measure of quality than six sigma and zero defects. If all variation is eliminated, the process performs exactly the same way every time. Predictability, whether in quality, time, or another outcome, produces a flood of obvious and hidden benefits. With six sigma and zero defects, on the other hand, if the process delivers a result that meets specifications, it allows wobble within the spec limits. Wobble equals unpredictability.

More importantly, the management of variation is well established. The late W. Edwards Deming built a career around it. The primary methodology is *statistical process control*, in which measured variation is plotted on control charts. Too much variation shows up on the charts, triggering investigation and, where needed, corrective action. Those doing the measuring and charting, and sometimes the correcting, are the people in the process who do the job.

THE OEE FALLACY

The third misunderstood performance measure is *overall equipment effectiveness (OEE)*. Manufacturing companies around the globe have been persuaded that maintenance and improvement of productive equipment requires use of this metric. But does that make sense? OEE is a single, highly aggregated number. The causes of that number are in the order of thousands or hundreds of thousands. There is no possible way that, by regularly measuring OEE, a company will gain insights on ways to make equipment do what it is supposed to. The three components of OEE—availability, efficiency, and quality index—though one level closer to the processes, are still made up of too many variables to tell what to do. (OEE = Availability ratio × Quality ratio × Production ratio.) It is good to measure performances that are close to the source, non-value-adding to do so with remote metrics.

OEE does have a redeeming value: A company's initial OEE computation, when compared with OEEs from other companies, has shock value. Managements typically pay little attention to maintenance, and a very low OEE score says, "Wake up, management, it's your machines!" More specifically, it says that the machines are the causes of equipment unavailability, process inefficiency, and poor product quality.

The sudden popularity of OEE has a precedent: cost of quality. Few companies measure it anymore. Cost of quality had long since shocked management into the realization that quality failures have large effects on top and bottom lines. There was no need to keep measuring it, because the message had sunk in. Intensive quality management had become standard business practice. (Sometimes, though, re-measuring cost of quality, say, once every five years, would pay off. Ford Motor Company quickly comes to mind. Ford, a strong advocate in the 1980s of Deming, SPC, cost of quality, and other TQ pursuits, made quality "Job 1." In the 1990s, Ford's quality had sunk to the depths. Maybe Ford needed to see its deteriorating quality in financial terms—what cost of quality does—but had long since ceased cost-of-quality determinations.)

Actually, OEE is a weaker metric than cost of quality ever was. The ideal for cost of quality is a finite number: zero. What is the ideal OEE? One hundred percent is the maximum value, but is not a good answer. The main problem lies in the availability factor, the percentage of time the equipment is running versus the time it could be running. By formula it is:

$$\text{Availability rate} = \frac{\text{Operating time} - \text{Downtime (for setups, maintenance, etc.)}}{\text{Total operating time}}$$

The ultimate, 100 percent, really means that the equipment is so heavily used that not a single unexpected job could be accommodated. As Baudin puts it, if the machine's utilization is 100 percent, that "translates into 0 percent availability."[22] Given the volatility of demand, very high use means stretched out lead times and customers lost because they won't wait. The combination of high utilization and high variability is deadly; more on this in Chapter 13 under the topic, "Chronic Capacity Starvation."

OEE was hatched in Japan, which does not make it wise.[23] (Cost of quality originated in the United States, and never did assume importance in Japan.) The Japan Institute of Plant Maintenance, which began bestowing a maintenance award in 1964, has made OEE a factor in its continuing TPM awards. In 2005, JIPM presented TPM awards to 55 plants/companies outside of Japan, plus many within Japan. Issuing awards with OEE a factor becomes a stamp of approval for the metric. That elevates OEE's shock value for companies that have neglected the maintenance function and the TPM methodology. Once those companies see the light and become turned on to TPM, the OEE will have done its job and thus should disappear.

The main theme of Chapter 6 has been the power of process data and the weakness of allegiance to metrics, especially cost numbers. Furthermore, Chapter 7 calls into question the companion of management by metrics.

NOTES

1. Several of the aspects are topics of the eleven chapters of Joe Stenzel, ed., *Lean Accounting: Best Practices for Sustainable Integration* (Hoboken, NJ: Wiley, 2007).

2. An early reference is Robin Cooper and Robert S. Kaplan, "How Cost Accounting Systematically Distorts Product Costs," in William J. Bruns and Robert S. Kaplan, eds., *Accounting and Management: Field Study Perspectives* (Boston: Harvard Business School Press, 1987).

3. The following are articles with a main or secondary lean-accounting slant by Richard J. Schonberger: "Lean Extended: It's Much More (and Less) than You Think," *Industrial Engineer* (December 2005), pp. 26–31; "Mandate to Grow," *Cost Management* (March–April 2004), pp. 43–44; "How Lean/TQ Helps Deter Cooking the Books," *Journal of Cost Management*, lead article (May–June 2003), pp. 5–14; "Open-Book Management: Less than Meets the Eye," *Journal of Cost Management* (January–February 2002), pp. 12–17; "Performance Management for a World-Class Work Force, *Target* (4th Qtr. 1999), pp. 26–30; "Economy of Control," *Quality Management Journal*, lead article, vol. 6, no. 1 (1999), pp. 10–18 (reprinted in *IEEE Engineering Management Review*, 4th Qtr. 2000, pp. 28–34); "Backing Off from the Bottom Line," *Executive Excellence* (May 1996), pp. 16–17; "Product Costing as a Rare Event," *Target* (November–December 1994), pp. 8–16; "Less Scorekeeping as TQM Takes Root," *Journal of Cost Management* (Summer 1994), pp. 3, 4; "Lurking Issues in Cost Management," *Journal of Cost Management* (Summer 1991), p. 3; "World-Class Performance Management," in Peter B.B. Turney, ed., "Performance Excellence in Manufacturing and Service Organizations," *Proc. of the 3rd Annual Management Accounting Symposium,* San Diego (March 1989; American Accounting Association, 1990), pp. 1–5; "Non-Cost Cost Control: The Visual Factory," *OEM,* (May 1989), pp. 28–29.

4. Some draw this distinction: *Lean accounting* is making the accounting function lean, whereas *accounting for lean* means modifying accounting to promote lean everywhere else: Mark C. DeLuzio, "Accounting for Lean," *Manufacturing Engineering*

(December 2006), pp. 83–88. The distinction tends to become a blur, however, because lean is lean. That is, process improvement requires less in production, and less in accounting.

5. Economy of control is presented as a main topic heading in Richard J. Schonberger, *Let's Fix It! How the World's Leading Manufacturers Were Seduced by Prosperity and Lost Their Way* (New York: Free Press/Simon & Schuster, 2001), pp. 100–104, 259. See, also, Richard J. Schonberger, "Economy of Control," *Quality Management Journal*, op. cit.

6. Jim Huntzinger, "Limited Production Principles: Right-Sizing for Effective Lean Operations and Cost Management," Chapter 2, p. 39, in Joseph Stenzel, *Lean Accounting: Best Practices for Integration* (New York: Wiley, 2007).

7. Mark C. DeLuzio, op. cit., states that *standard costs* are arguably "wrong from the moment when they are developed," which tends to be once a year as part of the budgeting cycle. He faults the purchase-price variance because it "promotes the building of excess (and eventually obsolete) inventory balances," and encourages buyers to go for the "lowest-priced vendor" regardless of the vendor's capabilities. And he notes that *volume (absorption) variances* support the "notion of producing as much as possible, regardless of customer demand."

8. Traci Von Duyke, "Case Study: Ariens Co.: Lean Accounting Offers Visibility, Eliminates Guesswork," *Lean Accounting News*, available online only, www.leanaccountingnews.com/#igetit, March 28, 2007.

9. Marshall L. Fisher makes this point in "Bob Hayes: Forty Years of Leading Operations Management into Uncharted Waters," *Production and Operations Management*, Vol. 16, No. 2 (March-April 2007), pp. 159–168.

10. That approach, called "open-book management," was made famous in an article about its application at Springfield Remanufacturing Company in "The Open-Book Revolution," cover story, *Inc.* (June 1995). More on the negative side of the matter may be found in Richard J. Schonberger, "Open-Book Management: Less than Meets the Eye," *Journal of Cost Management* (January–February 2002), pp. 12–17.

11. Michael Hammer, "The Seven Deadly Sins of Performance Management," *Sloan Management Review*, Spring 2007, pp. 19–28.

12. An Internet search of "Deming 85%" brings up many citations. He discusses why the fault is with the management system in W. Edwards Deming, *Out of the Crisis* (Cambridge, MA: MIT Center for Advanced Engineering Study, 1982), pp. 65–67.

13. MBWA is one of the more memorable tidbits from the 1982 blockbuster by Thomas J. Peters and Robert H. Waterman Jr., *In Search of Excellence: Lessons from America's Best-Run Companies* (New York: Harper & Row, 1982), pp. 122, 246.

14. According to Deming, op. cit., p. 22, MBWA "is hardly ever effective. The reason is that someone in management, walking around, has little idea about what questions to ask, and usually does not pause long enough at any spot to get the right answer."

15. Chuck Rescorla, when he was vice president of manufacturing at Graco Co. in Minneapolis, did more than just walk around. He spent one full day every week visiting every work center, including doing a turn on a variety of machines in the work centers (personal visit and later contact with Graco from 1997 to 2005).

16. Noel Visser, former VP of Operations at Upright-Ireland, Dublin, Ireland, said he regularly walks around asking that what-have-you-changed question (Noel Visser, invited address, *World Class Manufacturing Conference*, London, October 23, 1991).

17. Kaoru Ishikawa; David J. Lu, trans., *What Is Total Quality Control? The Japanese Way* (Englewood Cliffs, NJ: Prentice-Hall, 1985), p. 198.

18. What actually happened was that the plant eliminated WIP storage and pick lists. In the new system materials went directly, just-in-time, from the co-extruder lines to a position in front of the pre-scheduled outgoing dock: Richard J. Schonberger, *Let's Fix It! How the World's Leading Manufacturers Were Seduced by Prosperity and Lost Their Way* (Free Press/Simon & Schuster, 2001), pp. 89–90.

19. Milliken, the giant textile company, had the good sense in the early days of its quality crusade (early 1980s) to adopt the term *opportunity for improvement (OFI)*, instead of *suggestion*.

20. Karl Manrodt and Kate Vitasek, "Getting Better All the Time," *DC Velocity* (May 2006), pp. 52–55.

21. Anthony D. Burns, "Sick Sigma: Question Authority and You'll Win," qualitydigest.com/sixsigma (May 2006).

22. Michel Baudin, "Not-so-Basic Equipment," *Industrial Engineer* (May 2005), pp. 35–39.

23. Research by Davies suggests that Western emphasis on OEE is misguided, shifting the focus of maintenance toward equipment management and utilization as opposed to teamwork in the cause of productive maintenance: Christopher Davies, "The Contribution of Lean Thinking to the Maintenance of Manufacturing Systems," doctoral thesis, Cranfield University, School of Industrial and Manufacturing Science, U.K. (academic year 2002–2003).

Chapter 7

The Case Against (Much of) Management Goal Setting

The metrics trap has a trap within the trap: the management goals that the performance metrics are beholden to. This chapter, elaborating on points made in Chapter 6, shows that dubious management goal-setting practices nourish the suspect management metrics. The reasons are that there are better ways to drive process improvement, and that backlash results from attempts to manage distant goals amid here-and-now demands of the work force.

Question to a group of managers: How many of you consider goal setting to be a basic part of your job?

All hands go up.

Next question: What would happen if you didn't set goals?

Lots of answers: Some say, "Nothing much." Someone says, "I guess they'd set their own goals."

Goals, of course, may be long-range, medium-range, and short-range. In this chapter we focus mostly on the downside of managing to medium- and short-range goals. We'll say only this about the high-level, long-range variety: They are fitting. They define the strategic direction of the firm. But, as pointed out in Chapter 6—and reiterated later in this chapter—tracking metrics monthly against strategic goals, which are by definition long-range, makes no sense.

GOAL REVERSAL

Performance management is overdue for an overhaul. Standard practice is for managers to set numeric goals, especially for output and cost. The goals are to serve as the main basis for motivating the work force, supervision, and support staff. Various incentives, scolds, and punishments apply pressure.

Before the modern era of lean- and quality-driven process improvement, those practices were all we knew. Today, with much better alternatives, the old approach comes off as heavy-handed and costly, ineffective, and unfair.

The new way has first-level production associates, in teams, setting their own targets, but not in output or monetary terms. Having received competitiveness training, they know their process-improvement targets must revolve around quality, response time, and flexibility. Common measures of success include reducing defects, rework, flow time, flow distance, changeover time, and required space. These are general aims that do not require the specificity of a numeric goal. Rather, continuity and rate of improvement are what counts.

Instead of goals and metrics, what is necessary is data capture: keeping track of everything that goes wrong—in other words, collecting process data. Team members record incidences of late or defective parts, lack of tools or instructions, equipment stoppages, and other common process failings. Beyond that, the technology tells what to keep track of. In electronics, for example, associates will want to keep track of shorts, gaps, off-polarity, and so on. Teams visually plot trends. The trends highlight needs for problem solving, that is, fixing the causes. Doing so moves the trend line for the performance metric (e.g., number of defects) in the right direction.

Sometimes, a management goal is aimed at energizing a worthy initiative. At EPIC Technologies, a contract electronics manufacturer based in Rochester Hills, Michigan, the initiative was lean manufacturing. Overall, the lean effort was highly successful. For example, its lead time to Respironics, a key customer, fell from two weeks to two days or less.

There were, however, setbacks. One followed management's setting of an ambitious goal for inventory turnover. Overly tight kanban quantities in bins sized too small led to stoppages and late deliveries. One reason was that the work force was not yet sufficiently flexible. Another was insufficient equipment. Thirdly, deliveries of electronic parts from the distributor were not quick enough. More problems arose in freight, which was not yet geared to handle frequent, small-lot deliveries.[1] In retrospect it is clear: Processes need to be improved to allow inventories to shrink. Inventory goal-setting just gets in the way and invites missteps.

Goals imply an absolute number to be achieved by some date. Such specifics may have all the power of New Year's resolutions. If not met by the date, the goal was unrealistic. If the goal is met, the tendency is to relax, even if more improvement is in reach. If the goal is to exceed the industry average or to match or beat the best, there is another problem. Your industry is probably not the best at much of anything. Industry benchmarks are a weak basis for improvement.

Instead of goals as absolute numbers, it often makes more sense simply to call for, and expect, rapid improvement—a trend going the right way at a steep incline on a chart. That was the approach taken with staffs of "troublemen" at Ameren, a $19 billion energy company operating in Missouri and Illinois. Troublemen are the first line of attack on power outages in the field. When they are unable themselves to fix a problem, it becomes a hand-off to a construction crew. The delay is bad for customers, and the additional costs are bad all around. Information on simple charts got everyone focused on process improvements. The chart for the troublemen displayed percentages of jobs handed off to construction in each geographical area. That percentage relates closely to how well the troublemen respond to trouble calls. From the charts, troublemen in each area could see how they were doing compared to those in other areas. Other trend charts, by department, kept supervisors apprised. Mike Lazalier, consulting engineer at Ameren, states that the troublemen percentages "were substantially improved without formally setting any goals." The improvements were "motivated by the pride of the supervisors and troublemen, the availability of data to make better decisions to level work loads, and the greater visibility of performance for coaching purposes." Lazalier opines that many of the people are probably setting their own informal goals.[2]

Where there is a lot of competitive ground to make up, the call may be for an *accelerating* trend. Over time, rate of improvement serves well as a learning-from-experience indicator. If a trend in reducing defectives is rising but at a decelerating rate, the down-curving trend line will be *tut-tutt*ing the team. The impact is greatest when the trend chart is large and visible to everyone: the team itself, peers in nearby work areas, and staff and managerial support.

However the goals are expressed—fixed number or rate of improvement over time—there is merit in setting and monitoring them at the work-center or cell level. You may agree with this statement: People tend to set tougher but more realistic goals for themselves than those set for them by higher authority. The box, "Kanban Quantities Set by Empowered Associates," offers an example of operatives developing their own kanban quantities.

Kanban Quantities Set by Empowered Associates

Nilish Gupta, the new CEO at Acmetech, has this dominant objective: fast implementation of lean with high involvement of the work force. Some of his staff are leery, saying that fast and high involvement seem contradictory. Gupta explains: An uninvolved work force will *slow* progress. Some associates will be indifferent, uninterested, and reluctant to change. A few may even be deliberately uncooperative. Fast requires active engagement of the associates. Moreover, tapping their experience and common sense will yield better, longer-lasting results.

That settled, Gupta and his staff plan the implementation. Normally, Gupta says, first step would be extensive training, then reorganizing by value streams (e.g., re-layout into work cells); then kanban, and so on. But that takes a long time, and Acmetech needs help *now*. Gupta explains his better idea: Learn while doing—starting with kanban. Here is how it works:

Supervisors give every production associate a simple form. It tells the associate to: (1) Count the number of idle pieces waiting for processing in your area. Enter that number on the form. (2) Use all your experience to estimate the minimum number of pieces you can get by with—enough to mostly avoid stoppages for lack of material. Feel free to discuss this with teammates. Enter your estimate on the form, and turn it in.

No explanations are given. Some employees will ask what's going on. The best answer is something like, "There's just too much costly inventory lying around. You'd feel silly if you ran your home that way—many spares of everything."

Completed forms go to a small kanban planning group for review. Sometimes the quantity seems too large, so someone takes the form back to the associate and asks, "Are you sure? Could you get by with less?" The final estimate becomes the kanban quantity, written on large poster board and mounted in the work force. The new rule is explained: "You may not exceed the kanban quantity, except with special permission."

(Continued)

Gupta and staff are elated with the results. The total of all the estimates will reduce the WIP inventory in the plant by more than two-thirds. Actually eliminating the excesses is something else. It requires stopping production for more than a week in the average process. That includes no shutdown at all in final assembly and shipment, and up to about four weeks' shutdown in a few far-upstream processes. During this "draining of the swamp" the work force is busy removing excess storage racks, pallets, and conveyors. Also, they receive training in what this is all about: making Acmetech a lot more competitive.

The next step is obvious to the associates: Close the yawning space gaps where the storage had been. Do so by moving the machines close together. By now they have received some training in flow and value streams. So the transformation from shops to work cells begins.[a]

---

[a]This scenario was actually developed for a small company in the remanufacturing business; see Richard J. Schonberger, *Let's Fix It! How the World's Leading Manufacturers Were Seduced by Prosperity and Lost Their Way* (New York: Free Press/Simon & Schuster, 2001), pp. 171–177.

"Doc" Hall, editor-in-chief of *Target*, says this about companies in which the people doing the work are engaged in "spontaneous daily correction and improvement": "If [those companies] don't make business mistakes, those who persist will financially blow out the target setters and keep going."[3]

GOAL BACKLASH

Bottom-up process improvement raises productivity and lowers costs. The reverse approach, goal-driven productivity and cost, not only lacks if-then logic; it easily backfires. If I am a work-center supervisor given a goal of raising productivity and cutting cost by 5 percent, my team and I are tempted—no, *likely*—to do the wrong things:

- Cut maintenance and training in order to free up equipment and labor for more production. Never mind the impending equipment malfunctions and breakdowns and the reduced employee skill levels stemming from insufficient training.
- Schedule longer production runs, which keeps equipment busy producing rather than idle for changeovers. Resulting excess inventories is marketing's problem, and the cost of it finance's problem.
- Forbid overtime with its premium wage costs. Without overtime, order promises may be stretched out, orders may be late, and some customers may run. Again, that's marketing's problem.
- Or, if the output goal trumps the cost goal, make overtime required, and make it difficult for associates to use vacation time. Some employees may react later, or

sooner, by abusing leave policies, or even quitting, but the immediate productivity goal will have been met.

On occasion, for the sake of an important customer or order, those kinds of short-term actions can be for the good of the company. For the sake of a management goal, they are bad all around.

These points are nothing new. Dr. Deming was saying these things in *Out of the Crisis* in 1982. Specifically, he said, "Goals are necessary for you and for me, but numerical goals set for other people, without a road map to reach the goal, have effects opposite to the effects sought."[4] He said it again in 1994: "A numerical goal accomplishes nothing. What counts is the method. . . ."[5]

VISUAL DRIVERS

Process improvement, especially of the continuous variety, does not happen without a push. We've seen the fallacies of goals as a pusher. Cost, a traditional goal, is cumbersome and costly itself. Each cost analysis is a discontinuous project done by well-paid staff people. Cost is a weak basis for analysis because it represents the process only indirectly—and is only one measure of value. Others, just as worthy, include quick response, quality, flexibility, and functionality. As a driver, *cost is unlean.*

Bedrock JIT/TQ and lean provide simpler, more direct, and more comprehensive ways to propel improvement. A long list of visual-management devices directly engages the work force. They include, from the quality movement, Pareto charts, check sheets, run diagrams, control charts, and so on. These and other tracking tools target key process variables: response times, quality measures, human and facility flexibility, and product performance. In total, the system keeps process ups and downs on display, and highlights and prioritizes process glitches and mishaps. Moreover, the tracking system is owned by the people who do the work. It is natural, then, that the same people be empowered to attack and correct faults as they are noted.

The cost analyst may fear that empowered associates, lacking cost data, will fail to give priority to improvements that promise greatest savings. That is hardly a concern. Common sense may be in greater supply among front-line associates than among staff professionals. So endowed, front-liners will easily grasp cost significance. For example, say that a Pareto chart identifies the most frequently occurring problem as difficulty in correctly aligning a part, requiring delay to get and use a clamping tool. The next most frequent problem, occurring only half as often, involves a broken tool, requiring calling in a tool-room mechanic. The broken tool, clearly much more costly to correct, gets first priority.

Sometimes the associates may, wisely, give priority to a problem that extends flow times over problems that merely are costly to fix. A cost analysis, in contrast, is not likely to provide such sensitivity to flow times.

Exhibit 7.1   Many Faces of Visual Management

5S/6S: Labels/color-coding, spider charts, etc.

Work flow: Kanban, takt time, standard work, product schematics, fail-safe devices.

Process data: Seven basic tools, near-miss tallies, skills matrixes, stack lights, videotapings, trend charts, customer feedback.

Outcomes: Project displays, before–after photos, walls of fame, awards won.

Clear-sight devices: Cells, customer IDs point-of-use stock, mid-level shelves, partitioned containers, shadow boards, staff support located in production areas, glass walls/doors, light, paint.

EXPANDED VISION

Visual management accomplishes directly and cheaply what conventional cost management cannot do effectively. Exhibit 7.1 provides a brief list of visual management's many manifestations. The remainder of this section elaborates on each item. The format is bulleted list, which is in keeping with the theme of visual management: simplicity—few words required.

5S/6S—The "Housekeeping" Side of Visual Management

- The aim is to catch hundreds of small, clutter-hiding process weaknesses that otherwise would go untended and unmanaged.
- Labels, color-coding, and addresses—for almost everything—create an orderly work environment.
- Spider diagrams or bar charts display results of 5S/6S audits.

Work Flow on Display

- Kanban removes excess stocks in which problems would otherwise accumulate unseen.
- Takt times (industry's term for the customers' usage rate) and recorded completions provide planned regularity that, when disrupted, is a symptom of a process problem.
- Standard work shows assembly schematics and specifies correct methods, times, allowed WIP inventory, and so forth.
- Some fail-safe devices are mechanical. Others employ visual and sometimes sound effects that call for halting the process and recording the trouble.

Process Data: Record, Sort, Visualize

- The seven basic tools (Pareto, fishbone, etc.), and other means, signal and prioritize nonconformities.

- Production associates record near misses, the data that drive behavior-based safety.
- Skills matrixes display employee versatility.
- Stack lights call for help and for recording causes of red or yellow conditions.
- Videotaping reveals ways to speed up setups and changeovers.
- Trend charts tracking quality, setup times, flow times, and so forth clang the alarms when good trends falter.
- Frequent feedback—from next processes, customers, and testing—triggers frequent corrective actions.

How Are We Doing?

- Poster boards display the status of associates' improvement projects (team members, task assignments, milestone attainments, results of projects completed).
- Before-and-after photos, prominent in the work centers, are a source of pride and praise as well as constant reminders that the improvement efforts are paying off and worth continuing.
- "Walls of fame" trumpet accomplishments with photos of team members and recognition they have received.

Clarified Sight Lines

- Work cells bring far-flung operations together, allowing team members to see and understand whole processes.
- Signboards identify cells or equipment dedicated to a given customer.
- Point-of-use location of materials, in mid-level shelves and in partitioned containers, reduces confusion and congestion, making replenishment quicker with less chance of error.
- Shadow boards do the same for tools.
- Staff support people located amid production in rooms with windowed walls and doors promotes communication, visual and otherwise.
- Paint, colors, and good lighting enhance all of the other visual devices.

OVERACTIVE DASHBOARDS

The management dashboard is another visual-management device, and a popular one. It did not deserve a spot in the visual-management listing of Exhibit 7.1, however. The problem with dashboards is, you can't connect the dots.

In light of the previous sections of this chapter, what can be put on the management team's electronic dashboard that makes sense? The usuals from operations are labor

Exhibit 7.2   Sample Dashboard Segment

Metric	Units	Weight	Goal	January	February
On-time delivery	%	0.12	98%	96%	99%

productivity, unit cost, output, on-time delivery, yield, inventory turns, and utilization. Add to that several more from product development, sales and marketing, and accounting. On-time delivery will serve to illustrate limitations of dashboard management.

Exhibit 7.2 shows a segment of a hypothetical dashboard (adapted from a real one). The metric "on-time delivery," measured in monthly percentage, occupies one of the action rows. The on-time goal is 98 percent. In January, actual on-time performance, 96 percent, didn't quite make it, and february, at 99 percent, beats the goal.

Great display! But what use is this information? The factors that make up on-time performance number in the high hundreds or more. Some factors, apparently, were deficient in January and fewer of them in February. The explanations are endless: In January, capacity was tight, orders were bunched up, the weather was bad, a new salesman made some ambitious delivery promises, a truck broke down, and some credit-check paperwork was misplaced. In February, the good month, a couple of burdensome orders got canceled, a sometimes-late supplier delivered on time the whole month, the cranky pick-list system began to work better, a new product was simpler to build, and a vacant supervisory position was filled. Every one of these factors and many more are composed of large numbers of subfactors. (The five *whys* reveal a mother lode of those subfactors.) And the main factors and subfactors occur or don't occur with random abandon.

"You can't connect the dots" means you cannot drill down from high-level metrics to root causes. (The opposite, rolling up low-level numbers into high-level metrics, is possible. But doing so will have averaged out the valued causal information.) With no way to go from the good or bad dashboard number to a treatable cause, the monthly dashboard metrics are not useful. The weighting factor, 0.12 for on-time delivery, allows all of the metrics to be compressed into a single number for the month, a metric with no redeeming utility whatever.

Is there any value at all for dashboard metrics? Yes, but not for any monthly purpose. On the other hand, auditing long-term trends is a valued and vital role for the senior staff. A many-month sequence washes out the high randomness of single-point dashboard numbers. The extension of the on-time delivery numbers shown in Exhibit 7.3 illustrates.

Over the seven months, January through July, on-times have headed rather sharply downward. Probably the executive group should look into it, although they may already know of special reasons that do not call for action. For example, maybe they are

Exhibit 7.3   Extension of On-Time Delivery Numbers

Metric	Units	January	February	March	April	May	June	July
On-time delivery	%	96%	99%	96%	94%	95%	91%	91%

quite sure that a severe shortage of supplier capacity for a key material is a dominating cause, one that affects all their competitors as well.

What this example illustrates is that using the dashboard as a basis for action each month is an unsound practice. Using the numbers on an audit basis, to size up long-term trends, is worthwhile. But, then, throw out the fancy electronic dashboard, which begs frequent attention to factors that warrant only infrequent audits.

Here is a postscript from a letter-writer to *CFO* magazine:

> There are no successful scorecards that tie into value programs, because the time horizons tend to be daily, weekly, or monthly, and value is the present value of future cash flows, hence a structural conflict. . . . [All] that useless data is itself an impediment to value-creating behavior, because it tends to make people try to game the system. . . . This is not to say measurement isn't important; it's vital, but scorecards are only a small part of the answer in operations and worse than useful in decisions about strategy.[6]

LEAN OVERSIGHT

With all this shifting of goal management to operating teams, what happens to senior management's essential oversight role? It needs to become leaner, with a primary concern for direction and rate of improvement, meaning looking at trends over several periods. This applies to aggregated, high-order metrics. It applies as well to process data posted in the work centers and accessed via some form of management by walking around (or flying around from site to site). Examples of MBWA were included in the previous chapter.

The MBWA form of *gemba*-like oversight involves two main kinds of performance data:

1. Detailed process data posted prominently in the work centers, to be frequently updated and frequently seen by everyone.
2. Other process outcomes that do not lend themselves to frequent (e.g., day-by-day) plotting. Examples are stepwise reductions in flow distance, space, and setup times. They are plotted as often as weekly or as they occur. They typically stem from successive improvement projects undertaken by work-center teams.

In either case, the role of walk-around managers is to learn, praise, and offer help: immediate help when needed, but always with a main focus on the longer term. If a trend has turned in the wrong direction and has stuck there for some time, such as several weeks or months, it is up to management to become more involved. Managers and the operating group may look to more or different resources that would help get the trend turned in the right direction. The same oversight comes into play if the rate of improvement has been tapering off over several weeks or months.

When trends or rates do get back on track, or if improvement rates accelerate, management's role is to participate in recognition and celebration events. The best form is the sharing rally in which teammates make presentations of what they did and how they did it. Present at the rally are associates from other work centers who may be able to exploit good ideas in their own areas. This is a key to knowledge transfer and elemental in knowledge management. Equally important is the presence of still higher executives, who need to be there to gain visibility and appreciation for what's going on in process improvement.

The best-developed examples of sharing rallies are those conducted regularly for some 20 years at Milliken, the textile and chemical manufacturer. Tom Peters described the Milliken rallies in his online column in 1985:[7]

The "Corporate Sharing Rally" [which the Milliken president has also called "Fabulous Bragging Sessions"] effectively and quickly pushes ideas from one end of the 60-plant organization to the other.

[The rallies] are held once per quarter, at corporate headquarters. As many as 200 people, at all levels, attend from around the system, some from hundreds of miles away.... (Milliken has had to expand the meeting site several times to try to accommodate all who want to attend.) The sessions last for two days, and the president or chairman attends every minute of them.

Dozens of teams give crisp, five-minute reports in rapid-fire succession. Reports are made from all quarters. Teams consist of secretaries and MIS people as well as machine operators. Each report describes the team's program and quantifies its impact. Peers score every effort on several dimensions from presentation style to quality of the program.

Only a few rules mark the sessions: (1) no negative comments are allowed, (2) no excuses of "we could have done it (or done better) *if* X, Y, or Z had cooperated" are allowed, and (3) quality of the program is as important as the amount of saving or revenue improvement. All who are present at the sessions take home some award, although those who do well take home a higher grade of award. Each award is signed by the president, framed on the spot, and presented before team members leave the session.

Each bragging session has a theme. One might focus on cost reduction, another on sales increases, another on customer listening, another on quality improvements, and so on. Presenters at the quarterly sessions often have spoken several times at local preliminary bragging sessions within their factory or sales unit. The top winners in the quarterly session make presentations at the president's meeting, where all the senior Milliken people gather.

Bragging and sharing has become a way of life at Milliken. The competition to become a presenter has grown keen. "Peers are really tough on each other," says [president Tom] Malone. "I grade almost every presentation as excellent."

Besides these corporate events, Milliken regularly runs sharing rallies with and for supplier and customer companies. Typically, the presenters are company presidents. They share their process-improvement successes as suppliers and customers of Milliken. Because they want to impress their Milliken partners, and everyone else, these rallies stimulate the companies to come up with good stories. Everyone learns from everyone else. Process improvement is well served.

Part II has been mostly about concepts, including a few that can especially retard process improvement. In Part III, we shift from disputable concepts to valuable practices.

NOTES

1. Interview with Steve Fraser, EPIC General Manager, summer 2006; plus case study: Rebecca A. Morgan, "Implementing Lean Throughout the Extended Enterprise," *Target* (5th Issue 2005), pp. 39–41.

2. Mike Lazalier, "Coax, Don't Squeeze: Use Metrics to Influence, not Aggravate," *Industrial Engineer* (April 2007), pp. 26–31.

3. Robert W. Hall, "Building a Vigorous Working Culture," *Target*, 3rd issue (2005), pp. 17–26. Also, e-mail dated September 27, 2006, to most of those who spoke at the second annual Lean Accounting Summit, which took place in Orlando, Florida, September 21–22, 2006.

4. W. Edwards Deming, *Out of the Crisis* (Cambridge, MA: MIT Center for Advanced Engineering Study, 1982), p. 69.

5. W. Edwards Deming, *The New Economics for Industry, Education, Government*, 2nd ed. (Cambridge, MA: MIT Center for Advanced Engineering Study, 1994), p. 41.

6. Richard Bassett, to "Letters," *CFO* (March 2007), p. 14.

7. Found in September 2006 at: tompeters.com/col_entries.php?note=005131&year=1985.

Building a Competitive Fortress

Part III has the aim of unlocking secrets of why some companies are able to carry on successfully for decades. A presumption is that long-lived companies have fortress-like characteristics: bulwarks that fend off competition. The reality, though, is that fortress walls need continually to be strengthened, but often aren't. Of the four chapters in this section, the first three present ways of raising the bulwarks, and the fourth gives examples of failures to keep the walls strong.

The topic of Chapter 8 is building a strong culture and embedding it deeply in the organization, a culture such as one of customer service, à la Nordstrom. Chapter 9's bulwark-building way is an iron-fist, make-your-numbers-or-else *modus operandus*— the kind made famous by General Electric. Chapter 10's approach is intensive management of process improvement, and here the best-known model is the Toyota production system.

How do those three competition blockers relate to the book's best-practices theme? For one thing, a strong culture provides its own, unique practices, and they may be potent enough not to require much help from conventional process-improvement methods. Make-your-numbers, deeply entrenched in business, how-ever, tends to interfere with the upstart new regime of best practices. In many companies the two have reached a state of uncomfortable co-existence. Process-improvement practices, including the full lean tool set, have a different kind of problem: lack of a single Big Idea. That lack may help explain why so many companies mount a strong lean and total-quality effort but fail to keep it going.

Chapter 11 fills in with a kind of fortress building that has its own Big-Idea impact. It is rallying around a unique business model, one so successful that it energizes its inside and external stakeholders to participate at high levels. Best of all, this kind of model generates innovative new streams of best practices. The host companies gain an edge over others that are limited to conventional lean/quality improvement. Dell and Wal-Mart, the best-known current paragons of unique business models, are global leaders in developing lean pipeline methodologies.

Chapter 8

Fortress by Culture

For a few companies, the key competitive asset is a long-lived, deep-seated culture that reaches out beyond the company. Four examples come to mind: Nordstrom, 3M, Medtronic, and Hewlett-Packard. Of the four, the first two have retained most of their strong cultures to the present, but the latter two appear to have lost some of their cultural punch. The four cultures are not at all alike. Each revolves around a different component of business excellence.

NORDSTROM: CUSTOMER SERVICE IS OUR BUSINESS

Nordstrom, which began as a small Seattle shoe store in 1901, now has its upscale clothing department stores in cities throughout the United States. *The Nordstrom Way*, as detailed in a 1996 book by that title,[1] boils down to this: Do whatever is necessary to make it right for the customer. Nordstrom's company storytelling includes the one about the customer who dashed to the airport after last-minute shopping, leaving her airline tickets on a sales counter; whereupon the saleslady grabbed some money from petty cash, hailed a cab to the airport, paged the woman, and handed her the ticket.[2]

This kind of culture may be more prevalent in retailing than elsewhere. Being face-to-face with customers exerts a pull toward doing what's right for them. That pull can be harnessed to offset opposing inclinations that reside in the complex makeup of human beings. Many communities throughout the world have at least one smallish retailer recognized for maintaining such a culture over many years or even generations of family ownership. Nordstrom is special in that it is not smallish. Its sizeable stores, nearly 200 of them, have opened in cities across the United States. But that expansion is relatively recent. When companies grow quickly, it becomes ever more difficult to hang onto an exceptional culture. Having Nordstrom family members—currently the family's third generation—still in executive and board positions surely helps provide continuity. Has rapid growth diminished the company's service culture? Apparently not. Nordstrom ranked fourth best of 25 companies in *Business Week*'s inaugural 2006 ranking of best providers of customer service.[3]

Has Nordstrom's attention to customers led the company to pursue lean methodologies—which aim for quick, flexible, high-quality customer response? The answer is, yes and no. No, Nordstrom is not known for giving attention to the classic Toyota-system brand of lean. But yes, Nordstrom has had a good deal of success with another lean avenue, initiated in 2000.[4] Nordstrom executives had become dismayed over quarter-by-quarter and year-by-year slippage of same-store sales revenue and company profit margin and stock price. So, belatedly (as compared with a few other major retailers), they threw out their mess of an ordering and inventory system and installed a quick-reaction Wal-Mart-like one with point-of-sale sensitivity.[5] The results show up clearly in Nordstrom's inventory turnover data. From 1990 to 2001, its inventory turns meandered downward, from 4.4 to 3.8. Since then they have vaulted to a 33-year high of 5.4 in 2006. In addition, benefits show up in percentage reductions in sales, general, and administrative (SG&A) costs for five years straight. SG&A reductions are a natural but under-appreciated product of becoming lean. Overall, and more important, Nordstrom appears again to be, in the United States, the top-performing upscale department-store chain.

3M: CLOSET INNOVATION[6]

The founding of Minnesota Mining and Manufacturing Co., later shortened to 3M, was a year later than that of Nordstrom. In 2002, 3M published *A Century of Innovation: The 3M Story*,[7] celebrating and documenting the company's 100 years. From sandpaper to Scotch Tape, from Tartan Turf to Post-it notes, 3M has been one of the globe's top companies in developing commercially successful products. Aside from its innovative prowess, 3M was among the more active western companies in learning and applying JIT in the 1980s. In its JIT implementation efforts, however, the company may have been hampered somewhat by a weak component of its overall strong technical capabilities. We consider the innovation culture first, then JIT and the technical-capabilities issue. (A *BusinessWeek* cover story, labeled "3M's Innovation Crisis" in the early 2000s, is presented as more of an annoying interruption than an innovation killer.[8])

3M's culture of pragmatic innovation has nothing to do with a founding family and progeny, as at Nordstrom. Rather, 3M is known for its lab-centered "bootlegging": allowing inventors and scientists free rein to use company facilities to pursue their own ideas. According to *The 3M Story*, "Regardless of their assignment, 3M technical employees are encouraged to devote up to 15 percent of their working hours to independent projects."[9] The "15 percent rule," as it came to be called (really permission rather than a rule), emerged from the development of Scotch masking tape by technologist Dick Drew. He had pressed on with his idea even though his superiors, William McKnight and Richard Carlton, disapproved. McKnight and Carlton were won over and an informal bootlegging practice solidified into the centerpiece of a company culture.

Before long and over time, more elements were added. In the 1940s, McKnight saw that Drew, who had parlayed Scotch masking tape into even more popular Scotch cellophane tape, was unhappy. Drew's freewheeling style did not mesh well with structured tendencies in the fast-growing company. McKnight's response was to advise Drew to hire some people and run his own inventing and developing operation. Drew did so, starting up the Products Fabrication Laboratory (Pro-Fab), staffing it with "misfits" like himself, and focusing it on creating better backings and coating processes. "During its 20-year lifetime, the lab was known for product breakthroughs that led to Scotchlite reflective sheeting, Micropore surgical tape, foam tape, decorative ribbon, face masks, and respirators. In addition, the lab experimented with adhesives that, almost four decades later, led to the blockbuster product, Post-it notes."[10] In addition, Pro-Fab became the model for 3M Technical Centers that through the years have become a key instrument in the company's new-product successes.

Other enhancements to the culture of innovation have been folded in. Technical Forum (1951) brought in Nobel laureates and sponsored specialty subgroups such as polymer chemistry or coating processes.[11] Tech Forum also created an annual Inventor Recognition Program. Genesis Program (1984) provided grants aimed at encouraging technical entrepreneurship—and some funding freedom to go along with the 15-percent rule. Other grant and recognitions programs to spark creativity include the Carlton Society, Engineering Achievement Award of Excellence, Alpha Grants for non-technical innovations, and the Technical Circle of Excellence and Innovation.[12]

Nor have the manufacturing people been neglected. For them, 3M created the Corporate Quality Achievement and the Process Technology Awards. Moreover, in the 1970s, the director of engineering borrowed Technical Forum concepts in getting engineers to share manufacturing process and equipment design technologies. Various manufacturing specialists organized themselves into minichapters, each with a specific focus, such as adhesives and ceramics. Minichapter people became inside consultants, spreading their knowledge around the company.[13] On the training front in the 1980s, 3M put hundreds of its manufacturing people through outside and on-site training on just-in-time and total quality.[14]

Are these overtures to the manufacturing side of the house sufficient to make 3M, dominant in product innovation, also an achiever in process improvement? The inventory/leanness data say yes: Since 1979, its worst year on the inventory scale, 3M's inventory turnover has risen at an average rate of 1.8 percent per year (see Exhibit 8.1). Its turns improved or held steady in all but five of those 26 years.

That performance notwithstanding, I tend to think that 3M, along with such companies as Kodak and DuPont, have not lived up to their potential in process improvement. Typical processes are mixing, coating, and extruding (e.g., to produce sandpaper, tapes, nonwoven sheets, and films). It is natural that such companies (and here I'm not referring particularly to 3M) should be strong on the chemistry of the processes, but weak in the mechanics of them. In staffing, they are likely to be long on chemical engineers, short on mechanical and manufacturing engineers. Or if plentiful, the latter will lack clout. As a result, putting certain of the lean concepts into practice becomes problematic. Not getting their due are, especially, quick changeover, small-lot processing and handling, and containerization. These are high-impact elements of the lean core in this kind of continuous-process manufacturing. Moreover, in chemical-oriented industries there is the long-standing preference for quality sampling out of large batches, which saves on inspection costs but is directly contrary

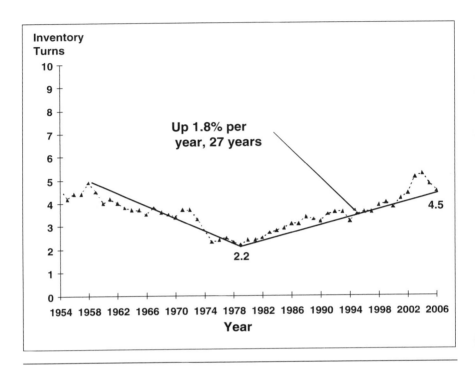

Exhibit 8.1   Inventory Turnovers at 3M

to lean's most basic landmark: small lots. (Other lean-core elements, such as work cells and kanban, are comparatively low in priority in process industries.)

The strong focus on process chemistry extends to the production work force. Operators tend to take pride in mastery of a specialty, so that those expert in mixing know little about coating and vice versa. That specialization inhibits cross-training and process rotation. It also has a retarding effect on instituting operator-centered TPM, given the tradition in the process industries of plant maintenance as its own proud and separate specialty.

All these factors add up to a hurdle in the way of these companies becoming highly flexible and quickly responsive to customers. These comments also appear to apply, more or less, to manufacturers of confectionary products, certain other processed foods, and cosmetics. The chemistry of the food or cosmetics is foremost, and matters such as small lots take a back seat. So manufacturing is complicit with marketers, who, in those industries, usually have long traditions of relying on warehouses high in finished goods to fill customer orders. That never works well, given the impossibility of forecasting item demand accurately. As long as manufacturing fails to provide the happy alternative—of quick, flexible, small-lot manufacturing—constrained performance will persist.

SAVING LIVES AS COMPANY CULTURE: THE MEDTRONIC EXAMPLE

Of all kinds of organizations, the most likely to be under the sway of a dominating culture should be one that saves lives. No doubt plenty of fire departments, emergency medical facilities, and rescue services fit the description. But our interest is in large corporations whose very size militates against existence of strong, enduring cultures.

For a big company that makes life-saving products, to really feel absorbed by what its products do, the link to lives saved must be clear and direct. Car-air-bag manufacturers come to mind. They know when their product fails, because they get sued. When its air bags save people, those are opportunities for the company collectively to feel proud. Most air-bag deployments, however, did not save someone's life. Rather they greatly reduced injuries. I have visited companies in the business, and have done training for one of them. They do give emphasis to their public-interest mission, but not to the extent of building that into a pervasive culture. As second- or third-tier automotive suppliers, their main concerns are staying in the good graces of the automakers and battling with competitors (and perhaps the courts).

How about, then, manufacturers of devices that ward off death by heart attack? One such company, Medtronic, did build a dominating culture around improving, extending, and saving patients' lives. Founded in 1949 by Earl Bakken and his brother-in-law, Medtronic has grown to 235th in the 2006 edition of the *Fortune* 500. The company developed the first wearable cardiac pacemaker in 1957. With growth it has added many products for treatment of heart disease, vascular illnesses, diabetes, neurological disorders, and other medical conditions. Open Medtronic's current web site and the first thing you see, in large letters, is, "Every 6 seconds, Medtronic helps improve another life."

Bakken, now 82 years old and retired from the Medtronic board, is the inspiration behind the culture suggested by that slogan. In a 1989 book, *Reflections on Leadership*, he discusses the tradition of his meeting with small groups of new employees. During those sessions he presents each employee with a Medtronic medallion and explains the corporate mission it represents. The medallion features the corporate symbol, a rising human figure. Above the figure is the company motto, "Toward Man's Full Life." Bakken urged the new employees to keep it nearby—"on their desks or at their work-stations—to remind them of the great things they are accomplishing as partners with the worldwide medical community in the struggle against disease and pain."[15]

Fifteen years ago a visitor to company headquarters in Minneapolis would see and hear a lot about these things, and more: the frequent interactions of Medtronic people with thankful patients and doctors; the "Customer First" buttons; the visits to surgical suites and recovery rooms; doctor visits to Medtronic facilities; the annual Holiday Party, which fetes flown-in patients who have avoided death or a diminished exis-tence. According to a Medtronic acquaintance, it's usually a tear-jerker. Earl Bakken still returns from his long-time Hawaii home to Minneapolis to participate in the Holiday Party.

No doubt the culture suffers a bit from absence of Bakken's full-time personal involvement. Moreover, part of the company's growth has been by acquisition, each new company having its own traditions. Interviews with Medtronic people at three of the company's sites[16] do not clearly indicate whether, or the extent to which, the Bakken culture has lost ground.

Even if, as at Nordstrom, new generations of the Bakken family were there in high places working to perpetuate what the senior Bakken started, preservation of the culture would probably be a challenge. Like every other company in the pharmaceutical and medical-device industry, the high energy expended in seeking and celebrating regulatory-agency approvals leaves that much less left for acknowledging patients whose lives have been saved by the industry's products. No such impediment exists, however, at Hewlett-Packard, our last example of a dominant culture.

THE "HP WAY"[17]

David Packard and William Hewlett, founders of the Hewlett-Packard Corporation, passed away in 1996 and 2001, respectively. "[O]bituary writers noted their enduring legacy was not the multi-billion dollar tech giant—it was the HP Way." So said the *Palo Alto Weekly* in "The Rise and Fall of the HP Way."[18] The original "Way," set down in print by the founders in 1957, is in the company's web site. Its seven elements do not look like the stuff of a legendary business culture. Executives in many other companies have announced similar-sounding intentions. Some of the words refer to profit, growth, success, and listening to customers. Others were in the vein of, "We trust our employees," "Everyone has something to contribute," and so on. Apparently, though, Hewlett and Packard, and successive management teams, put their weight behind the ponderous words.

In my own working relationships with several HP business units in the 1980s, when people talked about the HP Way I detected no hints of cynicism. And in most companies cynicism abounds (which may explain why Dilbert cartoons, initiated in 1989, are still going strong). HP people seemed to treat the Way as something only insiders could really understand. When pressed for an explanation, HP'ers would usually talk about openness, trust, honesty, concern, and respect for the employee. The "Rise and Fall" includes comments of former HP'ers about these things. They talk about "how co-workers were reassigned to new jobs rather than sacked; how the company for a time implemented a shortened work week for all employees so certain individuals would not lose their jobs"; also about how Hewlett and Packard would refuse "short-term contracts, so they would not have to lay off chunks of their work force after the contract was over. Packard said they didn't want to run a 'hire-and-fire operation.' "

In my JIT/lean roles at the HP sites, I had, at first, no more than passing interest in the HP Way. That changed. The main lean effort was to convert from functional departments and "autonomous build" to cellular assembly with cross-trained, job-rotating cell teams and kanban parts movements. New responsibilities of assembly operatives were for line balancing, material handling, quality, ownership and upkeep of their own facilities, tracking hourly performance against the rate, collecting data on everything that goes wrong, and team problem analysis and correction. To take on these responsibilities they would need to work closely with engineers, buyers, maintenance, payroll, hiring/ training, cost analysts, and other experts. It sounds like a daunting challenge that might take years to achieve. But these HP plants had the HP-Way advantage. Unlike almost any other company in the 1980s, in HP plants engineers' desks were often out on production floors intermixed with fabrication, assembly, and testing. Engineers and managers already had habits of taking coffee and eating company-furnished pastries and apples with the assemblers and equipment operators. The way was greased for working together on successful lean conversions, which at HP usually took weeks, not years.

In most large companies, a lean conversion would be slowed by corporate red tape and complex decision processes. Not at HP, with its Way-derived policies of high autonomy at each plant. That autonomy could be seen in plant size and staffing policies. When success with its product line pushed a plant's population up to about 500 employees, it would split amoeba-like into two plants.

Regarding staffing, HP favored decentralized expertise in design engineering, purchasing, and accounting. In other multi-plant companies, these would be mostly centralized at corporate headquarters. HP's size-limited plants were trusted largely to run themselves with family-like familiarity. That environment is conducive to working together rather than fighting the functional and factional battles common in very large facilities.

Plant-level autonomy might be thought to hinder knowledge transfer. But openness, another HP-Way element, prevailed. The company's first major cellular-lean implementation (in which I was not involved) took place in 1982 in an HP printer plant in Vancouver, Washington. Soon thereafter, people in other company plants had learned all about it and put their minds to doing it themselves.

Some strong company cultures (e.g., that of Nordstrom) are largely indifferent to conventional lean practices. The HP Way, however, turned out to be a welcome mat for cellular lean, along with total quality and supplier partnerships. My impression is that the thoroughness, speed, and ease of implementing JIT/lean at several of HP's plants in the 1980s may exceed that of any other company since that time. Those implementations have received their share of published recognition.[19]

Alas, as claimed in the *Palo Alto Weekly*, HP may have, to some extent, lost its Way. Some say that apparently began when an outsider, hard-charging Carly Fiorina from Lucent, became CEO. At one point, Fiorina got 80,000 employees voluntarily to go on a shortened work week. She followed that by cutting the work force by 6,000, "leaving some employees feeling they'd fallen for a 'bait-and-switch.' "[20] Further, Fiorina championed the merger with Compaq, which was publicly and bitterly opposed by William Hewlett, then still living. Merger with another large company could not help but water down the HP Way. (In financial and other respects, however, the merger seems to have turned out well.)

Recent events suggest that the HP Way may be under more stress. The new chief information officer, Randy Mott, had worked IT magic earlier in his career at

Wal-Mart and then Dell. He was hired at HP to do the same thing: Consolidate vast numbers of different information systems and data warehouses so that HP marketers, financial managers and others would be able to see the whole. That sounds like good medicine, except that large measures of autonomy are lost in the process.[21] In retrospect, it is a wonder that the Way lasted so long, given the volatility of the electronics industry along with the many years of rapid growth of HP. Time will tell whether HP has regressed to the point of adopting the common but often-discredited make-your-numbers business-management system described in Chapter 9.

NOTES

1. Robert Spector and Patrick D. McCarthy, *The Nordstrom Way: The Inside Story of America's Number 1 Customer Service Company* (New York: Wiley, 1996). Spector and McCarthy were outside observers. Another Nordstrom book in the same vein and vintage, but written by a Nordstrom insider, is: Betsy Sanders, *Fabled Service: Ordinary Acts, Extraordinary Outcomes* (San Francisco: Jossey-Bass, 1997).

2. Robert Spector, *Lessons from the Nordstrom Way* (New York: Wiley, 2001), pp. 199–200. Spector maintains that Nordstrom has made use of "corporate story-telling," now not a unique practice, for "most of its century-long existence."

3. Jena McGregor, "Customer Service Champs," *Business Week*, March 5, 2007, pp. 52–60.

4. The story of Nordstrom's turnaround since 2000 has been well publicized, and was briefly reviewed in Monica Soto Ouchi, "Nordstrom Board to Change," *The Seattle Times* (April 15, 2006), p. E1.

5. Bob Buchanan, long-time retail analyst at A.G. Edwards, says, "Nordstrom is one of the few department-store retailers that really understands ... and embraces the technology," cited in Monica Soto Ouchi, "Microsoft Shops for More Sales as Retailers Use More Technology," *Seattle Times* (January 16, 2007), pp . C1–C2.

6. References include: Eric Von Hippel, Stephan Thomke, and Mary Sonnack, "Creating Breakthroughs at 3M," *Harvard Business Review* (September–October 1999), pp. 47–57. Gordon Shaw, Robert Brown, and Philip Browniley, "Strategic Stories: How 3M Is Rewriting Business Planning," *Harvard Business Review* (May–June 1988), pp. 41–50. Rosabeth Moss Kanter, John Kao, and Fred Wiersema, *Innovation: Breakthrough Thinking at 3M, DuPont, GE, Pfizer, and Rubbermaid* (New York: Collins, 1997).

7. *A Century of Innovation: The 3M Story* (St. Paul, MN: 3M Company, 2002).

8. The cover story's subtitle is "How Six Sigma Almost Smothered Its Idea Culture": Brian Hindo, "At 3M, A Struggle between Efficiency and Creativity," *Business Week* (June 2007), pp. 8–14 in the magazine's Indepth section.

9. Ibid., p. 21.

10. Ibid., p. 26.

11. Ibid., pp. 32–33.

12. Ibid., pp. 41–42.

13. Ibid., p. 44.

14. I participated in some of that training.

15. Earl Bakken, *Reflections on Leadership* (Minneapolis, MN: Medtronic, 1989), p.18.

16. The interviews were with Medtronic acquaintances at the Minneapolis home base (April 2006), the Physio Control subsidiary in Redmond, Washington (May 2006), and the Xomed subsidiary in Jacksonville (June 2006).

17. David Packard, *The HP Way: How Bill Hewlett and I Built Our Company* (New York: HarperBusiness, 1995).

18. Jocelyn Dong, "The Rise and Fall of the HP Way," *Palo Alto Weekly*, online edition (April 10, 2002). In agreement with the article, lean-manufacturing expert Jeffrey Liker says, "The founders are gone, and the HP way is mostly gone," *Wall Street Journal* (June 19, 2006), pp. B1, B3.

19. References that I know of include two articles on JIT/total quality implementation at HP's computer systems division: Richard C. Walleigh, "What's Your Excuse for Not Using JIT?" *Harvard Business Review* (March–April 1986), pp. 38–54; and Mehran Sepehri and Rick Walleigh, "Quality and Inventory Control Go Hand in Hand at Hewlett-Packard's Computer Systems Division," *Industrial Engineer* (February 1986), pp. 44–51. Six HP case studies are included in Richard J. Schonberger, *World Class Manufacturing Casebook: Implementing JIT and TQC* (Free Press, 1987): cases 2 and 3 focusing on kanban and operator involvement at HP, Fort Collins, Colorado; case 11, the HP Personal Office Computer Division, Sunnyvale, California; case 13, the HP Computer Systems Division, Cupertino, California; case 17, the HP printer plant, Vancouver, Washington (the name, disguised as Ultrix Corp., no longer needs the disguise); and case 24, HP's disc-drive facility in Greeley, Colorado.

20. Dong, "The Rise and Fall of the HP Way," op cit.

21. Peter Burrows, "Stopping the Sprawl at HP," *Business Week* (May 29, 2006), pp. 54–56.

Chapter 9

Vengeful Numbers

The management system that for decades has dominated big business, particularly publicly traded companies, is described by these related terms: management by the numbers; top-down management; and command-and-control. Under that system, some companies employ vigorous earnings management, which means manipulating plans, goals, resources, and programs to achieve targeted earnings rather than putting best feet forward and seeing what earnings ensue.

The price companies pay for numbers management can be high.[1] Hope and Fraser, in *Beyond Budgeting*, report on the annual planning and budgeting that starts the numbers cycle:

> The average time consumed is between four and five months. It also involves many people and absorbs up to 20 to 30 percent of senior executives' and financial managers' time. Some organizations have attempted to place a cost on the whole planning and budgeting process. A 1998 benchmarking study showed that the average company invested more than 25,000 person-days per billion dollars of revenue in the planning and performance management process.[2]

Those costs are just for initial planning and budgeting (which, according to another study, influence only 2.5 major decisions per year[3]). The costs balloon in the quarterly review and control phases, preceded by monthly data collection, reporting, and review.

Besides the cost, the system has acquired a reputation for ruthlessness: Make your numbers or you're out. While some of that does occur, the greater ruthlessness lies in misallocations of resources. Everybody who does it knows that resources are hijacked; and the stock market knows it. Still, it is the way of doing business in some of the world's most admired and successful corporations, such as General Electric, Honeywell, and Emerson Electric. If there were no good alternatives or examples of high success by other means, we would have to accept management-by-the-numbers as good business, and never mind the faults.

But there *are* attractive options. A clear alternative is to generate good business numbers by managing the means rather than the ends. In *Profit Beyond Measure*, by Johnson and Bröms, managing by means is the central theme.[4] The means are, in a prominent context, *the processes*. The surest way to manage the means is through continuous process improvement, much of it bottom-up, with little command and spare managerial control. As Jim Womack put it, "If managers focus on their process, the performance metrics will come right; but if managers focus on their numbers, the process is likely never to improve."[5] There is no need to review process-improvement methodologies here. Rather the task in this section is to examine the make-your-numbers system—that is, to contemplate its flaws and consider the opportunities for gain by turning away from it, thus to rely more on continuous process improvement.

WHERE THE NUMBERS COME FROM AND TAKE YOU

The numbers that managers are beholden to come largely from a cost and volume collection system. Accumulated actual numbers get bounced against budgets, standard costs, and other numeric goals, typically weekly but sometimes even daily. Managers at the business-unit level keep watch. Their oversight role is to detect and try to correct for slippage before executives at headquarters see end-of-month reports. At corporate, negative variances sound the alarm. Business-unit management must cut spending, alter production schedules, chop programs, reduce training and maintenance, slow down hiring, delay payments on accounts, air-freight incoming materials, work overtime, and exhort the work force.

None of this is done because it is good business. It is to avoid the greater consequences if slippage is still there when quarterly data arrive at HQ. Slippage requires that the business-unit president and some staffers go to corporate and detail what's been done, try to explain why it didn't work, and then face the music. If deficiencies persist another quarter, corporate may do the cost cutting, reduce the business-unit's budget, shift production and programs to another business unit or an outsource, and even downgrade or fire someone. There is little in the numbers that points right at causes of the deficiencies, because all the goals, standards, and budgets are highly aggregated. (As discussed in Chapter 7, goal-setting itself is a shaky undertaking, *and not a necessary management function*.) So some of the budget cutting and cost cutting is across-the-board rather than precisely selective.

Nor are the by-quarter actions taken for good business reasons—except to the extent that the investment community values continuity and predictability. Is that a valid business concern? Let us consider the matter using a hypothetical company, Multiproduct, Inc., and after that a real company, Emerson Electric.

CONTINUITY AND PREDICTABILITY VERSUS MAGNITUDE

Is the shortest distance between two points a straight line? Yes, according to executives at Multiproduct, Inc., who have presided over 40 straight years of increased earnings per share and return on investment. No, says a classic 1962 study of economic development, R&D, and policy formation, which found superiority in unbalanced (zigzagging) patterns of growth and success.[6] No, also, says a new book, *Pop! Why Bubbles Are Good for the Economy*. It is about how bubbles in the economy (e.g., the "dot.com" bubble) unleash large bursts of entrepreneurial energies that create new infrastructures, facilitate learning, and rapidly roll out new technologies.[7]

The 40-straight years of gains at Multiproduct became, no doubt, their own agenda, and dominated the company's strategic planning. Each successive executive team would have felt the increasing pressure. Quarter by quarter and year after year, the CEO would have been congratulated and egged on by Wall Street analysts, who are predisposed to care more about predictable numbers than their magnitude. Stock analysts, after all, are honored and rewarded for their ability to predict. And executives of numbers-driven publicly traded companies generally are in conference calls with stock analysts every quarter, and sometimes more often. (The U.S. Chamber of Commerce, fretful of the effects of CEOs feeding Wall Street their quarterly earnings targets, is trying to do something about it. It is urging executives to end the practice, labeled a "self-inflicted wound by American CEOs."[8])

So we have on the one hand cases such as that of Multiproduct, Inc., indicating that, when done intensively with great discipline, numbers management can yield impressive long-term results. On the other hand are the deficiencies: that meeting the required numbers is not done for best business reasons, that it sacrifices resources and their worthy uses, and that it leaves cash on the table. Exhibit 9.1 is a portrayal of two alternative financial outcomes for Multiproduct over the period 1965 through 2005. The straight line represents the continuously upward 40-year performance.

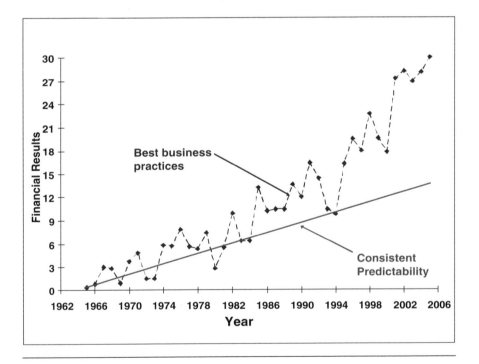

Exhibit 9.1   Hypothetical Business Outcomes at Multiproduct, Inc.

The zigzag line is a projection of Multiproduct's performance if good business practices had been foremost, with financials left unmanaged and treated strictly as a result. The graphed outcomes could be any of the usual financial measures—earnings per share, revenue growth, stock price, and so on.

The zigzagging pattern labeled Best Business Practices in the exhibit is the sort that the 1962 research and *Pop!* found to be superior in results. The numbers-management alternative is the straight line labeled Consistent Predictability. Though there is no way to prove superiority of Best Business Practices (zigzag), it makes sense. If management has the capability to manage the means directly—using best practices—the results should exceed what would obtain from managing the ends indirectly. Though Wall Street would be poorly served on the predictability dimension, the net advantage in earnings should result in long-term higher stock prices, as well as larger paid dividends to stockholders.

Kenneth E. Boulding, well known among systems theorists, penned a poem about system complexities. It aptly speaks to why it might be best to give up on predictability:

A system is a big black box
Of which we can't unlock the locks
And all we can find out about
Is what goes in and what comes out.

Receiving input-output pairs,
Related by parameters,
Permits us, sometimes, to relate
An input, output, and a state.

If this relation's good and stable
Then to predict we may be able,
But if this fails us—heaven forbid!
We'll be compelled to force the lid![9]

But is there a happy medium? Can't a company serve stock analysts with reasonable consistency and at the same time intensively manage the processes—without forcing the lid? The example of Emerson Electric Company sheds some light on the question.

EMERSON ELECTRIC: FORTY-THREE YEARS UPWARD

Emerson Electric Company, 126th on the 2006 *Fortune* 500, manufactures a broad assortment of industrial and consumer products. Every year for 43 years, from 1957 to 2000, Emerson's by-the-numbers system produced increasing earnings and dividends per share. Thirty-five years into that period, CEO Charles Knight said, "We concluded that, to maintain a premium stock price over long periods of time, we needed to achieve growth and strong financial results on a consistent basis—no swings of the pendulum. . . ."[10]

Not that Emerson paid no heed to emergent best practices in operations. Just-in-time manufacturing had made a start in a few Emerson plants in about 1984. It became an official corporate initiative in late 1985 in a meeting of company officers, all business-unit managers, and key staffers at corporate headquarters in St. Louis. Propagation of JIT—labeled internally as the "War on Inventory"—included presentation events at Emerson's scattered U.S. sites. (I was an invited participant in 20 of the events between 1985 and 1988.) The best way to judge the results is by JIT/lean's prominent metric, inventory turnover. From 1958 to 1981, Emerson's turns were on a downslide, from a respectable 5.2 to a miserable 2.5. It remained stuck at 2.5 until 1984. With the launch of JIT and the "War," it got unstuck right away, rising to 2.6 in 1985, followed by 3.0, 3.3, 3.3, and, in 1989, 3.6—a 44 percent improvement in the five years. Then the improvement slowed to a crawl—for the next 10 years.

What happened? For one thing, the main force behind JIT was executive VP William A. (Bill) Rutledge, a dynamo much liked and respected throughout the company. He suffered serious heart failure in 1990. After bypass surgery he resumed part-time duties at Emerson for a while, dying in 1994. JIT's fade at Emerson correlates well with that of Mr. Rutledge.

JIT was probably suffering from loss of high-level interest anyway, given the relentlessness of the company's earnings management. Charles Knight's 2005 book, *Performance without Compromise: How Emerson Consistently Achieves Winning Results*, mentions JIT only once, on page 93.[11] And at that he refers to it by the limiting term "just-in-time inventory management," rather than what it was generally called, just-in-time manufacturing.

While JIT was slipping at Emerson, other major manufacturers had been discovering it, or rediscovering *JIT*-renamed-*lean*, throughout the 1990s. Finally, in 1999, Emerson followed suit, resurrecting the effort under the changed name, *lean manufacturing*. The main impetus was growing disappointment with margins and Emerson's stock price. The *Wall Street Journal* aired the situation in a May 1999 story, "For Its Profit Streak, Emerson's Reward Is a Laggard Share Price."[12] Lean's effect at Emerson was the same as JIT's more than a decade earlier: Its inventory turns rose sharply. Knight also cited "valuable benefits for our customers . . . [including, in some divisions] meeting lead-time requirements that are as small as one-third of their level when we started . . . [and] late deliveries . . . cut in half."[13]

BEYOND THE FORTY-THREE YEARS

Emerson's 43-year string of increasing earnings ran out in 2001—an overall bad year financially at Emerson. That was an unlucky break for David N. Farr, who in 2000 received the CEO's baton from Knight. However, for Mr. Farr the pressure was off. He could manage differently if he and his executive team chose.

Now, seven years later, it looks as if Farr did choose to manage differently. Invited to write an epilogue to Knight's book, Farr said, "[It was] our choice not to worry about starting a new earnings string." Studies of other high-performing companies "revealed that they did a superior job of balancing sales growth, operating margin improvement, free cash flow, and return on total capital. . . . [We] tended to emphasize margin improvement over asset efficiency." So, he said, "We intensified efforts to streamline inventories and implement principles and techniques of lean manufacturing across the front offices and factory floors; it was all about speed and using less invested capital. . . ."[14]

By these statements, Farr appears to be clear on the intertwined benefits of lean on company success. Farr is upping the firm's attentiveness to customers. His call for speed, a dominant customer requirement, is the main deliverable from lean manufacturing and lean office processes. Free cash flow and less invested capital are financial by-products of lean. They come from reducing investments in inventory, freeing up capacity, and selling more to happier customers. They come, as well, from reduction of SG&A (sales, general, and administrative) expenses, a result of lean-derived process simplifications and overhead shrinkage. Oh, and without even trying, Farr's multi-faceted approach to management has Emerson's earnings and dividends per share rising again, year by year. Emerson watchers among the financial-analyst community should be doubly happy. They see good financial results, and they see that Emerson is getting those results through business improvement rather than through the back door of earnings management.

As a postscript to this tale about Emerson, here is a brief recount of how infectious diseases like numbers management can migrate. It concerns Diebold, the ATM machine company that acquired a bad name when it plunged into voting machines. Various U.S. states and precincts were adopting voting machines for 2004 and 2006 elections. Diebold's very public troubles had to do with glitches in quality, security, and delivery for its machines. In 2004, Thomas Swidarski, who had enjoyed quiet success in Diebold's ATM business, took over the elections business. After he made many staff changes, the bumps in the business were smoothing out. In December 2005, the board fired CEO Walden O'Dell, naming Swidarski in his place. O'Dell, according to *Fortune* magazine, "liked deals and was frankly bored by ATMs. . . . A former executive with Emerson Electric, O'Dells top priority was to make the numbers." *Fortune* goes on to say that Swidarski, however, "is more focused on the customers than he is on Wall Street."[15]

WHEN FINANCIAL ANALYSTS SEE BEYOND THE FINANCIALS

It is unusual, but not unheard of, that the talk among stock analysts about a certain company is as much on what generates its financial performance as the financials themselves. Companies in that sweet position include 3M and Apple for product innovation, Southwest Airlines for service with a smile, Dell, Inc. for quickness in all things, Wal-Mart as fanatic cost-trimmer, and Toyota for its production system.

Sometimes even an out-of-the-public-eye manufacturer of workaday products can capture analysts' attention for things non-financial. Illinois Tool Works may fit that description. ITW makes frequent acquisitions of little-known industrial-products manufacturers. Its success formula for each acquisition is simple. To shake out the weaknesses at the outset, ITW applies a comprehensive 80-20 analysis to the acquired company.[16] The 20 percent of products and customers, suppliers and part numbers that are producing 80 percent of gains get favored at the expense of the laggards. ITW has been doing this "since the early 1980s," applying it especially to its hundreds of acquisitions since then, and with gratifying results on the usual financials. ITW's grade in the leanness studies is *A*, based on its 20-year upward trend in inventory turnovers at a rate of 3.2 percent per year. (More about ITW in Chapter 12.)

Eighty-twenty works as an enhancer to most of the lean/Toyota system agenda, which thrives on narrowly focusing on best customers, products, parts, suppliers, job classifications, distribution centers, and brands of machine tools. Extend that even to factory designs. Intel's "copy exactly" strategy, taken up by other multi-plant companies, is to develop a single plant design and copy it at its facilities worldwide.[17]

As for the Toyota production system (TPS), it is a large set of basic process-improvement concepts and tools that blend well with those of quality and related areas. A few of the world's most admired companies, Dell and Wal-Mart in particular, are not known for mastery of that set, and instead have found their own way of becoming ultra-lean: Each has a powerful business plan. The next chapter, continuing this Part III discussion on building a competitive fortress, highlights and contrasts the two extremes: basic process improvement à la TPS, and unique business models such as those of Dell and Wal-Mart.

NOTES

1. An early, well publicized source of this point about managing by the numbers was Robert H. Hayes and William J. Abernathy, "Managing Our Way to Economic Decline," *Harvard Business Review* (July-August 1980), pp. 67–77.

2. Jeremy Hope and Robin Fraser, *Beyond Budgeting: How Managers Can Break Free from the Annual Performance Trap* (Boston: Harvard Business School Press, 2003), p. 5.

3. The 2.5 major decisions refer to those "with the potential to boost profits by at least 10%." The research, done by Marakon Associates, surveyed 156 large companies: reported in Carol Hymowitz, "Two More CEO Ousters Underscore the Need for better Strategizing," *Wall Street Journal* (September 11, 2006), p. B1.

4. H. Thomas Johnson and Anders Bröms, *Profit Beyond Measure: Extraordinary Results through Attention to Work and People* (New York: Free Press, 2000).

5. Jim Womack, e-mail letter to a subscriber of the Lean Enterprise Institute (November 21, 2006).

6. A.O. Hirschman and C.E. Lindblom, "Economic Development, Research and Development, Policy Making: Some Converging Views," *Behavioral Science*, 7 (1962), pp. 211–222.

7. Daniel Gross, *Pop! Why Bubbles Are Good for the Economy* (New York: HarperCollins, 2007).

8. Lorraine Woellert, "Goodbye Quarterly Targets?" *Business Week* (April 2, 2007), p. 12.

9. Found in http://www.mcs.vuw.ac.nz/~kris/thesis/node26.html.

10. Charles F. Knight, "Emerson Electric: Consistent Profits, Consistently," *Harvard Business Review*, January-February 1992, pp. 57–70.

11. Charles F. Knight, *Performance Without Compromise: How Emerson Consistently Achieves Winning Results* (Cambridge, Mass.: Harvard Business School Press, 2005), p. 11.

12. Carl Quintanilla, "For Its Profit Streak, Emerson's Reward Is a Laggard Share Price," *Wall Street Journal*, May 11, 1999, pp. A1, A8.

13. *Ibid.*, p. 115.

14. Knight, *Performance without Compromise*, op. cit., p. 227.

15. Barney Gimbel, "Rage Against the Machine," *Fortune*, November 13, 2006, pp. 84–94.

16. ITW's web site (www.ITW.com), August 2006.

17. "Working with Intel," an Intel advisory to its semiconductor contractors, explains the "copy exactly!" strategy: http://supplier.intel.con/construction/training/working1.htm, August 18, 2000.

Chapter 10

Process Improvement: Stretching Company Capabilities

Earlier chapters have shown that, by the inventory-turnover yardstick, most of the 1,400-odd companies studied have had mediocre-to-poor success with lean manufacturing and related initiatives. Those that have done well, and done so over the longer term (the smaller portion of some 1,200 companies for which we have 15 or more years of data), later tend to plateau or backslide. Accentuating the point are the starkly poor longer-term leanness scores for Japan, and even for Toyota, and the declining or non-improving scores in the past few years for seven other global areas.

Why is this so? On the surface it makes no sense. The basic, proven tools of process improvement number in the dozens. Most are low in cost, are rooted in simplicity, produce relatively quick results, and are common sense (unless your sense has been warped by years of working in a batch-and-queue environment). The aim of this chapter is to explore a few possible explanations, and consider what to do about them. Candidates include meddlesome stock markets, instability in the form of flitting from one management initiative to another, blindly doing what everyone else does, avoiding what's difficult, and measuring the wrong things. Besides those, one more culprit will dominate this discussion: losing interest or motivation for lack of a Big Idea. Weak results may also be partly owing to the sheer *number* of best practices—more than many companies seem to be able to cope with. To work up to these issues, we begin by taking a closer look at best practices in continuous process improvement.

BEST PRACTICES: SOME FOR STUDY, SOME TO DO, SOME FOR TRAINING

Best practices are of several types, notably (1) study, (2) do, and (3) training. *Study* employs tools and procedures for analyzing processes. *Do* means change the process itself. Exhibit 10.1 has *study* on the left and *do* on the right. The following discussion contrasts those two, along with *training* (omitted from the exhibit), in regard to importance as well as purpose. (Since most readers will be familiar with the practices themselves, the discussion need not go on page after page explaining each.)

The *do* practices are essential. They are the targets of process improvement. The *study* items, on the other hand, are worthy but *not* necessary. Lillian Gilbreth, one of

Exhibit 10.1   Two Types of Best Practices

Study	Do
Ishikawa's seven basic tools: flowchart, check sheet, Pareto chart, fishbone chart, histogram, scatter diagram, process control chart[a]	Product/value-stream-focused units (e.g., cells)
Spaghetti chart	Quick changeover
Videotaping	Pull/one-piece flow
Process benchmarking	Kanban (queue limitation)
Value-stream mapping	5S "housekeeping"
Value-add/Non-value-add analysis	Visual workplace
Suggestion system	Stack lights (trouble lights)
Time study	Under-scheduling of labor
Intensive observation	Heijunka (load-leveling) box
Process simulation and modeling	Repeating, mixed-model scheduling[b]
Kaizen events	Takt-time (rate-based) scheduling
Six sigma projects	Point-of-use material deliveries
Quality function deployment (QFD/House of quality)	Point-of-use equipment and accessories
Design of experiments (DOE)/Taguchi analysis	Process-capable equipment
	Down-sized equipment
	Down-sized, exact-count containers
	WIP stockroom removal
	Conveyor removal
	Wall removal
	Stand-up, walk-around assembly (chair removal)
	Standard work
	Design for manufacture and assembly (DFMA)
	Fail-safing
	Total productive maintenance (TPM)
	Behavior-based safety
	Reduction of job classifications
	Cross-training/job rotation
	Skills certification
	Pay for skills/knowledge
	Cross-careering
	Line-stop authority
	Quality at the source
	Self-inspection/next-process checking
	Operator implementation of own suggestions
	Backflush inventory accounting
	Supplier reduction
	Supplier certification
	Supplier collaboration

(*continued*)

Exhibit 10.1   (Continued)

Study	Do
	Supplier-managed inventory
	Shared trucking/"bread-man" deliveries
	Cross-docking
	Direct shipment
	Activity-based costing audits for infrequent competitive decisions

[a]At one time, Ishikawa's seven tools included stratification but not flowcharting. Kaoru Ishikawa, David J. Lu, trans., *What Is Total Quality Control?: The Japanese Way* (Englewood Cliffs, NJ: Prentice-Hall, 1985), p.198. Later, however, flowcharting replaced stratification in many lists of the seven tools.

[b]Mixed-model scheduling is sometimes viewed as a second stage of load leveling, the first stage being leveling the day-to-day schedule of end units. The second stage of leveling acts on models of those end units, converting large batches to small ones. A good explanation of the two-levels viewpoint is in Daniel T. Jones, "Heijunka: Leveling Production," *Manufacturing Engineering* (August 2006), pp. 29–36.

the pioneers of scientific management, is reported to have once said, "There is too much study of work that should be eliminated, not studied."[1] Some companies' continuous-improvement agendas, though, do not distinguish between the study and the do, which may improperly elevate study tools to equality with do practices. DJO, Inc. (formerly, dj Orthopedics), an impressive, award-winning best-practice implementer, cites the following "eight basic steps . . . : value-stream mapping, kaizen blitzes, making the factory visual, streamlining the internal and external supply chain, creating a demand-based scheduling system, implementing a line-of-sight management system, and launching a benchmarking program ."[2] The first, second, and eighth steps are ways to *study*, and the other five are things to *do*.

STUDY, ANALYZE, TRAIN

Study is, of course, valuable. Study works to increase gains and minimize missteps. But we are looking for reasons why, with so potent a list of best practices, the global results have been disappointing. Too much study, not enough doing, may be part of the answer. Add to that, too much training in study methods, and not enough in what to do. Perhaps more to the point, study and analysis, and training in them, are the full-time job of many staff people (technicians, accountants, engineers, etc.). Staff analysts may, therefore, tend to feel they have the mandate and the duty to hog the process-improvement show. That may help explain why work force empowerment, a strong movement in 1980s and early 1990s, has, in many companies, become an afterthought. Companies' formal statements about their lean and six sigma programs often include words about involving their people. Words, though, are not the same as deeds.

Of the various study and analysis tools, some are ideal for continuous, all-employee process improvement. The first two listed in the exhibit—seven basic tools and spaghetti chart—are easy to learn and apply. Their focus is on process data: the process talking to those collecting the data. Discussion follows.

Charting the Value Streams

Flowcharting or mapping of any kind, including videotaping and spaghetti charting, tends to be an eye-opener. It exposes glaring delays and wastes, often easily eliminated in the *just-do-it* mode. This analysis tool dates back at least to the work of Frank Gilbreth, who in 1921 presented "Process Charts: First Steps in Finding the One Best Way" at an annual meeting of the American Society of Mechanical Engineers (ASME). In 1946, ASME standardized a set of five flowcharting symbols.[3]

Fundamental in all kinds of process mapping is the view that value-adding elements are good, and non-value-adding elements are bad. Of the ASME's five icons, the circle stands for a value-adding operation. The other symbols represent non-value-adding operations, targets for excising: arrow for a transport, upside-down triangle for a storage, big *D* for a delay, and square for an inspection or check.

Two-Stage Process Mapping

Deeper analysis entails two-stage flowcharts (which may have been a part of Gilbreth's 1921 presentation). The first stage tracks the process as it is; the second stage is the process as it is planned to be, or is after improvement. Nadler's 1967 book, *Work Systems Design: The Ideals Concept*, proposed in high detail a two-stage design procedure that goes well beyond before-and-after flowcharting. Defining the existing process or system is Nadler's first stage. Specifying the "technologically workable ideal system target (TWIST)" is the second.[4]

Noted management scientist Russell Ackoff had the same idea. His 1978 book on problem solving advocated "idealized design," which uses prospective rather than retrospective problem formulation. He believed that "idealized design also facilitates participation of all stakeholders, the generation of consensus among them, and the extension of their concepts of feasibility."[5]

With similar intent, Rother and Shook more recently developed a two-stage approach called *value-stream mapping (VSM)*, which calls for a present-state and a future-state map.[6] Given VSM's high popularity as a lean tool, it warrants extra comment. One use of VSM is just to map the process in its present state. Detailing the as-is process can be of immense value. It starkly reveals many useless, time-wasting, costly steps that need to be excised. As Pauley and Flinchbaugh say, "What's important is . . . the team discussion that generates understanding, . . . which leads to new insights . . . ." They are critical of the tendency for map-building to be "delegated to an engineer or junior staff." That loses the main value, that of a team of people connected to the process doing the mapping in order to understand and learn.[7]

A common perception is that the future-state map is equally valuable. It is not. The reason is that the future state commonly becomes a set of numeric goals. That encourages management by goals and metrics, rather than just-do-it process improvements. Chapters 7, 8, and 9 explained the difference.

Focus—Value Streams' Main Idea

What sets the value-stream idea apart from garden-variety flowcharting is its tie-in with the first and most important of the *do* practices in Exhibit 10.1: defining product/value-stream-focused resource units. The best way to think about a value stream, or value chain, is as a business segment focused on a product family, or, sometimes, customer family. There is probably nothing more effective, in process improvement, than breaking up the functional silos and realigning the processes by the work flow in a product family. The work cell is a microcosm of this realignment. The focused factory and plants-in-a-plant are enlarged variants. Linking a focused factory to a supply chain or customer chain extends the scheme further.

Why are organization and layout by flow, or value streams, highest on the do list? It clears the fog. Instead of seeing only your operation, process, shop, or department, you see a whole flow segment. You see, and your team may produce, a complete subassembly, product, or service. An office cell-team's expanded sight lines may take in a complete order-entry process, or warranty-claims process, or purchase-receipt-pay process. A more complete value-stream segment may take in supplier-to-customer fulfillment. Without such visibility, it is hard for people to know why frequent small-lot deliveries make sense, why cross-training is important, why machines should be set up quickly for short runs, and why greater output can just be producing waste. Without flow visibility, "common sense" tends to favor a job-holder doing just one thing, avoidance of machine setups, and production and transport in largest possible lots.

Plants-in-a-plant and cells have been high on manufacturing companies' do lists since well before the advent of value-stream mapping. However, where organizations have the disease of entrenched silos, involving some of the infected actors in value-stream mapping, may prove to have curative powers.

Time Study—For Timing, Not Control

The roots of process analysis reside in the rich soil of scientific management, dating back to the late 1800s. The movement features the work-study methods of the aforementioned Frank and Lillian Gilbreth, Frederick W. Taylor, and others. Besides several kinds of flowcharting, scientific management gave us *time study*—by history, by stopwatch, by work sampling, and by predetermined methods using tables of data. Today, time study for setting labor standards and controlling productivity is out of favor. It is seen as counterproductive, non-value-adding, and contrary to modern principles of work force management—and good riddance. However, time study for weighing alternative methods and for synchronizing, leveling, and balancing flow remains high on the list of useful process-analysis tools.

Training in *How* and *What*

Training, our third category of best practices, subdivides further into *how* and *what*. *How* concerns training in methods of studying, analyzing, and executing process improvement. The topics include problem-solving, the scientific method, and so forth. *What* concerns training in what to *do*, that is, the targets of improvement. Learning about the targets must be first, with the highest priority. People need to know about cells, kanban, cross-training/job rotation, and quality at the source; why they are best practices; and their impact on competitiveness. With knowledge and understanding about these and other *do*'s, they may proceed directly with implementation. There is no requirement that implementation should wait for processes to be studied, or for training in how to study the processes. What I am suggesting is that companies may be training too much on how to study and analyze and too little on what to change to make the processes effective.

Do's and Don'ts

Still another category of best practices is *don't*s, which refers to targets for removal. There may be almost as many of them as *do*'s, because they tend to be opposites. Examples of *don't*s include layout by common function (silo creation), economic order quantity, push scheduling, distance-spanning conveyors, WIP stockrooms, kitting, monument machines, multiple suppliers for each part number, quality by lot-inspection, labor reporting, and control by cost variance.

LIMITATIONS AND OMISSIONS

The business unit that actually applies all of the *do*'s in Exhibit 10.1, a long (though not comprehensive) list, probably does not exist. The typical company's process-improvement repertoire includes only a small number of them. Frequently, practices that once had been in use later fall into disuse. With so lengthy a list, it is all too easy for a facility to pick the easier ones (mechanistic, inside the factory, and inside the organization) and shelve the fuzzier, more complex ones (humanistic, in the support functions, and in the supply and customer chains). Practices set aside often have greater, more-enduring benefits. Their omission reduces the likelihood that the firm will be able to keep pace with disruptive events—in technologies, product lines, markets, suppliers, regulations, executive teams, and competitors. Many of the biggest and most enlightened companies have brow-furrowing omissions.

Eastman Kodak, for example, has been among the more active companies in best-practice training since the mid-1980s.[8] Yet only since 2002 has the company seriously tackled its huge distribution inventories.[9] Kodak's performance on the inventory metric had improved impressively since 1970. By finally addressing its largest inventory horde, in distribution, Kodak's improvement trend has advanced from impressive to outstanding. (See the Kodak inventory-turnover in Exhibit 4.1. Also from Chapter 4, see the Kodak discussion and graph on its improving *rate* of improvement in Exhibit 4.7.) This is not to single out Kodak for putting aside, for more than a decade, supplier collaboration—what was perhaps its greatest improvement opportunity. As will be discussed in Chapter 17, inaction on the distribution side of the business has been the norm in most consumer-goods companies. (Kodak has long been mostly, but not exclusively, a consumer-goods company.) Kodak may be ahead of most others in seriously attending to the issue.

Overlooking a glowing opportunity is not the exception but, I think, the norm in most of the world's premier companies and plants. Sometimes what is overlooked seems inconsequential. Plantronics, the world's leading producer of lightweight communications headsets, offers an example. Since the late 1980s, its plants, mainly in Mexico, have invested heavily in best-practice training. Staff at Plamex (the name given to Plantronics in Mexico) have not only listened and learned; they have implemented many of the practices in Exhibit 10.1. As a result, raw and in-process inventories have fallen from weeks' to hours' worth. In the 1990s, materials moved in fits and starts through warehouses and kitting stations, back and forth between stockrooms and production, and outbound. Today, incoming materials mostly go directly from dock to point-of-use or to stock. While other *maquiladora* plants cling to kitting, the Plamex plants have mostly eliminated it—and the excess labor, inventory, double-handling, documentation, source of mistakes, delays, and costs that go with kitting.

Unlike the large majority of assembly plants in Mexico, China, and other less-developed countries, Plamex has been converting long, many-person assembly lines to cells. Plamex, though, has yet to implement a companion improvement: getting rid of the chairs and converting to stand-up, walk-around assembly. With few exceptions (e.g., soldering), Plamex assemblers sit at single stations rather than stand and take steps among two or more stations, which would thus provide greater work content per assembler.[10] The deficiencies of sit-down assembly are taken up further in Chapter 16.

DROWNING IN THE BASICS

These examples have helped make the point that the *do*'s in Exhibit 10.1 are a full plate. The list is so lengthy as to be intimidating. It is akin to the list of things each of us should do to maintain good physical and mental health. Along with such long lists, there is no overriding Big Idea to center on. For an individual, examples of a Big Idea are belief in and allegiance to God, country, or family. For a business, it could be the customer (Nordstrom) or stock price (General Electric). When there is nothing so dominant—and there is not in the arena of continuous process improvement—things fall by the wayside. Companies fail to live up to their potential, with risk of losing ground to competitors.

What can be done? The best answer is to keep importing energy so the effort does not run down. From system theory, information equals energy. (More familiarly, in system science, information = negentropy.) Companies need to bring in new information and renew information on topics that have lain fallow. They need to do so from various sources. Keep going to the same sources, or the standard ones for your industry, and you are likely not even to encounter some of the best practices given in Exhibit 10.1.

A problem with this prescription is that there is too much information. For example, perhaps 10 or 20 times as many books are turned out yearly on management and manufacturing practices today as were published 20 years ago. (Nielsen Book-Scan found that 1,446,000 book titles were sold in the U.S. in 2006. Of that number 1,123,000, or 78 percent, sold fewer than 99 copies.[11]) It is easy today to publish, and to do so without great expense. Finding pearls of wisdom in the large mix is a challenge.

The best way around this obstacle is to go to the sources. Instead of a kaizen publication, third removed, go to Imai's seminal 1986 book. It presents various tools of continuous improvement (but does not mention kaizen *events*).[12] Instead of someone's article on benchmarking, study Camp's trail-blazing 1989 work. Camp's book is not about benchmarks, it is about benchmark*ing*, the search for best practices, residing mostly outside one's own industry.[13] Caterpillar does it right. Cat's CEO Jim Owens says, "We've benchmarked many different industries and then our own best-in-class facilities and created our own recipe book."[14] For total productive maintenance, the source is Nakajima's small 1988 book, which says little about periodic and predictive maintenance (80-year-old western plant-maintenance concepts) or "doing your PMs"; it is mainly about maintenance as a primary responsibility of operators.[15] If most of the books in the company library fail to cite original sources, and have few or no references or bibliography, you should wonder how much the authors really know about their subject.

The Internet is not much help. It is organized in backward chronology: newest first; original works deeply buried, and often or usually not there at all. Also, what's hot gets plenty of pages; what's not, but is substantive and enduring, is buried or not there.

Broadly knowledgeable, experienced people are excellent sources of information. If they are your own (not consultants), your company should be on the improvement pathway. Good results should have been showing up in the usual ways. They include, in the short term, reduced flow times and lead times; and in the long term, upward-trending inventory turnover. (Inventory trend in the short run, a few months or even two or three years, is easily biased by complex combinations of changes in products, sales channels, competitive actions, and so on). In most companies, though, knowledge and experience are restricted: too few people learning too few topics. It is time to step up the training and broaden the coverage.

We've looked at the long and the short of constructing a competitive fortress using basic process-improvement methods as the building materials. In a few rare cases, taken up in the next chapter, a powerful business model becomes the fortress.

NOTES

1. Ben B. Graham, *Detail Process Charting: Speaking the Language of Process* (New York: Wiley, 2004), Chapter 1.

2. Bruce Vernyi, "dj Orthopedics, LLC: Lean Medicine Cures Chaos," *Industry Week* (October 2005), pp. 42–44. dj Orthopedics was designated as a 2005 *Industry Week* "best plant." Other public accolades to the company include an article: Lea A.P. Tonkin,

"Lean Teaming at dj Orthopedics, LLC: Vista, CA and Tijuana, B.C. Mexico Share Lean Learnings," *Target* (3rd qtr. 2002), pp. 41–44.

3. Ben B. Graham, op. cit.

4. Gerald Nadler, *Work Systems Design: The Ideals Concept* (Homewood, IL: Richard D. Irwin, 1967). In my early life as an industrial engineering student, then a practicing IE, I greatly admired Nadler's Ideals. And why not? I was an IE, an analyst. The tools of process study attract analysts like bees to nectar. Nadler, author of many books, is IBM Chair Emeritus in Engineering Management at the University of Southern California.

5. Russell L. Ackoff, *The Art of Problem Solving* (New York: Wiley, 1978), see p. 48.

6. Mike Rother and John Shook, *Learning to See: Value Stream Mapping to Add Value and Eliminate Muda* (Brookline, MA: Lean Enterprise Institute, 1998).

7. Dennis Pawley and Jamie Flinchbaugh, "The Current State: Progress Starts Here," *Manufacturing Engineering* (October 2006), pp. 71–81.

8. Richard Schonberger was among those doing the training at Kodak.

9. Jonathan Katz, "Meeting at the Crossdock," *Industry Week* (May 2006), p. 50.

10. These observations about Plamex come from my own visits there, plus discussions with Plamex people over the years, and a phone interview with a Plamex official in April 2006.

11. This total does not include the hundreds or thousands of self-published books that are not sold by established stores. Cited in "Harper's Index," *Harper's* (June 2007), p. 13. See also, www.bookscan.com.

12. Masaki Imai, *Kaizen: The Key to Japan's Competitive Success* (New York: Random House, 1986).

13. Robert C. Camp, *Benchmarking: The Search for Industry Best Practices That Lead to Superior Performance* (Milwaukee, WI: ASQ Press, 1989).

14. Ilan Brat and Bryan Gruley, "Global Trade Galvanized Caterpillar," *Wall Street Journal* (February 26, 2007), pp. B1, B7.

15. Seiichi Nakajima, *Introduction to TPM: Total Productive Maintenance* (Portland, OR: Productivity Press, 1988; originally published in Japan in 1984).

Chapter 11

Unique Business Models (Big Ideas)

Every two years, IBM asks CEOs and government leaders what their topmost hot buttons are. In 2006, two items stood out: business-model innovation and collaboration with other companies.[1] Collaboration is a topic for other chapters. Business-model innovation is the subject of this one.

Business models get a place in this chapter because of a connection. It turns out that, based on the leanness studies, the number-one manufacturer (Dell) and the number-one retailer (Wal-Mart) fit the innovative-business-model notion to a T. Moreover, in some respects, their business models seem to be more potent and robust than the basics of process improvement, including the lean core.

INNOVATIVE BUSINESS MODELS

A business model is different from a business plan or strategy. Plans and strategies are temporary, lasting for a few months or maybe a year or two. A business *model*, on the other hand, is for the long haul. IBM chairman Samuel Palmisano spoke to *Business Week* about why surveyed executives should rate business-model innovation highly, as compared with product innovation. Companies must have innovative products, and there had better be continuous successions of them, because "your competition's going to react to what you've just done." Business-model innovation, though, is "much tougher to react to."[2]

The ideal business model would be overwhelmingly favorable to customers and clearly superior competitively, easy to understand, and hard to deny or object to. With those attributes it would readily rally employees, suppliers, and stockholders in its service.

The business models of Dell and Wal-Mart come close to fitting that ideal. They have simple names: *Dell-direct*, and at Wal-Mart, *everyday low prices*, abbreviated in the retail industry as EDLP.[3] The models have been instrumental in the companies' success through nearly all of their histories. They work so well that they wow outsiders and inspire insiders to keep developing innovations: ways to make Dell ever-more direct and Wal-Mart the home of everyday ever-lower prices. Moreover, Wall Street pays nearly as much homage to these companies' business models and the management innovations they inspire as to the financial outcomes that are investors' normal preoccupation. Each company's leading-edge *modus operandi* are presented next (the feats of both companies pop up in other chapters as well). A final point of closure to the chapter contrasts unique business models with the continuous-process improvement pathway to success.

DELL-DIRECT

As a slogan, Dell-direct means the customer gets her order within just days of placing it, electronically or by phone. As a full-fledged business strategy, there is much more to it. What brings in customers is that they get to customize their orders (Dell's modular designs of its computers helps).[4] Moreover, they know the quality will be good, the technology up-to-date, and—necessarily—the price will be right. How can a company deliver ultra-short lead times, high quality, and flexible choices at a low cost? This is exactly the combination of results delivered by what has been variously called Japanese production management, the Toyota production system, JIT/TQC, and lean/sigma. Yet Dell is not known, especially, for its prowess in applying the TPS/ JIT/TQC/lean/sigma tool set.

Dell does it differently. Its forte is customer-producer-supplier synchronization. To illustrate, here is the Dell challenge, as conveyed to me by Dick Hunter, Vice President, Americas Manufacturing Operations, whom I spent a couple of hours with in February 2004. Tomorrow, he said, I should log onto the Dell web site, select any PC, and print out the configuration details and price. Wait a day, then look for what had been selected. Probably, he said, I would find changes in configuration and/or price. I didn't need to do this, because I already knew what this was all about—what Hall calls "two-knob control."[5] One knob allows Dell to adjust and control the supply side; the other knob influences the demand side.

As explained in *Information Week*,[6] it works like this: "Many times a day" Dell receives electronic data on the state of its supply chains: amount and location of inventories and capacity to make more. On that basis, marketing will, by offering special deals, steer customers away from components and subsystems in a state of impending shortage, and toward excesses.

All parties benefit. Suppliers get relief from production and order-filling problems. Dell avoids supplier outages and late deliveries. And via the special deals the customer gets more for the money. For example, the deal may be a larger monitor for just $10 more, or maybe a lower price if the customer will accept the laptop that weighs 3.5 pounds instead of the 3.2-pound model. If the customer must have the lighter-weight model, the customer gets it for whatever price is in the current catalog or web site. The lighter model is not likely to be out of stock, just relatively low.

What happens at the customer end of two-knob control is called, in behavioral psychology, *shaping behavior*. Dell calls it *demand shaping*.[7] In business, shaping comes in many forms. Some forms are outright manipulation and not for the good of the customer. A typical example is the pharmaceutical company that, by bombarding consumers with TV ads, gets them to use an expensive medication that is no better than aspirin. Other forms of shaping are for the general good, for example, lower prices for off-peak usage of power or airplane flights. Still another form is sale-driven retailing, which brings us to Wal-Mart's contrary—to common retailing practices—business model.

WAL-MART AND EDLP

Wal-Mart is king of the chain stores. Its impact on all others is huge. Regarding chain stores in general, Virginia Postrel observes that they "do a lot more than bargain down prices from suppliers or divide fixed costs across a lot of units. They rapidly spread economic discovery—the scarce and costly knowledge of what retail concepts and operational innovations actually work."[8]

Wal-Mart shows the way to the rest in multiple ways. In particular it shows the folly of sale-based retailing, at least in its competitive niche. The kernel of its innovations is its business model, everyday low prices. EDLP requires everyday lowered costs, the more so in discount retailing, which is where Wal-Mart lives. Retail is highly inventory-intensive, much more than manufacturing. Lowering costs in retail, therefore, is largely a matter of reducing inventory costs. Dominant ways are getting lower prices from suppliers, cutting logistics costs, and accelerating turnover of inventories. The Wal-Mart innovation machine attacks all three.

As a passive concept, EDLP is one of cost avoidance. The usual alternative, sale-driven retailing, causes multiple costs to rise as sales generate spasms of non-value-adding activity. The extra costs begin with advertising the sale. Then, bringing in large lots of sale items overloads the logistics system and requires enlarged warehouses, stockrooms, and truck fleets. Jerky schedules cause administrative and wage costs to rise for the manufacturers, the logistics entities, and the retailer. Manufacturers' costs go up because they must produce and ship in occasional large "sale" lots, which forces them into the undesirable batch-and-queue mode.

Wal-Mart's persistent efforts to get better prices from suppliers are not passive. They are dotted with breakthrough practices. Some are of Wal-Mart origin. Others were modest concepts devised elsewhere that Wal-Mart captured and made big. An example is a movement called *quick response (QR)*. Giant textile manufacturer Milliken got QR started in 1986[9] by bringing together key department stores and apparel houses to face up to the giant competitive threat from the Far East. Those at the meeting came away with plans for sharing demand, production, and shipping data.

Though a manufacturer instigated QR, retailer Wal-Mart soon took over the movement and elaborated it by levying various new requirements on its suppliers. These include *vendor-managed inventory (VMI)*, in which suppliers are obliged to manage Wal-Mart's inventory replenishment via electronic access to the retailer's point-of-sale data.[10]

In 1991, to tighten its VMI links, Wal-Mart elected to phase out of dealing with sales representatives and brokers in favor of direct dealings with manufacturers.[11] Related to that, it began requiring that producers ship direct to Wal-Mart distribution centers (DCs) or to stores. Instead of infrequent large-batch shipping to fill somebody's downstream warehouse, the new mode became one of *continuous replenishment*: frequent shipments synchronized to daily barcode-scanned retail sales. For manufacturers, the system calls for still more. It recommends extending the synchronization to production schedules and purchasing. Raising the ante, Wal-Mart became the world leader in upgrading to radio-frequency identification (RFID), opening up more ways of tightening supply and synchronizing to real demand.

For its own DCs, Wal-Mart pioneered cross-docking, in which a truckload of an incoming item does not go into warehouse storage. Rather, it is split into small lots for loading directly into multiple trucks for immediate transfer to retail stores. Wal-Mart reportedly delivers 85 percent of its merchandise using cross-docking.[12]

Topping all this off, more than 2,000 of Wal-Mart's suppliers have seen fit to locate empowered staff to the mega-retailer's Bentonville, Arkansas, home base, there to collaborate on both strategic and tactical issues.[13] The ring of 20 office parks housing these suppliers has acquired the nickname "Vendorville."

Vendorville is serious business, and the business is collaboration. Doing it successfully begins inside each firm. The supplier's enmeshed *lean team* consists at least of operations, sales/marketing, and finance. Together they can, with counterparts at Wal-Mart, cover the essential bases: joint impacts on sales and market share, effects on operational and supply-chain capacities, and projected changes in cost and cash flows. This is quite unlike the usual approach: separately at each company, sales booking orders that are thrown over the wall, clashing with operational realities, and, later, finance seeing whether they made money; or, alternatively, to keep capacity busy, production making product in large lots and sending it to storage, sales offering price and other inducements to move the excesses, and, again, finance seeing whether any money was made.

In putting suppliers and Wal-Mart'ers in everyday, face-to-face contact, Vendorville works great. Still, it cannot resolve many supply-pipeline problems without astute uses of information technology. Again, this is a Wal-Mart strength. Though the company spends less on IT per sales dollar than major competitors, it leads them in results. Part of the reason may be that Wal-Mart develops most of its IT in house rather than using off-the-shelf systems. Moreover, Wal-Mart's IT personnel commonly have prior experience in merchandising, and, later, are frequently promoted out of IT and into an IT-using function.[14] This connectivity helps ensure that it is not IT for technology's sake, but for furthering the company's multiple ambitions.

Wal-Mart orchestrates the collaborative process like no other company. It is tough love, though. Suppliers, whether Procter & Gamble or Acme Power Bars, are not protected but are openly exposed to the harsh realities of the global economy.

Creation of Vendorville (in effect, "Collaborationville") was an unnatural act. Far-flung suppliers with plants around the world had to move staff, often city people, to small-town Bentonville, Arkansas. They do it not only because huge sales volumes are in the offing, but also because working with Wal-Mart, the innovation machine, makes them better.

It may even make them better as to one aspect of ethics. According to a story in the business press, no Wal-Mart employee, whether buyer, store manager, or executive, may accept any kind of gratuity—not even a cup of coffee. Vendor reps accustomed to bestowing small (or large) gifts, in expectation of at least some extra leverage, know they cannot do it in Bentonville. Ann Fandozzi, a Chrysler manager, says Wal-Mart's policy is "incredibly hard to believe." Fandozzi was commenting on the firing of Julie Roehm, high-flying Wal-Mart marketing executive, formerly with Chrysler, who was fired in part over alleged freebies. One of Wal-Mart's largest suppliers, Procter & Gamble has what are thought to be strict policies on gifts. But P&G executives may accept business meals that are "minor in terms of the overall relationship with the giver." "At Wal-Mart, where executives double up in hotel rooms and rent compact cars, the rules are even stricter."[15]

Yes, Wal-Mart currently has a "kick-me" sign on its posterior (in the United States, anyway; in Mexico, where Wal-Mart's market share is larger than in the United States, the retail giant is revered[16]). In the world of business, the sign reads "follow me," for Wal-Mart's mastery of pipeline management. (Chain stores with long tentacles have become popular targets for being "Wal-Martyred." An Internet search comes up with sites saying Best Buy sucks, Home Depot sucks, Starbucks sucks, and Tesco sucks; also, Macy's sucks because Federated Stores has acquired many beloved old-name department stores and renamed them *Macy's*.) Freeman[17] suggests how Wal-Mart could deflect criticism and turn it to advantage. He says they could do so by publicly and persistently pointing to how it makes things better for its diversity of stakeholders. A company that is just for shareholder value is socially selfish; one that maximizes *stakeholder* value is selfless.

THE BASICS VERSUS UNIQUE BUSINESS MODELS

We sum up this chapter with a brief comparison between the two ways to build a dynastic fortress that have been presented. First is the basics of process improvement, characterized by simplicity and common sense. They provide quick payback at low cost. For example, any setup-time reduction immediately reduces the cost of labor to perform setups and justifies reducing the lot size and investment in inventory. Most important, the basics deliver continual improvement in the eyes of the customer: quicker response, better quality, greater flexibility, and higher value. Bremer calls these four benefits "soft savings."[18] Oh? I'd say that they are among the best ways to pump hard money into the top line (sales revenue) and bottom line (earnings). Whatever the four are called, today's executives should realize that serving customers in these ways is the foundation of business success. But the usual money-denominated factors easily blur vision.

A more fundamental limitation has been presented. Though the many tools of the basics produce abundant improvements, each tends to be too small to attract much attention from high management, investors, customers, suppliers, and other parts of the organization. Lack of a large idea or a few dominant targets and results makes the basics susceptible to fadeout.

The second fortress-builder is the Big-Idea business model. Enough has been said on the plus side of such models. But they, too, have their limitations. For one thing, they may be fragile. What could crimp Wal-Mart, home of EDLP in big-box stores? Maybe small-box stores. How about Dell's direct-to-the-customer model? An article in the business press[19] reports that in hundreds of smaller Chinese cities, "Dell doesn't sell as effectively as its rivals." In part, that is because in China "even some business customers want to see products before they buy." The China factor, plus competitive pressures in the West, has pushed Dell into retail sales. An agreement for Wal-Mart to sell Dell computers was announced in May 2007.[20]

Does that signal the demise of the Dell-direct business model? Maybe all that is needed is to broaden the model by re-targeting Dell's quick-reacting supply-production-delivery processes to include retail. As for the Dell-direct slogan, Michael Dell could announce to all that the upgraded but otherwise intact mantra-of-the-enterprise is Speed in All Things (or a cleverer expression of that idea). Actually, that is an apt description of what Dell-direct has grown into, and what has driven Dell's success. Speed relentlessly cuts costs for Dell and its suppliers, generates cash in faster than cash out, accelerates exposure of all manner of problems and causes, and tightens bonds with suppliers and their suppliers. Finally, it enables Dell to sell and deliver with UPS speed to both business and home customers even as it offers wide configuration choices.

Rarity is another limitation. This discussion has focused on just two companies because of the paucity of other strong examples of uniquely potent business models. Are there other good examples now, or others in the making, that we should know about? If so, they should be scoring wins on some of the same criteria as Wal-Mart and Dell: (1) having had their models prominently featured in the press for years, and (2) doing well on the leanness scale of long-term squeezing of inventories.

As another example in retailing, how about Costco, an emerging, strong competitor of Wal-Mart? Customers love Costco, and growing numbers of reports in the press tell why.[21] Costco restricts price markups, its executives content themselves with modest remuneration, and its employees are treated well (uncommon in retailing). However, in leanness it gets a grade of C for flat inventory turnovers since 1994. Also, Costco obtains low purchase prices by switching from brand to brand and model to model, which is in conflict with long-run supplier partnership and regularized ordering. In other words, Costco jerks the supply chains. (Target, another competitor, does too.[22]) In contrast, Wal-Mart's collaborative agreements give high consideration to leveling out demands on suppliers' capacity, because it helps reduce suppliers' costs and therefore Wal-Mart's.[23] As for Wal-Mart's strongest international competitors, U.K.-based Tesco, though an innovator, gets a C, and France-based Carrefour a D, on long-term inventory turnover.

Though powerful business models are uncommon, every company should always be active in developing one that will work for it. Such model building generally starts small in one business function, such as Illinois Tools Works' 80-20 analysis model developed by the company's acquisition team. If such a relatively modest-scope model should turn ITW into a launching pad for innovative extensions, the model may become another Dell-direct.

That is not to say Dell and Wal-Mart have all the right answers. Yes, both are world champions of pipeline management, based on collaboration and innovative IT solutions.

But both companies' external muscle surrounds plenty of internal fat. Both are in need of a broadened commitment to process improvement, one in which all their employees continually gather and assess every process botch and blunder. Both companies rely too much on their best and brightest for innovative ideas and their IT systems for data. Neither has quite managed to create a merger of model, mission, and mindset—to transform and upgrade its business model into Marine-Corps-like cultural pride.

There is no such thing as a company "built to last" (to use the phrase that became the title of the Collins and Porras bestseller[24]). The quest is simply to survive and thrive longer. Getting there requires the union of a dominant business model and comprehensive continuous improvement driven by all the people in all of the processes. That elusive combination, if achieved, should function as an innovation generator, acquiring "flywheel-like momentum" (to use the captivating mental image that Collins introduced in his earlier book, *Good to Great*[25]). To bring this discussion back down to earth, the two chapters in Part IV present a few very good companies and what they do right—and sometimes wrong.

NOTES

1. "Innovation: The View from the Top," *Business Week* (April 3, 2006), pp. 52–53.
2. Ibid.
3. Rahul Jacob, "Beyond Quality and Value," *Fortune* (Autumn–Winter 1993), pp. 8–11.
4. Thomas F. Wallace and Robert A. Stahl, *Building to Customer Demand* (Cincinnati, OH: T.F. Wallace & Company, 2005), p. 61. Contrarian research suggests that modular design may have practical limits. The reasoning is that a very high degree of modularity could "undermine the innovative process by reducing opportunities for breakthrough advances": Lee Fleming and Olav Sorenson, "The Dangers of Modularity," *Harvard Business Review* (September 2001), pp. 20–21.
5. Robert W. Hall, "Distributed Excellence and the Dell Model," *Target* (2nd qtr. 2000), pp. 6–11.
6. Chris Murphy, "Imagining What's Possible," *Information Week* (September 8, 2003), pp. 52–56.
7. Thomas L. Friedman, *The World Is Flat: A Brief History of the Twenty-First Century* (New York: Farrar, Straus and Giroux, updated and expanded edition, 2006; original, 2005), p. 519.
8. Virginia Postrel, "In Praise of Chain Stores," *Atlantic Monthly* (December 2006), pp. 164–167.
9. "Quick Response: Slow but Inevitable," supplement, Automatic Data Collection Management Section, *Manufacturing Systems* (August 1994), pp. 8–15.
10. Mary Lou Fox and Kevin Moore, "Getting Started with Vendor-Managed Inventory," *APICS—The Performance Advantage* (July 1994), pp. 52–53.
11. Karen Blumenthal, "Wal-Mart Set to Eliminate Reps, Brokers," *Wall Street Journal* (December 2, 1991), pp. A3, A14.

12. Ray Kulwiec, "Crossdocking as a Supply Chain Strategy," *Target*, 3rd Issue (2004), pp. 28–35.

13. Michael Barbaro, "Wal-Mart's Vendors Bring Glitz and Glamour to Its Hometown," *Seattle Times* (July 7, 2005), pp. E1, E6.

14. Laurie Sullivan, "Wal-Mart's Way," cover story, *Information Week* (September 27, 2004), pp. 36–44.

15. Gary McWilliams, Suzanne Vranica, and Neal E. Boudette, "How a Highflier in Marketing Fell at Wal-Mart," *Wall Street Journal* (December 11, 2006), pp. A1, A16.

16. John Lyons, "In Mexico, Wal-Mart Is Defying Its Critics," *Wall Street Journal* (March 5, 2007), pp. A1, A14.

17. R. Edward Freeman, "The Wal-Mart Effect and Business, Ethics, and Society," *Academy of Management Perspectives* (August 2006), pp. 38–40.

18. Michael Bremer, "The Missing Link: Driving Improvement Results to the P&L," *Superfactory* web site (February 2006).

19. Louise Lee, Peter Burrows, and Bruce Einhorn, "Dell May Have to Reboot in China," *Business Week* (November 7, 2005), p. 46.

20. Christopher Lawton, "Dell to Rely Less on Direct Sales," *Wall Street Journal* (May 25, 2007), p. A3.

21. Nina Shapiro's report about Costco says, "The company is proving Wall Street wrong by adhering to a radical idea: Treating customers and employees right is good business," in "Company for the People," *Seattle Weekly* (December 15–21, 2004), pp. 21–29.

22. According to a supplier of Makin Bacon to both Wal-Mart and Target, Wal-Mart's orders are steady, but Target is enthused some years, uninterested in others; for example, a couple of Christmases ago, "Target ordered a boatload of product for the fourth quarter. I had no clue the order was coming": Charles Fishman, *The Wal-Mart Effect: How the World's Most Powerful Company Really Works—and How It's Transforming the American Economy* (New York: Penguin Press, 2006), pp. 56–57.

23. "Wal-Mart has done away with [the promotion cycle], to the quiet relief of some suppliers who still endure the cycle at other retailers. . . . Smooth out and rationalize the demand from consumers. . . . That makes the supply more predictable. Everyone saves—customers and companies." Fishman, ibid., p. 61.

24. James C. Collins and Jerry I. Porras, *Built to Last: Successful Habits of Visionary Companies* (New York: HarperCollins, 1994).

25. James C. Collins, *Good to Great: Why Some Companies Make the Leap. . . and Others Don't* (New York: Harper Business, 2001) .

Part IV

What Goes Wrong: Impressive Companies and Their Weak Spots

Every company's way of doing business is dotted with flaws and blind spots. A few of the more common and severe of the weaknesses are the subject of this chapter. A small number of companies have been selected to demonstrate. In some cases, to help make a point, a strong practice or company is laid side by side with a deficient one.

Topping the list of practices that weaken is growth-to-a-fault, the kind that leaves lean/TQ in its dust. That topic, the theme of Chapter 12, compares and contrasts four rapidly growing companies. Two of them, Toyota and Danaher, are widely admired for their lean expertise although the leanness data contradict that admiration. The other two, Harley-Davidson and Illinois Tool Works, have been able to achieve both high growth and strong leanness.

Chapter 13 considers two more common failings: lack of continuity and mismanagement of knowledge.

Chapter 12

Does Rapid Growth Put the Brakes on Lean?

The business of business is building long-term wealth. Growth alone can be the driver. Growth coupled with intensive lean-based process improvement is a surer route, for two reasons: (1) Lean throws off free cash flow for acquisition-based growth. (2) Lean improves customer response, thereby enabling organic growth with existing and new customers. Pressing the growth accelerator too hard, though, can seriously strain best-practice capabilities. As they say about long punts in American football, it's out-kicking your coverage.

FOUR COMPANIES IN TWO PAIRS: TOYOTA/HARLEY AND DANAHER/ILLINOIS TOOL

Four companies serve to illustrate: Toyota, Danaher, Harley-Davidson, and Illinois Tool Works (ITW). All four are notable for their lean prowess and have been pressing the pedal for growth—Toyota and Harley organically, Danaher and ITW largely though acquisitions (see the box). Long-term growth for each of the four companies is 5 percent or more per year, which is rare among the 1,200-plus companies in the global database. All four have enjoyed strong long-term gains in earnings and cash flow.

One more company, Graco, Inc., one of the world's eminent lean manufacturers, winds up the chapter. Three years of acquisitions have not been easy even for Graco to digest and "lean out."

Four Companies' Lean Credentials

Toyota

The world's strongest automaker, with 2006 sales of $179 billion, Toyota originated and is still widely viewed as the epitome of lean. Citations to that effect are endless and need not be cited here. What is new about Toyota is its press for growth and apparent determination to be the world's largest automaker.[a]

Danaher

Danaher is an $8 billion diversified manufacturer headquartered in Washington, D.C., with about 200 global manufacturing and distribution sites. The lean community has long considered Danaher as one of the West's most lean-committed manufacturers. Danaher's web site (October 2006) says the company was conceived on a fishing trip in the early

(Continued)

1980s, with a "vision of a manufacturing company dedicated to continuous improvement and customer satisfaction." An Internet article labels Danaher "a poster-child for kaizen and lean manufacturing success."[b] Bill Waddell refers to Danaher as a "lean darling" that "was formed around a lean vision from the get go."[c] *Business Week* has chimed in with a glowing article on Danaher's superior, long-time financial performance as well as its strong lean credentials.[d]

Harley-Davidson

This well-known $5.6 billion manufacturer of motorcycles celebrated its 100th anniversary in 2003. As a subsidiary of AMF Corp. from 1969 until a management buyout in 1981, Harley's fortunes steadily deteriorated. In 1983, under withering competition from Japanese makers, Harley's new owners successfully petitioned the International Trade Commission for five years of tariff relief. That would, they hoped, buy time to sufficiently upgrade performance. Central to the upgrading was a three-pronged management initiative: total quality, employee involvement, and material-as-needed (MAN), the latter being Harley's equivalent of JIT/TPS/lean. The implementation was so successful that in 1987, one year early, Harley petitioned the ITC for termination of the tariff protection.[e]

Illinois Tool Works

ITW, a $14.1 billion diversified manufacturer, has acquired some 700 companies. Those acquisitions have benefited from ITW's unique way of finding and prioritizing the critical value streams: its 80-20 process (which was reviewed in Chapter 9). ITW's web site says that process includes "all aspects of the business.... This includes finding ways to simplify our product lines, customer and supply base, and business processes and systems. In the end, 80/20 improves quality, productivity, delivery, innovation, market penetration, and ultimately, customer satisfaction."[f]

---

[a]Hans Greimel, "Report: Toyota Hustling to Top GM," *Wall Street Journal* (September 18, 2006), p. C3. Ian Rowley, "Who's That in GM's Rearview Mirror? Toyota," *Business Week Online* (September 21, 2006).
[b]Jon Miller, "The Kaizen Turnaround Kings at Danaher" (August 21, 2006); found at gembapantarei.com (October 7, 2006).
[c]Posted on a lean accounting–focused discussion thread by independent consultant William H. Waddell (September 26, 2006).
[d]Brian Hindo, "A Dynamo Called Danaher," *Business Week* (February 19, 2007), pp. 56–60.
[e]Found on web sites: Harley-Davidson.com; and Harley.munising.com (October 7, 2006).
[f]ITW.com (October 7, 2006).

There are striking differences, however. Toyota's and Danaher's inventory numbers peaked years ago and have been worsening since. Harley's and ITW's have kept going up, and up. Exhibit 12.1 through Exhibit 12.4 display the trends.

As shown in Exhibit 12.1 and Exhibit 12.2, Toyota's sales have soared at an average rate of 5.0 percent for 20 years, and Harley's sales are up 5.3 percent per year for 16 years. Inventory-turnover trends for the two companies are opposites, Harley with a plus 3.9 percent annual rate and Toyota with a minus 4.0 percent annual rate. Harley's improvement stretches 20 years starting from its bottom-most year, 1986. The downtrend for Toyota spans 13 years since its high year, 1993, which in turn followed five years of no improvement. That totals 18 years of no improvement/decline.

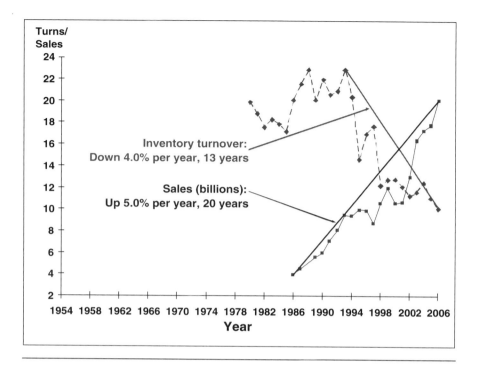

Exhibit 12.1   Sales and Inventory Turnover at Toyota Motor

Danaher's average sales growth, 5.8 percent per year over the past 16 years, accelerated to 7.7 percent per year for the most recent 11 years. ITW's sales rate is 5.0 percent for 20 years, rising to 5.4 percent in the most recent 15 years. In inventory turns, ITW's annual rate is plus 3.2 percent for 20 years, while Danaher's is minus 2.2 percent for (like Toyota) 13 years.

WHAT THE FINDINGS SHOW

What can we make of these findings? Harley-Davidson's long-term record shows that a motor-vehicle manufacturer is able to achieve high rates of improvement in inventory turns and organic growth at the same time. Toyota has not been able to do both. Illinois Tool's long-term data show that a diversified manufacturer can maintain fast-paced acquisition-based growth and rapidly improving turns at the same time. Danaher has kept acquiring and growing, though while losing ground on the leanness scale. Harley and ITW seem to emerge as unsung heroes of lean coupled with rapid growth.

Danaher's 2.2 percent average annual decline in inventory turns is modest, at least compared with Toyota's 4.0 percent. But why did Danaher's turns slide at all? Some acquisition-minded companies troll for turnaround companies; others seek already excellent companies to acquire. At least two of Danaher's large acquisitions, Fluke

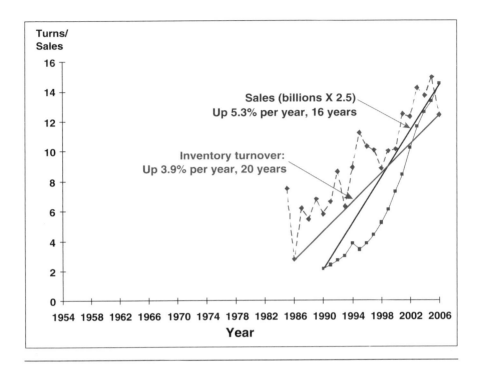

Exhibit 12.2   Sales and Inventory Turnover at Harley Davidson

and Hach, appear to have been the latter. Prior to acquisition, both were in the leanness database and graded *A*. Fluke (electric testing instruments), when acquired in 1998, had grown its sales an average of 6.5 percent in the prior 7 years; and it had improved its inventory turns at an average annual rate of 3.2 percent for 18 years. Hach (water-quality testing instruments), acquired in 1999, had grown sales at a 6.2 percent rate for 7 years and improved inventory turns at a 3.3 percent rate for 20 years. See Exhibit 12.5. At acquisition the two companies were turning their inventories three to four times yearly, which was below Danaher's five-plus turns. So the acquisitions would have had a negative effect on Danaher's total turns. However, the two companies' good, 18- and 20-year rates of improvement and strong lean capabilities perhaps should have, by now, become positive contributors to the parent company's turns.

Overall, Danaher appears to be a strong company making good acquisition choices. Excellent upward trends in cash flow and earnings serve as evidence. Were I to visit some of Danaher's facilities, no doubt I would emerge with strongly favorable impressions. If I visited others—newer units that may have overwhelmed the purveyors of the Danaher business system,[1] and older ones where some of the ardor has been lost—I would expect not to be so impressed. Looking at the composition of Danaher's 12-year downward trend line shows that, as with Toyota, most of the decline is owing to increases in purchased materials and finished goods. But also, as with Toyota, work-in-process turns have worsened a bit, too.

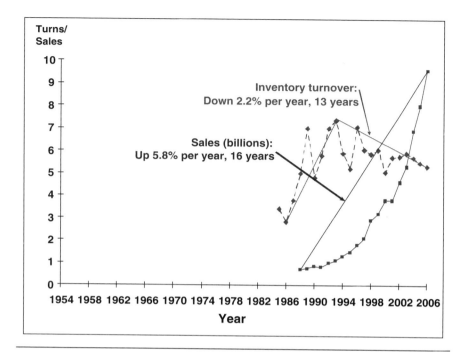

Exhibit 12.3   Sales and Inventory Turnover at Danaher

Finally, as with Toyota, Danaher's fast growth may be diverting it to some extent from pressing hard for lean—in the factories as well as in the pipelines. Alternatively, maybe Danaher's present senior management team has become more financially driven. Either way, Danaher appears to have faded some as a "lean darling." Does it matter? Following brief speculative commentary about Toyota, we consider historical lessons from IBM.

At Toyota, long considered conservatively managed, has the lure of becoming the biggest and grandest made it a bit reckless? Has its current executive team gone the way of nearly all other publicly traded corporations in the world, pushing more for short-term financial numbers than long-term improvement-driven wealth?

Maybe not; the strategy might be to deliver more knockdown punches to already-reeling General Motors and Ford, plus other under-performing global automakers. Using its great wealth, Toyota can afford to rapidly expand, flooding multiple global markets at the same time as its biggest competitors are forced to shrink.[2] Toyota ends up with a lot of new plants—and customers—making it all the harder for Detroit and Western Europe to come back. In that strategy, Toyota would hope to retain its strengths in leanness and quality, but be willing to endure some losses thereof if it cannot be avoided. Maybe such a strategy could work. However, it entails long-term risks, as detailed in the next section.

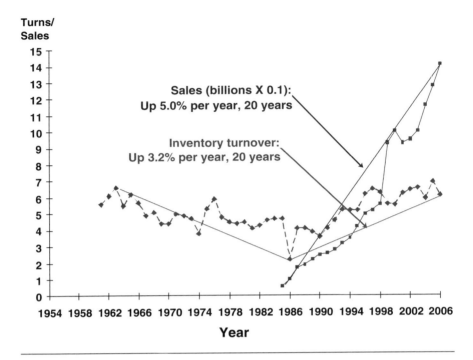

Exhibit 12.4   Sales and Inventory Turnover at Illinois Tool Works

IBM AND TOYOTA: WILL HISTORY REPEAT?

Exhibit 12.6 displays two similar patterns about three decades apart. On the left is IBM's precipitous decline in inventory turnover over a 24-year period. The first number, 24.8, means that in 1961 IBM's total inventory was only about two weeks' supply. In that era few companies ever achieved such leanness. But that was the year the company introduced its Selectric typewriter, a giant hit product employing electronics. New supply lines and diverse new suppliers may have been main reasons why inventory turns plunged. By 1985, IBM's turns had hit bottom at 2.1, which is equivalent to about six months' supply. The declining turns did not hurt IBM's sales, which skyrocketed through the decline and beyond. Contributing factors were a succession of enormously successful electronic products. They include the 360- and 370-series mainframe computers, plus various disk storage systems and peripherals. They grew sales but required complex delivery and supply lines criss-crossing the globe.

The right side of Exhibit 12.6 shows the same pattern for Toyota. Its sales have kept growing rapidly even as its inventory turns have plunged. What all this suggests is that leanness doesn't matter. But read on.

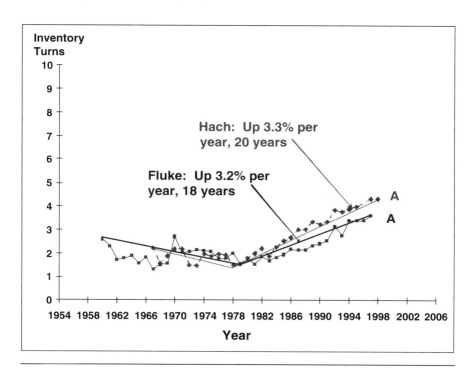

Inventory Turns vs Year

Exhibit 12.5   Pre-Acquisition Inventory Trends at Hach and Fluke

Exhibit 12.7 fills in some of the critical blanks, showing what happened to IBM's earnings and stock price. We see that investors loved IBM, greatly bidding up its stock price between 1961 and 1973. But after 12 years of badly worsening inventory turns—which show up on financial statements as shrinking cash flow—they'd had enough. IBM's stock quickly went from strong buy to sell now. Ironically, while IBM was still in a state of chaos—parts, subassemblies, and finished products all over the globe making hard work of trying to get where needed—investors started buying again. There was a simple reason: IBM had developed the personal computer. Though PC sales never were more than a small fraction of IBM's total sales, and the PC was mostly a money-loser for IBM, it didn't matter. Wall Street believed the PC would become as big a success as the mainframes, and the stock price soared.

IBM's earnings peaked in 1984, and one year later its inventory turns hit bottom. The company had gone from sprinter-lean to couch-potato-fat. Huge sales revenues were being eaten up by costs, so earnings fell, and the share price did, too. By 1993, the third of three years of red ink, the share price had fallen 50 percent. Meanwhile, IBM had got on the lean pathway. Its inventory turns improved at a rate of 2.8 percent per year in the 21 years from 1985 through 2006. (That impressive rate does not show up well in Exhibit 12.7 because of the graph's stretched-out vertical scale.) Of course, IBM's improving leanness will have brought it ever closer to customers. That fits well

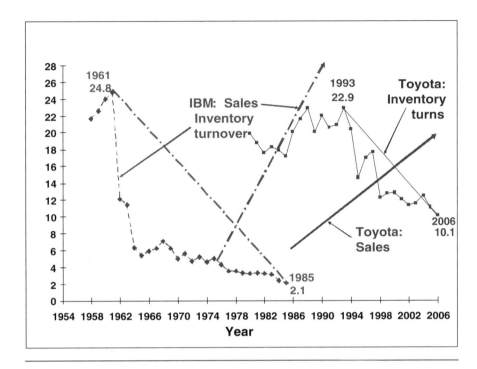

Exhibit 12.6   IBM Pattern: Repeating at Toyota

with the mandate of Lou Gerstner. Hired in 1993 out of RJR Nabisco to fix the broken behemoth, Gerstner "totally reorganized the company around customers."[3]

For IBM, inventory was a leading indicator—by 12 years for share price and 23 years for net earnings. There are good reasons why long-term declines in inventory turns should similarly affect the large majority of inventory-intensive companies, though the years of lead will vary. The multiple negative effects of low attention to process improvement, with inventory growth as a telling metric, are the following:

1. Growth of inventory gobbles cash, so earnings (bottom line) will be negatively affected.
2. Growth of inventory puts distance between makers and users, so users up and down the value chains will get worse service. Some final users will shift orders to other makers. Poor service will deter other potential users from becoming customers. Sales (top line) will be negatively affected.
3. Growth of inventory lengthens time to discover causes, so quality and other processes will deteriorate—more customer defections. Sales (top line) will be negatively affected.
4. These effects are compounded the longer the deterioration in process management persists.

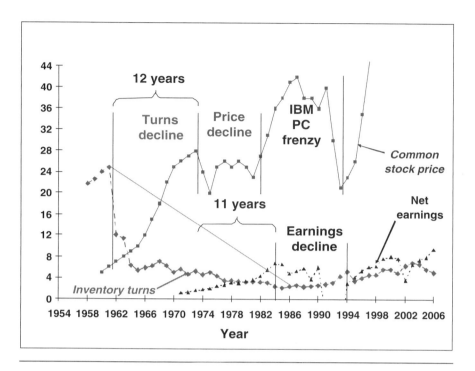

Exhibit 12.7   IBM: Inventory, a Leading Indicator

---

5. The longer the deterioration, the more likely that knowledge, habits, and systems of best-practice process improvement will be lost, and will be difficult and costly to regain.

A few companies may not experience much lag-effect deterioration of share prices and earnings. That would be the case if their competitors' process-management performance were inclining downward at a steeper angle. However, all companies that cut back on process improvement will experience the five negatives cited above.

There are no signs of Toyota's share price falling after its own 13 years of worsening inventory turns, nor of that at Danaher. But, for the five reasons cited, both companies are likely to be experiencing the negative lag effects—the more so if their downward trends do not turn upward before long.

GRACO: IN A GROWTH SPURT

Graco, Inc. is a midsized ($816 million) manufacturer of liquid spraying, dispensing, and pumping equipment (not the Graco that makes baby and toddler products). This company, whose headquarters and main manufacturing center lie alongside the

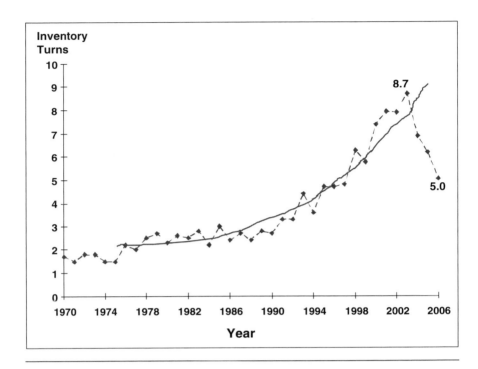

Exhibit 12.8   Graco, Inc.: Long-Term Accelerating Improvement Curbed by Three Years of Acquisitions

Mississippi River in Minneapolis, is little known to the public. But I know them rather well, from two on-site visits over a few years, plus considerable interview-based research. Graco's substantial business success has been fed by intensive lean efforts. That includes the lean core within Graco's plants. Beyond that are practices rarely found elsewhere that simplify and synchronize flows forward to the customer. More on that in Chapter 17.

Evidence of Graco's stellar lean performance is shown in Exhibit 12.8: an upward trend with strong upward concavity—until the past three years involving three acquisitions. (In an earlier stage of writing this book, Graco was to join Dell, Wal-Mart, HP, and NEC in Chapter 4 as one of the foremost examples of "improving the rate of improvement.") Before that, Graco had been typically conservative about growth. (As noted author Michael Treacy put it, executives generally don't plan for growth systematically, though they know just what to do to cut costs.[4])

Graco's three acquisitions, accounting for 11.2 percent of its 2005 sales, drew the company's inventory turns downward from 8.7 to 5.0. From data in the Graco annual report, it appears that composite inventory turns for the three were about 4.5, which is nearly 50 percent lower than Graco's prior 8.7 turns. It may take a few years for Graco to effectively digest the acquired companies. Another sizeable acquisition in July

2006 suggests that Graco, which had long been content with organic growth, may be shifting its sights somewhat toward growth by acquisition.

Is Graco now growing too fast? It stands to reason that there is an optimal rate of growth, different for every company—not a fine line, but a zone. For a well-managed company, grow much slower and you start losing talented people for lack of challenge and the likelihood of restricted remuneration. That happened at R.W. Lyall, a small California manufacturer, which finally induced its risk-averse owners to make an acquisition.[5] Grow much faster, and your good management practices can't keep up and regress toward average. Lean companies may be especially vulnerable, because lean is, by nature, precarious. The four chapters in Part III, especially Chapter 10 on "stretching company capabilities," explain that vulnerability. As for Graco, the spate of acquisitions may have caused but a temporary setback in its lean journey, though more, sizeable acquisitions would surely have long-term negative effects. Continuity is difficult, which is the main point of Chapter 13.

NOTES

1. The Danaher business system is featured in Brian Hindo, "A Dynamo Called Danaher," *Business Week* (February 19, 2007), pp. 56–60.

2. "Toyota Motor Corp., to fuel sales expansion further around the world, vowed Friday to maintain an unprecedented pace of capital spending—well more than $10 billion a year— in the next several years, putting pressure on Detroit and other rivals already struggling to cope with challenges from the Japanese auto maker." Norihiko Shirouzu, "Toyota to Maintain Spending, Pressure on Detroit," *Wall Street Journal* (October 9, 2006), p. A12. Also, Norihiko Shirouzu, "Toyota Races to Rev Up Production for a Boom in Emerging Markets," *Wall Street Journal* (November 13, 2006), p. A1.

3. Robert J. Herbold, *Seduced by Success: How the Best Companies Survive the 9 Traps of Winning*, (New York: McGraw-Hill, 2007), p. 46.

4. By contrast, Treacy says, "successful growth companies such as Wal-Mart and Dell are so focused that they are able to pursue many goals simultaneously": cited in Scott Thurm, "Leadership: The Best Ways to Grow," *Wall Street Journal* (October 25), 2004, pp. R1, R4.

5. The R.W. Lyall case is presented in Richard J. Schonberger, Karen A. Brown, and Thomas G. Schmitt, "Your Lean Team: Use It or Lose It," *Target* (1st qtr. 2003), pp. 13–21. See also Richard J. Schonberger, *Let's Fix It! How the World's Leading Manufacturers Were Seduced by Prosperity and Lost Their Way* (New York: Free Press/Simon & Schuster, 2001), pp. 155–157. Update: After losing lean leader Mo Vasquez to a company visiting Lyall on a benchmarking trip, Lyall finally did make its first acquisition.

Chapter 13

Losing Their Way—or Not

Lean and TQ are temporal. Like good news, they come but usually don't stay. This book presents three main reasons. From Chapter 5, lean's popular definition—attack on wastes—is unexciting to executives, marketers, and customers. From Chapter 10, lean/TQ is a collection of an overwhelming number of best practices from which to cherry-pick, but no Big Idea. In this chapter, it is *executive-level discontinuity.*

The investigation combines trend data, web and library searches, interviews, and, where applicable, personal visits to the companies. Findings group into two general ways by which companies tend to be diverted from the lean/quality pathway—or, in a few cases, to stay on it. The two section headings are stated in the negative. Discontinuity upstairs, which often lords over other issues, is first. The other main diversion is chronic capacity starvation, which may sound odd because lean begins with the presumption of excess resources that must be winnowed down. But just as too little inventory can wreck a lean effort, so can too little capacity.

DISCONTINUITY IN THE EXECUTIVE SUITE

There is nothing like executive-level discontinuity to neutralize a fine process-improvement effort. There appear to be too many examples to count, and not many of the opposite kind: companies that have remained devoted process improvers for enough years to include changes in the executive suite. We'll begin with one of the rarities, and then give a few prominent examples of the many companies that regress.

CONTINUITY, MILLIKEN STYLE

The best example of a company that keeps improving its processes may be Milliken, the giant South Carolina–based textile and chemical company. Privately held Milliken carries the name of its current board chairman, Roger Milliken, who turned 90 in 2005. He was named president in 1947 and in 1988 became chairman and CEO, a position he stepped down from recently. That Mr. Milliken has run the company for so many years provides one kind of continuity. The kind we are interested in, continuity in process improvement, dates back to 1981, when company officers set in motion Milliken's Pursuit of Excellence.[1] Many executives and managers enrolled in Philip Crosby's Quality College and attended Dr. W. Edwards Deming's four-day seminar, and soon put that learning to work company-wide. With total quality as the foundation, Milliken has carefully selected additional best practices to weave in:[2]

- Just-in-time production and supply were added in the mid-1980s. Milliken generally has stayed with the *JIT* label rather than its *lean* reincarnation.

- Milliken was the launching pad, in the 1980s, for quick response (QR), the forerunner of continuous replenishment à la Wal-Mart. Soon Milliken's design center at Spartanburg headquarters was adorned with a large banner, "Milliken—Home of Quick Response."

- Milliken was one of the first in its industry to abolish piece-rate incentives, doing so in 1989.

- Milliken implemented several JIT projects in its chemicals business (consisting of two plants). They included the 1988 opening of a new plant, a radical plant design with *two* reactor groups, the smaller of the two aimed at running small batches just in time. Standard chemical plants have one reactor group and can economically run only large batches.[3] The chemical industry as a whole still has not learned much, as indicated by its low rank among industries on leanness (see Chapter 18).

- Milliken designs a lot of its own machines for the same reason: avoiding getting boxed into large lots by monument machines.

- I learned, in a visit to Milliken in 1988, that company policies have long favored having enough capacity. In an approving follow-up letter to Milliken, I said, "That opens up the options. Many other companies—in textiles and otherwise—have none, because there are no hours left in the week when things go wrong." "Chronic Capacity Starvation in the Face of Unpredictable Demand" is the heading of a later section of this chapter.

- By 1992, Milliken had reduced its supplier base to 2,200—from 9,500 in 1980.[4]

- Few companies in the world can match Milliken's annual per-employee numbers of suggestions (called *opportunities for improvement—OFIs—*at Milliken[5]): typically in the fifties in the early 1990s, and up to around 100 in 2002, 2003, and 2004. Avoiding a non-value-adding accounting exercise, OFIs are not costed out. How are these numbers possible year after year? President (retired) Tom Malone's widely used term is "trust curve."

- Few companies place as much emphasis on visual management as Milliken does, and has done since the 1980s.

- Milliken was one of the West's early adopters of quality function deployment, a natural add-on to its early-1980s total-quality commitment. Generally, though, Milliken resists chasing management fads, and tends to go its own way with those it finds merit in. One example is six sigma. Launched in recent years, Milliken's six sigma involves only a few projects, each big ones, some taking as long as a year. They focus not on small things, but on customer and business processes.

- The Milliken Performance System, adopted in about 1995, focuses on total productive maintenance and daily management systems for operations. Fifty-seven plants have been recognized with the TPM Prize awarded by the Japan

Institute of Plant Maintenance. Milliken had found that many of Japan's Deming Prize winners chose to pursue the TPM Prize next, which seemed to make sense as a next step.

• Milliken does not use the term *kaizen*. They have "just-do-its."

• Milliken is number 38 on *Fortune* magazine's 2006 list of "100 best companies to work for."[6]

• Milliken's successes stand in stark contrast to its peers' in its dominant industry, textiles, and its secondary one, chemicals. From Chapter 18's ranking of 33 industries on the long-term leanness scale, textiles/sewn products is second last, in 32nd place, and chemicals is third last, in 31st place.

What explains these many indications of outstanding long-term dedication to best practices and process improvement? One word: continuity.

DISCONTINUITY: MANY EXAMPLES

When it comes to the opposite, *dis*continuity, Ford Motor Company is the flashing-light billboard example. In the 1980s, Ford proclaimed, *Quality Is Job 1!* By the 2000s, that slogan seemed to have been written in disappearing ink.

Other examples are endless. For their lean losses, the previous chapter found Toyota and Danaher to be big surprises. Going back to the West's first years of JIT-cum-lean, standouts in discontinuity include General Electric and Westinghouse. Wiremold, Steelcase, and American Standard round out the following discussion of inconstancy upstairs. Interwoven are reviews of what happened when Westinghouse sold its best manufacturing plants to Eaton Corp. and when Wiremold was acquired by Legrand of France.

General Electric: Early Advice from Toyota

GE may have been the first Western company to hire Toyota experts for advice on applying JIT production. The Toyota team was brought in mainly to help fix the company's poor-performing white-goods business centered in GE's massive Appliance Park in Louisville, Kentucky.[7] By May 1983, on a visit to the dishwasher plant at Appliance Park, I found concrete results: Thirty miles of conveyor had been reduced to six. Green-yellow-red pull cords were staged along the assembly line for assemblers to signal the state of the line and stop it for quality or other problems. A photo from an earlier book of mine shows a stamping machine with a large sign mounted on top saying, "Fabricate Junction Box Bracket: Point of Use Manufacturing."[8] That and other machines formerly located in distant shops had been moved to points of use on the assembly line where they were down-geared to produce just in time. Other component parts were moving right to points of use rather than being shuttled three times through two overhead departments. Raw/WIP inventory turns had increased from 11 to about 16.[9]

By that time, JIT had made an impact in several other GE businesses.[10] On May 4–5, 1983, GE Corporate Engineering assembled 60 managers from various business units for a "Just-in-Time Workshop" in Washington, D.C.[11] Some of the participants were speakers, reporting on JIT achievements at their plants. Later, the JIT advocacy cadre took up residence in the GE Production Management and Systems Consulting department, assisting in development of JIT in numerous GE businesses.[12]

It didn't last. In 1984, GE sold its small kitchen-appliance business—its most advanced in JIT manufacturing—to Black & Decker. That was the beginning of GE's sell-off of several manufacturing businesses and acquisition of a TV network, and finance, leasing, and insurance businesses. Before long, Ed Spurgeon, JIT Program Manager, and others on his staff in corporate consulting began to retire. No doubt, some GE businesses have continued to pursue JIT/lean. As an ardent collector of information on such topics, though, my files include only one reference to JIT at GE after 1986.[13] I doubt that long-time (now retired) CEO Jack Welch and other high-level GE executives ever developed a sustaining interest in the subject matter.

Westinghouse—Reincarnated as Eaton Cutler-Hammer

The story at Westinghouse is similar though more drastic, because the discontinuity there included a full-scale move out of manufacturing and into the entertainment business. Before going that direction, though, Westinghouse followed a JIT pattern similar in some ways to that of GE.

The official launching pad for JIT was the Westinghouse Productivity and Quality Center in Pittsburgh. When I first visited the PQC in late 1984, what I saw was an automation laboratory. It had all manner of equipment being tested and refined for use in the company's factories. My PQC hosts were apologetic, because they had got "JIT religion": Simplify and improve processes, and put off the high costs and complexities of automation.

Masterminds at the PQC had developed *OPTIM*, an innovative way to rapidly get JIT and process improvement going throughout the company.[14] As explained in a PQC "Executive Summary" dated 1985, each business would develop OPTIM's *time–cost profile*. In some ways resembling value-stream mapping, OPTIM is "a graphic representation of the buildup of cost with time, as a product or service passes through its entire cycle in your business operation."[15] The Summary cited six completed OPTIM examples with cycle-time reductions such as 50 percent, 66 percent, and 90 percent, along with large reductions of scrap, inventory, and floor space.

But OPTIM and the profile are examples of the kind of overly structured corporate programs that, I think, often smother local initiative. *Total Quality Focus*, a monthly newsletter of the Westinghouse Distribution and Controls Business Unit, included a column in each issue entitled "OPTIM Update." The column reviewed the business unit's inventory numbers as compared with the "$15.7 million per month [that] is required to meet the year-end inventory objective of $115.9 million, or 13.5 percent AGI/SB" (meaning average gross inventory as a percent of sales).[16] This aspect of OPTIM is the kind of heavy-handed, misguided use of numeric management goals that yields more negative than beneficial results (see Chapter 9, "Vengeful Numbers").

In a few corners of Westinghouse, local initiative would not be smothered. The best example is the Controls Division, which transformed its six plants into roaring JIT/lean successes in about 1984 and 1985. Best known was the Asheville, NC, plant,[17] to which 3M Corp. and other companies sent large numbers of people on benchmarking visits. Plant manager Vinod Kapoor led the transformation.[18] Included were making over the plant into six focused factories, doing most other aspects of the lean core,[19] reducing the number of accountants from 16 to 8, and achieving two- to six-fold flow-time reductions in the office. Scuttlebutt around the company told of how Kapoor sent large amounts of buffer stock "to the corner." "Get by without it," he said, which put people to work doing what was necessary to comply. Later, promoted to a division executive, Kapoor refocused on another of the division's plants, in Fayetteville, NC. There he was faced with people's reluctance to cut lot sizes. So he went to the records and changed them—set lot sizes to *one unit*. That generated hue and cry and complaints. Kapoor just told those who grumbled to solve the problem, which they did.

But later, the roof fell in on Westinghouse as an industrial power and a JIT leader. The company, which had bought the CBS broadcasting company and had been selling off industrial businesses, decided in 1997 to get rid of all remaining manufacturing.[20]

That was not the end of the story. In 1994, the Controls Division, along with JIT adherents Kapoor and division head Spencer Duin, was sold to Eaton Corp., which housed the division in its Cutler-Hammer business unit. This was Eaton's largest acquisition, bumping its sales up by 20 percent. It also appears to have been a lean acquisition. Eaton's inventory turns, 6.5 in 1994, rose to 6.7, 7.1, and 7.4 in the next three years.

Meanwhile, Eaton had mounted its own strong JIT effort in the early 1980s.[21] Its inventory turns had been stuck at about 2.6 from 1970 through 1976. Then, for the next 21 years, Eaton's turns rose smartly, making its leanness grade an *A* through most of the 1990s. (The grade is still *A*, though the improvement trend has tapered off and become jerky since 1997.) Substantial JIT improvements in Eaton's truck components plants contributed to the grade. Examples, in Tennessee, circa 1985: In Shelbyville, throughput time to produce shafts fell from 8-to-10 days to 28 minutes with WIP cut 98 percent; in Kings Mountain, throughput time to machine transmission cases fell from 1-to-18 days to 2 hours with WIP cut from 22-to-23 days to 4.[22] Later, Eaton's Automation Products Division in Watertown, Wisconsin, removed the incentive-pay system for the hourly work force and reduced labor classifications and grades by 60 percent. These steps smoothed implementation of the lean core. Results at Watertown included 40 percent reduction in floor space, 50 percent in lead time, 60 percent in total inventory, and 75 percent in WIP.[23]

Under its new parent, Cutler-Hammer's JIT experts kept up the pace. On a 1996 visit to C-H's home-circuit-breaker business based in the Caribbean, I found extensive implementations of the lean core. Machined and molded parts went by ship, a one-day sail, from the company's Puerto Rico plants to assembly cells in Santo Domingo,

Dominican Republic. Given the stringent user-safety requirements for electrical products, these operations placed high emphasis on quality, sometimes through installation of fail-safing devices.

After all that JIT/lean activity in the 1980s and 1990s, it was startling in 2005 to read this opening paragraph of an article in *Target*: "When Eaton Corporation introduced lean concepts to its 200+ plants worldwide in 2001, expectations . . . were high ." The story continues, saying that the dream faded because of "varying interpretations, the perspectives of different consultants, and inconsistent metrics." The solution: Senior management introduced the Eaton Lean System in 2003.[24] This begs the question: Are there no senior people at Eaton aware of the company's pioneering lean achievements in the 1980s? Or its seasoned lean expertise and continued successes in the 1990s?

Wiremold (U.S.) and Legrand (France)

Few Western companies have been as acclaimed for their lean achievements as Connecticut-based Wiremold, producer of specialized electric power raceways, strips, and other wiring items.[25] Shingo-Prize winner (1999) Wiremold was favored with savvy, consistent, lean-focused direction from CEO Art Byrne and his staff. A 2002 article reviews Wiremold's JIT/lean ascension. From lean's beginnings in 1991 to 2000, Wiremold grew fourfold, both organically and through acquisitions.[26] A former Wiremold executive recalls that "we had hundreds of companies visit us, and all of us, beginning with Art, were very open about what we did."[27]

Then, in 2002, privately held Wiremold was acquired by Legrand, a large, publicly held electrical-products company headquartered in France. The same former executive tells what happened.

> When Art and I retired they promoted the two individuals into our positions that we recommended. And then Legrand proceeded to hire from the outside a CEO and CFO for "Legrand North America" who did not understand lean and showed no interest in learning it. And slowly, piece by piece, much of what was created over the ten years was undone. Not intentionally, but every time they ran into a problem they would come up with a "traditional" non-lean solution. At this point every senior manager and almost every middle-level manager that was there in 2002 is gone, and I am told the lean culture has virtually disappeared.[28]

It is not that Legrand was clueless. It seems to have been among continental Europe's early birds in discovering and thriving on JIT. Its inventory turns had hit bottom at 3.3 in 1984, but then rose steeply, to 6.9 in 1993. Then, as in other companies, perhaps the JIT bloom faded. Legrand's long-term leanness grade was *A* in the mid-1990s, fell to *B* in the late 1990s, and rose back up to a shaky *A* in the year following Wiremold's purchase in 2002; see Exhibit 13.1. It still retains the *A* although its inventory turns fell a bit from 2004 through 2006. Legrand continues

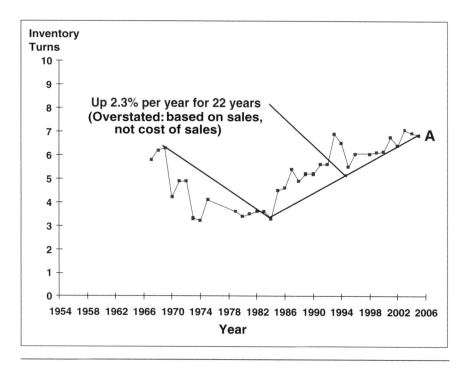

Exhibit 13.1   Inventory Turnover at Legrand (France)

to make acquisitions, including eight in 2005, but, if Wiremold is a fair indication, Legrand may be frittering away prime value that may have come with those eight.

American Standard: Losing Its DFT Edge

At American Standard, until recently one of the world's largest producers of bathroom and kitchen fixtures (that business unit was sold off in 2007), lean's name was not *JIT*. It was *demand-flow technology* (DFT), a term coined by the John Constanza Institute of Technology, a lean training and consulting company employing innovative training systems. DFT includes all of the lean core. Articles in *Fortune, Business Week,* and the *Wall Street Journal* spoke glowingly of how, under CEO Emmanuel Kampouris, American Standard had prospered from the DFT treatment, which was launched in 1990.[29] The company's inventory turnover graph (Exhibit 13.2) appears to confirm statements in the articles about soaring inventory turnovers and cash flow, and so on. We cannot know its turns for the first two years of DFT, because the company was privately held then. The graph appears to show, however, that turns about doubled, to 10.8 in 1994, the date of the first *Fortune* article. (That met the qualifications for an *A* on leanness. The grade fell to *B* as turnover plunged in the 2000s, and finally to *C*.) For several years, American Standard's annual reports were peppered with discussions about DFT. But by

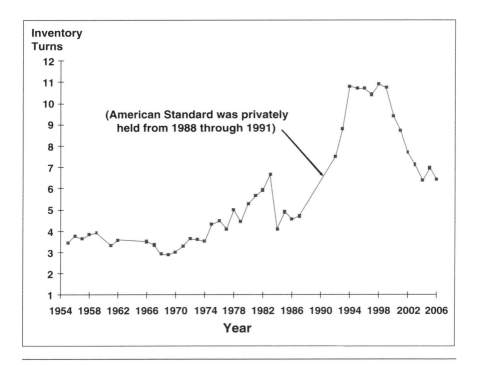

Exhibit 13.2   Inventory Turnover at American Standard

2001, after five years of flat turns, and then three of sharply worsening turns (and after a new CEO took over from Kampouris—in 2000), the DFT halo was off. That year's annual report told of finding just the ticket to revive its operations: six sigma. Six sigma is good medicine, but not as a replacement for the lean core.

Steelcase: Playing Catch-up

Usually, it is an advantage to be privately held. On the process-improvement scale, it did not turn out that way for office-furniture maker Steelcase, which was private until 1997. In the late 1980s, Steelcase avidly educated its managers in JIT/TQ practices. I was among those brought to the company's Grand Rapids home base, in 1988 and 1989, to conduct training sessions. These were two-day seminars fused with detailed specifics from plant tours and meetings with managerial teams. I knew the industry fairly well, having conducted the same kinds of tailored events at two of Steelcase's main competitors. The first was privately held Haworth in 1983 and 1984. The other was publicly traded Hon Industries in 1986 and 1987, and again in 1990. The three companies' JIT enthusiasms had different effects. Steelcase quickly went all out for JIT, and then almost as quickly put it on the back burner. A-graded Hon became one of the most impressive JIT implementers on the planet and, it seems, still is today.

Haworth (Holland, Michigan) has not, to my knowledge, emerged as a JIT/lean/TPS stalwart, but may have done well on the TQ side of process improvement: Haworth's web site highlights its "exacting standards of quality," including being a finalist for the Baldrige, the U.S. national quality award.

Industry Week told of Steelcase's early JIT flurry (referred to in the company as "world-class manufacturing," or WCM). The 1991 story featured former CEO Frank Merlotti speaking about manufacturing cells and a focused-factory layout in the company's new Context plant. Merlotti stated that at Context, typical customer lead times fell from 12 to 6 weeks, and production flow time was at 5 days compared with 25 to 30 days in a traditional plant. Ninety percent of the 5,400 employees in the company's Grand Rapids plants were organized into 560 teams, all receiving eight hours of training in WCM's five points: quality, faster throughput, elimination of waste, focused factories, and employee involvement. Participation in the teams was mandatory, and, after first making supervisors the team leaders, the company switched to having teams elect their own leaders. Enthused about the teams, Merlotti did his part by becoming a listener when teams made presentations on their process improvements.[30]

In another lean move, the old 1956-era desk plant was realigned into five focused factories, which cut total travel distance from as much as 35 miles to as little as 200 feet, and which reduced a 28-day flow time to 5-to-7 days.[31] Steelcase Canada was also achieving these kinds of JIT/lean successes.[32]

Most of the company, though, was unmoving. To try to learn why, I interviewed former WCM honchos Rob Burch and Larry Barton, along with current managers John Duba (head of the company's lean office), John Levandoski (in the supply-chain group), and Dr. David Mann (generally in charge of Steelcase's revitalized lean effort).[33] The interviews, plus my own recollections of legacy issues, reveal numerous reasons for inaction.

First, the 1990s saw a big upturn in business. To cope, the company put most of the WCM and employee-empowerment agenda on hold and ratcheted up the still-dominant batch-and-queue system. The sad irony is that when demand is outstripping capacity, the ills of batch-and-queue are magnified. All measures of performance deteriorate.

There were related factors: The labor force was stretched, and people moved to off-shifts were unhappy about it. Merlotti's employee-involvement initiatives shriveled. Although the work force was never unionized (three UAW drives had failed), it may as well have been, since union-like labor rigidities were ingrained at Steelcase. For example, there were many job classifications, which inhibited shifting people to where the work is; and a posting system rather than who-is-right-for-the-job governed the filling of openings. Worse, Steelcase was enmired with a piecework pay system. As David Mann put it, "We were emphasizing flow and reduced inventory, but at the same time we were paying employees by the piece—rewarding people to build inventory!"[34] The work force resisted any talk about changing these accustomed practices. Steelcase just let these weaknesses persist, because, according to one of the interviewees, management "didn't like people not to be happy."

Moreover, there were too many suppliers, and purchasing was thought of as a dead end. The heads of operations were weak and irresolute; they tried organizing into business units and tried reengineering, but follow-through was lacking. Plant managers were rewarded for the usuals, including keeping machines busy and making as much as possible, whether needed or not. In most Steelcase plants, high walls separated and de-synchronized the four main segments in the flow of production: machining, welding, paint, and trim. Most of the plants were excessively large, which requires unlean long-distance handling and denies well-contained value streams. (In 2006, the production area in one Grand Rapids plant had been "trimmed" to nearly 800,000 square feet; Chapter 16 is mostly devoted to issues related to excessive plant size.) Focus, value-steams, extended cells, and silo-bashing had not taken root. Finally, one of the interviewees opined, Steelcase was in a position of strength; there was no burning platform to shake up the system.

All that changed in the new century. The office-furniture industry had enjoyed its best year ever in 2000. Then orders sank. In the aftermath of 9/11/2001, customer companies curtailed expansion plans and quit buying. Furniture manufacturers, including Steelcase, laid off thousands and shuttered plants. Now there *was* a burning platform, one that was especially combustible for Steelcase. From a newspaper story, Steelcase "had to play catch-up with several large competitors, including Herman Miller and Muscatine, Iowa–based HNI [Hon Industries], which have long embraced production efficiency."[35] Actually, Steelcase had begun to rejuvenate its JIT/lean effort in the late 1990s. New, no-nonsense executives knew what needed to be done, and Duba was hired to run the new lean office. Piecework was killed in 2000, containers were downsized, and new lean success metrics, such as reducing number of moves, were instituted. Finally, today, Steelcase appears to have its lean act together.

With the usual caution that for a single company inventory turnover is an imperfect indicator, here are the numbers for the industry's big three: Steelcase does not meet the 15-year requirement for full membership in the database, but its inventory turns have stayed at around 14 for most of the 10 years of data we do have. Hon hit 23.6 in 2001 but has slid since then to 16.5—dropping it from an *A* grade to a *B*. Herman Miller hit 33.7 in 1999 but has lost ground since, down to 24.7, also reducing its grade from *A* to *B*.

CHRONIC CAPACITY STARVATION IN THE FACE OF UNPREDICTABLE DEMAND

This book maintains that the greatest lean deficiencies lie not in operations, but in the pipelines. While other chapters explore that, here we examine the main obstacle to getting it done in operations, through the lean core. The blockage is between the two main elements of manufacturing: fabrication of components, and assembly of them into finished products. Often the two take place in the same factory or same multiplant campus, where it is easy to see the problem: Assembly has achieved one-piece flow (or close to it); fabrication is still in large batches. Pallet- and rack-loads of WIP sprawl at the interface. The lean team is somewhat embarrassed, but is able to show that now, after impressive reductions in machine setup times, the fabrication batches are much smaller than before. Quick setup, providing *adaptive capacity*, is elemental in the lean core. But it has its practical and financial limits. The team recognizes the other option, more machining capacity, but that is unaffordable.

But is it? How much of that unaffordability is an artifact of numbers management? Two kinds of numbers intertwine here. One is monetary, and that subdivides into holding down expenditures, holding down debt, and realizing profits. The other is machine utilization. It is easy for the CFO to pull up utilization numbers and proclaim that the equipment is under-used. That squelches talk about spending on more machines.

A rare few academics, consultants, and manufacturers fight off those arguments. One is Michael George and two co-authors. Their book, *Fast Innovation*, convincingly shows how high capacity utilization combined with high variability in task times creates severe delays.[36] It is a generalizable relationship, which in its original application to factory facilities, was developed in the 1930s by European mathematicians Felix Pollaczek and Alexander Khintchine.[37] In applying the Pollaczek-Khintchine formula to innovation, George, et al., state that at 95 percent utilization the design time for a task that on average takes 5 days jumps to 30 days.[38] In the same vein, Professor Rajan Suri's Center for Quick Response Manufacturing at the University of Wisconsin–Madison calls for "spare capacity" to reduce lead times.[39]

Prominent among manufacturers is Milliken, which, as mentioned earlier in the chapter, years ago established policies favoring plenty of capacity. Another is Precor, producer of high-end treadmills and related workout equipment. Most companies just fatalistically allow the capacity crunch, and the attending sea of troubles, to persist. I'll present the good example, Precor, then some of the more typical kinds.

PRECOR: NO CAPACITY EXCUSES

Chapter 12 described how Illinois Tool Works gets the most out of its many acquired companies through rigorous 80-20 analysis. Precor is one of those companies. Acquired by ITW in 1999, Precor is an outstanding example of application of the lean core. Included in that, Precor reduced its supplier base from 2,000 to 240, and nearly all of those 240 either operate in the supplier-managed-inventory mode or replenish based on "faxbans" from Precor's shop floor. I'll skip the rest of the details (including exceptional attention to safety and ergonomics) and get right to the point about Precor and capacity.

Precor makes treadmills and other fitness equipment for the home market. But its bread and butter is selling heavy-duty models to the giant fitness chains and clubs. Often, when Precor wins a contract, it is to ship a large number of "bikes" (their term for treadmills) and other equipment for the opening of several new stores. Those sudden, unpredictable, high-volume orders are the kind of extreme variation that, as predicted by the Pollaczek-Khintchine equation, can bring a manufacturer to its knees. Not Precor: For the 80 percent of products so identified by 80-20 analysis, the machining building includes a large number of dedicated milling machines. Here are the advantages:

- *Marketing:* When customers call, sales need not be overly concerned about whether capacity is available. They can book the order and promise quick delivery.
- *Operations:* Dedicated equipment can immediately begin making good parts, with few delays and setup adjustments.
- *Inventory costs:* They are inconsequential, because plentiful dedicated equipment allows making parts on demand.

Precor is no longer an ITW company. It was sold in 2002 to Finland's Amer Group, producer of sporting-goods, a good fit with Precor's line of exercise equipment. Amer's leanness grade is *C*. Notably, however, Amer's inventory turns jumped from 7.2 in the year of the Precor acquisition in 2002 to 8.0 in 2003, before falling in 2004, 2005, and 2006.

THE NORM: CAPACITY DEPRIVATION

In earlier discussion of JIT's advent at GE, I expressed admiration for staging metal-working equipment at points of use along the dishwasher assembly line. There was no possibility, though, of putting the tub- and door-molding machines lineside. The tub halves and doors were, for plastic-molded parts, very large. Therefore, the mold-presses to make them were giant-sized, as was their acquisition cost.

Following my 1983 visit to the plant, I offered a few positive comments in a thank-you letter to my host. I also mentioned a large unresolved issue: "the imbalance between the production rate in tub and door injection molding and the rate of use of tubs and doors" in final assembly. Lack of capacity in molding meant the mold-presses had to operate many more shifts per week than final assembly. That produced large inventories of large parts in a department storage area removed from the assembly line. There had to be plentiful extra inventory to allow down time for maintenance, model changeovers, and scrap and rework. I said in the letter that dealing with these issues by adding more molding capacity is probably too expensive.[40] Now I disagree with myself. My guess is that the sharp-pencil people at GE saw that the molding machines had sufficient capacity *per week*; therefore, there was no need for more capacity. That way of thinking flies in the face of the JIT/lean objective of synchronizing production stages *per minute*.

SWEP International in Landskrona, Sweden, producer of compact brazed heat exchangers, has a strong lean effort going—which is the case with many manufacturers in the Nordic countries; see regional rankings in Exhibit 2.6. (SWEP is owned by U.S.-based Dover Corp., which was graded a strong *A* on leanness until the 1990s, when declining turns lowered the grade to *B*, and then *C*. Since bottoming out in 2000, Dover's turns have improved, perhaps driven partly by astute acquisitions and also by lean efforts such as that of SWEP.) But now lean at SWEP has become rather like driving in a construction zone. You know exactly where you want to end up, but the quick-and-easy ways to get there are blocked. For SWEP, each blockage looks a lot like the others: lack of enough brazing-furnace capacity. By accounting and raw utilization numbers, they have plenty of furnaces. But diligent efforts to link press lines with brazing by kanban, along with takt-time scheduling, clearly reveal the reality. In fall 2006, I spent a day-and-a-half with about 60 SWEP people: the president, plant manager, sales and accounting people, and so on. The last topic, to wind up the day's discussion of lean and related matters, was to rank the big issues in order of importance. The group was in full agreement: The number-one issue was lack of capacity. Given the many complex problems always present in manufacturing, it is rare to have such unanimity and understanding.

Another example comes from one of this book's admired manufacturers (featured in Chapter 12): Graco, Inc. The mother plant in Minneapolis has five focused machining and assembly cells. At first the cells were organized around the group-technology concept. Improving on that, they were reorganized as product-family cells. Most manufacturers stop there, except for shrinking and tweaking. Graco pressed on, reorganizing them again as market-family cells (see the box, below). The result is world-class machining cells and world-class assembly cells. The remaining challenge, and it is a big one, is how to tightly link the two. It is the common problem: There simply is not sufficient machining capacity. For example, at any point in time, machining may be producing 30 part numbers, but assembly is using 300 part numbers. So the machining and assembly cells are physically separated by WIP storage. Graco managers are very much aware of this, but the cost issue looms.

Focus: Product Families Good, Customer/Market Families Superior[a]

For many or most manufacturers, production technologies do not line up well with market segments. Where they do, organizing production cells by market/customer families yields a host of benefits. Each cell becomes a member of a value stream that takes in production support, marketing, sales—and, don't stop there—engineering, finance, accounting, and purchasing. The result is mini-companies, each with a full complement of functions. Bring in the customers to meet *their* providers in *their* mini-company.

Where products spill over into many markets, cells focused on product families is the best the company can do—in the short run. In the longer run, however, the company should be looking for ways to shift the product line somewhat, so that at least some of the products line up with customer families and value streams.

---

[a]This concept is central in Principle 1 of 16 "customer-focused, employee-driven, data-based principles." See Richard J. Schonberger, *Let's Fix It! How the World's Leading Manufacturers Were Seduced by Prosperity and Lost Their Way* (New York: Free Press/Simon & Schuster, 2001), p. 236.

One of Parker Hannifin's units provides a third example.[41] This business, producing hose connectors in Cleveland, had been a traditional batch-and-queue facility. That changed in 2006. Under a new lean-savvy plant manager, the facility went all out for lean. In just a few months, two plants were consolidated into one, as large racks and pallet boxes were emptied. Taking the freed-up space are 10 newly organized value-stream-focused assembly-test-pack cells. Each is fed by four or five automatic screw machines just across a main aisle. The screw machines fabricate the main component parts. In the consolidation, 16 of 54 screw machines were eliminated. Each of the remaining 38 machines was rebuilt for quick setup in one of Parker's other business units. For all that, it was taking three times longer to cycle through the product line in machining than in the assembly cells. As a result, there were still racks and bins full of machined parts, made in too-large batches, ahead of assembly. If each of the 16 machines had been retained and assigned to the cells, machining capacity would have been nearly a third greater, thus bringing machining in closer sync with assembly. With more machines, several probably could be dedicated to high-runner parts producing close to the usage rate in assembly—with zero setup time.

Here again is the issue of capacity deprivation. The machines were already owned and long-since paid for. Why be so quick to cut valuable capacity? Aside from space limitations, a likely suspect is machine-utilization numbers, which so often lead to wrong decisions. With 54 machines, the utilization percentages probably were below 50 percent, before the quick-setup renovations. The numbers-watchers would say, "too many machines—and now we can eliminate the machines, and a whole building, too!"

Another factor is generalizable to many companies. In its long history this hose-connectors business unit was devoid of anything smacking of JIT or lean before 2005. Why? One reason may be lack of financial incentives to improve. In 2000, Parker Hannifin installed Donald Washkewicz as its new CEO. Various indicators of deficient financial performance got Washkewicz searching for reasons. He found one. This old-line maker of a large variety of industrial products was still practicing markup pricing: Just add an increment, usually 35 percent at Parker, to costs. The *Wall Street Journal* put it this way: "No matter how much a product improved," the company gained nothing in profit margin. "And if the company found a way to make a product less expensively, it ultimately cut the product's price as well." Under Washkewicz, a new pricing system was installed and quickly began paying large dividends. It sets prices based on competitive factors such as quick response, performance, quality, and uniqueness.[42] This example once again illustrates how connected are the different elements of the business. An obsolete pricing practice, which markup pricing surely is, can be one more reason why best lean or six sigma efforts fall short.

The new "strategic pricing" model at Parker may even inspire company-wide efforts to find out what its costs really are—which conventional cost accounting does not do. One of Parker's divisions appears to have done just that. The case study comes from the 2006 Lean Accounting Summit in Orlando. In all the papers presented, there were only one or two that reported really significant implementations. One was about

Parker's Racor Division, Beaufort, South Carolina. They make engine ventilation and hydraulic filtration products. With plentiful lean achievements under its belt, the plant turned to its accounting and performance-management practices—and began eliminating burdensome transactions and controls. As Harley Davidson did two decades ago, Racor developed a simplified "total-conversion-cost" methodology. The twin advantages are better costs with less non-value-adding fuss.[43] What will become of this innovation at the division level? If Parker is like most companies, it will end up being stalemated later at corporate. Under CEO Washkewicz, maybe that fate can be avoided.

Scheduling and Pricing Options

Cutler-Hammer's circuit-breaker business in the Caribbean was capacity constrained, too, but exacerbated by wildly variable demand for thousands of permutations of breaker models. Demands poured into C-H's Spartanburg, South Carolina, distribution center from 8,000 distributors before being batched and passed on to the Caribbean operations. Order fill rates and on-times per unit of inventory were substandard. Adding machining capacity in Puerto Rico and assembly cells in Santo Domingo could solve the problem, and probably without breaking the bank. But there were better answers.

One is simply to get much more out of existing capacity. The lean way to do this is to cease producing to the volatile orders coming from Spartanburg. Instead, schedule the larger-demand items to a fixed daily/hourly rate (the takt time), changeable only about monthly. Let Spartanburg hold sufficient inventories to handle the uncertainty. Not doing so means that *every* link in the chain is holding inventory. And every production stage is squandering capacity doing scheduling flip-flops. Dan Jones wrote a clear, concise piece further detailing how leveling the demand works and why.[44]

Even stronger options are available on the demand side of the business. Cost analysts at C-H headquarters estimated that for a given SKU, the cost of processing an incoming customer order is a flat amount regardless of the quantity ordered. On the other hand, a staff expert in Caribbean operations estimated that low-volume orders cost 3 to 4 times as much manufacturing support as high-volume ones. Therefore, C-H should raise the prices of onezie-twozie orders for a single SKU, so that distributors are less likely to place such orders. This greatly improves overall margins and at the same time frees up production capacity and improves on-times and fill rates. (For more on simple pricing solutions and how lean/TQ and pricing affect each other, see "Pricing for Speed" in Chapter 6.)

For Barilla SpA, an Italian pasta maker, the problem, in the late 1980s, was not insufficient capacity. It was being forced by its distributors into maintaining ridiculously excessive capacity. As detailed in a Harvard case study,[45] Barilla sold its line of packaged pastas to its retailers largely through third-party distributors. Sales at retail were about flat. But the distributors' stock-replenishment practices resulted in highly volatile orders placed on Barilla, such as 80,000 kg of pasta one week and 4,000 kg the next. Barilla knew what to do. Ask the distributors for their daily shipments to retailers. That quantity, hardly changing from week to week, would be Barilla's production and delivery schedule—and its effective capacity. The distributors resisted, but Barilla persisted. Finally, after five years, Barilla had some success with the distributors. The new ordering, production, and delivery mode is known as *continuous replenishment* (see the Wal-Mart discussion in Chapter 14.)

WIP in the Dungeon

Evidence of insufficient machining or sheet-metal capacity can often be spotted in a quick plant walk-through. Volkswagen, in Puebla, Mexico, is a case in point. It is a fine-looking plant, assembling (when I was there in 2001) Jettas, Cabriolets, Old Beetles, and New Beetles. Most elements of the lean core are active, and job classifications have been reduced from 750 to just one. But changeovers on the two main press lines are infrequent, which produces large lot sizes of 10 critical stampings. The excess WIP cannot go direct to body weld, so it has to go into storage. WIP is a lean eyesore and a gobbler of prime space. So at VW-Puebla it goes to the basement, taken there by tuggers pulling trailers of stampings to the elevator and on down.

The lean way to stamp out the WIP is to run smaller lots more in tune with usage in body weld. That would require many more changeovers per day, which can be justified only by very quick setups on the presses. While progress had been made on setup times, they were taking much longer than the 9 minutes, 43 seconds that GM had achieved in 1990 at its McKeesport, Pennsylvania, stamping plant. (That was the time recorded in a nationwide competition, and not its average setup time.[46]) Moreover, changeover times at VW were unstable. Charts beside the stamping lines tracked the time taken on every setup (every manufacturer should do this!), showing high variation (e.g., five minutes) on both sides of the mean. Variation of that kind—anywhere, in any process—requires *extra WIP* in front of the next process. Low variation, on the other hand, allows setting precise, tightened kanban limits. So, at VW-Puebla some combination of three solutions to the WIP-in-the-dungeon problem needed to be sorted out: (1) quicker setups; (2) stable setup times; and, most expensive, (3) another press line.

These points about capacity interacting with variation concern a common, serious misconception in managing physical resources. We end the chapter by shifting gears, from physical to knowledge resources and their management.

KNOWLEDGE *MIS*MANAGEMENT

Peter Drucker titled his 1969 book *The Age of Discontinuity*.[47] Judging by the examples in the previous section, we can only say, "quite so." In the same book, Drucker famously stated that "these new industries ... will employ predominantly knowledge workers...." Today, we include knowledge of best practices in process improvement. Yet companies that invest heavily in developing that extensive knowledge easily give it up. Not only that, in some cases, after as little as a decade, there seem to be no remnants of that knowledge. Magnified by many companies, it is a colossal waste of resources.

For all its good sense and breadth of benefits, the lean core clearly is not self-sustaining. It needs plenty of help. Other chapters point out that lean/TQ is too many things, that it favors cherry-picking, and that it is weak externally, in the pipelines. It needs structure, meaning systematic devices, and lots of them. Diverse examples follow.

RALLIES AT MILLIKEN

Few companies retain and boost their process-improvement expertise as well as textile giant, Milliken, featured earlier in this chapter. It is not enough that the Milliken family astutely oversaw the company for decades. Family in high places can as easily weaken a company (e.g., Ford) as build it. At Milliken, a slew of management devices prop up process improvement. They regularly count and make a big deal of OFIs (opportunities for improvement, aka *suggestions*). Large signboards display upgraded capabilities, awards, recognition, and results. Internal sharing rallies, and external ones with partner organizations, take place at scheduled intervals, spreading the wealth of best practices. (Daimler-Chrysler has adopted a similar practice in which suppliers give presentations to peers at Daimler-Chrysler events quarterly.[48])

PRESENTATION EVENTS AT BAXTER

For many years, Baxter Healthcare has regularly held process-improvement events at all facilities. Teams make their presentations locally. The best of those go to regional events, where they present and hear presentations from other plants in their business unit. The best of those go to a fine hotel or resort somewhere in the world for the company's annual awards celebration, where they make their presentations to the company's most senior people.[49]

TRADITION AT HP

The famous pronouncement of Tevye, the milkman in *Fiddler on the Roof*, resonates: *Tradition!* At Hewlett-Packard, tradition is the stuff of the culture known as the HP Way, which boils down to respect for people (see Chapter 8). Among the best of the best practices in process improvement is high involvement of the work force, built necessarily on that same foundation of respect. Coupling that with the constancy (until recently) of the HP Way helps explain why HP was among the earliest and most successful western practitioners of JIT.

SPREADING THE WORD BY WEB SITE AT WEBSTER PLASTICS AND PHILLIPS PLASTICS

Some companies have gained inspiration to excel on lean/TQ by going after public awards, honors, and certifications. That route usually has not held up over time. There is reason to think that might change. Just look at the web sites of Webster Plastics and Phillips Plastics. Both include long lists of awards and recognition. Given the growing role of the Internet in finding a supplier, in this case of plastic components, these lists provide the companies with impressive credentials. They have become valued marketing tools. Marketers typically are lukewarm about lean and total quality, but here is a way to draw them in.

POST-IT NOTES AT SIMPSON LUMBER

In 1988, I visited a Simpson Lumber sawmill. A point of interest was its use of CEDAC: cause-and-effect diagram and cards. Also known as *fishbone charts* or *Ishikawa diagrams* (after their originator, Kaoru Ishikawa), the Simpson CEDAC diagrams were festooned with Post-it notes. Over the course of an improvement project, each time an idea was tried out, another note was stuck on the diagram. The notes provided a simple-to-update history of each improvement—a large, visible journal.

WHITEBOARDS AT SCHWEITZER ENGINEERING LABORATORIES

Ed Schweitzer, founder and CEO of Schweitzer Engineering Laboratories (SEL), was addressing an audience of several hundred at the company's 7th Annual Supplier Day. Schweitzer had put his company on the JIT/TQ/lean/world-class journey in 1989. He remains a strong advocate, with "keep it simple" as the effort's centerpiece. But, using whiteboards as an example, he told the audience, liberally sprinkled with SEL people, that things had gotten out of hand. Electronic data collectors are everywhere, he said, and the data-collection system has people constantly typing data into a computer where it enters a "digital Valhalla," never to be seen again. Schweitzer made it clear: Whiteboards need to be put up everywhere, as was the case when SEL was a much smaller company. This simple, convenient device must be accessible to everyone, as a highly visible way to record whatever goes wrong and whatever needs fixing.[50]

YEARBOOKS AT NIHON RADIATOR

On my first trip to Japan, executives at Nihon Radiator showed me a library of "yearbooks." Each one documented that year's improvement projects. The booklets, around 100 to 150 pages, contained graphs, tables, hand-drawn sketches, and photos of project participants. These volumes have effects similar to Milliken's keeping count of OFIs year after year. Keeping the quantity up becomes ingrained. Also, the booklets provide a history of what was tried in the past, how it worked, and where.

PERSONAL KNOWLEDGE IN PUBLIC FILES
AT MITSUBISHI ELECTRIC

In an earlier book, I cited Jeffrey Funk's report of his two years in the engineering department of a Mitsubishi Electric business unit in Japan. Every scrap of information that the engineers encountered went into public files (ordinary file cabinets), cross-referenced for easy retrieval. Engineers must comply or be seen as not team players. Information hoggers (the western norm) were not wanted. This is systematic knowledge management, 1990s style.[51] Today, no doubt, the information goes into computer files—which should make it more accessible, though less permanent.

COMPANY HISTORIES FOR PRESENT DECISIONS AT MARS

A final example, that of systematic memory preservation and aggrandizement, comes from Mars, the candy-bar maker. I learned of this about 10 years ago. In planning new plant locations around the world, Mars conducts deep analysis of plant-location decisions in the past. Its database is organized by year, location, reason for selecting that location, and comments about those reasons. Some of the reasons have stood the test of time. For example, the site for one plant was picked because it looked to be the best location for national distribution and also a low-cost facility purchase. Another site promised minimal-quantity, just-in-time transport. Hindsight analysis, however, pinned down cases of overly ambitious demand forecasts that resulted in a premature plant opening. In other cases, factors such as labor cost, now-discredited economy-of-scale beliefs, and questionable accounting practices were getting in the way of good decisions based on product and market needs.

Maybe companies need to have a position called *company historian*, charged with intervening in every significant issue, strategic or tactical. The aims would be to combat institutional forgetting and to avoid reinventing the wheel, especially the wobbly sort. Further, they would include overseeing the kind of learn-from-hindsight due diligence described above for Mars; and ensuring that the company emphasizes refresher training, not just the hot, new thing. An abiding sense of process-management history is one more way to raise people's appreciation for continuity.

As with all phenomena, physical or social, lean/TQ is subject to the law of entropy: Everything runs down. Organizations, however, can combat or stave off that fate. As von Bertalanffy put it, "Living systems can avoid the increase in entropy, and may even develop toward states of increased order and organization."[52] What is required is importing *negentropy* from outside the system. As noted in Chapter 10, negentropy is energy in the form of information. The company, business unit, or plant that is weak on process improvement needs just that: plenty of external information infused into every corner, every subsystem, of the business. Even the best companies tend to bring in vital information selectively, as we see with examples in Part V.

NOTES

1. Malcolm Baldrige National Quality Award 1989 Winner Milliken & Company, found in www.quality.nist.gov/Milliken_89.htm.
2. Unless otherwise noted, sources for this information are a combination of my own recollections and notes from visits to Milliken in the 1980s, plus later phone and e-mail contacts with the following Milliken executives: Sam Gambrell, former head of industrial engineering; and Craig Long, head of six sigma and quality.

3. Richard J. Schonberger, "Take Out What Doesn't Add Value by Doing It 'Just in Time,'" *Chemical Processing* (April 1992), pp. 58–59. The information source for the article was Sam Gambrell (industrial engineering) and Tom Malone (president), December 17, 1990.

4. Aleda Roth, "1992 OMA Leadership Forum on Cutting-Edge," *OMA Newsletter*, 6, no. 2 (Summer 1992), pp. 1, 12.

5. In the 1980s, Milliken called its suggestions "error cause removal" (ECR). That negative term was thrown out in the 1990s, and replaced by the positive, *opportunity for improvement.*

6. Robert Levering and Milton Moskowitz, "And the Winners Are . . . ," *Fortune* (January 23, 2006), pp . 89–128.

7. Zachary Schiller, "GE's Appliance Park: Rewire, or Pull the Plug?" *Business Week*, (February 8, 1993), p. 30.

8. The photo is shown in Richard J. Schonberger, *World Class Manufacturing: The Lessons of Simplicity Applied* (New York: Free Press/Simon & Schuster, 1986), pp. 11–12.

9. Or maybe inventory turns had doubled: "GE's Automated Assembly Line: High Product Quality with 50% Less Inventory," *Modern Material Handling* (May 6, 1983), pp. 41–45.

10. In 1983, GE already had assigned an individual, Edward V. Spurgeon, as Program Manager—JIT. In spreading the word, Spurgeon published "Batches of One: The Ultimate in Flexibility," *Production Engineering* (September 1983; pp. unknown).

11. Richard Schonberger was an invited speaker at the GE JIT conference.

12. A case study reports on application, as of 1982, of JIT purchasing at GE's Transportation Systems Business (rail locomotive and heavy-vehicular electric drive motors): Richard J. Schonberger, "JIT in Purchasing at GE, Erie," in *World Class Manufacturing Casebook: Implementing JIT and TQC* (New York: Free Press/Simon & Schuster, 1987), Chapter 25, pp. 212–233.

13. Jack Bergman, "VAM (Value Adding Manufacturing) in Action," presentation at Productivity's The Best of American Conference (April 23, 1990). Bergman's paper listed JIT as one of three elements of VAM at GE Nuclear Energy, and cited two years of flow-time reductions in feed powder, pellets, and rods.

14. OPTIM was featured in Thomas A. Stewart, "Westinghouse Gets Respect at Last," *Fortune* (July 3, 1989), pp. 92–98.

15. "Reaching for Quality," unpublished eight-page OPTIM Executive Summary, Westinghouse Productivity and Quality Center (May 1985).

16. From the July 1990 issue.

17. Report on the Asheville plant in "JIT Urgency Revealed During APICS Summit" (no author), *P&IM Review with APICS News* (August 1986), pp. 26–30; Vinod K. Kapoor, "Implementing JIT: Some Lessons Learned," *Automation* (May 1989), pp. 40–41; S.S. Cherukuri, "Westinghouse Electric Corporation, Construction Equipment Division, Asheville, NC Plant: Creating Employee Ownership," *Target* (November–December 1993), pp. 51–53.

18. According to a paper, "Implementing Just-in-time: Some Lessons Learned," by Vinod K. Kapoor (circa 1986), Kapoor first learned about JIT in 1980 from a monograph, "Improving Productivity: Some Case Studies by Mitsubishi." Westinghouse had invited a delegation from Mitsubishi-Japan to the United States, including a visit to the company's

new plant in Asheville. Following presentations, Mr. Tagaki, leader of the Japanese team, gave Kapoor the monograph, which was full of JIT lore. Kapoor inhaled the contents and went right to work transforming the plant.

19. Vinod K. Kapoor, "Just-in-Time and the Focused Factory," *Manufacturing Systems* (December 1989), pp. 47–49.

20. Timothy Aeppel, "How Westinghouse's Famous Name Simply Faded Away: Media-Struck CEO Didn't Follow Through on Promise to Keep Industrial Lines," *Wall Street Journal* (November 20, 1997), p. B-10.

21. Eaton's early JIT activities included inviting me to do a one-day seminar at the company's Engine Components Division in Kearney, Nebraska (September 14, 1983).

22. From author's old notes; original sources not preserved.

23. Earl W. Hildebrandt, "Workshop Report: Manufacturing Excellence Through People," *Target* (Spring 1988), pp. 20–23.

24. Lea A.P. Tonkin, "Clear Line of Sight to Excellence at Eaton Cutler-Hammer in Milton, ON," *Target*, 5th Issue (2006), pp. 20–27.

25. See, for example, Art Byrne, "How Wiremold Reinvented Itself with *Kaizen*," *Target* (January–February 1995), pp. 8–14; Thomas Fairbank, "Implementing Kaizen at the Wiremold Company: The Role of the Kaizen Promotion Office," *Conference Proceedings: The Best of North America: Becoming Lean*, Productivity, Inc., Chicago, IL (November 4–5, 1998), pp. 672–696; Clare Ansberry, "Deadline Scramble: A New Hazard for Recovery: Last-minute Pace of Orders," *Wall Street Journal* (June 25, 2002), p. A1.

26. Jeff Schaller, "Standard Work Sustains Lean and Continued Success at Wiremold," *Target* (1st qtr 2002), pp. 43–49.

27. E-mail correspondence, Orest Fiume, former Wiremold chief financial officer, to a large number of activists in the lean-accounting movement (October 3, 2006; slightly updated by Mr. Fiume, November 12, 2006).

28. Ibid.

29. Shawn Tully, "Prophet of Zero Working Capital, *Fortune* (June 13, 1994), pp. 113–114; Shawn Tully, "Raiding a Company's Hidden Cash," *Fortune* (August 22, 1994); Joseph Weber, "American Standard Wises Up," *Business Week* (November 18, 1996), pp. 70, 74; Jeffrey A. Tannenbaum, "Why Are Companies Paying Close Attention to This Toilet Maker?" *Wall Street Journal* (August 20, 1999), p. B1.

30. John H. Sheridan, "Frank Merlotti: A Master of Empowerment," *Industry Week* (January 7, 1991), pp. 24–27.

31. Robin Yale Bergstrom, "Probing the Softer Side of Steelcase," *Production* (November 1994), pp. 52–53.

32. Bruce MacDougall, "Steelcase Canada Ltd.: A Smarter Way to Work," *Target* (September–October 1996), pp. 37–40.

33. The telephone and e-mail interviews with former and current Steelcase managers took place in June through November 2006.

34. David W. Mann, "Leading a Lean Conversion: Lessons from Experience at Steelcase, Inc.," *Target* (3rd qtr 2001), pp. 28–39.

35. James Prichard, "Office-Furniture Makers Finally Sitting Prettier," Associated Press story in *Seattle Times* (May 6, 2006), p. E4.

36. Michael L. George, James Works, and Kimberly Watson-Hempbill, *Fast Innovation: Achieving Superior Differentiation, Speed to Market, and Increased Profitability* (New York: McGraw-Hill, 2005).

37. George Anders, "How Innovation Can Be too Much of a Good Thing," *Wall Street Journal*, June 11, 2007, p. B3.

38. George, et al., op. cit., p. 315.

39. See box on Quick Response Manufacturing in "Mining Boom Spurs Innovation," *Manufacturing Engineering* (March 2007), pp. 75–78.

40. Schonberger letter to Doyle Jones, GE Appliance Park (June 3, 1983).

41. Personal visit to the Parker Hannifin plant in September 2006.

42. The article cites one estimate that more than half of companies still use markup pricing: Timothy Aeppel, "Seeking Perfect Prices, CEO Tears Up the Rules," *Wall Street Journal* (March 27, 2007), pp. A1, A16.

43. Brian Maskell (BMA Inc.) and Mark Kovtan (Racor Division, Parker Hannifin), "Lean Accounting at Racor Division, Parker Hannifin," *Lean Accounting Summit Conference*, Orlando, FL (September 21–22, 2006).

44. Daniel T. Jones, "Heijunka: Leveling Production," *Manufacturing Engineering* (August 2006), pp. 29–34. See also B. J. Coleman and M. Reza Vaghefi, "Heijunka: A Key to the Toyota Production System," *Production and Inventory Management Journal* (4th qtr 1994), pp. 31–35.

45. Janice H. Hammond, "Barilla (A), (B), (C), and (D)," HBS case nos. 9-694-046, and 9-965-064, 065, and 066 (May 17, 1994).

46. See photo and discussion of the 9 minute, 43-second stamping-line changeover in Richard J. Schonberger, *World Class Manufacturing: The Next Decade* (Free Press/Simon & Schuster, 1996), pp. 31–32.

47. Peter F. Drucker, *The Age of Discontinuity: Guidelines to Our Changing Society* (New York: Harper & Row, 1968), p. 40.

48. John Prehn, Hames Hare, Kurt Vogler, and John Casey, "A Little Help from Their Friends," *Quality Digest* (March 2007), pp. 28–33.

49. The process-improvement events are resident in Baxter's long-standing Quality Leadership Process, which was inaugurated in 1985 and rolled out company-wide in 1988–89.

50. SEL was founded in the garage of Edward O. Schweitzer III in 1981, had grown to about 350 employees by 1999, and had grown to some 1,400 employees by 2007.

51. Cited in Richard J. Schonberger, *World Class Manufacturing: The Next Decade* (Free Press/Simon & Schuster, 1996), pp. 223. Original source: Jeffrey L. Funk, *The Teamwork Advantage: An Inside Look at Japanese Product and Technology Development* (Portland, OR: Productivity Press, 1992), pp. 149–149.

52. Ludwig von Bertalanffy, *General System Theory: Foundations, Development, Applications* (New York: George Braziller, 1968), p. 41.

Leanness: A Changing Landscape

We've seen that lean companies all too easily develop middle-age spread. At the same time, other companies, sometimes under the radar, have been on long-lasting, successful diets, and have become the new, global lean leaders. That is the message of the opener for Part V, Chapter 14.

Toyota gave us the lean core. Today's biggest successes in becoming lean have a lot to do with innovative practices that the lean core tends not to address. Some of the new lean exemplars are retailers, one being Wal-Mart. This chapter adds to what earlier chapters have said about practices perfected at that retail giant. A growing number of other store chains are doing well in the same dominant measures of retail success. One success parameter is ability to turn over stock quickly while keeping store shelves filled and avoiding stockouts. Another is doing so even as styles and seasons change, by squeezing out traditional weeks and months of reaction time with producer-suppliers.

While retail is a whining engine of lean innovation, it cannot rival manufacturing in ultimate leanness. Retailing requires full shelves, whereas the never-reachable ideal in manufacturing is zero inventory. Thus, the global grand champion of lean—at least in terms of the heights of inventory turnover—must be a manufacturer, namely Dell, Inc.

The four chapters in Part V are a diverse mix. The topics are:

- *Chapter 14:* The lean crown goes to Wal-Mart and Dell. Why Toyota lost it.
- *Chapter 15:* Special ways of becoming lean.
- *Chapter 16:* Designing the physical facilities so they do not clash with lean/TQ ideas.
- *Chapter 17:* Establishing strong external linkages.

Global Lean Champions: Passing the Torch

Chapters 4 and 11 have already crowned Dell in manufacturing and Wal-Mart in retailing as the new kings of lean. That may be news to many or most of the lean community, who continue to hold Toyota in highest esteem as the paragon of lean. However, its many-year performance on the inventory-based leanness scale has been poor. That does not mean anything is wrong with the Toyota *system*. It is still good as ever, as far as it goes. As for Toyota itself, the data suggest that it has not been intensively and effectively practicing a full set of lean tools.

Who is? Maybe nobody. Dell's and Wal-Mart's lean tool sets do not appear to be all that full, either, because neither is known for zealously practicing the lean core. Their advanced applications of lean in the pipelines is their chief capability. This chapter begins with relatively brief commentary on those Dell/Wal-Mart proficiencies. Following that is a close, comparative look at Toyota the company: how the world's premier automaker and money machine has faded in measures of leanness, and the long-term effects of that on its (or any company's) competitiveness.

WHERE LEAN COUNTS MOST: TIGHTENING THE CHAINS

The Dell and Wal-Mart advantage is no big secret. Anyone who reads the stories about them in the business press should roughly understand. The usual shop-floor formula that most lean-inclined companies focus on—cells, kanban, TPM, 5S, one-piece flow, kaizen events—are not the big deal. (Dell's newest domestic plant, opened in October 2005 near Winston-Salem, North Carolina, is a beehive of conveyorized automation, which is contrary to lean's vision of simplicity. Moreover, the plant is huge–750,000 square feet.[1] Chapter 16 reviews the disadvantages of very large production facilities.) Rather, in the forefront are their high-impact collaborations: across functions within each company and extending to the same in their supply-chain partners.

HOME-GROWN, OR BORROWED AND ENHANCED

Successes of Dell and Wal-Mart in lean management stem largely from home-grown practices targeted at ever-higher-velocity flows through supply chains and out to customers. Others have been borrowed but then nurtured into practices that change the industry. Some of the innovations are in physical logistics. Wal-Mart's leadership and advanced implementations in such areas as barcode/RFID-driven suppliers, vendor-managed inventory, direct shipment from suppliers, and cross-docking are well known.[2] Among its more recent ways to further quicken response and reduce inventories are: creating high-velocity warehouses;[3] elimination of slotting fees, thereby reducing overhead costs in accounting;[4] revamping store selections to accelerate turnover of popular items and sharply reduce total inventories;[5] and cutting trucking wastes by 25 percent.[6] Economics professor Jerry Hausman (MIT) has calculated the net *Wal-Mart effect* on the economy. He estimates that, between 1997 and 2001, the superstores (Wal-Mart's and, derivatively, its competitors) reduced annual inflation of food prices by 0.75 percent. "These guys have done much more than any antipoverty program," he says.[7]

Dell controls its supply pipelines better than any other company. It is equally masterful on the shipping side. Dependably quick delivery is so important to Dell that it rejects moving all its production to low-cost China. That competitive advantage would not be possible with very long shipping distances. Thus, for the sake of quick shipping, Dell maintains production within the United States, with assembly plants in Texas, North Carolina, and Tennessee. For the same reason it assembles in Brazil, Ireland, Malaysia, and China, and is bringing plants on line in India and Poland in 2007.

Other dominating excellences of both Dell and Wal-Mart are in application of information technology for synchronizing supply actions to current (not forecast) sales. Chapter 11 detailed some of the physical and IT innovations. Further comments on the IT practices follow.

IT DRIVERS

Among major retailers, there is high realization of the necessity to follow Wal-Mart's lead in IT-based inventory management (see Wal-Mart in Chapter 11). Best examples are three global clothing retailers whose success formula is to change styles, and restock stores accordingly, dozens of times per year. They are Italy's Benetton and Spain's Zara,[8] both of which have their own apparel plants, and Sweden's H&M Hennes & Mauritz, which doesn't.[9] (Who owns the manufacturing source is not all that critical.) Benetton had lost some of its quick-response edge, but has regained much of it. Five years ago, Benetton replenished its stores with new clothes monthly; now it is as often as once a week.[10] Even major fashion houses such as Louis Vuitton, Gucci, and Ferragamo are getting quick.[11] Other examples include most of the big-box retailers and many of the convenience-store chains.

With these and other retailers' demands spurring them on, some of their major suppliers have followed suit, though it is against their nature. I'm talking about packaged-goods manufacturers such as Colgate-Palmolive, Gillette, Johnson & Johnson, Kodak, L'Oreal (France), Mattel, and Rev Holdings (Revlon). All are graded *A* on leanness. Dominated by marketers, who always want more inventory, these kinds of companies must have a strong marketing reason to consider a strategy involving less. Wal-Mart and its retailing emulators seem to have succeeded in supplying that reason.

And what about Procter & Gamble, often cited for its tight partnership with Wal-Mart? That linkage was firmly established in 1988, when P&G established a dedicated Wal-Mart team. Since then, the two companies have established joint scorecards and performance measures. They do a joint demand forecast. P&G manages the inventory in Wal-Mart's DCs based on access to Wal-Mart's on-hand stock balances. P&G even placed a customer-service rep in Wal-Mart's accounts payable group.[12]

Nevertheless, P&G has faltered on leanness. Its grade had been *A,* but it fell to *B* in 2004, and then, in 2006, all the way to *D,* for a 10-year decline. Its big acquisition of Gillette in 2005 pulled down P&G's inventory turns sharply, because, in 2004, Gillette's annual turns were a lot lower, at 3.3, than P&G's were, at 5.7.

Distributors are another type of supplier, some distributing to manufacturers and others to retailers. Among the strongly *A*-graded distributors in the leanness database are Avnet for electronics, W.W. Grainger for industrial supplies, Nash Finch for groceries, and Tamro (Finland) for pharmaceuticals. In the past, distributors were esteemed by their customers for carrying a lot of inventory. That may still be the norm. Through collaboration with customers and their suppliers, however, the best distributors now have been achieving high-velocity continuous replenishment with both their customers and their own suppliers.

For savvy retailers and suppliers, smart IT is a logistics tool. Dell's IT-driven compression of both supply and demand pipelines is more than that. It is the centerpiece of its business model, *Dell-direct.* As discussed in Chapter 11, that model and how it is executed are unique; no other company has anything to compare. While other electronics companies are not copying the Dell business model, many surely are pressed by direct or indirect competition with Dell to become adept themselves in IT-driven tightening of their pipelines.

In comparison, manufacturers in other sectors are slow learners. They are eager to practice the lean core, which is within their own direct control. That is easy compared with the typical nobody-in-charge pipeline excesses. A company that lacks customer or competitive pressure to face up to the pipeline challenges needs to generate its own urgency. Reading books about supply-chain management, investing in SCM software, and attending SCM conferences is not enough.

COLLABORATION BEFORE IT

IT solutions are hollow and problematic if not built on a firm foundation. Deep-seated cross-functional actions that break up the silos open the doors to equally deep collaborations with external partners. Harnessing IT power works well only after the internal and external human collaborations.

No company is quite as systematic about this as Wal-Mart.[13] As a Harvard Business School case study puts it, "Although Wal-Mart had developed a reputation for bargaining hard, it had also progressively tried to build partnerships with a widening circle of suppliers."[14] From another case study more than a decade ago, Wal-Mart "has an 80% time advantage over a typical competitor in the industry."

Its rapid replenishment cycle (twice weekly versus the typical every two weeks) results in "asset turnover of about four times the industry average."[15] And, from a 1992 citation, "One [Wal-Mart] system allows 2,000 vendors to see immediately how their merchandise is selling."[16] These case reports from the past demonstrate that Wal-Mart has been developing its collaborative capabilities for many years.

Now Wal-Mart does its collaborations systematically, beginning with mundane data purification. With that in mind, in 2003, Church & Dwight (C&D) found itself squarely in Wal-Mart's sight lines. C&D, famous for its Arm & Hammer baking soda, also produces about 600 other products. Wal-Mart asked C&D to select one product line and clean up all the electronic data for the products. Then C&D would collaborate with Wal-Mart to ensure that both companies were using the same product names, descriptors, and attributes. C&D's IT department searched out data from its various departments; eliminated errors and redundancies; reweighed, counted, and measured; and so on.[17] With a firm foundation of clear, accurate, up-to-date data, the rest of the collaborative agenda is likely to go smoothly—as it does with Procter & Gamble (P&G).

Some 300 P&G people work in Wal-Mart's home town, Bentonville, Arkansas, "devising cross-marketing and other tie-ins." Says Tom Muccio, head of P&G's Wal-Mart team until his retirement, "The people were paid by P&G and sat in P&G's office, but it was like they were working for Wal-Mart and P&G equally."[18]

Any company can buy or develop software. That Wal-Mart and Dell have IT superiority follows from their many years of intensive formation of collaborative planning at a detailed level. With Dell, in the volatile electronics industry where suppliers are mostly oceans away, the collaborative process is at arm's length. Its impressive-looking results on the inventory turnover scale say that distance has not been a serious impediment.

TOUGH LOVE

The question arises: Doesn't the lean core also include close partnerships with suppliers? It does. A partnership, though, can be tight or standoffish, benevolent or in-your-face.

The classic lean partnership follows the model as it developed in Japan three or four decades ago. The partnerships were shaped by Japan's cartel-like *keiretsu* system, aka Japan, Inc., once thought to be a bulwark of Japan's industrial might.[19] *Keiretsu* are highly protective of all members, which means the prominent, wealthy companies help the smaller, weaker ones, financially and otherwise. It is a teacher–pupil kind of partnership. The bigger companies, those higher on the pyramid, are the teachers. They do extensive missionary work with lower-level suppliers, the subservient pupils, to bring about quality at the source and deliveries by kanban.

In the *keiretsu* that Nissan belonged to, former high-ranking Nissan managers were running many of the group's smaller companies. "This made it very difficult for Nissan to refuse to buy from these *keiretsu* companies, even when they were not competitive."[20] Shaky, low-performing companies that would have gone bankrupt elsewhere in the world rarely did when *keiretsu*-protected. Call it the teach-them, pamper-them, shelter-them model.

When those practices came across the oceans along with JIT and TQC, the teach-them part, along with supplier reduction, made good sense. The rest did not. In the West, it was swim or sink—and, by the way, reduce your prices 7 percent yearly. Call it the bittersweet model of supplier partnership.

Wal-Mart suppliers, newer ones anyway, might like that term: "Bittersweet, yes—fits our situation to a T." But most who supply to Wal-Mart benefit enormously. They must learn and apply Wal-Mart's leading-edge technologies and joint strategic planning. Both parties' best interests are in keeping the relationship going. According to one report, Wal-Mart "is reliable." In contrast, "You can be out of Target on a week's notice. Wal-Mart doesn't play that game."[21] The game Wal-Mart does play, though, is intensive and demanding. A Wal-Mart supplier becomes a stronger, more efficient one, better able to survive, maybe even thrive in today's high-risk, business world. It's tough love, sincerely Wal-Mart.

These lessons have not been lost on Japan. The *Wall Street Journal* explained that when major manufacturers began to restructure, the *keiretsu* that had propped up the money-losers no longer were "big happy famil[ies]" but became "a bit dysfunctional."[22] Nissan Motor is an example. When Carlos Ghosn of Renault took the reins at Nissan in 1999, he set about dissolving Nissan's *keiretsu* ties with hundreds of suppliers, sticking with just four of them. Soon Mazda and Mitsubishi Motors began to do the same.[23] The closed relationships gave way to open supplier selection, introducing beneficial competition. At Toyota, though, founding family members may have resisted these changes to the status quo.[24]

Wal-Mart and Dell, and their dual (internal to external) collaboration practices, have elevated global standards of competitiveness. However, Toyota and its famous production system still are held in high esteem. We turn now to a deeper look at that company and system.

TOYOTA: MIXED MESSAGES

In sea-life outings, sighting a whale sends everybody to that side of the boat. The nagging concern: Is anyone left to see what magnificence might be stirring in the water on the other side?[25]

In manufacturing, Toyota is the whale. We're all watching, talking about, listening to, and emulating Toyota. And why not? In its category and most others, too, Toyota has long been the best and the richest. It is number three on *Fortune*'s 2007 list of the World's Most Admired Companies. (But not its dealerships, which "continue to score poorly in customer satisfaction."[26]) Its production-management system (plus other excellences) got it there. Keeping watch on the other side of the boat seemed unnecessary. Toyota itself seems not to have kept that watch.

That shows in the form of rising, level, then plunging inventory turnover. In 1983, Toyota was turning its inventory 18.3 times per year—excellent, unmatched in its industry and most others.[27] Over the next five years, its turns rose higher, to 22.9 in 1988. Five years later, in 1993, it was still 22.9—no improvement. And then the plunge, down to 10.1 turns in 2006. Toyota's balance sheets break down total inventory into its three components. High growth of finished vehicles and for-sale parts in the pipelines since 1993 is the main offender. Toyota's finished goods rose from about 12 days' supply in the early 1990s to 26 days' worth in 2006. Its other inventories have grown to a lesser degree: raw materials from 2 to 5.1 days' worth, and WIP from 3 to 5.4 days' worth.

Meanwhile, Honda's inventory turns improved steadily from 1979 to the 2000s (raw and WIP turns somewhat, and finished-goods turns greatly), dropping off some in the past four years. Even troubled General Motors has been able to elevate its turns, over a 32-year time span since 1974. Lean, by itself, is no ticket to financial health. With its lean trend, though, GM has staved off a much worse financial plight. Every tick upward in inventory turns generates cash flow and quick-response benefits, helping keep the Grim Reaper away.

Exhibit 14.1 shows trends for the three automakers. Others in the industry (not shown) are a mixed bag, some with poor trends, others good ones. Long-term though unsteady improvement trends are the case for DaimlerChrysler, Ford, Nissan, Renault, and India's Tata Motors and Hindustan Motors. Except for the two Indian companies, these are, like Toyota, global manufacturers. Supporting international operations makes inventory management difficult. Yet some firms, automotive and otherwise, are able to keep "leaning out" their inventories while stretching their supply lines across continents.

Chapter 20 reviews the motor-vehicle industry—from cars to trucks to combines to motorcycles—in more detail. Here, because we've taken Toyota to task, we offer a few more comments on why it is still the giant of the automotive industry even as its application of its own lean system seems to have faltered. Also, we address the implications, for Toyota or any other high flyer, of long-term weakened performance on the inventory metric.

[Personal demurral: In 1981, I became one of the earliest westerners to be a convert to and apostle of (through various published works) the lean practices that had been honed at Toyota. I gave no thought to looking for flaws in how Toyota does its business—until the company's sharp downslide in inventory turns began to reveal itself in the late 1990s. When the data talk, you have to listen, even when it goes against dominant mindsets—yours and others'.[28]]

THE LONG AND THE SHORT OF TOYOTA

As compared with all other automakers, Toyota is about the best and among the worst on two common business measures—wealth generation and long-term inventory trend, respectively. Precise explanations for this best–worst oddity would require a good deal of study of a complex company in a complex industry. Such penetrating analysis is lacking, but a few likely explanations suggest themselves. They are

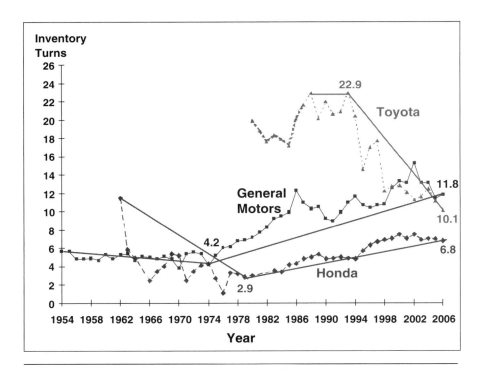

Exhibit 14.1   Toyota Declining, Honda/GM Gaining

expressed here in the form of several hypotheses. (From my dictionary, a *hypothesis* is something "highly probable" but as yet unproven.) Six hypotheses, numbered from H1 to H6, follow.

- *H1*: Rapid and accelerating global growth has generated wealth for Toyota, but it has fallen behind in matching that growth with sufficient human talent to keep up and maintain quality and tight internal and external coordination.

  Discussion: The business press has been reporting on Toyota's quest to be the world's biggest automaker (see rapid-growth discussion in Chapter 12). This strategy is puzzling. Long thought of as a conservative company, Toyota has been admired for excellence in process improvement, made the more possible because of its former slow, careful global expansion. For example, in 1994, the Chinese government imposed restrictions on foreign automakers in order to give its domestic makers an advantage. "Toyota was not willing to play ball."[29] (GM, VW, and Ford were, and GM has become strong and profitable in China.)

  A 2004 lead article in the *Wall Street Journal*[30] says, "Torrid growth has spread thin the company's famed Japanese quality gurus." (Similar stories have peppered the business press for the past three years.[31]) The story includes examples. At Toyota's flagship North American plant in Georgetown, Kentucky, quality problems are growing in cars assembled there. Contributing to that, assemblers are violating some aspects of "standard work," and are sometimes misidentifying the proper part to install in the next model coming down the line. Toyota's new standard-bearer plant in Tsutsumi, Japan, is devising solutions. One remedy is contrary to TPS/JIT/lean principles. Tsutsumi is replacing lineside racks holding different parts for different models with in-sequence kits of parts prepared offline by logistics employees. But kitting is a non-value-adding activity that injects delay and inventory, raises labor and administrative costs through double handling, takes responsibility away from assemblers, and introduces one more potential source of error. (Art Smalley, expert commentator on Toyota and TPS, authored a several-page critique of this material-handling practice. He recognizes the deficiencies but suggests some benefits; for example, there is less clutter in the work areas.[32])

- *H2*: The methodologies that make up TPS/lean are too numerous even for Toyota to keep good tabs on and allegiance to. (See "Drowning in the Basics" in Chapter 10.)

  Discussion: The H1 note about the turn toward kitting is supportive of this hypothesis. In the news also are stories about training lapses within Toyota. Two articles are specific to the NUMMI (New United Motors Manufacturing, Inc.) plant in Fremont, California, a joint venture between Toyota and GM that began in 1984. The first article states, "The Toyota management which runs the plant sought to re-emphasize the workforce's employment of TPS."[33] The second says much the same thing, pointing out the need for operatives to know about things like kanban.[34] In other words, the work force may have received TPS training and learned kanban in the past, but the learning had faded and required "re-emphasis."

  Another report is about "Toyota University" in Gardena, California. Established in 1998 to train Toyota employees, the facility a few years ago began admitting trainees from other companies. Most paid for the privilege, but as a public service Toyota offered training free to Los Angeles police and, in 2005, the U.S. military. Toyota's quality woes and recalls, however, have halted the training of outsiders, so that the university could concentrate on training its own.[35]

  Those examples of lean stumbles may just be isolated exceptions. However, Katsuaki Watanabe, the new (as of June 2005) president of Toyota Motor Company, seems concerned. Reportedly, in about 2002, he and colleagues "began pushing the company's powerful manufacturing gurus to re-think Toyota's much-admired 'lean production.'" They found out that most of its machines "were too big, clunky and slow." Besides attacking the monuments, new goals include "coming up with a new type of low-cost factory," cutting assembly lines' length in half, and halving the number of components.[36] These goals sound like those of a company new to lean, not the world's foremost epitome of it.

- *H3*: The company's rapid and accelerating global growth clashes with its traditional insularity and has been a principal cause of fast-growing pipeline inventories and lead times.

  Discussion: Historically, Toyota's plants and those of most of its suppliers had been clustered around Toyota's headquarters in Nagoya, Aiichi Prefecture, nicknamed "Toyota-City." As "Doc" Hall puts it, "No other auto company has ever had operations so geographically concentrated. . . . Communication by see-and-do was easy."[37] With the Toyota system having grown up in that compact, simplified environment, it may be harder for Toyota than other auto-makers to adapt its lean/quick-response system for global operations. The advantages of clustering are missing in North America as well, a result of Toyota's strategy—for political reasons—of locating each plant in a different state or province.[38] Lack of experience in managing globally may partly explain Toyota's growing inventories of purchased materials and finished vehicles.

  In contrast to Toyota, Honda's plants historically were stretched out along Japan's 2,000-mile archipelago. Honda also was the first Japanese automaker to begin manufacturing in the United States. Today, Honda imports about one-third of the vehicles it sells in the U.S. market, whereas Toyota imports about half. That is a lot of Toyota cars spending weeks on the ocean. Having more experience outside of Japan may partly explain Honda's long-term improvement in inventory turnover versus Toyota's worsening trend (though Toyota's absolute numbers still are higher). Some western automakers have many decades of global experience. For example, Ford established Ford of Britain in 1911.[39] Continental Europe did not open its trade barriers, thereby admitting Japanese car makers, until 1999.[40]

- *H4*: Toyota's superiority in manufacturing engineering offsets its declining leanness/growing inventories.

  Discussion: Toyota's excellence need not be, or stay, in lean operations. In manufacturing, the essential locus of success lies way before that—in engineering. Most years, the quality of Toyota vehicles has been at or near the top. More than assembled in, that quality has to be engineered in: the design of the product; of the suppliers' components; and of the tooling, the plants, and the plant facilities.

  Toyota's factories may now have better equipment than any other automaker. And why not? Toyota has far more wealth to invest. James Harbour, chairman and founder of the *Harbour Report*, is far more knowledgeable than I about the industry, and he says Toyota spends twice as much on its factory equipment and facilities than most competitors.[41] Maybe that is somewhat overstated, but considering the source, the opinion can hardly be discounted.

  Toyota, and Honda as well, exceed western competitors in flexibility to quickly launch new models and to run multiple models down a production line. The root of that daunting capability is platform design, which takes place in engineering. More than just vehicle architecture, platform flexibility is integration of product design and equipment design. Specifically, it integrates (1) a small number of standard car or truck platforms on which various models can be built, with (2) flexible equipment that can handle a variety of models.

It takes many years for these engineering-based strengths to build and become entrenched. Sometimes that deep-set expertise can go too far. As with any other function, engineering can be too dominant in a closed-minded way. More on that topic in Chapter 15.

- *H5*: Resistance at Toyota to management ideas originating elsewhere has had negative effects on the company's pursuit of lean.

  Discussion: Systems theory, brought out of the classroom in recent years to help explain strong and weak performances in business, distinguishes between open and closed systems. Toyota has been used as an example of the former, that is, open to the import of information and ideas. Some evidence, though, suggests the opposite, that of closed-system tendencies. For example, the public's long-term high regard for the quality of Toyota vehicles contrasts with its low regard for the quality of Toyota's dealerships.[42] That suggests that quality at Toyota stops at the shipping dock and is not treated as a system-wide concern.

  Deeper evidence: Toyota is the fulcrum of Japan's largest *keiretsu*, consisting of nearly 250 companies linked by cross-stock ownership and decades of mutual support. Many or most of Toyota's suppliers belong to that *keiretsu*. Meanwhile, most other *keiretsu* have been undergoing breakups, opening their members to outside influences, to best-practice innovations, and to tougher competition. Supplier-partners weakened by over-protection may have contributed to Toyota's growing inventories, and also to higher costs of its purchased materials. Toyota's CEO Katsuaki Watanabe was head of purchasing in the late 1990s. He became upset at the suggestion from a rival that Toyota was paying too much for parts as compared with peers. He spearheaded an effort to get suppliers active in designing the cost out of parts[43]—on undertaking of Western origin called DFMA.

  The Japanese automakers, especially Toyota, have been slow to embrace potent "foreign" ideas, such as modular supply and smaller, leaner factories.[44]

- *H6*: While the quality, including fuel efficiency, of main competitors' products has risen to about equal that of Toyota,[45] customers' perceptions lag. Thus, Toyota is still able to outsell and out-earn makers of other nearly as good cars and trucks.

  Discussion: Perception of quality has long been recognized as ranking sometimes as high as actual quality as a determinant of what the customer will buy.[46] As for fuel economy, *Business Week* reports that "GM has 23 models that get 30-plus miles per gallon—more than Toyota or Honda."[47]

  Why haven't poor rankings of Toyota dealerships translated into poor perceptions overall? Maybe it's because car dealerships are notoriously abhorrent to the car-buying public. We car buyers have become resigned to it and see no reason to expect Toyota dealers to be any better. The best automakers aggressively and successfully demand quality from their independently owned suppliers; there is no reason why they should not be equally ardent about quality of the dealerships, which also are largely independently owned.

Most big companies have down years that they recover from in a later cycle. By many measures, Toyota is hardly down. No doubt some of the six hypotheses, and Toyota's downward trend in inventory turnover, are issues that are already matters of concern at the company. Moreover, it still has the prestige and wealth to attract the best talent in its industry and from other industries as well. Toyota may continue to dominate its industry for many years.

The greater issue for this book concerns the majority of companies and why they cannot master or retain mastery of the lean and total-quality fundamentals. Chapter 15 explores that question.

NOTES

1. John S. McClenahen, "Factory of the Future," *Industry Week* (February 2007), pp. 21–22.

2. Wal-Mart is "identified as the king of crossdocking," in Ray Kulwiec, "Crossdocking as a Supply Chain Strategy," *Target*, 3rd issue (2004), pp. 28–35.

3. K. Hudson, "Wal-Mart's Need for Speed," *Wall Street Journal* (September 26, 2005), p. B4.

4. J. Adamy, "New Food, New Look," *Wall Street Journal* (November 21, 2005), p. R8.

5. K. Hudson and A. Zimmerman, "Wal-Mart Aims to Sharply Cut Its Inventory Costs," *Wall Street Journal* (April 20, 2006), p. B2.

6. J. Covert, "Wal-Mart Boosts Truck Fuel Efficiency," *Wall Street Journal* (April 25, 2006), p. B3A.

7. Mar Whitehouse, "How Wal-Mart's Price Cutting Influences Both Rivals and Inflation," *Wall Street Journal* (November 25–26, 2006), p. A4.

8. "Zara can design, produce, and distribute a new garment in three weeks," Kasra Ferdows, "New World Manufacturing Order," *Industrial Engineer* (February 2003), pp. 28–33.

9. "While traditional clothing retailers design their wares at least six months ahead of time, H&M can rush items into stores in as little as three weeks," Steve Hamm, "How Smart Companies Are Creating New Products—and Whole New Businesses—Almost Overnight," *Business Week* (March 27, 2006), pp. 69–71. See also Kerry Capell and Gerry Khermouch, "Hip H&M," *Business Week* (November 11, 2002), pp. 106–110.

10. Stacy Meichtry, "Benetton Picks Up the Fashion Pace," *Wall Street Journal* (April 10, 2007), pp. B1–B2.

11. Christina Passariello, "Louis Vuitton Tries Modern Methods on Factory Lines," *Wall Street Journal* (October 9, 2006), p. A1; Carol Matlack, Rachel Tiplady, Diane Brady, Robert Berner, and Hiroko Tashiro, "The Vuitton Machine," *Business Week* (March 22, 2004), pp. 98–102; Alessandra Galloni, "At Gucci, Mr. Polet's New Design Upends Rules for High Fashion," *Wall Street Journal* (August 9, 2005), pp. A1, A5. On Ferragamo and others, Cecile Rohwedder, "Making Fashion Faster," *Wall Street Journal* (February 24, 2004), p. B1.

12. Michael Graen and Michael Shaw, "Supply-Chain Partnership between P&G and Wal-Mart," in *E-Business Management: Integration of Web Technologies and Business Models* (Dordrecht, Netherlands: Kluwer Academic Publishers, 2003), pp. 155–172. Alternate source: http://citebm.business.uiuc.edu/IT_cases/Graen-Shaw-PG.pdf.

13. B. Saporito, "Is Wal-Mart Unstoppable?" *Fortune* (May 6, 1991), pp. 50–59.

14. P. Ghemawat, K. Mark, and S. P. Bradley, "Wal-Mart Stores in 2003," Harvard Business School case study 9-704-430 (October 2003).

15. Society of Management Accountants of Canada, "Becoming a Time-Based Competitor: Appendix A Case Study," Management Accounting—Guideline 22 (January 1994), pp. 39–42.

16. Wendy Zellner, "O.K., So He's Not Sam Walton," *Business Week* (March 16, 1992), pp. 56–58.

17. Laurie Sullivan, "Slow to Synch," *Information Week* (June 7, 2004).

18. Sarah Ellison, Ann Zimmerman, and Charles Forelle, "P&G's Gillette Edge: The Playbook It Honed at Wal-Mart," *Wall Street Journal* (January 31, 2005), pp. A1, A12.

19. "Sumitomo: How the '*Keiretsu*' Pulls Together to Keep Japan Strong," *Business Week* (March, 31, 1973).

20. Risaburo Nezu, "Carlos Ghosn: Cost Controller or Keiretsu Killer?" *OECD Observer* (April 2000), p. 17.

21. Quoted in Charles Fishman, *The Wal-Mart Effect: How the World's Most Powerful Company Really Works—and How It's Transforming the American Economy* (New York: Penguin, 2006), pp. 56–57.

22. M. Williams, "When *Keiretsu* Lose Their *Way*, It's Time for a Name Change: The One Big Happy Family That Long Was Japan Inc. Now Is a Bit Dysfunctional," *Wall Street Journal* (April 27, 2000), pp. A1, A12.

23. Akio Okamura, "Beyond the Keiretsu," *Automotive Development & Production* (September 2005), pp. 20–22.

24. Emily Thornton, "Mystery at Toyota's Top," *Business Week Online* (April 26, 1999), p. 52.

25. Metaphor borrowed from a National Public Radio "Morning Edition" report (October 28, 2005). Susan Spaulding, a national security consultant, said the Pentagon's homeland defense agency, NORTHCOM (U.S. Northern Command) was doing whale watching by expending high activity on natural disasters—hurricanes, floods, earthquakes—but little on its primary mission of anti-terrorism.

26. David Welch, "Staying Paranoid at Toyota," *BusinessWeek* (July 2, 2007), pp. 80–82.

27. Data prior to 1983 are not usable, because Toyota was legally two companies—the manufacturing arm and the distribution arm—with two separate financial reports.

28. So much is said about Toyota's excellence that negative evidence tends to be pushed aside or discounted. This sort of tendency, arising in a variety of fields, has been called *publication bias*, "the tendency of scientists to report findings that support some point . . . but to bury examples that undercut it ." "You hear stories about negative studies getting stuck in a file drawer. . . ." Sharon Begley, "New Journals Bet 'Negative Results' Save Time, Money," *Wall Street Journal* (September 15, 2006), p . B1.

29. Gordon Fairclough, "GM's Chinese Partner Looms as a New Rival," *Wall Street Journal* (April 20, 2007), pp. A1, A8.

30. Norihiko Shirouzu and Sebastian Moffett, "As Toyota Closes In on GM, It Develops a Big Three Problem," *Wall Street Journal* (August 4, 2004), pp. A1–A2.

31. A more recent example: Amy Chozick, "Toyota's Net Shows Sting of Rapid Growth," *Wall Street Journal* (May 10, 2007), p. A3.

32. Other benefits, to the assemblers (fewer parts-selection errors, easier training, and more value-added time), are offset by the opposite for the new material handlers (more chances for errors, more people to train, more non-value-added work): Art Smalley, "Toyota's New Material-Handling Systems Shows TPS's Flexibility," www.lean.org/community/ registered/articledocuments/tps_flexibility2.html (October 15, 2006).

33. Patrick Waurzyniak, "Lean at NUMMI," *Manufacturing Engineering* (September 2005), pp. 73–84.

34. Tim Simmons, "NUMMI Plant a Model for Ailing Car Industry," *Tri-Valley Herald Online*, CA (March 5, 2006); cited in *Superfactory Newsletter* (March 13, 2006).

35. Mike Spector and Gina Chon, "Toyota University Opens Admissions to Outsiders," *Wall Street Journal* (March 15, 2007), pp. B1, B4.

36. Norihiko Shirouzu, "As Rivals Catch Up, Toyota CEO Spurs Big Efficiency Drive," *Wall Street Journal* (December 9, 2006), pp. A1, A6.

37. Robert W. Hall, personal correspondence (October 9, 2004).

38. The North American plants have other deficiencies besides their dispersed locations. Though some Toyota plants in Japan have the flexibility to build more than six different vehicle models, most of its eight U.S. plants are limited to one or two: Norihiko Shirouzo, "Toyota's New U.S. Plan: Stop Building Factories," *Wall Street Journal* (June 20, 2007), pp. A1, A14.

39. Gary S. Vasilash, "Speaking European at Ford," *Automotive Design and Production* (April 2006), p. 52.

40. Stephen Power, "Europe's Car Makers Face Turmoil as Japanese Gain in Market Share," *Wall Street Journal* (October 14, 2004), p. A1.

41. Interview (September 2005). Mr. Harbour, and the *Harbour Report*, have long been among the most authoritative voices on the state of the automotive industry.

42. David Welch, "Staying Paranoid at Toyota," op cit.

43. Norihiko Shirouzu, "As Rivals Catch Up, Toyota CEO Spurs Big Efficiency Drive," *Wall Street Journal* (December 9, 2006), pp. A1, A6.

44. "Unlike the U.S. and European automaker, the Japanese auto industry has shown few visible initiatives toward modularization": A. Takeishi and T. Fujimoto, "Modularization in the Auto Industry: Interlinked Multiple Hierarchies of Product, Production, and Supplier Systems," 1st draft (February 28, 2001).

45. Norihiko Shirouzu, "Big Three Gain on Japanese Rivals," *Wall Street Journal* (June 2, 2006), p. A8.

46. One of many sources on the power of perception in the quality arena is: David A. Garvin, *Managing Quality: The Strategic and Competitive Edge* (New York: Free Press, 1988), pp. 49ff.

47. David Kiley, " 'Just as Good as Toyota' Is a Tough Sell," *Business Week* (December 11, 2006), pp. 38–39.

Chapter 15

How Overweight Companies Get Lean

This chapter examines special (not routine) ways that fat companies or business units have become lean. Most special of all are ways to pump up the human organization and keep its best people challenged. The chapter also looks at a common phenomenon: a company that once had employed the lean agenda with success, lost interest, and some years later stoked the lean embers and has them throwing off heat again. The discussion then turns to two common, critical tendencies that stand in the way of getting, or rejuvenating, process improvement. One is the products themselves—how they, and their components, tend to proliferate destructively. The other is company education and training, which often appear to be watered down, even in companies that have their own "university."

IMPORTING/EXPORTING LEAN EXPERTISE THROUGH ACQUISITIONS AND MERGERS

For the lean-driven company, one route to success is paved with astute acquisitions, mergers, and divestitures. Chapter 4 explored that topic as a side issue. Here the matter comes up again, this time with emphasis on the expertise angle. Deliberately or accidentally, some acquirers end up with additional lean/total quality know-how and experience that rivals the value of the acquired company itself. Two examples follow: Cardinal Health's acquisition of Alaris Medical and Terex's of Genie Industries.

CARDINAL HEALTH: ACQUIRING MORE THAN JUST A COMPANY

In 2004, when Cardinal Health, the medical-products giant, bought Alaris Medical, Alaris was an attractive catch.[1] Its shares traded at a solid $20, and it had recently been invited to join the New York Stock Exchange. It had strong credentials in process improvement with inventory turns at 4.8. That is higher than that of all 10 roughly similar U.S.-based medical-products companies represented in the leanness database.

Four years earlier, Alaris enjoyed the singular dishonor of being the most heavily debt-laden medical-device company in the United States. Its share price had fallen to 31 cents, and it had been booted from the NASDAQ exchange for not meeting their minimum requirements, given the combination of low share price and negative net worth. On-time deliveries were 80 percent in an industry where hospitals expected overnight response, and first-year warranty repair rates were a high 13 percent. Seeing

Alaris's stock price spiraling downward, hospital customers were backing off. Salespeople were spending 40 percent of their time on quality matters and on trying to put a healthy face on the company so as not to lose customers.

In an effort to stem the bleeding, Alaris hired David Schlotterbeck as president and CEO. Schlotterbeck was a rare commodity, having led or been in the thick of several prior lean/TQ transformations. They began in the mid-1980s with CalComp, where he was vice president of R&D. At Alaris, Schlotterbeck touched off a solid recovery featuring quality-based process improvement. Alaris's warranty repair rates fell to 2.5 percent. Its infusion-pumps business suffered only one product recall in the next four years, as compared with 47 recalls among Alaris's two other major competitors. Alaris's achievements on the lean front were written up in *Target*.[2]

Prior to Alaris, Schlotterbeck was president and CEO of Pacific Scientific, producing motion control, process measurement, and safety products. Pacific needed help. The share price was languishing at about $11 in 1997, having fallen from the $20s. Sales were down, and product offerings were a conglomeration of 13 lines. In fixing the company, Schlotterbeck explains, "we took a very rapid approach, since by now, the methodology was well understood." Within months inventories were down, profits up, and the share price had risen to the mid-to-high teens. Soon, larger competitors were noticing and tendering offers to buy Pacific Scientific. One offer turned into a hostile takeover bid at a price of $20.50. The share price kept rising to an unsustainable $24. To avoid the takeover, and possible investor lawsuits for rejecting it, the board put the company up for auction. By January 1998, three companies, Emerson Electric, Square D, and Danaher, had negotiated offers to buy Pacific Scientific, each for more than $30 per share. The winner, at a $30.25 price, was Danaher—happily another believer in process improvement.

Prior to Pacific Scientific, Schlotterbeck was executive vice president and COO from 1991 to 1994 at Nellcor, also a medical-products company. It was another successful turnaround.

No doubt, when Cardinal Health acquired Alaris, it was for more than just the company. Cardinal needed someone to spearhead a lean/TQ effort, and Schlotterbeck had the credentials. Experienced, high-level executives and turnaround artists are plentiful. But those with process improvement as the leading-edge strategy for elevating a company's fortunes are rare.

TEREX ACQUIRES A LEAN GENIE

Terex, producer of construction equipment headquartered in Westport, Connecticut, has been on an acquisition binge, growing sales from $1.8 billion in 2001 to more than $7 billion in 2006. Its purchase of Redmond (Washington)-based Genie Holdings in September 2001was special. Rarely do acquisitions have as large an effect on company management as Genie has had for Terex. Hall states that Genie is "relatively mature in lean and quality, becoming 'Toyota-like' in process improvement." And, "Genie's system is being used as the model to transform all of Terex." It is the platform for the Terex Business System, which is meant to take in more than just operations. Thirty-eight members of the Genie leadership team have been dispersed to various Terex business units.[3] A few remarks about Genie's deep-set lean expertise follow. We begin in the past tense in order to show its lengthy history of gaining that expertise, and then describe the company in more recent terms.

Genie, producer of construction hoists, lifts and booms, began with a total-quality initiative in the early 1980s. Assisting were consultants from Delta Point. Colin Fox, lead consultant, had earned his lean/TQ spurs in the early 1980s at Omark Industries of Portland, Oregon, which was one of the first non-Japanese companies to plunge fully into JIT/TQC. By the time of my first visit to Genie, in 1994, when the company was still small and local, Genie had achieved a good deal. It had reduced manufacturing flow time from 3 to 4 weeks to 3 to 4 days and cut work-in-process inventories 60 percent. Thirty JIT suppliers delivered every day (American Steel twice daily), commonly in pre-kitted sets. Assembly was mixed-model with a large (80-foot) lift interspersed with a few smaller lifts for good balance. Electrical cells, in the middle, were on pull (kanban) links to the main line. Ninety-five percent of orders for service parts, a large business, were shipped same day.

Production in the aluminum building was all cellular: welding fabrication, then out to the next building for paint, and back for subassembly and final assembly. Two carousels in the center held fabricated masts vertically. The build rate for masts was 35 per day. Beside each carousel was a vertical stand holding about 52 kanban disks. A carousel opening was the authority to fabricate another mast section. Work orders had been almost abolished in favor of kanban, the exceptions being a few items from long-lead-time suppliers.[4]

By 2006, Genie had systemized process improvement.[5] Each plant has a "Moonshine Shop" where skilled operators take turns working on carts, fixtures, and other devices for tryout in operations. A tooling shop applies higher precision to devices needed to provide and hold tighter tolerances. A third support area keeps track of changes and progress on improvement projects, and coordinates revisions. The Mooseworks (the name taken from the old TV show, *Northern Exposure*) is an experimental production area. There, Genie people thoroughly study production processes; they develop and build their own right-sized production equipment, and continually come up with new wrinkles for leaner performance. In assembly, an overhead monitor visible to everyone tracks completions at each work-station against a takt time. Slow stations are candidates for improvement or for rebalancing the work. (Precor, featured in Chapter 13, uses the same system for tracking work-station completions, with the aim of improving the slowest.) Genie's lean journey has not been impaired by the common trap of growing production by enlarging its manufacturing buildings. Each of Genie's six major focused factories is 200,000 square feet with 400 employees. (Chapter 16 includes discussion of the unlean nature of large manufacturing buildings.)

For some 20 years, Genie has hosted carloads and busloads of visitors, especially from Boeing, whose main operations share the same Puget-Sound region with Genie. Many companies have learned a good deal from Genie about lean, total quality, and related topics. Now, through ownership, Terex is the beneficiary.

CHALLENGE PEOPLE, OR THEY STAGNATE—OR THEY'RE GONE

When Terex acquired Genie, the 38 experts from Genie's leadership team who fanned out at Terex got a new lease on their work lives. They had already led the transformation at Genie, and now they had a new challenge, no doubt with high potential for reward. (Colin Fox, from Genie, became a Terex executive vice president.) Had Genie stayed put, plenty of its best people, with all that knowledge and experience, would surely have been hired away. Boeing, growing fast and enamored with lean, needed them. The same was true for another area company, Paccar, ranked second best among 54 motor-vehicle manufacturers on long-term leanness (see Chapter 20). Genie could have taken the Graco route, adopting a new grow-by-acquisition strategy. That would have provided an alternative outlet for suppressed talent. But the Terex option presented itself, and Genie took it.

Illinois Tool Works is the esteemed model of how to grow by acquisition, putting to use its own unique lean formula (80–20) at each new member of the ITW family. In 2005, ITW began implementing a new innovation. Executives began training a wide assortment of managers in how to make acquisitions.[6] By early 2007, some 160 people from sales, auditing, engineering, plant management, and so on had been trained with the expectation that they would seek out great companies to bring into the ITW fold.

The results have shown up quickly. After an off year, 2006 produced a new company record: 53 acquisitions valued collectively at about $1.7 billion. That is a per-unit average of $32 million. That is well within the ballpark of ITW's typical acquisitions—mostly smaller makers of industrial parts, supplies, and end-products. Such modest-sized targets are plentiful. The usual big-company way of finding and studying good candidates—a small team of high-powered acquisition specialists—would be hard pressed to do more than scratch the surface. For its part, ITW had never even had an acquisitions and mergers team, instead relying on small numbers of high-level executives and managers to find candidate companies. So now ITW has a large, eager cadre scouring the global landscape. They study, they travel, they make PowerPoint presentations at headquarters, they negotiate, and they deliver a new company to keep ITW growing. And they follow through by ensuring that the newly acquired get "80-20'ed," thereby squeezing out weak practices and maximizing gains.

Other companies have their own ways of keeping their people from going stale—and decamping for greener pastures:

- *Wiremold:* Plentiful lean improvements at Wiremold (wire management systems for buildings) freed up employees to staff an in-house JIT group. That allowed the company largely to wean itself off outside consultants, while also providing a more interesting and rewarding work life for those in the JIT office. Wiremold spokesman Jeff Madsen sees the transition to an in-house group as a key to sustaining the lean culture.[7]

- *Freudenberg-NOK:* At FNOK (oil-sealing devices mainly for the automotive industry), improvement is spelled *GROWTTH—Get Rid Of Waste Through Team*

*H*armony. As one of its plants achieves excellence in lean, it puts some of its best lean implementers into GROWTTH teams that take temporary assignments at other FNOK sites that need help. To keep this going, the company keeps adding plants, often in close geographical proximity to customer sites for maximum customer focus.[8]

How did all this get started? Joseph Day, who, as FNOK's chairman, gets much of the credit for the company's continuing lean successes, explains. "For the first 18 months or so, we had Toyota-trained teachers in our facility showing us the way." But the preference of those visitors was less to teach and more to do it themselves, which Day refers to as "sort of a drive-by kaizen." FNOK launched its own training unit called The Lean Center, which turns out internal experts via 10-week learning/doing programs.[9]

- *Hon Industries:* At HNI, each quarter brings another group of operators into the Rapid Continuous Improvement (RCI) department. There they study improvement tools in the lean core and apply their skills along with full-time RCI staff on projects.[10] Thus, unlike Wiremold and FNOK, it's not just the professionals and managers who have their chance at uplifting work opportunities.

- *R.W. Lyall:* This small producer of plastic pipes and connectors for household gas delivery has been a popular benchmarking site in its Los Angeles locale. Lyall's lean successes, largely generated by the production work force, led to assignment of several operators as a lean manufacturing implementation group.[11] But the plant was too small to continually challenge and inspire the lean team. Meanwhile, the owners had been studying a few other manufacturers for a possible acquisition. Loss of the lean-team leader to one of the visiting benchmarking companies prodded the owners to act. They bought a small, local manufacturer, which provided new pastures to which Lyall's best people could extend their expertise.

Of course, many companies do not have large concerns about retaining their lean/ TQ talents. They are too bogged down with organizational complexities, bad habits, and rigidities to achieve much development of those talents. Ways to deal with that matter follow.

COMBATING BUREAUCRATIZATION AND INERTIA

Among the various descriptors of lean, one of the most fitting is *simplicity*. However, many lean initiatives, in large corporations anyway, are mind-numbingly complex: elaborate, multi-layered plans; heavy-handed assessment visits by corporate; and a full set of goals and metrics of the kinds faulted in Chapters 6 and 7.

A complex plan, though, is better than little or nothing. And still today there are plenty of companies that are too busy with daily business to have any time for process improvement. Jerry Feingold and Bob Miller say that is often the case in the medical-devices sector, which is Miller's milieu. (Miller is director of advanced factory management at Advanced Bionics of Sylmar, California.) How can that be? Miller explains; "The price charged for these products is determined by insurance reimbursement, long product-development cycles, critical reliability, and manufacturing processes that are very change- and risk-averse." So, "there's not much incentive for top executives to adopt a lean program."[12]

Inertia at the top, though, need not stifle a process-improvement effort. Most of the lean/TQ menu costs little. People at plant level and below should, without budgetary assistance, be able to at least run pilot projects. An improvement such as a work cell or a quick setup pays for itself almost right away. That should trigger some or all of the following:

1. *Prove the worth.* A quick, visible payoff (less space, less inventory, shortened flow path) should convince those who thought the ingrained practices were just fine. The Gillette example in the next chapter elaborates on this way of proving the worth.
2. *Impress senior management.* Busy executives are results oriented. Payoffs from a pilot effort are a good way to get high-level attention. Executives can be impressed by people who take the initiative to save time and money without fuss, bother, and funding.
3. *Engage senior management.* Lean/TQ results are easily packaged into a simple presentation, with before-and-after photos and numerical results. Hourly people as presenters make it more impressive. Inviting senior people to such presentations over and over generates cooptation. Disinterest gives way to advocacy fueled by better understanding of the methods and power of best practices.
4. *Generate interest elsewhere in the facility.* A demo project, done right (e.g., sparkling clean, new paint; better lighting), has a *wow* factor. It becomes a source of pride and praise for those involved. People in nearby areas want to be next.
5. *Free up space for replicating the improvement elsewhere in the facility.* Typically crammed plants lack room for large-scale change all at once, and doing it in staged phases provides a way forward.

A pilot project at Advanced Bionics in 2003 captured most of these five points. The facility, a subsidiary of Boston Scientific, produced implantable neurostimulators to treat deafness and intractable pain. Plant management saw the need for a lean initiative, but nothing had been done to that point. The pilot, referred to as a kaizen event, began in the electrode line, which was capacity and space constrained. Bob Miller led a cross-functional team of eight that got itself trained only in the basics. They rejected a big, time-consuming training project featuring conflict resolution, consensus building, goal-setting, and so on. As Miller put it, such training "tends to have a stale, canned feel to it. Everyone has been through more training on these topics than they can generally stomach . . ." Instead, they went right to work organizing a cell with one-piece flow, and installing kanban and 5S . Those steps plus others raised capacity and output 30 percent in the same floor space. Invited to a presentation at the end of the week, the vice president of operations said, "So where are you going to do the next one?" More projects followed, led by a core group that carried the method to other areas, the main improvements being sharp reductions in throughput times.

But pilot projects and kaizen events can do only so much. As Miller put it, "My ultimate goal was (and is) to move away from kaizen events as our main lean implementation and incorporate the concepts as part of our daily work."[13] (Chapter 5 similarly discusses continuous improvement as opposed to discontinuous project events.)

As for the daily work, it starts out much leaner if the product design people have properly addressed the commonality issue, our next topic.

COMMONALITY

Special things are costly, complex, and time-consuming. Common things are the opposite. There is ample room for both in business and industry. In product and component design, there is always plenty of latitude for industry to find and remove what is unnecessarily special. Our discussion considers the penalty of not doing so, addresses obstacles to achieving commonality, and gives examples from a company in electric lighting.

THE FULL PRICE OF MODEL PROLIFERATION: UNDOING LEANNESS

Agility—a capability to quickly produce or serve about anything the customer might want—is expensive. Andy Grove, former CEO of Intel, describes the bottom axis of a scale in which products and services grow more full-featured, complex, and expensive. This, he feels, is a common pitfall of large companies. He calls for a "shift left" on the features scale, toward "keep it simple, stupid."[14]

Exhibit 15.1 may be that kind of scale, showing the danger of getting too far to the right. A company with few products, lower left on the straight line, is in a precarious existence. Additions to its product lines raise the company's return on investment, based largely on synergies and filling lulls in capacity with alternate products. The good times fade as the company moves along the upward-curving confusion curve. Increasing complexity, losses of focus, and growth of overhead eat up the synergies. Confusion stems also from more products competing for schedule time on the same resources. More products mean more engineering changes, and more growth of overhead and complexity.

Lean and total quality combat the confusion by injecting simplified solutions. Most important is drawing the growing number of products into focused families or value streams. With that, disruptive influences stand out for easier reduction. For two of its product families, Plug Power Company holds all engineering changes for release twice monthly, rather than a continual bombardment hitting many parts of the system.[15]

Those and other simplifications more than keep that wolf from the door, until the product line grows beyond reason—a tipping point, if you will. By the time the

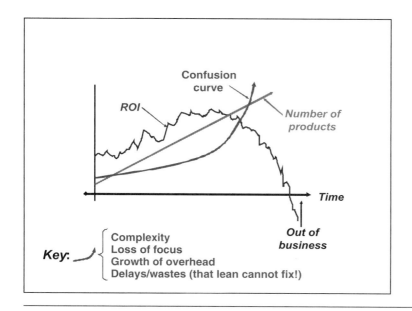

Confusion
curve

ROI

*Number of
products*

Time

*Out of
business*

Key: ⎰ Complexity
⎱ Loss of focus
Growth of overhead
Delays/wastes (that lean cannot fix!)

Exhibit 15.1 Focus on Money-Making Products

confusion curve crosses the number-of-products line, the company is already sinking
fast, toward red ink. If the product offerings keep growing, the company is hopelessly
bogged down in the four confusion factors: complexity, lost focus, high overhead, and
delays and wastes that no amount of lean can fix. Finding Ford Motor Company in
precisely this situation, new CEO Alan Mulally began telling groups of employees,
"We have been going out of business for 40 years."[16]

GOOD PRODUCT DESIGN AND THE COMPLEXITY FACTOR

Design of the product (or service) may exceed all else in impact on competitiveness.
Fortunately, a good deal is known about good product design. The state of the art is a
set of teachable concepts, the guidelines—software, too—known as *design for
manufacture and assembly* (DFMA). Yet, for at least five reasons, DFMA is not
often a company's strong suit.

First is a paradox: In most cases, good design strongly favors use of common rather
than special component parts. As Baudin puts it, "Every time we use the same part on
two models, we eliminate one opportunity to make a mistake."[17] However, if you are a
design engineer, standard parts are contrary to *your* standards. If you are to use parts
designed for some previous product or model—no doubt, by someone else—what,
you may wonder, are they paying you for? Moreover, "no engineer ever got noticed by
carrying over his predecessor's design . . . even if it saved big money."[18]

The designers' mindset needs to be altered, which may not be all that difficult. It
takes exposure in the form of DFMA studies, workshops, and see-for-yourself visits to

where DFMA is well established. The logic and necessity for DFMA is convincing. The clincher may be this realization: Using standard parts with few fasteners frees me, the designer, to focus my talents on features that are important. Otherwise, I'll be frittering away much of my expertise on mundane dimensioning issues or designing another screw.

Second, few companies have performance measures and reward-and-recognition structures that encourage DFMA. There is no lack of suitable measures for posting on trend charts or displaying on before-and-after schematics or photos. Example metrics include, per end product or assembly: number of fasteners and connectors, total number of parts, percentage of common parts, and percentage of models in which a given part is used. Other measures relate to simplifications in assembly, such as avoiding the need to invert the unit, avoiding alignment steps, and reducing the number of assembly and handling steps and time required.

Third, there is the problem of unfriendly search routines for finding an existing part that will do the job. The need is for an easily accessible and efficient library of existing specs and drawings. Without that, the engineer's tendency is to just design a new part. This situation is changing. Advanced search engines automatically code and classify parts by shape for quick, visual retrieval.[19]

Fourth, product engineers and process engineers typically do not work together. Thus, designers lack visibility into how their designs enhance or detract from producibility.

Fifth, in design, the right hand usually resists talking to the left. In multi-divisional companies, each division retains too much sway over specs for its own product models. Externally, the problem is too little interaction of product designers with suppliers' product and process engineers. These deficiencies limit the scope of standardizing parts, and the benefits thereof.

World-class DFMA requires fixing all five deficiencies: knowledge of DFMA fundamentals, appropriate recognition and reward, efficient search mechanisms, product and process engineering interaction, and joint design activities among divisions and echelons in the value chain. As one wag put it, "As a design engineer, I can design more waste into a value stream in one afternoon than a sea of lean thinkers can take out in a lifetime."[20]

GETTING DFMA GOING FOR LOW- AND HIGH-MIX PRODUCTS

Genlyte, second largest North American producer of electric lighting fixtures and controls, has grown rapidly, largely by acquisition. A sparsely staffed headquarters in Louisville, Kentucky, oversees its 16 divisions and 35 factories. Genlyte's policy is to provide high-end support but leave most management to the local entity. In decentralized corporations, high-end support refers mostly to allocating capital, plus providing centralized administration in limited cases where there are clear economies of scale. The formula has worked well, judging by Genlyte's 10 years of consecutive earnings growth. And in leanness, Genlyte grades *A* for its 18 years of improvement in inventory turns at a 2.4 percent average annual rate.

At headquarters, though, the operations staff believed something should be done to help infuse a high commitment to DFMA in the divisions. To that end, a large portion of its January 2007 manufacturing symposium (by teleconference) was devoted to the topic. Engineers at three of Genlyte's companies presented their successful applications of DFMA.

Some of Genlyte's plants produce consumer lighting, a relatively low-margin business with prices driven down by big-box retailers such as Lowe's, Home Depot, and Wal-Mart. The high-volume, low-mix nature of such consumer-goods manufacturing is a natural for DFMA. Product/part standardization can be a key to survival.

In the main, though, Genlyte is in the commercial lighting business. Customers are mostly ordering specialized lighting fixtures, either uniquely designed or selected from a thick catalog of options. It is an attractive business with higher margins than for consumer lighting. However, the agility to respond quickly to special orders is expensive, and can eat up those profit margins. Here is where DFMA comes in. The need for costly agility plummets as engineers adopt relatively small numbers of standard materials, sizes, shapes, finishes, and so on that can accommodate a very large number of customer-specified designs.

Along with those benefits comes a bonus. Ordinarily, the job-shop nature of producing for commercial applications requires a high degree of vertical integration. The manufacturers feel they cannot do much outsourcing to lower-cost contract producers, because that would lengthen design and production lead times. And lead times are often the difference between getting or losing a contract. Standardized components change the equation. For contract manufacturers, standardization chops the long lead times. For a company like Genlyte, that opens the door to more outsourcing—for low costs, high quality, and quick response.

Many manufacturers, similarly focused on high-margin, specialized products, have too long considered vertical integration a necessity. In the global economy that strategy will erode competitiveness. Commonality, at the materials and components levels, opens the door to a rosier future.

Commonality gets briefly addressed again in Chapter 17. In winding up this chapter we turn to the fourth major ingredient for overweight companies to become lean: diffusion of knowledge.

PIECEMEAL COMPANY TRAINING/EDUCATION AND IMPLEMENTATION

Genlyte has the right idea. Though a decentralized company, it recognizes the need to get its business units up to speed on the critical DFMA issue. Its manufacturing symposium got that ball rolling. The question is: why hadn't the training industry long since provided companies like Genlyte with that kind of best-practice learning?

For one thing, the training sector, that part specializing in process improvement anyway, appears to have undergone a reversal as to the makeup of its audiences. In the

1980s and into the 1990s, attendees at public events were heavy on people from big companies, light on them from medium and small ones.[21] Increasingly, through the late 1990s and to the present, it's the reverse. Big Industry seems to have internalized much of its training. It has its own experts, and it brings in consultants now and then to provide more specialized expertise. So much is known about process improvement that there is not much need to broaden the training and development in best practices. Or so the likely thinking goes.

Judging by the generally poor results shown by the leanness studies (A-graded Genlyte excepted) and elaborated on in the 14 previous chapters, the big-company thinking looks to be unsound. The old guard read everything, organized book-study groups, went anywhere and everywhere to learn, and experimented extensively with acquired knowledge. But the old guard has retired. Big-company training may have become less intense and more fractionated—in a word, *bureaucratized*. Moreover, it is myopic. When large companies were outward looking they could sift the many good and less good ideas. With training internalized, companies seem frequently to be getting stuck on training their people in a narrower set of slow-to-adapt practices and concepts.

Meanwhile, medium and small companies have seen threats to their survival. Those that supply bigger companies are under the gun to control process quality and respond to demands quickly and dependably. They feel they must learn how. Those that produce end products are facing competitors that have learned, so they must do so, too. Though large companies have always spent far more on outside training than smaller ones, that gap has probably narrowed, and in some quarters, closed.

Getting people trained in the right things is not easy. A dominant finding of this book is that process improvement is many-faceted, and that the facets are strongly interlinked. A conventional cost system clashes with process-improvement efforts. Traditional engineering and marketing mindsets lead to unlean proliferations of parts and models. Managements' partiality for goals and high-level numbers pulls people's concerns away from their zones of influence. The relative ease of attacking internal wastes draws attentions away from the bigger targets of improvement—the long, problematic lead times in the external pipelines.

Training is inadequate if it does not steer the enterprise toward the interconnections, the greater sources of meaningful improvements, and, in general, the bigger picture. Globalization should be guiding us onto that training vector, though so far it seems not to. Small and medium companies may provide some of the impetus to bring curiosity and enthusiasm back into the learning environment.

Prime examples of learning gone awry are central in the discussion of flow-through facilities, which will appear in Chapter 15.

NOTES

1. These comments about Alaris and Cardinal Health come from personal correspondence with David L. Schlotterbeck, CEO of Pharmaceutical and Medical Products at Cardinal

Health (January 2006), as well as my own visits to three of Schlotterbeck's places of employment: CalComp, several visits in the mid-1980s; Alaris Medical, on August 4, 1999, and August 8, 2005; and Cardinal Health, on November 16, 2005.

2. Lea A.P. Tonkin, "Alaris Medical, Inc.'s Fast Track to Lean Implementation Improvements," *Target* (3rd qtr 2002), pp. 41–44.

3. These remarks about Genie come from Robert W. Hall, "Uncorking the Genie from the Bottle," *Target*, 2nd issue (2006), pp. 6–14.

4. These comments about Genie's lean beginnings come from my own notes, dated 1994.

5. Hall, ibid.

6. Ilan Brat, "Turning Managers into Takeover Artists," *Wall Street Journal* (April 6, 2007), pp. A1, A8.

7. Jeff Schaller, "Standard Work Sustains Lean and Continued Success at Wiremold," *Target* (1st qtr 2002), pp. 43–49.

8. Richard J. Schonberger, Karen A. Brown, and Thomas G. Schmitt, "Your Lean Team: Use It or Lose It," *Target* (1st qtr 2003), pp. 13–21.

9. Russ Olexa, "Freudenberg-NOK's Lean Journey: An Interview with CEO and Chairman Joe Day," *Manufacturing Engineering* (January 2002), pp. 34–45.

10. Lea A.P. Tonkin, "Winning Performance at the Hon Company in Cedertown, GA," *Target*, 5th issue (2006), pp. 31–34.

11. More on R.W. Lyall may be found in Richard J. Schonberger, *Let's Fix It! How the World's Leading Manufacturers Were Seduced by Prosperity and Lost Their Way* (New York: Free Press/Simon & Schuster, 2001), pp. 155–157.

12. Jerry Feingold and Bob Miller, "Leading a Lean Initiative from the Ranks," *Quality Digest* (December 2006), pp. 40–44. Also, the same authors delivered a longer version of the article at the Institute of Industrial Engineers Lean Manufacturing Solutions Conference, Orlando, FL (December 4–8, 2005).

13. Ibid.

14. Lee Gomes, "Andy Grove Enters New Post-Intel Role as Activist Capitalist," *Wall Street Journal* (November 1, 2006), p. B1.

15. Robert W. Hall, "Plug Power," *Target*, 1st issue (2007), pp. 6–14.

16. David Kiley, "The New Heat on Ford," *BusinessWeek* (June 4, 2007), pp. 33–38.

17. Michel Baudin, *Lean Assembly: The Nuts and Bolts of Making Assembly Operations Flow* (New York: Productivity Press, 2002), p. 225.

18. Kiley, ibid.

19. Lawrence S. Gould, "Search by Shape," *Automotive Design & Production* (March 2007), pp. 60–61.

20. Mike Shipulski, "Successful Design for Assembly," *Assembly* (March 2007), pp. 40–46.

21. These impressions of audience composition are based mainly on records of attendance at JIT/lean/TQ-oriented public presentation events organized by the former Management Research Corp. from 1984 through 2000; the Shingo Prize from 2002 through 2004; and various universities and professional organizations from the early 1980s to the present.

Chapter 16

Flow-Through Facilities

Tenets of good, lean design of production facilities seem often to be poorly understood. Or, if understood, situations conspire to sway manufacturers away from them.

A big offender has to do with size. But not size of equipment. Manufacturers have come to understand lean machines. The opposites, widely referred to as *monuments*, are handmaidens of batch-and-queue processing. They were justified by now-discredited economy-of-scale notions fed by spurious cost-accounting practices: loopy calculations that could find lower unit costs for producing monumental volumes of items destined to sit in storage.

Though manufacturers no longer see scale as making sense for equipment, the same is not the case for factories. Are growing sales volumes stretching the capacity of the present plant? The automatic response has been, and still often is: build an addition. The larger plant, so the thinking goes, will yield scale economies.[1] That dubious notion is this chapter's first topic. The second topic has to do with unlean production lines: too often long and few, instead of short and many. The final topic brings in the bigger picture: tying pricing and making money to good flow-through facility designs.

FACTORIES: GROWTH IN MULTIPLES

Siemens Energy & Automation in Philadelphia is housed in a 175,000-square-foot plant (about 16,000 square meters). It has been enlarged four times and is home to three focused product lines or value streams. A strong lean effort was well underway when I visited six years ago. After the tour, I had to ask one of my hosts, manufacturing projects leader James Tafel, if they wished they had three or four smaller plants instead of the single large one. "Yes!," he said, "one building for each of our focused product families!," which are process automation, measurement and control, and dimensional measurement (mostly for the automotive industry). In the age of lean, most companies that end up with several product lines under one large roof could come to the same conclusion. In the old days of separate shops and departments, the disadvantages of outsized factories were less apparent.

Still, the preference for bigger plants persists. (The jury is still out on big versus small distribution centers. "[S]ome companies believe smaller is better," though "Wal-Mart isn't one of them."[2] A common accommodation for giant DCs is "warehouses within the warehouse."[3]) Given the option of two smaller plants instead of one big one, construction and operating costs seem to favor the latter. With a second plant there is the cost of an extra wall, another set of utilities, and higher heating and cooling expenses. Then there is the presumption that more than one plant will increase overall costs of material transport and handling.

The additional construction and utilities costs are valid. The point about material transport and handling is sometimes valid, often not. Regardless of those costs, lean favors small plants over large ones. That is because a large, single plant is physically and socially unwelcoming to the most important of all concepts that underpin lean: organizing resources by product families or customer families—that is, by value streams. Further discussion follows, beginning with the handling/transport issue, and then the value-stream angle.

LARGE PLANTS: HIGH HANDLING AND TRANSPORT COSTS

Whether a large plant was built that way or has grown outward by add-ons, it will be forever plagued by long material-handling distances. In a 50,000-square-foot plant (roughly 5,000 square meters), flow distances from receiving and shipping docks can be considerable. If the plant is square, the wall-to-wall distance is more than 200 feet (or 70 meters). In a 500,000 ft^2 plant (some 50,000 m^2), end-to-end travel, about 700 feet (or 220 meters), becomes a large source of cost and delay. Engineering will be called upon to devise some kind of material-handling automation. If the product is at all heavy, the plant will soon be an obstacle-course of whizzing forklifts or tugger-trains. Or it will be distance-spanning, mostly overhead, conveyors. Either way, the handling gear is a large, intrusive, non-value-adding (NVA) investment. For, say, a car or refrigerator assembly plant, the NVA conveying apparatus can rival the cost of all the value-adding equipment in the plant.

Half that cost revolves around getting incoming materials to productive work centers and finished goods to shipping docks. Just as significant are the costs of moving work-in-process from feeder to user cells, shops, production lines, or departments. For either purpose, vehicular handling has the advantage of flexibility, an esteemed attribute. Process improvement often includes re-configuration of space. But vehicular handling, besides its tendencies to do damage or injure people, gobbles a lot of real estate. Overhead conveyors, because they take up only "free" air, are a popular alternative. Within a few months of their installation, however, some of the conveyor and some of the pickup and put-down points will prove to be wrongly placed, inhibiting layout improvements. Machines, even fairly heavy ones, are movable, as are assembly lines and cells. Overhead (or in-floor) conveyors, once installed, do not want to move.

Handling costs in big factories are enough of a concern that the automobile industry has taken extreme measures. I'm not talking about the idea of simply cutting dozens of "point-of-use" receiving docks into factories' outer walls. That means shortening dock-to-line handling distances, with origins in Japan's auto industry, is old news. Buick was retrofitting its main assembly plant in Flint, Michigan, that way in 1982, when Buick hosted a meeting of the Repetitive Manufacturing Group (which became the Association for Manufacturing Excellence). Ford's Wixom, Michigan,

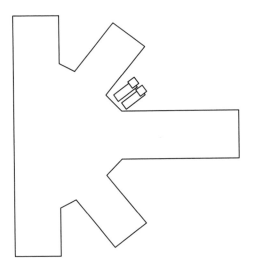

Exhibit 16.1   Adam Opel's Star-Shaped Assembly Building

factory, producing its luxury cars, had done that kind of retrofitting by the time I visited the plant in May 1987.

What is extreme are two car factories designed with odd-angled outer walls to greatly increase area for point-of-use docks. One is an Adam Opel AG plant in Rüsselsheim, Germany. Automobile production on the site goes back to 1899, when a plant there manufactured the "Lutzmann patent motor car." One hundred years later, after many iterations, the plant was redone as an eight-pointed star, but missing three of the points because of blockage by rail sidings at one end.[4] Exhibit 16.1, a sketch of the plant, shows five wings (star points) where production takes place. Four of the five house the main production line, which is decoupled so that a problem in one wing does not stop the entire line. The fifth wing prepares the door and cockpit modules for insertion into the main line. Receiving docks can be situated anywhere along the walls of the five wings, so that distances to points of use are short. The exhibit shows a pair of incoming trucks at unload docks where two of the production wings come together, which is deep within the production zone. The building's large central area is not near to the receiving docks. But no matter; no production takes place there. It is the plant's "nerve center," with plentiful meeting rooms and information boards. The plant, like most in the auto industry, is massive (520,000 ft^2). Unlike most, this one avoids much of the high costs of in-plant transit by greatly shortening distances from docks to points of use.

The second odd-shaped plant is at "Smartville" in Hambach, France, where Daimler-Chrysler (as a 75 percent owner) assembles the Smart car. The very small (for the auto industry) plant is in the shape of a plus sign. As with Adam Opel's star design, the reason is to provide plentiful outer walls for receiving to points of use along the assembly line. That purpose is all the more vital for Smart, because the plant acts as a system integrator as well as assembler. It is surrounded by seven focused factories that produce seven major modules and deliver them just in time to the Smart assembly lines. There, assembly time is only 4.5 hours, compared with 20 hours in a VW plant producing the Polo. Of the 1,800 employees in Smartville, 1,100 are employed by the module suppliers: Magna Systeme Chassis for the spaceframe; Magna Unipart for doors; Surtema Eisenmann, paintshop; Siemens VDO, cockpit; Dynamit Nobel, plastic body panels; ThyssenKrupp Automotive, powertrain and rear axle; and Cubic Europe, surface decoration.[5]

Even if the Smart plant had been designed in the usual rectangular shape, it would be relatively small. That is because the number of component parts it assembles into a car is a small fraction of the 3,000 or so of a typical small-car assembly plant. The seven on-site suppliers acquire most of those parts and assemble them into modules, relieving Smart of the burden of handling so many parts. The example illustrates a point: The more the parts, the bigger the plant. The opposite truth is: The fewer the parts, the smaller the plant.

SMALL PLANTS: MATERIAL HANDLING BY MANUAL PUSH

The material-handling requirements of a small plant are modest. Overhead conveyors, with their rigidities and inflexibility, are unlikely; they would look like wasteful over-engineering. Because distances are short, material handling may be mostly by manual push—using wheeled carts, trolleys, and pallet jacks. Lean principles favor manual push, to the point where a not-unusual measure of lean success is number of fork trucks retired.

Today, after several years of lean under its belt, the Boeing large aircraft plant in Everett, Washington, is a showcase of small wheeled handling carts. One can stand almost anywhere in the plant and count a few hundred push or pull trolleys.[6] This plant, housing the 767, 777, and the new 787 Dreamliner, is said to be the largest building of any kind in the world. (Boeing, too, has become a systems integrator, and no longer is proud to say it houses the world's largest machine shop. Even with deliveries of preassembled modules, its aircraft are huge and require a huge plant for final modular build.)

Push handling is friendly toward process improvements, especially re-layouts and material handling itself. Also, carts and trolleys can bump into and nick things, but do not imperil people. These are among the advantages of small plants over a big one. They offset, many times over, the material transports out in the weather that might be necessary on a manufacturing campus with two or more plants.

Value-Stream Organization: Plant-Size Effects

Actually, a production complex of small plants may require very little plant-to-plant transport. The reason is the attraction of making each plant a focused factory, a mostly self-contained production unit organized around a value stream. In the ideal, each focused unit has its own receiving docks, with incoming materials going directly to points of use. It may also have its own shipping docks for direct transport to the customer.

Focused-factory campuses come in different configurations. One extreme is a campus that requires considerable plant-to-plant transport, and the other, very little. The first kind has one or more plants fabricating semi-finished products, which must go to the next plant for complete assembly, and then onward to the paying customer. The second is more self-contained, typically by housing both fabrication of parts and assembly of them into finished products.

Plant-to-Plant Transit in a Focused-Factory Campus

General Electric's joint venture with Prolec in Monterrey, Mexico, has the first kind of focused factories, four of them.[7] The product is custom-designed electric transformers primarily for Mexican power companies. Three of the four factories produce components—tanks, coils, and cores—for the fourth, which assembles, tests, and ships completed units. This arrangement entails a good deal of transport from the three component plants to the assembly plant. Would it be smarter to consolidate into one or two self-contained plants? No; the large size and space requirements for a transformer and its main components would require a very large factory with all the disadvantages that have been mentioned. The four-plant configuration makes good sense.

Precor (featured in Chapter 13), producer of high-end treadmills, also has the first kind of focused-factory campus. Two of its three smallish plants produce the finished product, one focused on "bikes" and other fitness machines for the retail market, the other for commercial customers (e.g., fitness centers). The third factory produces components (e.g., stamped and machined items and subassemblies), which then get transported to the other two buildings for final processing.

Precor could break up its component-parts factory and move all the machining and stamping equipment into the two assembly plants. The plants would become self-contained focused factories. That is probably not practical, because it would require a great deal more fabrication equipment. Again, it would require larger buildings with their disadvantages.

These two examples illustrate a point: Both GE/Prolec and Precor have products too large and heavy to effectively produce in fully self-contained, focused factories. The factories would be overly large and cumbersome, and require excessive investment in duplicate fabrication machinery. The logic of that is not lost on Smart, which designed a small assembly plant for producing cars—small ones, but still heavy and space-gobbling. That the vast majority of the world's other auto-makers have been slow to follow suit is a mystery. That slowness looks to be a main reason why the typical car assembly plant is anything but lean. More on that in Chapter 20.

Self-Contained Focused Factories

Other companies have products more amenable to more self-contained kinds of factories. There sometimes are administrative reasons for grouping two or more on a single campus. The following are examples:[8]

- *Dell.* At its Round Rock, Texas, headquarters, Dell (Chapter 4) has three self-contained factories on its large campus. One assembles servers; a second, high-end desktop computers; and a third, lower-priced PC models.
- *Fluke.* Danaher's Fluke business unit in Everett, Washington, has two focused factories: one for high-volume, mostly hand-held electronic testing instruments, and the second for large, heavy instruments. Both are nearly self-contained, packaging included at the ends of assembly cells.
- *Excel Pacific Diecasting.* This very small Melbourne, Australia, manufacturer had one plant with facilities for both aluminum and zinc. In 2004, Excel took over a nearby building so that it could contain the two kinds of diecasting in two focused factories.
- *Takata Seat Belts.* Takata's Monterrey, Mexico, production is in two focused factories. One is devoted totally to Honda, the other to Toyota and Daimler-Chrysler. Both are self-contained and in different areas of the city.
- *3M Corp.* and *Hewlett Packard* have long had policies favoring smaller plants, each focused on its own product families and self-contained like individual small companies. 3M's plants tend to be in scattered, smaller cities and towns. HP's practice has been to house products in modest-sized plants, and to split off products and people to a new plant in another city when the plant's population grows to 500 or so (see Chapter 8 for more on this).

In these examples, the plants are smaller than 200,000 square feet (usually much smaller) and self-contained to the point of minimal plant-to-plant transit. Dell and Fluke produce end products for consumer and business customers, and their plants are focused by product family. Excel and Takata produce components that go into customer-companies' end products. Excel's plants are focused by type of material. Takata's are focused by both product family and customer family, which is the ideal form of organization—where the situation allows it. 3M's and HP's plants are mostly product-family focused. In each case, lean is well served.

Wrong-Way Planning for Expansion

For all the advantages of growth by multiple small plants, many companies automatically think first of an addition to the present plant. *Assembly* magazine's third annual Assembly Plant of the Year award, in 2006, went to Lear's two-year-old Montgomery, Alabama, automobile seat plant. Lear built it there mainly to supply a new, nearby Hyundai assembly plant.[9] Judging by the detailed description of this plant's achievements—in lean, quality, ergonomics, safety, customer delivery, self-directed teams, training, and employee involvement—there should be more awards. As is typical, though, "Lear decided to build a flexible plant that could easily be expanded in the future." The plant is currently nicely sized for the product, at 94,000 square feet. The way to add capacity is not by expanding. The logical way is by a second plant, probably with the same equipment and dedicated to an alternative family of customer models. The Lear plant outsources the metal-working, so costly, heavy equipment of that type would not be a factor bearing on the issue.

In 1999, U.K.-based Invensys christened a new plant in Tijuana, Mexico, to produce UPSs (uninterruptible power supplies) for its Powerware business unit (later sold to Eaton Corp.). The impressive factory, of about 150,000 square feet, is fully organized into cells, the production area is ringed with glass-walled meeting and training rooms, and the rest rooms look to be among the nicest of any factory in the state of Baja, California. On grand opening day, the plant manager took visiting dignitaries through the facilities, proudly pointing out the features—including, on the east side, a "soft wall" for future expansion. Later, I mentioned the merits of a second small plant as opposed to the deficiencies of an addition. But the wall is soft, and add-on thinking runs deep.

In 2005, I visited Amore Pacific's main cosmetics plant just south of Seoul, Korea. The production lines have undergone an impressive lean transformation—from stretched out and space consuming, to compact and cellular with cross-trained operators frequently rotating jobs. But then I heard the plan: to consolidate the company's present four plants in different parts of Korea into one large one, for which land had already been acquired. I had pointed out the fallacies of enlarged factories in a seminar the previous day. So my critique of this plan drew smiles and knowing nods. No doubt, however, it was too late to stop "progress." Big-plant thinking is seductive.

What to Do When Lean Creates Yawning Excess Space

"The big old plant now has huge swaths of unused space, even after converting some of it to the distribution center."[10] That quotation cites a familiar result of lean/six-sigma/TQ successes. It refers to the situation at a Batesville Casket Company factory in Manchester, Tennessee, which has 428,000 square feet under roof. Also familiar is what Manchester hopes to do about it. It is "looking for a new complementary product to take on to absorb space, and to provide more jobs, for no one is laid off because of [process improvement]."[11] Of course, in finding a complementary product, the plant will no longer be a caskets-focused factory. The simplicity of being focused on a single, dominant value stream will be gone, succeeded by a variety of complexities. The management may be wishing the plant had not been built so large in the first place, and a few may joke about a radical solution to the problem: swinging the wrecking ball at the excess space.

PRODUCTION LINES: TOO LONG, TOO FEW, TOO UN-ERGONOMIC, TOO MIND-NUMBING

Long production lines are the norm for many products having large numbers of parts. Nothing much distinguishes these lines from those in Henry Ford's day—except for line-stop authority. Today's lean lines have an *andon* cord to pull or button to press when there is a problem. Assemblers have authority to stop the line to get the problem fixed right away. Baudin observes, however, that doing so is "such a daunting prospect for assemblers that they practically never do it." Why not? Because, he says, the cost of stopping an entire assembly line of cars is prohibitive. It's the cost of idling all the assemblers and their equipment, plus stoppage of a revenue stream of more than $10,000 per minute.[12]

This does not mean that line stop is a bankrupt tool. It can and does work in assembly of less expensive products, such as small appliances, rider mowers, and small motorcycles. In cars, where the concept apparently originated, it will work if a long assembly line is subdivided into several segments, called "chunks" in auto-motive. (The concept has long been known about, but rarely applied, one exception being a Toyota plant in Kyushu, Japan, dating to about 1993.[13]) Each chunk of cars in active assembly is separated by a buffer-stock of four or five idle cars that serve to decouple the chunks. Under this arrangement, assemblers may be expected to stop their segment many times per shift to ensure that end-of-line quality is excellent.

Fill-and-pack lines have their own, unique issues. When I visited a Gillette plant producing deodorants, shaving accessories, and related personal-care products, it was coping fairly well with the plant-size bugaboo, but not with the line-length issue.[14] At 120,000 square feet of manufacturing floor space, the facility easily accommodated the necessary tanks for bulk materials, plus several fill-and-pack production lines, each a partial value stream focused on a product family. Running multiple products on multiple lines was part of Gillette's and the plant's effort to get closer to the customer, a worthy objective. The design of the lines—narrow-width and single-channel—fit the lean ideal of one-piece-at-a-time flow. (Wide lines with many units per cross-section are the unlean norm in foods and beverages, though not in personal-care products.) Still, the lines were excessively long. Stretched between each pair of work-stations were segments of non-value-adding conveyor holding dozens of units. The lines also included one or more accumulators, islands of just-in-case inventory. One accumulator held, by my rough estimate, 5 to 8 minutes of stock. That's a lot considering the high line speeds.

DESIGNED FOR FAILURE

Engineers have traditionally designed fill-and-pack lines that way for three reasons:

1. They are pressured, by faulty productivity and accounting metrics, to run the lines ever faster, to the point that equipment and materials will conspire many times per

shift to malfunction. The extra inventory on extra lengths of conveyor and accumulators provides breathing room—a bit of time to rush to the problem and un-jam or reload the offending device, while the rest of the stations keep humming.

2. The news media's stock shot or clip of a factory is of a powered conveyor loaded with inventory, in a moving but non-value-adding state. The scene is ingrained in our minds.

3. Conveyors and accumulators are mechanical, so engineers like them.

All that just-in-case inventory and conveyor, however, are out of tune with basic lean and total-quality concepts. On the gel-deodorant lines, the length also raised issues of possible open-air contamination along early segments of the line (before the unit is inverted and reaches the cover-and-cap stations). Personal-care products need to be made in a reasonably clean-air environment though not a class-10,000 clean-room. There is some particulate matter in the air.

The knock on the conveyor-as-safety-stock plan is that it amounts to designing the lines for failure. Lean/TQ calls for exposing and solving problems rather than covering them up with buffer stock. In packaged consumer goods production, loaded conveyors equal value subtracted.

The lean/TQ solution is to replace each long line with three or four compact cells. Each cell has a full set of equipment, except the conveyors are so short that they hold only a couple of idle units between each value-add station. Though the company must pay for three or four times as many pieces of equipment, most devices in a fill-and-pack line are not the break-the-bank variety. As an offset, there is the disinvestment of cutting out conveyor and accumulator segments and shrinking total required space. With three or four cells, the same product output will obtain at slower speeds. Thus, the equipment may be simpler and cheaper and less prone to jam-ups. In the case of the odd machine that is very expensive, it may be feasible for two cells to be situated back-to-back in order to share that machine.

Whatever the cost, the dividends are high. They accrue mainly from being able simultaneously to run three or four times as many product SKUs as before. As it is in this Gillette facility, dozens of product models (when you consider all the fragrances, sizes, labels, and so on) constantly compete for scheduling time on the production lines. Not having enough lines limits the company objective of getting close to the customer. A further limitation is the considerable time it takes to change a line from one model to another.

A typical scenario that goes along with multiple cells is segmentation into two modes of production: (1) For a high-runner SKU, there is a dedicated cell—no changeovers; just run the product at the average sales rate (the true customer takt time), which over a few months may fluctuate from, say, 18 shifts per week to 10. When it is 10, the cell doesn't produce on third shift; but during the lulls it gets maximal attention so that it will not malfunction when it does produce. (2) For the lower-demand majority of SKUs, quick changeover—several per day or per shift—allows running small lots close to the ideal of continuous replenishment. Because

Gillette is a major supplier to Wal-Mart, the global fount of continuous-replenishment lore and push for it, an upgrade to cellular in Gillette's factories is all the more attractive.

What to do with the freed-up floor space? How about an in-plant distribution point, especially for customers like Wal-Mart that prefer not to incur the costs and problems of extra shipping and storage stages in the supply pipeline.

PILOT TEST

The above scenario, using a real Gillette facility, is widely applicable, especially in packaged-goods companies. Regardless of the industry, shortening long production lines, eliminating distance-spanning conveyors, and shifting to compact cells yields large benefits. The scenario lacks one remaining element: an execution plan. Production must continue during the shift from lines to cells. So the plan needs to be phased, one line at a time.

In my own discussions with my hosts at Gillette, the favored plan was to start with a pilot test of the whole idea—to prove the worth of several cells replacing a single line. (Advantages of pilot tests were discussed in Chapter 15, in "Combating Bureaucratization and Inertia.") Because cellular production is still uncommon in the packaged-goods sector, people will be reluctant to forge ahead. The financial people would be among those who might need convincing. Marketing people should become the strongest cheerleaders—if only the ideas could get their attention. While my hosts in manufacturing were enthused, the ideas did not, to my knowledge, get much further. Steven Levitt, co-author of *Freakonomics*, may have hit on a key reason why. In a keynote address, he said this to the 3,200 attendees at the 2006 conference of the Council of Supply Chain Management Professionals (CSCMP): "Corporations are reluctant to experiment even though it would show them how to be successful."[15] A pilot test is an experiment aimed at correcting weaknesses in the plan and erasing doubts among the doubters.

SIT OR STAND?

The Gillette plant is in an industry whose goods usually end up on the shelves of drug and grocery stores. They tend to be processed and packaged in plants where production associates work in a stand and walk-around posture. The work is healthful and conducive to task variety.

It is quite different in factories producing apparel and many kinds of electrical and electronics goods. Most of the world's production of those products takes place in developing countries. Typically, assemblers are in a sitting position all day long doing the same operation hundreds or even thousands of times per shift. They soon have chronic physical problems: sore backs, shoulders, necks; maybe also elbows, forearms, wrists, and fingers. If the task time is just 10 seconds, which is a common number, they must repeat the task nearly 3,000 times per shift. They dislike the work, the job, and maybe the employer. They don't like the pay, either, because these narrow-skill, easily learned jobs are at the low end of pay scales. They cannot readily find better jobs, because their resumes are brief, maybe listing just a single job skill. Yet, if nearby plants provide employment options, they tend not to stay long. They quit in the forlorn hope things will be better at the factory across the street.

There is a social penalty, too. Most of the work force come from small villages in rural parts of the country. It is scary to come to the city and get a job in a huge factory. Making a friend, such as the person to the left or right on the assembly line, helps. But about the time you have made a friend, she can't stand the job anymore and quits. And the whole cycle of woe repeats itself in the new place of employment.

If the employer is a multinational, it may know better. For assemble-and-pack work, companies in developed countries have mostly abandoned long production lines and their mindless, low-work-content, sit-down jobs. They convert to multiple cells in which everyone is cross-trained and swapping jobs, sometimes as often as hourly. In a cell each assembler, tester, or packer performs two, three, or more of the tasks that on a production line are each assigned to two, three, or more people. Cell members stand and take steps among two or more adjacent work-stations.

The company is willing to offer higher pay for these multi-skilled associates for the competitive advantage of greater flexibility. Multi-skilling provides good-looking resumes. Still, the multi-skilled are not quick to bolt because they have reasonably good jobs. There is task variety, and the ambulatory job design is ergonomically beneficial. Learning and rotating through all the stations in the cell provides whole-process visibility. That can generate ideas for process improvement and some degree of intellectual fulfillment for cell-team members.

All the advantages of cellular assembly apply equally in developing countries. In dense manufacturing areas, such as southern China and northern Mexico, there is an even stronger case for tossing the long production lines and replacing them with cells. While the lines were designed with stultifying 10-second sit-down jobs, in the cellular configuration the work content per person expands to a reasonable 30 seconds. The cell is a small, compact unit in which everyone learns how to do every job. There is time to think and even to record process problems when they occur. With a bit of encouragement, better yet a systematic process, common-sense ideas for improvement will spill forth. The work force is slow to turn over, and the plant's good reputation for treating people well gives it best hiring choices. And the chairs are gone.

BI-MODAL VALUE-STREAM DESIGN: COST AND PRICE EFFECTS

One of lean's most basic principles is organization by value streams. In many cases, this effort congeals around two basic product families, standards and specials. The standard products are high-volume, low-mix, and the special products are low-volume, high-mix. Separation of the two yields a blizzard of benefits regarding processes, schedules, equipment, maintenance, skill levels, training, and staff support.

They extend to customer service, sales and marketing, engineering design, purchasing, logistics, quality management, costing, and pricing. The benefits relate to the simplicity of standard products and the complexity of specials. Standard products are easy, taking less of everything and thriving on low-cost repetition. They flow rather than jerk through staff and plant operations. The specials are difficult, taking uncommon expertise and costly, non-repeating resource usage and actions.

The last two items on the benefits list, costing and pricing, are at the business end of enlightened separation of standards and specials. The idea is to offer customers this alternative: a standard product at a very attractive price, or any of many non-standard versions at much higher prices. But few manufacturers are able to get their act together enough to put such practices into effect.

Sometimes it takes price pressures from mega-retailers to get manufacturers to do the math and act on it. Tesco or Target or Wal-Mart need only say, "We'll buy a million a year from you if you make it to our specs and cut the price from $10 to $6.50 each." Suddenly, the manufacturer is able to get its financial, marketing, operations, and other functions talking together. They soon see how to set up a dedicated value stream—one with simple, repetitive processes—that will yield a profit even at $6.50. Other product variations, those sold at lower volumes to other customers, remain managed more or less as specials requiring the $10 price. Or maybe $9, because costs are lower now that the specials are managed separately, and now that there is less congestion with the high-volume product getting its own resources. (See also "Pricing for Speed," in Chapter 6.)

A few manufacturers have gravitated toward their own versions of the standards/specials duality. A previous book offered Queen City Steel Treating Company of Cincinnati as a good example. This heat-treating job shop organized its customers into three tiers. The top two, Queen City's key accounts, represent the standards value stream, which they subdivided further. Tier 1 are customers with high-volume, common heat-treating needs. Tier 2 are those with substantial volume and considerable process commonality. Tier 3 represents specials, customers placing low-volume orders irregularly with little process commonality. The tier-3's were seen as interrupting "our ability to service the upper tiers." Queen City's policy was still to serve the third tier, but they pay more and wait longer. If they balk, Queen City would not mind if those lesser customers defected to the competition. The policy of favoring the top-tier customers amounted to "renting furnaces to our volume customers."[16]

This chapter, narrowly aimed at good engineering of manufacturing facilities, is in contrast with the broad issues taken up next: external linkages in Chapter 17.

NOTES

1. The excessive-size issue was briefly explored in Richard J. Schonberger, *Let's Fix It! How the World's Leading Manufacturers Were Seduced by Prosperity and Lost Their Way* (Free Press/Simon & Schuster, 2001), pp. 130–132.

2. "Small May Be Beautiful, but Wal-Mart's Sticking with Big," *DC Velocity* (June 2005), p. 3.

3. David Maloney, "Fast Forward," *DC Velocity* (July 2006), pp. 93–97.

4. Gary S. Vashilash, "Opel's Approach in Rüsselsheim," *Automotive Development & Production* (September 2001), pp. 70–74.

5. William Kimberley, "The Smart Way of Building Cars," *Automotive Development and Production* (April 2004), pp. 14–16; Brandon Mitchener, "Can Daimler's Tiny 'Swatchmobile' Sweep Europe?" *Wall Street Journal* (October 2, 1998), pp. B1, B4. See also www.autointell.com/nao_companies/daimlerchrysler/smart/thesmart1.htm.

6. Personal visit to Boeing-Everett on April 7, 2007.

7. Personal visit in September 1998.

8. Personal visits: Dell in January 2004; Fluke in April 2003; Excel in September 2004; and Takata in March 2004. (Excel was purchased by Hosico Engineering Group in March 2004.)

9. Austin Weber, "Lear Puts Quality in the Driver's Seat," *Assembly* (November 2006), pp. 26–38.

10. Robert W. Hall, "Batesville Casket Company Manchester Operations: 2006 AME Award of Excellence Winner," *Target*, 6th issue (2006), pp. 6–12.

11. Ibid.

12. Michel Baudin, *Lean Assembly: The Nuts and Bolts of Making Assembly Operations Flow* (New York: Productivity Press, 2002), pp. 96–97. The same point was made in Richard J. Schonberger, *Let's Fix It! How the World's Leading Manufacturers Were Seduced by Prosperity and Lost Their Way* (New York: Free Press, 2001), p. 146.

13. Toyota carved up the "traditional long, monotonous assembly line into 11 short ones, . . . [each] independently operated by a team of 20 to 25 workers held responsible for the stage of production quality. . . . Shorter, autonomous lines allow workers flexibility to stop their line if there is a hitch just by pulling an overhead cord." The same story refers to Toyota's getting rid of robots and other automation, which the company decided were contrary to its preference for simplicity. Nobuko Hara, "A People Plant: Toyota Leaves Robots Behind and Comes Out Ahead," *Chicago Tribune* (December 5, 1993).

14. Personal visit in September 1999.

15. Cited in "CSCMP Pulls Off Texas-Sized Conference," *DC Velocity* (December 2006), pp. 32–33.

16. Previously cited in Richard J. Schonberger, *World Class Manufacturing: The Next Decade* (New York: Free Press/Simon & Schuster, 1996), p. 149. Quotations are from Ed Stenger, former President of Queen City Steel Treating. A phone interview with Vincent Sheid of Queen City (December 29, 2006) confirms that the company still segments the customers in the same three tiers, though with somewhat less rigidity than in the Stenger era.

Chapter 17

External Linkages

Thomas Friedman, in his blockbuster book, *The World Is Flat*, offers this perception on the power of global supply chains: "No two countries that are both part of a major global supply chain, like Dell's, will ever fight a war against each other as long as they are both part of the same global supply chain." Friedman is quoting Glenn Neland, Dell's senior vice president for worldwide procurement. Neland refers to the prosperity and lack of wars enjoyed by Japan, South Korea, Taiwan, Malaysia, Singapore, Philippines, Thailand, and Indonesia. These (along with prominent but unmentioned China) are countries with a large presence in extended supply chains. In contrast, he cites the following conflicted countries for their lack of that presence: Iraq, Syria, south Lebanon, North Korea, Pakistan, Afghanistan, and Iran.

This thought-provoking idea, referred to by Friedman as the Dell Theory of Conflict Prevention (it's the title of a chapter in his book),[1] is surely an oversimplification. Not many supply chains are as tightly strung as Dell's. However, the sheer volume, if not the tightness, of crisscrossing global linkages may offer support for the theory.

Our quest here, though, is not to save the world from wars. It is to look to practices that will allow companies to survive and flourish. Other chapters have made the point that many companies are doing well on practices close to the action in operations but poorly on those more remote or external. This chapter drills into the matter more deeply. It begins with evidence of how dominant the external process issue is as compared with the internal. Then, for perspective, we look at where industry went wrong. Timeline analysis shows the poor state of process improvement 30 years ago; how it got itself turned around stoked by a growing list of best practices; and its current state of being bogged down on the externalities front. The chapter ends with the enlarged issue of risk in our globalized industrial environment.

EXTERNAL LEAN: HOW LARGE AN ISSUE?

Objective data show that the biggest opportunities for improvement are not inside the firm but in the pipelines. The evidence is found in the three components of companies' total inventory. The internal component is known as work-in-process (WIP). The two external components are purchased (raw) materials and finished goods. Some companies list just two categories. They may combine raw materials and WIP, calling it *RIP*, or put WIP and finished goods together as one number.

Exhibit 17.1 lists 25 companies and the percentages of their inventory that are purchased and finished. The 25 have been drawn at random from about 600 companies for which we have calculated component percentages. (We have not dug out component inventory data for the other 600-odd companies in the database.) The percentages are "eyeball" averages of the most recent four to six years. The data say that there is 2 to 10 times more room for getting lean external to the organization than inwardly.[2] Peter Bradley, chief editor of *DC Velocity*, in similarly addressing lean's expanded meaning, says "We're gonna need a bigger box."[3]

In the exhibit, the fourth column is the sum of the second and third columns, percentage of purchased and of finished goods. The sums range from 55 percent at NEC (Japan: electronics) and 57 percent for Atlas Copco (Sweden: construction and mining equipment, compressors, industrial tools, etc.) to 99 percent for Alberto-Culver (personal-care products, food seasonings, beauty supply distribution). The median is 84 percent. That leaves just 16 percent for work-in-process.

Exhibit 17.1   Purchased and Finished Goods as a Percent of Total Inventory for 25 Companies

Company	Percent of Purchased Materials	Percent of Finished Goods	Sum
3M	18	50	68
Alberto-Culver	8	91	99
Atlas Copco (Sweden)	3	54	57
BASF (Germany)	22	NA[*]	NA[*]
Blount	35	49	84
Checkpoint Systems	13	82	95
C.R. Bard	26	56	82
Dionex	39	49	88
Electrolux (Sweden)	23	74	97
Flexsteel	40	40	80
GenCorp	50	25	75
Gorman Rupp	56	4	60
Heinz, H.J.	22	NA[*]	NA[*]
Ingersoll-Rand	32	52	84
Johnson Controls	48	37	85
La-Z-Boy	28	52	80
Medtronic	24	61	85
NEC (Japan)	22	33	55
Parker Hannifin	14	47	61
Respironics	29	61	90
Schering Plough	22	40	62
Sony (Japan)	20	64	84
Svenska Cellulosa (Sweden)	46	48	94
Toyota (Japan)	17	68	85
Volkswagen (Germany)	17	72	89
Median	22	51	84

[*]Not applicable: finished goods combined with work-in-process rather than a separate component of total inventory.

The median for finished goods, 51 percent, is more than double that of purchased materials, at 22 percent. Discussions with Atlas Copco officers help explain this Swedish company's remarkably low 3 percent for purchased materials: Most of the company's production is assembly rather than fabrication. Steel and castings are just a small component of purchases. The much greater portion is semi-finished components used in assembly. Investor Relations Manager Mattheis Olsson explains that these components are purchased just in time from suppliers, with deliveries sometimes twice daily. Atlas Copco, he says, has been refining its JIT purchasing "for decades." Hans Ola Meyer, VP, Controller and Finance, adds that the end product variations specified by customers are made with small numbers of component parts, which are often shared by the company's decentralized business units.[4]

For finished goods, the low is *A*-graded Gorman-Rupp (pumps, mostly large and special-duty) at 4 percent. That low a percentage is characteristic of make-to-order production. None of the other companies in Exhibit 17.1 come close that percentage, the next lowest being NEC, much higher at 33 percent. A popular but flawed notion is that becoming lean is moving away from the make-to-stock mode and toward make-to-order. That ideal fits in some kinds of manufacturing but not at all in others; for example, nearly all packaged consumer goods must be made to stock. Make-to-order always adds costs of over- and under-use of resources, whereas make-to-stock, for all its faults, allows producing to a steady beat. These numbers in Exhibit 17.1 suggest that make-to-order is not common. More to the point, finished goods make up more than 50 percent of inventory value for this sample of manufacturers. Those inventories bloat the customer pipelines, degrading connectivity with actual customer demand. They are the greatest opportunity for lean-based improvement.

WHERE WE LOST—AND FOUND—OUR WAY

My earlier book, *Let's Fix It!*, detailed the fall and rise of western industry in two exhibits.[5] Now that history may be updated. The fall (first exhibit) occurred largely in the third quartile of the twentieth century. Average inventory turnover for a large sample of companies was becoming steadily worse. That was a telling symptom of degraded industrial performance. Companies were progressively losing touch with customers, and internal silos were rising ever higher. Suppliers were increasingly treated as a black box, and both suppliers and one's own work force were being seen by management as adversaries rather than as partners in process improvement. The overall effect was declining competitiveness, especially with surging Japanese export companies. That decline involved most of what the company does. Scrap and rework were getting worse, quality more unpredictable, labor less flexible, equipment less dependable and more time-consuming to set up, and flow paths longer. Schedules became less synchronized, storage areas bigger, and product designs more complex with proliferations of component parts. By continually adding to their supplier base— for "sourcing protection"—companies spread thin their capability to coordinate and share data with suppliers. Marketing promotions were causing ever-larger and more costly spikes in demand. Finally, performance was measured in now-discredited terms such as how busy the machines and work force are rather than whether they produce what customers want and need.

The rise (second exhibit from *Let's Fix It!*[6]), reversing those unfortunate trends, was driven by total quality, just-in-time, lean, and related concepts largely from Japan. Best practices of western origin (design for manufacture, pay for skills, continuous replenishment, cross-docking, and more) kept the good trend going—for a while. Exhibit 17.2 is an adaptation of that second exhibit, with emphasis on results that are gratifying, and others that are not. Ten of the results in the exhibit, those shown in regular type and above the dashed line, pinpoint areas of best improvement. Five causes for concern are in italics and below the dashed line.

For the 10 "best" items, largely deriving from lean-core practices, the rising arrow signifies long-term improvement. Those 10 cover quality, equipment, labor, lot sizes, layouts, lean positioning of resources, and moves toward fewer (but better) suppliers.

Inventory/control systems, seventh on the list, take in a lot of issues. The batch-and-queue mode encourages dependence on IT for scheduling, keeping inventory records, tracking the flow, and accounting for every move. By simplifying processes and getting away from batch-and-queue, companies are able to reduce much of that IT dependency, including fending off burdensome reporting that ERP systems tend to impose. Externally, however, IT is largely a positive force for simplification and streamlined operations. A prime example is IT for processing supplier and customer orders.

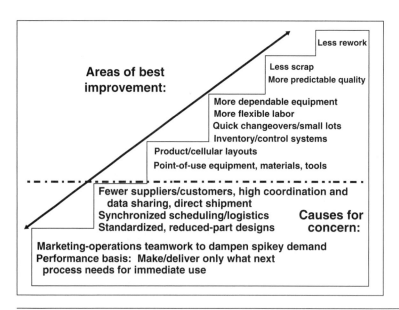

Exhibit 17.2   Areas of Best Improvement and Causes for Concern

The five causes for concern, below the dashed line, require efforts in the greater enterprise, taken up next.

CUSTOMERS AND THE LAWS OF REDUCTION

Most companies need fewer but better customers. The idea follows a general law:

The First Law of Reduction—Fewer customers, suppliers, operations, products, and components allow more intensive attention to those that count.

Rare is the company that does not have many unprofitable customers placing orders that overwhelm resources. Lesser customers divert attention from best customers, degrading overall performance. Trimming the customer list opens the door to joint planning with dominant ones. This starts with sharing information, especially about demand, capacities and capabilities, and inventories. Best customers may warrant direct shipment, bypassing one or more handoff and storage stages. But few companies are able to put together a multi-functional effort to effectively rationalize the customer base, thereby to set this in motion.

An exception is Nypro, one of the world's largest and most esteemed injection molders—with 55 facilities in 18 countries, including 20 in Asia and seven in Europe. The story of how, in the late 1980s, Nypro fired most of its 600 customers, retaining only its 31 biggest and best, is old news.[7] A long period of rapid domestic and global growth followed, with many of its plants dedicated to and located near a major customer's assembly plant. As next-door neighbor, each Nypro plant was positioned to learn a lot about its customer's processes, needs, and requirements. Armed with that knowledge, Nypro plants kept offering more value-added services to their customers. Nypro's current web site says the services include metal fabrication, assembly, program management, contract manufacturing, and a "high-velocity system" for delivering lean, high-quality results enterprise-wide.[8]

Nypro's expansion of services began slowly, but then later, out of necessity, shifted into high gear. Some of its big U.S. customers had started moving their assembly operations to developing nations, mostly in Southeast Asia. That would leave Nypro with a molding facility next door to a customer's empty assembly plant. Mainly to avoid that fate, Nypro stepped up a forward integration strategy, becoming an assembler as well as a molder. That way, a customer would not have to move assembly to China. Rather, it could transfer its assembly to the existing Nypro facility, which becomes its contractor for production *and* assembly—say of hand-held phones.[9]

HUI Manufacturing in Kiel, Wisconsin, has its own way of being selective about customers. This small company specializes in quick response to difficult metal-working issues of customers. HUI has defined its ideal customer. First, it is one found through what HUI calls "customer business development" selling. Second, it favors customers that value HUI's speed: production lead times of two weeks or less, which includes custom designs and sourcing of materials. Third, the ideal customer values

HUI's special combination of expertise in design engineering, and quick and complete (including paint) manufacturing.[10] HUI's web site screens in those kinds of customers and presumably screens out customers that just want some job-shop work done.

For some companies, the First Law of Reduction is too extreme. They want lots of customers, large, medium, and small. For them the law must be modified—to recognize levels of importance:

> *The Second Law of Reduction*—Reducing time and attention to lesser customers, suppliers, operations, products, and components allows time and intensive attention to those that count.

It is not easy to find companies that fully apply the second law to customers, One that does, though, is Rohm & Haas, producing specialty chemicals for paint and coatings, electronics, household goods, adhesives, detergents, personal-care products, and more. Its Emulsions business unit has organized 4,000 customers into four tiers in order of importance. The four are:

1. Partners, amounting to 2 percent of customers but 55 percent of gross profit
2. Potential partners, 27 percent and 13 percent
3. Strategically important customers, 17 percent and 13 percent
4. Other customers, 75 percent and 6 percent.

Under this alignment, major decisions on products and plants are planned jointly with best customers to ensure their needs are not compromised.[11]

Rohm & Haas grades a strong *A* on leanness, having improved its inventory turns at a yearly rate of 1.9 percent for 32 years. That puts the company in the top five among 106 chemical companies in the research, a sector ranked third from the bottom among 33 industries. (The industry ranking is in Chapter 18, Exhibit 18.2.) More to the point of this example, at Rohm & Haas the upward trend in leanness had stalled in the 1990s. Since organizing customers into tiers in the late 1990s, its inventory turns have jumped, from 3.8 in 1999 to 5.9 in 2006.

A quite different and indirect way to organize customers is by limiting product choices, which is another target of the laws of reduction. Done right, customers may still have it their way. The idea is to offer customers this alternative: a standard product configuration at an attractive price with quick delivery, or many non-standard options at higher prices with longer lead times. Some of Boeing's resurging financial health may be owed to just that kind of practice.

Historically, Boeing's customers could order any option or feature and Boeing would provide it. This meant that every airplane coming down the 747 or 737 line differed from every other one in tens of thousands of ways—and Boeing's cost structure suffered accordingly. Customers fussed over small design details right down to the facial-tissue dispenser in the lavatories. In the late 1990s then-vice president Alan Mulally complained that "The lavs and galleys are designing the airplane."

Finally, Ron Woodard, president of the Commercial Airplane Group, had had enough—and called for a switch to modular, standardized lavatories.[12]

Offering so many options was not the biggest problem. Rather it was the Boeing cost system, which was not capable of attaching the extra costs to each customer's plane. Thus, there were no incentives for customers to rein in their choices to save money. Finally, in the late 1990s, Boeing hired a new chief financial officer, the highly regarded Debby Hopkins, formerly with General Motors. Her new finance team revamped the costing system. That allowed a multi-functional team to define the specifications for a standard 737-400 with a standard, low price.[13] Today at Boeing, that is a standard best practice. Boeing "will still allow customers to choose equipment not on the approved list, but airlines that stray from the standard catalog will be required to pay any extra cost."[14]

SYNCHRONIZATION

Synchronized scheduling/logistics is the next area for concern from Exhibit 17.2. Companies that report 100 percent on-time may see that as the ultimate—perfect synchronization with the customer. That may be valid for FedEx or DHL. It rarely is for a manufacturer, because on-time delivery merely fills a customer's storage slot. Many days, or weeks, may pass before the items are actually needed and used by that customer, or another customer farther downstream.

Harley-Davidson is among the few manufacturers that have been fixing that broken system. Harley gains synchronization with its suppliers via automatic replenishment notices sent electronically to the suppliers; Harley's usage triggers the notices. This system was put into practice initially at Harley's Kansas City, Kansas, assembly plant, while its older plants in Milwaukee and York, Pennsylvania, remained running on a traditional forecast-driven supply chain.[15] Extension of automatic replenishment to Milwaukee and York are among the most effective ways for Harley to continue its long upward trend in leanness.

Relatively few manufacturers have done much to synchronize with upward or real downstream usage, maybe because it is difficult. For Barilla, the Italian pasta maker (Chapter 13), it took five years to gain the cooperation of its distributors to achieve synchronization with sales downstream in the food markets.

Manufacturers that supply to the Wal-Marts of the world have that kind of synchronization levied upon them. Others hide their heads inside their own operations and let their competitiveness deteriorate through inaction on the matter. An exception is Graco, the manufacturer of spraying equipment. The following discussion is on how Graco's success with the lean core paved the way for getting in sync with its distributors.

Exhibit 12.8, showed Graco's 29-year accelerating rate of improvement in inventory turns, which was halted and reversed in its past three years of acquisition-based growth. JIT/lean basics were responsible for the early phase of improvement. By the time of my first visit in 1997, nearly all its manufacturing was in product-focused cells, most of the other elements of the lean core had been attended to, and turns had risen from a low of 1.5 to 4.8. Since then, the company has continued to improve its cellular structure. Each cell has become a virtual small business with its own metrics, and is responsible for its product line, cradle to grave. While the best that most manufacturers can do is organize cells by product-family value steams, most of Graco's cells are focused both on a product family and a customer family.

There was not a lot more leanness to wring out of manufacturing, but plenty in the customer pipelines. In the second phase, several years of steep improvement, Graco eliminated its scattered branch warehouses. That abolished large amounts of inventory, which was the plan. Greater but unexpected benefits followed. Efforts with the lean core had honed Graco's quick-response capability: same-day shipment for orders received by noon. With no intervening branch warehouses, Graco's distributors directly benefited. The distributors slashed their own Graco inventories and switched from infrequent batch to frequent small-lot ordering. The effect at Graco was to even out its shipments, production, and purchasing. The newly smoothed, regular demand pattern simplified administrative processes, lowering those costs.[16]

Next steps would be to try to develop deeper collaborative relations with the distributors. Those efforts have been rebuffed. Graco has been unable to obtain forecasts or advance notices of shipment to final customers, has had no success in gaining access to point-of-sale data, and finds no interest in its proposals to provide a VMI (vendor-managed inventory) service. Distributors may not see much need for these changes, since they've already gained so much inventory reduction and fast response from Graco.

Johanna Småros lends support to that speculation by her case study of collaborative practices between four retailers and their manufacturer-suppliers. She found that "Sharing of POS data is considered moderately relevant [to retailers, because] it does not have a direct impact on the retailer's own operations...."[17]

Another reason for distributors' disinterest in joint planning may be that only a rare few manufacturers (e.g., Barilla and Graco) press for it. Moreover, there may be an impression that the advantages of collaboration are one-sided—in favor of the producer. The benefits would indeed start with the producer: better planning of capacity, staffing, and purchasing, and therefore lower costs. That those benefits, especially cost and reliability, would pass forward to the distributors is a point they may fail to see.

The popular term, *supply-chain management*, suggests that it is the customers' job to manage and improve relations with their suppliers. But here we've seen that customers—distributors in this case—are status-quo oriented. Nor is that uncommon. Often enough, suppliers have stronger management with better process-improvement practices than their customers. Supplier-producers, therefore, need to be aggressive practitioners of *customer*-chain management. Most producers, though, seem all too timid about pressing their customers for collaborative practices they know will competitively improve both parties. If only the few, such as Barilla and Graco, are pleading the point, that point is ground down and the inefficient, long lead-time, inventory-heavy customer chains remain.

In summary, Graco could not have slashed inventories and lead times in its customer pipelines without first having achieved a high state of leanness internally. In other words, success in pipeline management requires, as a prerequisite, some level of lean-based attainment internally. By extension, multi-functional teamwork inside the firm is a prerequisite to successful collaboration externally. Graco has good multi-functional teamwork, and so, as with Barilla, may ultimately succeed in its collaborative efforts with distributors.

STANDARDIZED PRODUCT DESIGNS

Third on the cause-for-concern list in Exhibit 17.2 is inadequate attention to standardizing product designs. Chapter 15 suggests factors that stand in the way of making progress on this DFMA basic. A few companies, mostly electronics, have done well (see Chapter 19). But DFMA efforts overall appear to be weak. Case studies talk a lot about standard work, from the lean core. However, case reports usually say little about standardizing parts or other aspects of DFMA.

Then there are the astonishing stories, usually from automotive because that is the industry that gets the most attention. One is about Ford's new CEO, Alan Mulally, who, for its shame effect, placed on a table in his office 12 different rods for propping up the hood on various Ford vehicles.[18] This is not to pick on Ford, because one can find similar stories for any of the automakers. (And Mulally knows what he is talking about. Some of the worst examples—of non-DFMA—came from Boeing, Mulally's former employer. But that was nearly a decade ago, before Boeing began its massive overhaul of designs and processes.) Because standardizing parts has rippling beneficial effects through most other processes and functions, for industry to be weak here is a deficiency of large proportions.

MARKETING-OPERATIONS TEAMWORK

The fourth weakness listed in Exhibit 17.2 is lack of joint planning by marketing and operations to limit their own causes of bumpy, lumpy demand patterns. Evening out demand bears bountiful fruit. One harvester of it is, again, Graco. Unlike most companies, manufacturing or service, Graco does not do promotions. In other words, the strong tendency for marketers to offer periodic sales, buy-one-get-one-free, special discounts, or end-of-period sales-boosting promotions is disallowed at Graco.[19] Promotions cause artificial demand spikes, which raise havoc in every business function including those of suppliers and carriers.

Marketers are not alone in creating demand spikes. Any batching done in operations, for production or for handling and transport, creates internal demand spasms. The lean core aims squarely at production batching. Secondarily, it attacks batched handling, mainly through more frequent, smaller-lot deliveries in cut-down containers triggered by kanban signals. However, too many companies still cling to in-plant kitting. A kit is a batch—and one that requires doubling handling and extra labor, and is another source for error. (Kitting for in-plant handling is unlean. Kitting for transport, on the other hand, is lean; for example, shipping complete sets of parts to make a TV or motorcycle or motor home is lean. Shipping a truckload of TV tubes, motorcycle handlebars, or motor-home windows is decidedly unlean.)

The packaged-goods sector has its own kind of batching—a batch in motion. It is the dozens or hundreds of items in a fill-and-pack line that are moving on a conveyor between value-adding stations, or circulating in an accumulator. Here, lean calls for (1) slashing the length of conveyor travel, (2) eliminating accumulators, and (3) cutting the width of side-by-side items in motion. If items are in single file, the moving batch is far more amenable to maintaining quality and integrity of flow than if the batch is wide. (For more on narrow-versus-wide conveyor channels, please see the Gillette example in Chapter 16.)

The most damaging of operations' batching practices is ordering from suppliers in multi-day or -week quantities. The usual reason is the view that smaller, more frequent deliveries incur extra transport costs that exceed the savings from reduced inventory batches. The gains from small, frequent deliveries, though, will always be under-estimated. You cannot put a price on the many benefits of getting closer in lead time to suppliers. The fixation is on the high cost of freight—"anywhere from 70 to 85 cents of every dollar spent on logistics," says one report.[20] So a cost-benefit analysis of small, frequent shipping is likely to include as benefits only the physical savings of having less inventory to store. Dan Jones speaks to the other side of the equation, saying that large-lot shipping never was economical, because trucks typically ran half empty.[21] JIT shipping, however, may employ small trucks with cube more fully utilized. And, whether with smaller or larger trucks, it employs milk runs: a truck route with pickup stops at multiple suppliers, or your finished-goods truck stopping for deliveries at multiple customers.

Milk runs require a high degree of joint planning, which can result in surprising accommodations. According to analyst Adrian Gonzalez, Schneider Logistics now transports after-market service parts for Ford and General Motors in the same trucks. Schneider had been serving both companies independently and finally convinced them to commingle their freight. Gonzalez says, "You see a Ford dealership next to a GM dealership but, before, Schneider would have to send two trucks. This is a win-win situation . . . with lower costs for Ford and GM, and better asset utilization for Schneider."[22]

To achieve innovative joint actions, there should be no such thing as a marketing strategy, or an operations strategy. The only permissible strategies should be multi-functional. Is there a proposal within marketing for opening up a new channel, selling to fast-food restaurants, for example? The proposal is likely to have a big impact on production capacity. It must be vetted through operations, so that what emerges is a joint marketing-operations strategy of selling to fast-foods and establishing pro-ductive capacity in the form of space, equipment, hiring, and training. We have been focusing on marketing and operations. But usually other functions, such as finance, would be affected enough that they, too, would join in the development and implementation of strategy.

MAKE/DELIVER ONLY WHAT IS NEEDED

The fifth concern, from Exhibit 17.2, is failure to heed lean's main mandate: to make and deliver only what is needed, precisely when needed. In most companies the stronger mandate is to hit traditional targets. Specifically, the lean core's main aims—short flow times with over-production disallowed—clash with unit-cost and cost-variance targets. Happily, most companies that take lean seriously, are able, more or less, to recognize that the cost-accounting system is a train wreck. While some companies have killed it, others just cease to allow it much sway over management decisions. In those cases, the lean core is not hobbled much by the conventional cost system.

Outside the core, the story is different. With some exceptions (e.g., auto seat suppliers delivering several times a day in model-mix sequence), little has changed. It still is make and deliver in large batches, and store in distribution centers for days or weeks—far out of sync with what is needed downstream. Accounting games bear much of the fault. One way to foil the destructive game-playing is to impose a no-nonsense performance metric that gives the pipeline inventories no place to hide.

JOINT INVENTORY: *NOT* PLAYING ACCOUNTING GAMES

Raleigh, NC, in 1985, was the site of one of IBM's first just-in-time/lean transformations. The high-powered task force in charge reconstituted far-flung batch processes for one major product line as a tightly linked assembly cell. It was situated right next to a little-used dock, where JIT deliveries of purchased materials arrived and went directly from dock to line. The application was advanced for its time, and even for today. A unique feature, conceived by the task force, was how they would assess the cell's performance with its JIT suppliers. What they devised was a measure they called *joint inventory*—simply the inventory already produced for IBM by each supplier plus that already received at IBM. The metric was aimed at dissuading managers from the nefarious practice of pushing inventory back on suppliers in order to look good. Joint inventory is a simple, effective way to deal with common supply-chain misdeeds.[23]

That was 20-plus years ago. Most of the methodologies for achieving lean pipelines are of recent origin. The methods, in large part honed in retailing, are equally effective in manufacturing. But manufacturers may just continue to do nothing much, unless pushed into action by a joint-inventory metric.

THIRD-PARTY LOGISTICS—AND FINANCE

If manufacturers or distributors lack motivation to deal with the pipeline issue, they may at least get some help from the 3PLs (third-party logistics companies). These new entities arise when logistics subsectors merge in various ways to provide a fuller range of services in which their clients—shippers and users—are not adept. Overnight freight handlers such as UPS, FedEx, and DHL make up one kind of 3PL. From mail-forwarders they've become distribution centers for filling orders that arrive electronically from IBM, Motorola, or HP. At UPS, the transformation includes acquiring six logistics companies, a brokerage, specialists in LTL (less-than-truckload) shipments, freight forwarders, and even a small Connecticut bank.[24] Former transport companies such as J.B. Hunt and Yellow Roadway travel another 3PL route. They have become multimodal and have added DCs where they perform light assembly and packaging. Warehousing and distribution companies have expanded the other way, into transport.

Nor is the 3PL movement just a western phenomenon. The 10th annual 3PL study, conducted in 2005, asked companies if they use 3PL services. More than 70 percent of responding companies say they do, a percentage that holds true for North America, Western Europe, Asia-Pacific, Latin America, and South Africa. For the same five regions, 77 percent to 90 percent of surveyed companies say their relationship with 3PLs is "very successful" or "extremely successful."[25]

While 3PL is fairly well established, another, related third-party service is emergent from the financial world. It organizes a financial supply chain for the flow of money that supports the movement of products and components. That movement, with all its fits and starts, risks and uncertainties, is a can of worms for suppliers, logistics companies, and users. A big question for suppliers is: when will I get paid? For users, it may be: how can I delay payment? For both, financing costs and turbulent cash flows is a large issue. It has to be, because purchased materials can easily make up 50 percent of manufacturing costs. Supply-chain finance providers, still a fairly new service, create order that may benefit all sides.[26]

Global hyper-competition creates rivals that didn't exist last year but emerge this year threatening your survival lunch. Counterfeiters flood the market with products that either look and function like yours, or are priced so low that customers don't care.

RISKY, FEARFUL WORLD

The World Is Flat[27] gets you thinking. It's scary out there. New companies can pop up anywhere and eat your lunch. Suspicious Internet chat causes governments to raise the security alarms, shutting down borders or greatly slowing entry of your JIT-managed goods. Powerful boats of armed-to-the-teeth pirates prowl the Straits of Malacca, looking to highjack the ship holding your container of goods. Counterfeiters aim to flood the market with cheap knockoffs of your premier product. Industrial spies and hackers steal your sensitive computer files, or simply shut your computers down. In some countries, movement of your materials incurs unpredictable delay for reasons of infrastructure, "adminis-trivia," or demands for under-the-table payoffs. To all that, add global warming, which may have something to do with increasing incidence of unpredictable hurricanes, tornados, blizzards, droughts, tsunamis, and the like. Disastrous weather can shut you down, and in any case can lead to rising prices of foodstuffs, fuels, and other commodities that ultimately affect your products' costs and availabilities.

Yossi Sheffi, author of *The Resilient Enterprise*,[28] tells what to do about these concerns: Map scenarios and develop countermeasures. Calculate probabilities of major disruptions and their severities. Conduct near-miss analyses. Run computer simulations using the scenarios, probabilities, and severities to improve your counter-measures.[29] Do these things thoroughly and systematically.

Left unsaid is who is to carry out the prescriptions. We can assume it will be done, if at all, in the usual heavy-handed big-industry way: Throw lots of well-paid professional people at the matter. Organize these players into project teams who fan out to dig the data necessary to do the mapping, the probabilities, and the simulations.

TURNING FEARS INTO DATA

Digging for data, though, is problematic. It is hit-and-miss, because outsiders—the project team members—do the digging. They are in a hurry (projects are like that), they do not know the territory, and they start with an empty sheet of paper. Best results are when a system of continual data-collection can be established. A good example is the requirement, in air traffic, that every near miss be recorded and reported. In the United States, a near miss in flight is when two planes become closer together than 5 miles, or are stacked less than 2,000 vertical feet apart. For those kinds of near misses, ones that occur frequently and are out in the open, data collection can be set up for regular reporting. Many kinds of risks, though, do not make it onto radar screens. Are there ways to bring these risks to light, and have data available when the project teams with their empty notebooks come searching?

Chapter 6 delved into a similar issue. The prescription was for the work force to continually record every frustration standing in the way of getting the job and the process done right. In this chapter, the concerns are broader than jobs and processes. In cases of highly critical near misses, either chronic or one-off, the emotional reaction of people is not frustration so much as fear:

- The temperature and pressure gauges are notoriously unreliable, so we've been ignoring them. But we're worried. (This was the situation that led to the 1984 Bhopal, India, chemical plant disaster that ended up killing or maiming tens of thousands.)
- We don't trust the O-ring seals (two Morton Thiokol engineers who anticipated problems that led to the Challenger space shuttle explosion that killed seven astronauts in 1986).
- I've been on the job only two weeks and they've got me navigating the complicated route through Paddington Station at rush hour (the train engineer who died, along with 30 others, in a head-on crash of his train with another high-speed train in the London tube in 1999).[30]

Other times, employees cannot follow procedures because there are none, or existing procedures are totally wrong for the situation. It might be the clerk, nurse, or pharmaceutical packing-line operator who must make a decision that, if wrong, could mean loss of a key account or someone's life, or a massive lawsuit—and personal loss of employment. Then there are the cases of associates who know there is no backup supplier of a critical part, or pumps that could keep the plant running in case of a flood, or know that customer data passing among company departments lack hacker/ competitor-safe encryption.

People need an outlet for such fears. And so do their employers, and society. A system that calls for all associates regularly to record job/process frustrations may just as well include fears, too. Why not label them problems, or risks? Because, to people, they are fears first, problems or risks second. And if Staci says, "Jennifer, why did you report that? You're a snitch!," Jennifer says, "Because they're requiring us to report fears. And you and I both have called them fears ourselves. So don't call me a snitch. I need this job."

WHY NOT INVENTORY—JUST IN CASE?

Robert Solow, winner of a Nobel Prize in economics, said, in a November 2001 talk, "Last year there were 100 elves working in the North Pole preparing toys for the Christmas season, while this year 95 of them will be making toys and five will be guarding the perimeter fence." Make that 90 making toys, five guarding, and five more dispersed to five huge distribution centers on the five largest continents—to stage and manage the inventories.[31]

The ordinary reaction to uncertainties and fears is to stock up: Fill your gas tank and your larder. If a business, fill your stockrooms. If a global enterprise, open more and bigger warehouses and DCs.

The preferred alternative is to become flexible. Every production or administrative associate masters and regularly performs several jobs. Every professional has been cross-careered. Engineers have done production work and have spent, or will spend, two or three years as a production supervisor or sales engineer. Buyers and accounts-payable people have swapped positions, which loses effectiveness in early learning periods but gives each of them valuable long-run business perspective and enhances their careers. And so on.

As for equipment, adaptive flexibility does not just mean quick setup and changeover. Just as vital is *surge flexibility*: equipment capacity to handle demand shocks, or sudden, unexpected but very welcome opportunities to serve a new or existing customer. When your company is called upon to perform in a pinch, it is often at the expense of a competitor. When the air clears, you emerge stronger and your competitor weaker. (For a good example, please see the Nokia/Ericsson story in Chapter 19, "When Things Go Wrong . . .")

Surge capacity can be global. For example, Intel has semiconductor plants around the world that are built to the same specs with the same equipment and same procedures (Intel's famed best practice called "Copy Exactly!"[32]). When there is a crisis in one plant or country, Intel's other plants can quickly ramp up and maintain commitments.

Various global calamities may have prodded companies such as Intel to step up their efforts on not having all their capacity in one place. A prominent example is the massive earthquake that hit Kobe, Japan, in 1995. Toyota was among those severely affected. A Sumitomo Motor Industries plant, Toyota's only source of brake shoes for its made-in-Japan cars, actually was in Osaka, not Kobe. But Sumitomo suffered collateral damage from the Kobe quake: It lost its gas and water supplies. The resulting shortage of brake shoes shut down production of 20,000 Toyota cars, with some $200 million in lost sales revenue.[33] The cause was not the inventory-frugal just-in-time system. It was the combination at Toyota of (1) having all production in just one geographical area, (2) reliance on a single source, and (3) no standardized design of the brake shoes, which presumably would have allowed flying in brake shoes from suppliers in the United States, Europe, or elsewhere.

Surge capacity provides time flexibility, but may be inflexible as to models. For example, a car plant that normally operates 10 shifts per week could readily surge to 15 by working three shifts. But it may produce only midsized cars—no compacts, no SUVs, no minivans. A situation at Dell in October 2003 demonstrated both time and model flexibility.

On that day, one of Dell's plants was put upon to build and ship 9,000 PCs, twice what it normally produced and more than its capacity upper limit, which was 8,000. At the start of second shift, things looked bleak for hitting 9,000. Surge capacity existed in another part of the plant, but it was designed for making printers. "In a quick meeting, the team decided to re-configure the printer production lines to make PCs instead, and to modify the shipping lanes for the added volume that night." The factory did it, building 9,100 PCs that night.[34]

High flexibility on top of planned surge capacity saved the day (actually the night) for Dell. Most companies, though, lack those capabilities. Instead, the main response to uncertainty is inventory. The five final chapters that make up Part VI bring in a good deal of hard inventory-based evidence on where the excesses and the excellences lie.

NOTES

1. Thomas Friedman, *The World Is Flat: A Brief History of the Twentieth Century* (New York: Farrar, Straus & Giroux, updated and expanded edition, 2006; original 2005), p. 522. Friedman admits that this theory is, in part, tongue-in-cheek, as was his earlier version, *The Golden Arches Theory of Conflict Prevention*, which he posed in his earlier book, *The Lexus and the Olive Tree* (New York: Farrar, Straus & Giroux, 2000).

2. Hall, in saying that the rewards of a major supply initiative "are higher than from internal lean," cites the cost of material, which "is typically 50–80 percent of total cost." Robert W. Hall, "The Lean Supply Chain Summit," *Target* (Third Issue 2007), pp. 48–59.

3. Peter Bradley, "We're Gonna Need a Bigger Box," *DC Velocity* (March 2007), pp. 34–36.

4. Phone interview and e-mail correspondence with Olsson and Meyer (March 8, 2007).

5. Richard J. Schonberger, *Let's Fix It! How the World's Leading Manufacturers Became Complacent and Lost Their Way* (New York: Free Press/Simon & Schuster, 2001), p. 31–36.

6. Ibid., Exhibit 12, p. 34.

7. See, for example, the Nypro segment in Schonberger, ibid., pp. 66–67.

8. Excerpted from www.nypro.com (March 1, 2007).

9. Brian Jones, president & CEO, Nypro Inc., "Competing in the Global Economy," keynote address, 16th Annual Shingo Prize Conference & Awards Ceremony, May 19, 2004, Lexington, KY.

10. Lea A.P. Tonkin, "HUI: What to Do When You Discover that Most of the Wasted Efforts and Delays Were Not on the Shop Floor," *Target*, 1st issue (2007), pp. 36–40.

11. Anthony J. D'Alessandro and Alok Baveja, "Divide and Conquer: Rohm & Haas' Response to a Changing Specialty Chemicals Market," *Interfaces*, 30, no. 6 (November–December 2000), pp. 1–16.

12. John Newhouse, *Boeing Versus Airbus: The Inside Story of the Greatest International Competition in Business* (New York: Knopf, 2007), pp. 121–122.

13. Jerry Useem, "Boeing vs. Boeing," *Fortune* (October 2, 2000), pp. 148–160.

14. J. Lynn Lunsford, "High Design: Boeing Lets Airlines Browse," *Wall Street Journal* (February 14, 2007), pp. B1, B12.

15. Laurie Sullivan, "Ready to Roll: Harley-Davidson's Three-year Effort to Build Closer Ties to Suppliers Is Paying Off," *Information Week* (March 6, 2004), pp. 45–48.

16. Communications with Graco management in February 2003, and in February 2007.

17. Johanna Småros, "Forecasting Collaboration in the European Grocery Sector: Observations from a Case Study," *Journal of Operations Management*, 25 (2007), pp. 702–716.

18. Monica Langley, "Inside Mulally's 'War Room': A Radical Overhaul of Ford," *Wall Street Journal* (December 22, 2006), pp. A1, A10.

19. Communication with Graco managers in February 2003.

20. Clifford F. Lynch, "Site Search," *DC Velocity* (May 2004), pp. 35–36.

21. "Little and Often," Daniel Jones e-letter, February 13, 2007.

22. Helen Atkinson (Quoting Adrian Gonzales, analyst at ARC Advisory Group in Dedham, MA), "Tailored to Fit," *DC Velocity* (August 2004), pp. 38–41.

23. Paragraph adapted from Richard J. Schonberger, "Supply Chains: Tightening the Links," *Manufacturing Engineering* (September 2006), pp. 77–92.

24. David J. Lynch, "Thanks to Its CEO, UPS Doesn't Just Deliver," *USA Today* (July 24, 2006), pp. 1B–2B.

25. The survey is roughly indicative. The numbers, though, are far too precise, because these kinds of surveys get only small percentage response rates. Peter Bradley, "A Successful Handoff?" *DC Velocity* (November 2005), pp. 55–59.

26. See, for example, Kate O'Sullivan, "Financing the Chain," *CFO* (February 2007), pp. 46–53.

27. Friedman, ibid.

28. Yossi Sheffi, *The Resilient Enterprise: Overcoming Vulnerability for Competitive Advantage* (Cambridge, MA: MIT Press, 2005).

29. One simulation package for "supply chain risk management (SCRM)" has been developed, with U.S. Department of Defense funding, by NewVectors Supply Chain Engineering, www.newvectors.net. Ray VanderBok, John A. Sauter, Chris Bryan, and Jennifer Horan, "Manage Your Supply Chain Risk," *Manufacturing Engineering* (March 2007), pp. 153–161.

30. These three examples are adapted from Sheffi, ibid., pp. 35–38.

31. Cited in Sheffi, ibid., p. 135.

32. Copy Exactly is explained to Intel contractors in "Working with Intel," http://supplier.intel.com/construction/training/working1.htm (August 18, 2000).

33. Sheffi, ibid., p. 19.

34. Sheffi, ibid., pp. 248–249.

Part VI

Why Industries Rank Where They Do

Chapter 2 grouped some 1,200 companies into nine global regions and ranked them on sustained leanness, as measured by long-term inventory turnover. Part VI uses the same measure, but this time groups the companies into 33 industrial sectors. The five chapters examine how those sectors are doing on lean/TQ, using turnover trends as partial evidence. Chapter 18 sets the stage. It ranks the 33 industries, best to worst on inventory performance.

The other four chapters look what is going on in a few of the industrial sectors. Three get their own chapters. Electronics comes first, in Chapter 19, because it seems to be the raw, leading edge of major trends in lean/total quality–driven global competitiveness. Next is motor vehicles, in Chapter 20, where lean got its start. Chapter 21 targets aerospace-defense, an upstart sector that, after years of ignoring lean, is agog with it, at least at the OEM level. Finally, Chapter 22 lightly reviews a few more of the 33 sectors. Included in the four final chapters are plentiful examples of individual companies and how they are faring in regard to best practices in process improvement.

Chapter 18

Leanness Rankings for Thirty-Three Industrial Sectors

This chapter groups about 1,200 companies into 33 industrial sectors.[1] Each company is included in as many as five industries. Although some of the companies (e.g., retailers) are represented in just one industry, more often it is two or three. For example, Canada-based Magna International is included in vehicular components, metal-working/machining, and light vehicles. It is in the latter because Magna has moved up the food chain from auto parts to contract assembly of cars for such customers as BMW and Chrysler. Large, diversified firms such as General Electric and Matsushita Electric Industrial are in up to five sectors.

In three cases, an industry sector large enough to stand alone is also an obvious component of a still larger sector: Semiconductors is treated separately and also included in electronics. Paper is both separate and within the wood (lumber)/paper sector. And apparel/sewn products is separate and also included with textiles.

THE INDUSTRY RANKINGS

Exhibit 18.1 lists the 33 industries in rank order, best to worst by long-term trend. (The scoring system, introduced in Chapter 2, is repeated below the exhibit.) Ranking first (leanest) is petroleum producers, with a 0.93 average score. The 43 companies making up the sector include 19 A-graded and only 2 D- and 1 F-graded. For the bottom-most industry, pharmaceuticals, the grading pattern is nearly the reverse: 21 pharma companies with D's and F's, and just five with A's.

A natural question is: How valid are the rankings? You need to know in order to assess your own industry and how it stacks up.

A good answer comes from tracking the rankings over the past four or five years (the number and composition of companies in the database was considerably smaller and less stable before that). Over that span, we have updated and recalculated scores, and re-ranked the industries several times as more companies' financial reports have become sufficiently available. The most reliable rankings should be for industries (1) made up of a larger number of companies, (2) whose rankings have not changed a lot, and (3) that are well represented by this database of larger, publicly held companies.

Exhibit 18.1   Industries Ranked by Long-Term Inventory Turnover

Rank	Industrial sector	Score	Number of Companies
1	Petroleum	0.93	43
2	Paper-converted products	0.89	57
3	Distribution-wholesale	0.86	47
4	Semiconductors	0.79	40
5	Electronics	0.77	226
6	Telecom	0.76	34
7	Paper	0.72	28
8	Metal-working/machining	0.71	241
9	Plastic/rubber/glass/ceramic	0.69	210
10	Major appliances	0.67	18
11	Pump/hydraulic/pressure	0.66	60
12	Vehicular components	0.66	102
13	Sheet metal	0.66	67
14	Machinery	0.64	111
15	Electric	0.61	86
16	Instruments/test equipment	0.61	41
17	Aerospace/defense	0.59	53
18	Personal-care products	0.59	32
19	Wood (lumber)/paper	0.58	49
20	Apparel/sewn products	0.56	49
21	Liquids/gases/powders/grains	0.54	316
22	Medical devices	0.53	43
23	Retail	0.53	131
24	Food/beverage/tobacco	0.53	134
25	Furniture	0.52	20
26	Basic metal processing	0.52	61
27	Motors & engines	0.52	61
28	Wire & cable	0.50	28
29	Autos, light trucks, bikes	0.50	38
30	Chemicals	0.36	106
31	Heavy industrial vehicles	0.35	50
32	Textiles/sewn products	0.28	43
33	Pharmaceuticals	0.02	66

Scoring basis–points:
2 — Clearly improving trend of at least 10 years
1 — Same, followed by 5 to 7 years of no improvement or decline
0.5 — 5 to 9 years of steady improvement
Zero — No clear trend at all—just up and down, irregularly
Minus 0.5 — At least 10 years of decline

On those three tests, rankings appear to be most reliable for 12 of the 33 sectors: semiconductors, electronics, metal-working/machining, plastic/rubber/glass/ceramic, pump/hydraulic/pressure, vehicular components, wood (lumber)/paper, liquids/gases/powders/grains, chemicals, heavy vehicles, textiles/sewn products, and pharmaceuticals. Those 13 industries are labeled "most reliable" in the leftmost column of Exhibit 18.2.

Exhibit 18.2 Reliability of Industry Rankings

Most Reliable	Reliable	Less Reliable	Questions on Ranking
4. Semiconductors	2. Paper-converted products (many private producers)	1. Petroleum (large rise in rank)	6. Telecom (small sample; large rise in rank)
5. Electronics	3. Distribution/wholesale (rise in rank)	13. Sheet metal (many private stampers; shifting rank)	7. Paper (small sample; subject to commodity cyclicity)
8. Metal-working/machining	14. Machinery (decline in rank)	15. Electric (large shifts in rank)	10. Major appliances (very small sample)
9. Plastic/rubber/glass/ceramics	22. Medical devices (rise in rank)	17. Aerospace-defense (large shifts in rank)	16. Instruments/test equipment (recent growth in sample size; plunging, then rising rank)
11. Pump/hydraulic/pressure	29. Autos, light trucks, bikes (decline in rank)	23. Retail (mix of low- and high-margin retailers)	18. Personal-care products (very small sample)
12. Vehicular components		26. Basic metal processing (large decline in rank)	20. Apparel/sewn products (many private makers)
19. Wood (lumber)/paper		27. Food/beverage/tobacco (large shifts in rank)	25. Furniture (very small sample; over-represented by office furniture)
21. Liquids/gases/powders/grains		28. Motors & engines (large decline in rank)	28. Wire & cable (small sample; large decline in rank)
23. Retail			
30. Heavy vehicles			
31. Chemicals			
32. Textiles/sewn products			
33. Pharmaceuticals			

The next column, "reliable," includes five industries. Some factor keeps each of them from the "most reliable" category. Paper-converted products is made up of a respectable 57 companies. That omits, however, hundreds of privately owned companies, especially small, locally owned cardboard-box companies; were they included, paper-converted products might or might not score and rank differently. Dwight Schmidt, Executive Director of the Corrugated Packaging Council, says there are about 1,500 box plants in the United States alone.[2] The rankings for the other four industries have been a bit unstable in the past four or five years: distribution/wholesale and medical devices have been improving, and machinery and autos/light trucks/bikes worsening.

"Less reliable," the third column, includes eight industries. Petroleum has made a large upward jump in rank, while basic metal processing and motors & engines went the other way. The sheet-metal sector does not include many small, privately held metal-stamping companies; also, sheet metal's rankings have been somewhat erratic. Large up-and-down changes in rank apply to electric, aerospace-defense, and food/beverage/tobacco. The retail companies are a bipolar mix of low-margin sellers avid for tight inventories (Wal-Mart) and high-margin ones (Tiffany) that are not.

The fourth column holds eight industries still more questionable as to rank. Sample size is an issue for all eight. Telecom has risen a good deal in rank. In apparel/sewn products, the 46 companies are but a tiny fraction of the thousands that exist in the world. Other factors are: The paper industry's cycles of global over- and under-capacity can overwhelm best lean intentions; instruments/test equipment's ranking has shifted erratically as several companies were added to the database; and wire & cable's rankings have sunk sharply.

WHAT THE RANKINGS SAY

What is the meaning of, say, the top or the bottom ranking? If I am an executive in paper-converted products (containers, packaging materials)—number 2 and in the "reliable ranking" column—I might be inclined to feel proud, even smug. The ranking reflects leanness, and lean has long been the hottest management initiative in manufacturing. On further reflection, I modify that inclination, because there is a burden in being in a high-ranked industry: Most competitors are very tough. If my company allows process-improvement practices to flag, we are likely to see serious customer defections to competitors who are still improving their responsiveness and flexibility. Also, before long, the effects of their faster pace of fixing problems and cutting inventories will translate into a cost/price advantage. Currently, 18 companies in paper-conversion are graded A (e.g., Canada's Quebecor; South Africa's Nampak, and Smurfit-Stone Container). If your company is one of the two graded D or F (MeadWestVaco is graded D+), or even those graded C, which number 28, you need to get on the lean bandwagon fast.

[*Caveat*: As has been stated in an earlier chapter, the inventory trend for a single company is indicative but sometimes not a fair and accurate gauge of excellence in lean management. Product line changes, acquisitions and divestitures, offshore moves, and so forth may skew inventory performance for a few years. (Sealed Air, graded *C*—and nearly a *D* or *F*—may still be digesting its 1997 acquisition of a larger company, Cryovac, from W.R. Grace. And more recently—more indigestion— it has expanded a good deal internationally.) Whatever the unfair grading for a single company, it washes out for groupings of them, especially in the larger, more stable industry sectors.]

On the other side of the coin, an executive in 32nd-ranked textile/sewn products might view that low rank (in the "most reliable" category) as a passport to business-as-usual. The opposite makes more sense: The textile company that improves its responsiveness—lean's main mission—gains a competitive edge. Still, the common attitude could be, "Why worry? This industry does not compete on leanness."

Ah, but it does. Chapter 14 gave examples of how the practices of leading-edge companies transforming the industry. Two of the cited companies are Italy-based Benetton and Sweden-based H&M Hennes & Mauritz, both graded *A* along with five others in the industry; two more are graded *B*. That compares with 11 graded *D* and *F* and 23 graded *C*. Benetton's innovations across supply chains were featured in two of my earlier books.[3] Another *A* would go to Zara, except that we do not yet have access to its financial documents for the required 15 years. Zara, a subsidiary of Inditex of Spain, may currently rate as one of the top-10 leanest-of-the-lean companies in all industries, as measured by quick response to sales trends in its stores, and faster-moving inventories.[4] As *Business Week* puts it, "Zara is the Dell Computer Inc. of the fashion industry."[5] Fast-growing, privately held American Apparel follows a similar strategy. (American Apparel's vertically integrated factory in downtown Los Angeles includes, at the sewing stage, organization into cell teams of six sewers, by color and silhouette.[6])

These examples make the point. Even companies ranked low in long-term leanness have a lot to gain from a strong lean/TQ effort, or to lose if it is lacking.

The remaining chapters of Part VI examine some of the industries in more detail. Three sectors—electronics, automotive, and aerospace-defense—get special attention in chapters of their own. The final chapter briefly looks at what is happening in other sectors.

NOTES

1. We have some data for two other sectors, printing and mining. They are not separately discussed or ranked because of unique features. Much of printing goes from raw paper to delivered result in scarcely any time or measurable inventory. Some mining goes from uncountable in-the-earth raw material to immediately delivered ore; other mining companies also refine ores into measurable semi-finished or finished inventories. In the future, we may try to capture and separately analyze companies that perform both mining *and* refining of ore.
2. Phone interview (November 21, 2005).

3. Richard J. Schonberger, *Building a Chain of Customers: Linking Business Functions to Create the World Class Company* (New York: Free Press/Simon & Schuster, 1990), p. 149; *World Class Manufacturing: The Next Decade* (Free Press/Simon & Schuster, 1996), pp. 140–141.

4. Richard Heller, "Galician Beauty," *Forbes* (May 28, 2001), p. 98; Jane M. Folpe, "Zara Has a Made-to-Order Plan for Success," *Fortune* (September 4, 2000), pp. 80–85; Kasra Ferdows, "New World Manufacturing Order," *Industrial Engineer* (February 2003), pp. 28–33.

5. William Echikson, "Streamlining: The Fashion Cycle High Gear," *Business Week e.biz* (September 18, 2000).

6. Eviana Hartman, "Nylon" (October 2006), pp. 70ff. Found on www.americanapparel.net.

Chapter 19

Electronics:
A Metamorphosis

Like the caterpillar that could only crawl until it took wing as a butterfly, electronics manufacturing is experiencing metamorphosis. Emergent from the cocoon is the new, high-flying electronic manufacturing services (EMS) subsector. Being freed of that burden has in turn transformed the OEMs into nimble overlords able to concentrate energies on rapid development of products and advances in process management. These sweeping changes began in U.S. electronics but are global today. In discussing those changes, the chapter begins with supporting leanness data, and then details the rise of the EMS subsector. A third section presents a few of the industry's trendsetters. A final topic concerns risk: how a small, unexpected event in this highly outsourced, globalized industry can trigger large-scale change in the competitive order.

ELECTRONICS—EARLY 1980S TO THE PRESENT

U.S. electronics, on its death bed in the early 1980s, was again global leader by about 1994. In but a decade, the likes of IBM, Motorola, Hewlett-Packard, Honeywell, Data General, and Digital Equipment Corp. had matched—no, *outmatched*—Japanese giants such as Hitachi, Sony, NEC, Fujitsu, Sanyo, and Toshiba. They did so, in part, through application of process-improvement methods that originated in Japan: JIT, total quality control, empowerment, supplier partnership, and so on. The U.S. group gained further mileage from an even more potent, western-grown improvement methodology: design for manufacture and assembly (DFMA). Now, another decade forward, some of the names of the top U.S. contingent have changed: Data General is gone, having been acquired by EMC. DEC was acquired, then merged, ending up within Hewlett-Packard. Dell and Apple have forged into prominence, both benefiting greatly from DFMA and JIT/TQ/lean.

One piece of evidence of all this comes from the leanness database. Most of the U.S. contingents were sharply improving their inventory turns through the late 1980s and into the 1990s. (Sixty-three of the companies that were in existence back then were clearly improving their turns for the required 10 years, versus just 31 that were not.) Data General and DEC had graded *A* on leanness prior to being acquired. The other six major U.S. companies named in the above paragraph were and still are *A*-graded.

In contrast, for two out of three Japanese electronics companies, long-range trend lines were flat or heading downward in the 1980s and into the 1990s. Of the six Japanese companies named above, four were not doing well on the inventory metric. Sony, the exception, was (and still is) *A*-graded. But Sony has long been known as a Japanese maverick. It is famed, for example, for not joining with other companies on technology standards (e.g., Sony's Beta videotape recorder). That tendency extends to forging its own ways in regard to running a company. NEC was cited in Chapter 4 for its accelerated upward inventory turnover pattern in the past 15 or so years, but its turns were mostly flat in the 1980s and into the 1990s. Toshiba's turns soared from 1962 to 1988, and then sank. Sanyo's plunged in the 1980s and stayed low in the 1990s. Hitachi's and Fujitsu's inventory performances were mostly static through the 1980s and early 1990s.

Today, five of those companies are graded *A* on leanness. The sixth, Sanyo, is moving in the right direction (graded *C*+, it needs 4 more up years to meet the 10-year qualification for the *A* grade). Moreover, electronics is a leader in helping to pull Japan out of its economic slump; nearly half of Japanese electronics companies in the database are now graded *A*. But electronics cannot do it alone. As shown in Chapter 2, Japan remains ranked worst of nine global regions for having by far the lowest composite long-term inventory-turnover score. Unlike electronics, other Japanese sectors have generally not improved their leanness scores.

This is not to say that *A* grades on leanness will uplift Japanese electronics to global supremacy again. Deutsche Bank analyst, Fumiaki Sato, has set Japan's electronics industry on its ear with what he says in his new book, *A Scenario for the Realignment of Japan's Electronics Industry*.[1] Sato argues that seven big electronics houses need to merge into just two giants. Matsushita, Hitachi, and Mitsubishi would form one mega-company; Sony, Toshiba, Sanyo, and Sharp the other. Companies keep growing through mergers in North America, the U.K., Australia, and elsewhere, often with good-to-brilliant results. Belatedly, perhaps, it's Japan's turn.

Of the 226 electronics companies in the long-range database, 188 are based in the United States or Japan. A close look at the remaining 38—from Europe and scattered other countries—shows long-term leanness scores and grades similar to those of the U.S. and Japanese companies.

TRANSFORMATION: FROM MODULES TO CONTRACT MANUFACTURING

The reengineering of electronics began in the mid-1980s with small moves toward modular suppliers. Companies such as Hewlett-Packard and CalComp were inviting their sheet-metal fabricators to load wiring and other components into metal frames and skins. Before long, electronics OEMs had other kinds of suppliers doing the same thing. That is, they began acting as system integrators and delivering modular subassemblies rather than separate parts to their OEM customers. In parallel, the

OEMs greatly reduced their numbers of suppliers and number and variety of parts per end product—the lean ideal of fewer and better.

The fewer-suppliers notion came from Japan as an element of JIT/TQC. Fewer part numbers was mostly a western concept. It is the main thrust of the practices known as *design for manufacture and assembly*, a body of work of Professors Boothroyd and Dewhurst at the University of Rhode Island, circa 1980. Western electronics manufacturers quickly became DFMA's most ardent users. A 1987 Boothroyd-Dewhurst book, *Product Design for Assembly*,[2] was both recognition of what was going on in electronics assembly and a template for how to do it right.

An early, notable application of DFMA is the IBM Proprinter. Featuring unidirectional push-and-snap assembly and minimal number and variety of parts, the Proprinter received *PC* magazine's 1985 product award. The printer from Japan that IBM had been marketing had 152 parts, and the Proprinter just 61.[3] IBM had designed the product for robotic assembly using IBM pick-and-place robots. Because many IBM factories around the world were equipped for that, the strategy would allow quick ramp-ups of production to match the expected strong surge in sales. But the Proprinter proved to be so simple to assemble, requiring scarcely any fasteners, that doing it robotically was seen as overkill. (Design for robotics, then not needing the robots, was a main point made by Boothroyd and Dewhurst in *Product Design for Assembly*.) So assembly of the highly successful product was done manually by cell teams in IBM's factories.[4] Actually, when a product is designed for assembly, choice of assembly method does not matter much. Do it robotically, with hard automation, with skilled or unskilled labor, or in a sheltered workshop,[5] any of which is likely to yield good quality at low cost.

Though the Proprinter got the most attention, other Western electronics manufacturers were applying the same simplified design concepts. Hewlett-Packard's 1985 annual report states that its Touchscreen II personal computer "has only 400 parts compared with 1,000 in an earlier model."[6]

There is some evidence that the Japanese electronics industry was slow to pursue DFMA, perhaps because of its foreign origins. As mentioned in Chapter 4, 18 years after the Proprinter, Sony planned to shrink its number of parts from 840,000 to 100,000 and Toshiba would cut its parts by 20 percent.[7] In this sort of thing, western makers had a long head start. It greatly reduces the burden of too many hundreds of loose parts from too many suppliers. The production cycle shrinks, while providing value-add strengthening of the supply base.

No one could have foreseen that these beginnings of modular supply with fewer suppliers and part numbers would structurally transform the electronics industry. In the 1980s, the OEMs did their own printed-circuit-board assembly. By 2000, hardly any did; they sold it off to what became electronic manufacturing services (EMS).[8] From virtually nothing, EMS has become a large component of the electronics sector. Though the movement began in the United States and grew large there, now by far the biggest (as of 2007) and fastest-growing EMS is Taiwan-based Hon Hai/Foxconn Technology Group.[9] Taiwan and Hong Kong are home to other large EMSs as well.

But rapid growth of EMSs is global. The western Big Five—Flextronics (Singapore), Sanmina-SCI, Solectron, Jabil Circuit, and Celestica (Canada)—had combined revenue of $54 billion in 2006.[10] (Flextronics was founded in the U.S. and later reincorporated in Singapore. Westerners dominate its board and executive team.) That is about one-quarter of product sales (not service revenue) of their five largest U.S.-based customers: Hewlett-Packard, Dell, Intel, Cisco Systems, and IBM. Led by Flextronics,[11] the major EMSs increasingly have moved up the food chain into design and production of PCs for HP and NEC, networking and telecommunications gear for Lucent and NTT DoCoMo, and phones for Nokia and Sony-Ericsson. (EMS is a young sub-industry. For assessment of long-range leanness, sufficient years of financial data are not available for Celestica or Sanmina-SCI; but they are for Flextronics, graded A; Jabil Circuit, D; and Solectron, $C+$.)

This transformation of electronics has unleashed freedom for component parts to move to the most capable entity, enabling each to focus on what it does well. Because of the lightweight nature of electronic components, the freedom of movement is geographical as well. The past 10 years have seen large-scale globalization of the industry, company by company. Whether factories are owned by the OEMs or by their EMS partners, the primary expansion has taken place in China, Singapore, India, and other Asian countries. For all the concern about giving away one's core competencies in the bargain, the business of obtaining suitable supplier-partners in those countries has itself become a core competency. OEMs adept at it have become highly secretive about their suppliers. As journalist James Fallows puts it, "Asking a Western company to specify its Chinese suppliers is like asking a reporter to hand over a list of his best sources." Fallows quotes Liam Casey in Shenzhen, China (sometimes referred to as Mr. China), saying, "Supply chain *is* intellectual property."[12]

Sometimes, especially in the case of semiconductor manufacturing, the full production cycle may include crossing the Atlantic and Pacific, and lesser oceans and seas, several times.[13] The off-shoring march to far-flung countries was led, again, by western companies. Japan's electronics giants were a step or two behind. As the *New York Times* put it, "The qualms are gone. Now even Japan's pride and joy, its top-end electronics manufacturers are coming to China."[14]

A parallel transformation extends the beneficial thread to the remainder of order-fulfillment. It is the merging of disparate logistics providers as described in Chapter 17 (in the section "Third-Party Logistics—and Finance"). This restructuring, applied strongly in electronics but other sectors as well, removes many sources of missteps and delays through the process stages, including unclogging the pipelines.

So much outsourcing and off-shoring introduces new challenges for the OEMs, and for the EMSs and 3PLs as well. Outsourcing, with a strong collaboration component, must become a core competency. Evidence from the leanness data suggests that two of the seven largest EMSs have had some success in mastering that competency: Flextronics and Solectron have sharply improved their raw-material turnover numbers in the past four to eight years. Because raw materials constitute from 55 percent to 80 percent of total inventory value for the six EMSs, tightened links with suppliers take out a lot of cost—and lead-time problems. The other five,

Benchmark Electronics, Celestica (Canada), Elcoteq (Finland), Jabil Circuits, and Sanmina-SCI, have seen little change in their numbers, and thus have been losing opportunities for competitive gain.

ELECTRONICS TRENDSETTERS

Of the 226 electronics manufacturers in the leanness database, 80 are graded *A*. Among those, 34 have been selected for their exceptionally long leanness trends and are listed in Exhibit 19.1 in rank order. (Please see the box, "Explaining the Rankings.") Dell heads the list with a 5.8 percent annual improvement for 17 years. Xerox is next, not for its rate of improvement, which is 2.0 percent, but for the very large number of years, 40, over which it has compounded the benefits of that 2.0 percent. Moreover, Xerox's rate of improvement has surged in the most recent 8 years.

Explaining the Rankings

The rankings are inexact. They are a weighting of the percentage rate of change and its time span. As spelled out in Chapter 1, time span is at least as important as rate, because of compound customer-allegiance and compound monetary-interest effects over time. Dell and Xerox illustrate those two factors, Dell with very high rate of improvement and Xerox with very long time span.

A slump—a large dip in a company's upward trend—is a penalty that pushes its rank downward. Motorola's 2.3% for 32 years would warrant a rank of third or fourth but for its 8-year slump from 1993 to 2000. That slump suggests that the rate and years of improvement overstate the company's attainment of lean expertise, thus lowering its rank to ninth.

When a company is down in the last 2 to 4 years, that indicates two things: (1) The company's current rate of improvement has fallen from what it was. (2) That was not long enough ago to suggest much loss of lean expertise. The net effect on a company's ranking is small. Thus Ericsson, with a down-trend in the last 3 years, still ranks highly, in sixth place, for its 2.4%, 32-year improvement trend.

Third-ranked Apple, Inc., is a special case. Its inventory turnover, which skyed to 375 (less than one day's total inventory) in 2001, has fallen since to 51 in 2006. Apple financial manager, Nancy Paxton, explains the very high numbers in 1999 through 2001: rigorous JIT with suppliers, plus use of contract manufacturing for most production. Since 2001, however, Apple has been opening retail stores. Because stores must be stocked with inventory, that brings down the company's inventory turnover numbers.[15] Apple's 3.9 percent, 25-year improvement thus may be said to greatly understate its lean performance *as a manufacturing company*. But Apple has chosen to be also a retailer, and the resulting lowering of its percentage improvement puts Apple third rather than first among electronics companies. Remarkably, though,

Exhibit 19.1   Standout Electronics Manufacturers Ranked by Long-Term Trend in Inventory Turnover

Rank	Manufacturer	Per-Year Trend (through 2006 unless otherwise stated) as of June 2007
1.	Dell, Inc.	Up 5.8%, 17 years
2.	Xerox	Up 2.0%, 40 years (strongly upward last 8 of the 40 years)
3.	Apple	Up 3.9%, 25 years (extremely high inventory turns in '99–'01)
4.	NEC (Japan)	Up 3.2%, 21 years (with long accelerating trend) ('05)
5.	Western Digital	Up 4.0%, 33 years (down last 4 of the 33 years)
6.	Ericsson (Sweden)	Up 2.4%, 32 years (down last 3 of the 32 years)
7.	Scientific Atlanta	Up 3.1%, 25 years (flat for 8 years in the middle of the 25) ('05)
8.	Honeywell	Up 1.7%, 31 years (down last 3 of the 31 years)
9.	Motorola	Up 2.3%, 32 years (slump '93–'00)
10.	Thomas & Betts	Up 2.5%, 30 years
11.	Philips (Netherlands)	Up 2.5%, 26 years
12.	International Game Tech.	Up 2.9%, 23 years
13.	IBM	Up 2.8%, 21 years (down last 3 of the 21 years)
14.	TDK (Japan)	Up 5.0%, 17 years
15.	Hewlett-Packard	Up 4.0%, 17 years (down a bit last 4 of the 17 years)
16.	Seagate	Up 3.9%, 17 years (down last 3 of the 17 years)
17.	Sony (Japan)	Up 3.6%, 17 years (down last 3 of the 17 years)
18.	Woodhead Industries	Up 3.5%, 20 years (slump '94-'01) ('05)
19.	CTS Corp.	Up 3.0%, 22 years (down last 3 of the 22 years)
20.	Molex	Up 1.7%, 18 years (down last 3 of the 18 years)
21.	Analogic	Up 2.2%, 21 years
22.	Pioneer Corp. (Japan)	Up 1.7%, 25 years (large slump '94–'98)
23.	Halma (U.K.)	Up 2.1%, 17 years
24.	Vaisala (Finland)	Up 3.7%, 20 years (large slump '99–'03)
25.	Fujitsu (Japan)	Up 4.7%, 15 years
26.	Toshiba (Japan)	Up 4.4%, 14 years (nearly arrow-straight)
27.	Casio (Japan)	Up 4.6%, 14 years
28.	Flextronics (Singapore)	Up 4.1%, 16 years (highly erratic first 11 of the 16 years)
29.	Tellabs	Up 2.9%, 23 years (down 4 and up 3 or past 7 years)
30.	Plexus	Up 2.1%, 19 years (with deep down-spikes; down last 4 of 19 years)
31.	Sharp (Japan)	Up 2.5%, 18 years
32.	Hitachi (Japan)	Up 2.9%, 14 years
33.	Canon (Japan)	Up 3.2%, 14 years
34.	Hoya (Japan)	Up 2.2%, 13 years

Fortune says that in 2006 Apple's 174 stores were "insanely lucrative," as measured by sales per square foot.[16]

Countering the 80 *A*-graded electronics companies are 31 with grades of *D* or *F*. Of those, the one with by far the worst downward trend in inventory turnover is Hutchinson Technology, Inc. (HTI), producer of disk-drive components for computers and data-storage peripherals. Hutchinson's main customers are hard-drive

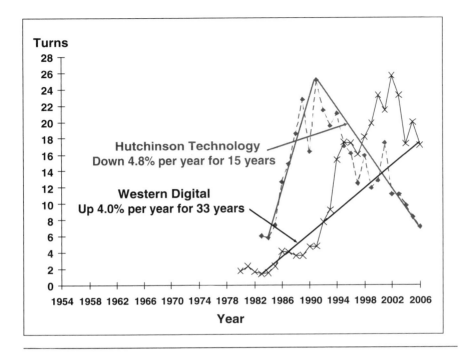

Exhibit 19.2   Contrary Inventory Turnover Patterns for Hutchinson Technology and Its Customer, Western Digital

manufacturers such as Innovex, Seagate, Western Digital, and TDK (Japan), all *A*-graded. Exhibit 19.2 shows the contrary trends for HTI (minus 4.8 percent per year for 15 years), and Western Digital (plus 4.0 percent for 33 years). The difference, astonishing because the two form a significant supply-chain linkage, needed an explanation. The component inventory breakdown for Hutchinson shows—especially in the past 8 years—much greater growth of finished goods than of work-in-process and purchased materials.[17] This suggests poor linkages and synchronization with demands of Western Digital and other customers. It's the big pipeline issue again—the problem, fully discussed in Chapter 17, to which neither supplier nor customer gives proper attention.

As is the case for any single company, Hutchinson's negative inventory performance could involve extenuating circumstances. People in the finance department there accepted my invitation to comment on what was to go into the book. Why should finished goods have skyrocketed? They point out that more than 95 percent of their product is exported to Asia. To better serve customers there, Hutchinson has established vendor-managed (HTI-managed) inventory hubs, which they also refer to as JIT hubs. HTI stocks those VMI sites with three to five weeks of inventory, which are on HTI's books. Before the hubs, customers would be invoiced at time of shipment from the United States. Other explanations have to do with process changes—more automation; the switch from mechanical to electromechanical products in 1996; and changes in product mix that were completed in 1991. Though the pipeline issue remains, these explanations cast Hutchinson in an improved light. In the logic of joint inventory (Chapter 17), though, it doesn't matter who legally owns the materials and bears their cost on the balance sheet. They are there, and they represent lead time and a customer-to-customer disconnect. Moreover, despite the extra inventory in the system, HTI is more vulnerable to global pipeline disruptions to serving its customers than before.

WHEN THINGS GO WRONG—AS THEY WILL IN A GLOBAL INDUSTRY

That topic, global disruptions, brings to mind how a small fire at a remote supplier plant resulted in a reversal of fortunes for two prominent mobile phone makers, Nokia and Ericsson. As a point of background, in April 2005, I had arranged a visit to Ericsson's headquarters in a Stockholm suburb, there to interview Jan Wassénius, vice president of supply. My purpose was related to this book. Specifically, Ericsson was to be included in Chapter 4 among the "strongly lean" elite. Those are the few companies that have improved not only in their long-term inventory turnovers but also in their *rates* of improvement. I'll explain why Ericsson ended up not being included.

Ericsson's graph had the characteristic concave upward pattern. By the time in 2005 that I was able to be in Sweden, I saw that the company's inventory turnover had slid downward for two years. But I went through with the interview. With deeper preparation, I might have learned something about how Ericsson had apparently fumbled its way out of a strong global position in mobile phones, ceding market share to Nokia. I knew about the new Sony Ericsson joint venture to produce and market the phones, but lacked the details about why. Sheffi relates those details as a dramatic story in his book, *The Resilient Enterprise*.[18]

On March 17, 2000, a lightning bolt ignited a small fire in a Philips NV semiconductor fabrication plant in Albuquerque, New Mexico. It was put out quickly, but the fab's no-dust clean-room status was severely compromised. To shorten the story, that created a global shortage of a chip necessary in the manufacture of new-model mobile phones. Nokia's response was massive, including sending its own engineers to Albuquerque and to other fabs of Philips to get the chip shortage fixed and to commandeer chip-making capacity not only from Philips but also other makers. Ericsson's response was meager in comparison. Its shortage ultimately amounted to millions of chips. By the end of 2000, with the chipmakers mostly caught up, "Ericsson announced a staggering 16.2 billion kronor (US$ 2.34 billion) loss in its mobile-phone division." Philips, whose chip-plant fire triggered the events, recovered with relatively small losses. Nokia's market share six months after the fire rose from 27 to 30 percent, and Ericsson's fell from 12 to 9 percent. In April 2001, Ericsson retreated, signing with Sony to form Sony Ericsson Mobile Communications.

And that is why Ericsson's inventory turnover numbers sank in 2003, 2004, and 2005. Mobile-phone processes are inherently lean compared with the complex telecom switching business that remains dominant at Ericsson. Sony Ericsson Mobile's balance sheet now carries the inventory, thus depriving Ericsson of the good inventory turns that were coming from the phones division.

Why did things turn out this way? Sheffi opines that Ericsson's weak response "reflected the more consensual and laid-back nature of Swedish culture, while Nokia had the more individualistic, aggressive culture of the Finns."[19] Maybe there is something to that speculation. However, preparing in advance for the no-warning but high-probability disasters in the globalized electronics industry requires high amounts of collective thought and planning, not individualization.

NOTES

1. Fukiaki Sato, *A Scenario for the Realignment of Japan's Electronics Industry,* 2007.

2. See, for example, Geoffrey Boothroyd and Peter Dewhurst, *Product Design for Assembly* (Wakefield, RI: Boothroyd Dewhurst, Inc., 1987).

3. I. Bettles, "Design for Manufacture and Assembly (DFMA)—The Boothroyd & Dewhurst Approach," in *Factory 2000, Third International Conference on Competitive Performance Through Advanced Technology,* York, U.K. (July 27–29, 1992). Found in ieeexplore.ieee.org/iel3/1194/4429/00171898.pdf?arnumber=171898.

4. "IBM Discovers a Simple Pleasure," *Fortune* (May 21, 1990), p. 64.

5. Anybody, including people with disabilities, can be an effective assembler where the product has undergone DFMA. See Karen Wilhelm, "Enabled Workers for a Sustainable Lean Business," *Target* (2nd Issue 2007), pp. 10–16.

6. Hewlett-Packard 1985 annual report, p. 7.

7. K. Ishibashi, "Sony Will Slash Parts List, in Bid to Boost Margins," *Wall Street Journal* (October 7, 2003), p. B5.

8. Robert W. Hall, "The Rise of Electronic Manufacturing Services," *Target* (4th qtr 2000), pp. 8–15.

9. A ranking of the top-10 EMSs, with sales revenue and one-year growth rate, was found (on March 9, 2007) in www.emsnow.com/spps/sitepage.cfm?catid=84.

10. Sum of data from each company's financial statements.

11. "Flextronics' most recent strategic expansion involves the original design and manufacture (ODM) of complete products, often before the company has a commitment from any customer": Jeff Ferry, "Flextronics: Staying Real in a Virtual World," *Strategy + Business,* Issue 37, Winter, 2004, pp. 1–9.

12. James Fallows, "China Makes, the World Takes," *Atlantic* (July-August 2007), p. 60.

13. Sheffi relates the routing of an Intel Pentium processor that powers a Dell computer: Japan to Arizona or Oregon; then to Malaysia; back to Arizona; out to Dell factories in Texas, Tennessee, Ireland, Brazil, Malaysia, and China; and finally to Dell customers anywhere in the world. Yossi Sheffi, *The Resilient Enterprise: Overcoming Vulnerability for Competitive Advantage* (Cambridge, MA: MIT Press, 2005), pp. 10–11.

14. K. Belson, "Japanese Capital and Jobs Flowing to China," *New York Times* (February 17, 2004), C, p. 1.

15. Correspondence with Nancy Paxton, Apple Investor Relations (March 12, 2007).

16. Jerry Useem, "Simply Irresistible: Why Apple Is the Best Retailer in America," *Fortune* (March 19, 2007), pp. 107–112.

17. From Hutchinson's annual reports.

18. Sheffi, op. cit., pp. 1–10.

19. Sheffi may have been led to this view by a news story quoting an official of a company that dealt with both Ericsson and Nokia, saying that "Ericsson is more passive.": A. Latour, "Trial by Fire: A Blaze in Albuquerque Sets Off Major Crisis for Cell-Phone Giants," *Wall Street Journal* (January 29, 2001), p. A1. Later in his book, Sheffi (ibid., p. 260) says Nokia's response was because its culture included "deep relationships and extensive communications with suppliers" and "broad and fast internal communications." Strong external and internal communications have long been advocated by "everyone" as good management. There is little point in giving it the "culture" label.

Chapter 20

Motor-Vehicle Industry: Earliest but Lagging

The long-term leanness rankings in Chapter 18 include four sectors in which motor vehicles has a presence. Of the 33 industries, motors/engines is 27th, autos/light and trucks/bikes is 29th, and heavy industrial vehicles is 31st. Vehicle components do much better, ranking 12th, which puts it comfortably into the top half of the 33 sectors. Overall, as judged by 10-or-more-year inventory trends, the automotive industry is not a high performer. Two quick reactions might be: (1) The OEMs have had success in getting their suppliers to adopt lean, but have lacked the incentives or capabilities to do much of it in their own business units. (2) Contrary to what is sometimes presumed, the OEMs are not simply pushing inventory and all its problems back onto suppliers. This chapter bores down into these propositions and related issues. To set the stage, we look at data for 55 automakers and then 91 suppliers.

MOTOR-VEHICLE PRODUCERS: HOW THEY RANK

Of the land-based motor-vehicle assemblers (cars, trucks, RVs, off-road, motorcycles; not boats or planes) included in the database, Harley-Davidson tops the leanness list with 3.9 percent per year improvement, and for 20 years. Toyota Motor, fount of lore in the lean core, ranks 52nd out of 55 companies. Its inventory turnover has not improved in 16 years and in the past 13 has been more than halved, from 22.9 to a still-respectable 10.1 turns. Toyota's decline averages 4.0 percent per year, nearly opposite in rate to Harley's rise. Toyota's financial records show that the decline is mostly owing to growth of finished goods, but also of purchased materials and work-in-process inventories. Exhibit 20.1 includes these two manufacturers in a leanness ranking of 55 motor-vehicle companies.

As with electronics (Chapter 19), the rankings are a weighting of the percentage rate of change and its time span. Because the trends for these motor-vehicle companies are so much more erratic than for the electronics group, the rankings here are less precise. The following discussion begins with an overview of the rankings, then a more detailed look, and finally comments about rankings on factors other than long-range inventory turnover trend.

Exhibit 20.1   Motor-Vehicle Manufacturers Ranked by Long-Term Trend in Inventory
Turnover

Rank	Manufacturer	Per-Year Trend (through 2006 unless otherwise stated)
1.	Harley-Davidson	Up 3.9%, 20 years
2.	Paccar	Up 2.1%, 38 years
3.	Honda (Japan)	Up 2.1%, 27 years (down a bit last 7 of the 27 years)
4.	Tennant	Up 2.1%, 31 years (improvement slow last 12 of the 31 years)
5.	Magna Int'l. (Canada)	Up 3.0%, 24 years (deep slump latter '90s; recovery last several years)
6.	Thor Industries	Up 3.6%, 15 years
7.	General Motors	Up 2.0%, 32 years (slump '87–'95; down last 3 of 31 years)
8.	Hindustan Motors (India)	Up 2.7%, 20 years (highly erratic last 7 of 18 years)
9.	JLG Industries	Up 3.7%, 23 years (deep slump '99–'04; recovery last few years)
10.	Ford	Up 1.9%, 32 years (down sharply last 4 of the 32 years)
11.	Hitachi Zosen (Japan)	Up 4.2%, 22 years (deep slump '96–'02)
12.	Terex	Up 5.3%, 11 years
13.	Tata Motors (India)	Up 5.5%, 13 years (slump '98–'03)
14.	Kawasaki Heavy (Japan)	Up 2.7%, 12 years (little last few years)
15.	Kubota (Japan)	Up 1.7%, 14 years
16.	Iveco (Netherlands)	Up 4.2%, 10 years (to '03)
17.	Nissan (Japan)	Up 2.8%, 11 years (down erratically for about 20 prior years)
18.	Fiat Auto (Italy)[a]	Up 2.0%, 25 years (slump '93–'98; down last 4 of the 25 years)
19.	Renault (France)	Up 2.0%, 26 years (down sharply last 8 of the 26 years)
20.	Porsche (Germany)	Up 1.7% erratically, 25 years (down sharply last 4 of the 25 years)
21.	Peugeot-Citroën (France)	Up 1.9%, 27 years (big slump '90–'97; down last 7 of 27 years)
22.	Alvis (U.K.)	Up erratically 13 years, then flat erratically 9 years ('03)
23.	Isuzu (Japan)	Flat erratically 28 years (sharply up last few of 28 years)
24.	Daimler Chrysler (Germany)	Flat erratically 10 years (up sharply prior few years; down last 6 of 10 years)
25.	AGCO	Flat 12 years (mostly up last 9 of the 12 years)
26.	Volvo (Sweden)	Flat 12 years (up from 10 worse years; up last 6 of the 12 years)
27.	Claas KgaA (Germany)	Flat 12 years
28.	Nacco Industries	Flat 9 years (up sharply from worse 8 years)
29.	Mitsubishi Motors (Japan)	Flat erratically 15 years (down sharply, 7 prior years)
30.	Navistar	Flat erratically 17 years (but way up from '60s & '70s) (to '04)
31.	Yamaha Motors (Japan)	Flat 14 years (up from worse 10 years)
32.	Scania (Sweden)	Flat 11 years (up from worse 6 years) ('05)
33.	Winnebago	Flat 23 years
34.	Trinity Industries	Flat 12 years (up a bit from worse years; down last 4 of 12 years)
35.	Toro	Flat 26 years (down erratically '86–'01, then up last 5 of the 26 years)
36.	Millat Tractors (Pakistan)	Flat very erratically 17 years ('05)
37.	Polaris Industries	Flat 15 years (trending down last 7 of the 15 years)
38.	Komatsu (Japan)	Down 1.5%, 17 years
39.	Caterpillar	Down 2.3%, 11 years (after up sporadically for 18 years)

40.	Deere	Down 2.8%, 13 years (up somewhat last 6 of the 13 years)
41.	Audi (Germany)	Down 2.7%, 16 years (down incline halted last 4 of 16 years)
42.	BMW (Germany)	Down 3.4%, 18 years (much less steeply down last 14 of the 18 years)
43.	Manitowoc	Down 4.2%, 10 years (after up sporadically for 24 years)
44.	Fleetwood Enterprises	Down 1.0%, 22 years (highly erratic last 10 of 22 years)
45.	Suzuki Motors (Japan)	Down 2.0%, 14 years
46.	Nissan Diesel (Japan)	Down 3.4%, 15 years (up somewhat last 7 of the 15 years)
47.	Daihatsu Motors (Japan)	Down 4.6%, 20 years (much less steeply most of the 20 years)
48.	Fuji Heavy-Subaru (Japan)	Down 3.1%, 11 years (in a sporadic, generally down trend for 26 years)
49.	Hino Motors (Japan)	Down 3.5%, 18 years (up somewhat last 5 of the 18 years)
50.	Mazda (Japan)	Down 3.6%, 17 years ('05)
51.	Volkswagen (Germany)	Down 3.8%, 10 years (after up for 16 years)
52.	Toyota Motor (Japan)	Down 4.0%, 13 years (after 6 flat years)
53.	Oshkosh Truck	Down 2.8%, 20 years
54.	Champion Enterprises	Down 4.5%, 12 years (after up sporadically for 25 years)
55.	Toyota Industries (Japan)	Down 5.5%, 13 years (after sharply up for 11 years)

[a]Results for Fiat are tentative, because of uncertainties in interpreting source data.

TRENDS: UPWARD, FLAT, AND DOWNWARD

Twenty-two motor-vehicle makers have generally upward leanness trends. Thirty-three others show no improvement or decline: 15 with no clear improvement and 18 trending downward. Of the downward group, 8 Japanese companies occupy the bottom 11 rungs, 45th through 55th: Suzuki, Nissan Diesel, Daihatsu, Fuji Heavy-Subaru, Hino, Mazda, Toyota Motor, and Toyota Industries. Three heavy equipment makers—Komatsu, Caterpillar, and Deere—sit together at the top of the bottom 18, in 38th, 39th, and 40th place, respectively.

Of the 23 upward-trending companies, the top two, Harley and Paccar (heavy trucks), look to be deserving of about equal rank. Harley's fine 3.9 percent rate is over a good-not-great 20 years; Paccar's good-not-great 2.1 percent stretches over an outstanding 38 years. Honda looks good in third place. Its rate is the same as Paccar's but over 11 fewer years, and with a bit of lost ground in the most recent 7 years. Tennant (industrial sweepers/scrubbers) rates 4th place for its long improvement record, but not higher because the good trend tapers off in later years.

The remaining 18 companies in the up-group have disruptions or flaws in their improvement trends. The 18 include 10 globally scattered car companies: 2 U.S. (GM and Ford), 2 French (Renault and Peugeot-Citroën), 2 Indian (Hindustan Motors and Tata Motors), 1 Canadian (Magna), 1 German (Porsche), 1 Italian (Fiat), and 1 Japanese (Nissan). The other 8 companies include 4 in construction or farm equipment (JLG, Terex, and Japan's Hitachi Zosen and Kubota), and 1 each of recreational vehicles (Thor), motorcycles (Kawasaki, Japan), heavy trucks (Iveco, formerly Netherlands—acquired by Fiat in 2004), and armored fighting vehicles (Alvis, U.K.—acquired by BAE in 2004).

THE IMPROVERS

With plenty of exceptions, the rankings generally descend with rates and time spans. Slumps seriously mar the uptrends for Magna (5th), GM (7th), crane-and-lift producer JLG (9th), construction-vehicle maker Hitachi Zosen (11th), Tata (13th), Fiat (18th), and Peugeot-Citroën (21st). Erratic (i.e., spikey) up-patterns, suggesting lack of consistency, apply to Hindustan Motors (8th) and Porsche (17th). Large recent-year declines plague Ford (10th), Renault (19th), and Porsche (20th). The ranking for Alvis (22nd) is lowered both for erratic trend and late-year decline. Shortened time spans, 15 years or fewer, push rankings downward for Thor, Terex, Tata, Kawasaki, Kubota, Iveco, and Nissan. Finally, Kubota (15th) has a combination of modest rate, 1.7 percent, and time, 14 years. (Note, about 12th-ranked Terex: By acquiring Genie—see Chapter 15—heavy-equipment manufacturer Terex may now be well launched on the lean pathway.)

Various sources suggest that most of the companies just named have had their lean and total-quality successes, and much of that expertise should still be there. Tennant was featured in a case study for its achievements in quality and JIT in the early 1980s.[1] Motor vehicles are but a small component of Kawasaki's product line. But for a few years in the 1980s, Kawasaki's motorcycle plant in Nebraska was the western world's number-one site for JIT/lean benchmarking visits. A case study on that plant was published in the same book as the Tennant case study.[2]

JLG received *Industry Week's* Best Plant award in 1999 for its lean-core attainments.[3] That year, though, JLG acquired Gradall, which added 25 percent to JLG's sales but pulled down its inventory turns: In 1998, Gradall's turns were 4.2 versus 8.4 for JLG.[4] Renault enjoyed a straight-arrow 2.2 percent annual improvement rate for 18 years—until 1998, when the trend reversed itself.

BATTLE OF THE CAR BULGE

Typically, auto companies try to keep their costly fixed capacity busy, even in years when their car models are not selling well. That factor may explain a lot of why GM, Ford, Daimler-Benz, Renault, and Peugeot-Citroën have experienced downward inventory turnover in later years of their upward long-term trends. It certainly does for Ford. The finished-goods (FG) component of its total inventory had hovered around 45-to-50 percent from the late 1980s through most of the 1990s. Since then, as Ford's inventory turnover plunged, its FG percentage jumped well up into the 60s. GM's component data show much the same pattern.

That phenomenon is easier to see for car companies in the flat and downward segments of Exhibit 20.1, because those companies have much longer and deeper plunges in their inventory turnover trends. The FG component for 51st-ranked VW had been below 50 percent from 1986 through 1989. Since then, as VW's total inventory turns have worsened, finished cars (and parts for sale) have zoomed up through the 60s, and to 73 percent of total inventory in 2006.

The car companies could get away with pushing unpopular car models onto their customers, the dealers. Lacking clout, dealers could do little about it. Now, in the

United States, growth of nationwide dealers—for example, AutoNation, the largest—changes the equation. With 334 showrooms and stores for nearly every different make and model, AutoNation can play one automaker against another. Its new ordering practices are based on mining customer data to reveal which of the thousands of car variations are in high demand. That information becomes the basis for each store's ordering from the carmakers. Total numbers of cars in the lots go down, and vehicles that are there turn over more quickly. H. Wayne Huizenga, the founder of AutoNation, likens this to the way Wal-Mart operates.[5] And that way starts with retailer sales and filters back to the producers, forcing them to produce what sells, rather than less-popular versions they might prefer to make.

NO CLEAR PATTERN

Fifteen companies are labeled "flat"—actually meaning *no clear pattern*—in Exhibit 20.1. Three of them, Isuzu (23rd), AGCO (25th), and Volvo (26th), get credit for their most recent upward trend. Ranking 28th is Nacco (forklift trucks and other products), flat for fewer years (9) but with an upward jump since the prior 8 years. (Comments about prior years, if not too remote, can indicate latent lean learning, or lack thereof.) Benefiting similarly are Navistar (30th), Yamaha (31st), Scania (32nd), and Trinity Industries (34th—rail cars and other products). The long, flat trend for Winnebago (33rd) suggests absence of current or prior lean expertise. Toro (35th) and Millat Tractors (36th) are erratic. Polaris (37th), fading in its last seven years, is at the bottom of the flat group.

Among these companies, undistinguished for their inventory trends, one nevertheless stands tall for its special approach to lean: Scania, the heavy truck and bus manufacturer. Johnson and Bröms devote a book chapter to Scania's single-minded pursuit, dating back to the 1950s,[6] of modular design of its trucks. The design objective is to have small numbers of standard parts that combine into small numbers of main modules that assemble into a very large variety of truck configurations. The effect is to allow customers broad choices—customized trucks—that cost much less to produce and service than is possible without the standardization and modularization. "Co-modularization" extends the benefits from Scania's trucks to its buses.[7] All of Scania's annual reports that we have looked at crow about these capabilities in several ways. For example, "Scania's new gearbox is a typical example of modularization. The various parts are combined in different ways to fit on everything from a light distribution truck or bus to really heavy rigs featuring Scania's most powerful engines."[8]

I am aware, from personal visits to its Kenworth truck plants, that Paccar also provides vast customer choice, and that Kenworth produces all that choice with high flexibility and quick response. (Kenworth is secretive, though, on the details. Its annual reports say nothing about this capability, and Paccar has been unresponsive to requests for further information.) In spite of flexibility, or maybe even because of it, Paccar has by far the longest trend of improving inventory turns of the companies in Exhibit 20.1. Why doesn't Scania measure up on the inventory-improvement metric?

There could be a dozen reasons. A statement in its 2005 annual report hints at one possibility. Because small numbers of its standardized parts go together modularly to provide high variety for customers, "this allows considerably longer production runs than is possible in a conventional production system."[9] *Aha!* Maybe small lot sizes and short production runs—basics of the lean core—are not given much weight at Scania. Maybe it is the accounting bugaboo: conventional, discredited cost accounting that "proves" unit costs go down with longer runs.

This is not to say that long production runs are always bad. In cases of fairly level demand, a standard, high-volume part might be produced synchronously to high-volume usage at next processes—maybe in a run of an entire month, until the switch to a new level rate.

DOWN-TRENDS

For the 18 companies in the "down" group, the ranking is still more unsettled. For example, the bottom five could be listed in any order. Oshkosh Truck has the least negative rate (minus 2.8 percent) but for 20 years. The other four have greater negative rates though for shorter time spans, 10 to 13 years. VW (minus 3.8 percent), Champion (minus 4.5 percent), and Toyota Industries (minus 5.5 percent) have good prior years, whereas Toyota Motor (minus 4.0 percent) had 6 prior years of no improvement.

Further up from the bottom, rankings 50 to 45, is a string of six more Japanese producers: Mazda, Hino (which became a subsidiary of Toyota in 2001), Fuji, Daihatsu (another Toyota subsidiary, since 1967), Nissan Diesel, and Suzuki. Their ranks could be in almost any order, because combinations of their negative rates and number of years seem nearly equivalent. RV-maker Fleetwood (44th) has a low negative (1.0 percent) but for 22 lately-erratic years. Heavy-equipment producer Manitowoc (43rd) has a high minus trend for 10 years coupled with other negative factors. However, current skyrocketing global demand for construction cranes, a Manitowoc speciality, should be driving its inventory turns upward.

German automakers BMW (42nd) and Audi (41st) have similar negative patterns. They had improved their turns dramatically in the 1980s. BMW's rose from 12 in 1981 to 19 in 1988. Audi's shot upward from 8 in 1978 to 21 in 1992. But both companies are now graded *D*, BMW for its plunge to 7.2 turns, and Audi for sinking to 12.9 turns.

Uppermost in the down group are three construction and farm equipment manufacturers, Deere (40th), Caterpillar (39th), and Komatsu (38th). Komatsu has the second smallest of the negative trends (minus 1.5 percent) over a clear-cut span of 17 years. Deere's and Caterpillar's worsening trends are much alike—and in both cases after long improvement stretches.

Deere's upward trend was one of the more impressive of any company—from 2 turns in 1954 to 12 in 1993, and concave upward in shape, signifying an accelerating rate. Its period of greatest improvement was the 1980s, when many companies had become enamored with JIT. And then came the backsliding, for 13 years, but with some recent-year improvement.

Some of Deere's units have had success in coping with huge finished inventories in forward pipelines. According to a 1994 report, at the East Moline Harvester Works, planters in the yard awaiting shipment were trimmed from 350 to 25. Moreover, they were assembled complete, which cut 40 hours of additional post-shipment assembly that had been required of dealers. These improvements were made possible by lean-core practices in Deere's factories, such as reducing production lot sizes from 30 days to 4 days.[10] These benefits must have been limited mainly to the Harvester Works and customers, because they did not show up favorably in Deere's balance sheet. To the contrary, Deere's inventory turns plunged from a high of 12 in 1993 to 5.6 in 2000.

The next part of the story is more favorable. A 2006 report on Deere's Commercial and Consumer Equipment Division refers to overhauls of IT, then logistics, then financial terms that had favored inventory buildups at dealers. Order-to-delivery times fell from several weeks to 5-to-7 days, and inventories from $1.4 billion in 2001 to $900 million in 2005.[11] Because 60 to 65 percent of Deere's total inventory is finished goods, these steps are meaningful—and may signal a renewed strong lean trend in both factories and customer chains. The next step is to do something about the supply chains, because purchased materials have grown steadily as a component of Deere's total inventory—from around 14 percent in 1992 to 24 percent in 2006.

Caterpillar's "Plant-with-a-Future" initiative,[12] featuring focused factories and most of the rest of lean core, fed its rising turns from 3 in 1982 to 6.2 in 1995. Since then, Cat's turns have slid steadily, to 4.6 in 2006. But here is a rare case where finished-goods growth is not the culprit. As a percentage of Cat's total inventory, FGI has fallen rather evenly from 66 percent in 1991 to 48 percent in 2006. WIP, on the other hand, has grown from 8 to 16 percent of inventory. One reason could be Cat's fast-growing remanufacturing business, which could require extra stocks of in-process parts. Remanufacturing is very lucrative for Cat,[13] which would justify some growth of WIP.

OTHER INDICATORS

As explained in Chapter 2, the leanness research focuses on inventory-turnover trend, not absolute value. We might expect, though, that the two are closely related. That turns out to be true for Harley-Davidson and Paccar. They are, respectively, number 1 and 2 in trend, and number 2 and 1 in absolute value. (Absolute values are not included in Exhibit 20.1.) Specifically, in 2006, Paccar turned its inventory 19 times and Harley 12 times. Harley, over the past three years, is also the most profitable of the motor-vehicle group with a net profit (before taxes) margin on sales of about 28 percent, and Paccar appears to be third, at 14 percent. Porsche, number 2 in net margin at about 19 percent, had an excellent 14 inventory turns in 2002, but has slid since then to 12 in 2006. (Porsche, like most companies in Europe, does not report cost of goods sold, so its inventory turnovers are computed on total sales and therefore overstated. For company-to-company comparisons, we adjust the overstated numbers downward by 15 percent.) That four-year decline knocked Porsche down to 20th place in the leanness rankings. Four years mean little, though, and Porsche may have the lean expertise to push its turns back up again before long.

Just about as many companies do not fit the mold of present turns closely correlated with long-term trend. Among the counter-intuitive examples are Daihatsu (Japan—small cars), Hindustan Motors (India—cars, buses, trucks), Kubota (Japan— farm machinery), and Toyota Motor. Daihatsu, lowly at 47th rank, has turns that at 16 are better than Harley's. Similarly, Toyota Motor, ranked low at number 52, has high turns (10). Hindustan and Kubota are the opposite. Respectively, they rank high (8th and 15th) on long-term trend, but are low in turns (5.4 and 4.2).

As for the link between turns and profit margin, there is no point in giving it further attention. Chapter 3 explains that improving leanness always spins off free cash and so improves the financials. But while some companies, in doing so, reach the heights in profitability, others merely owe a precarious survival to strong performance on the lean scale. With so many prominent car companies (e.g., GM and Ford) and their suppliers (Dana, Delphi, Metaldyne, Renold in the U.K., and others) mired in red ink, or worse, at this writing, motor vehicles makes the point.[14]

NINETY-ONE MOTOR-VEHICLE SUPPLIERS

Ninety-one components makers have been ranked in the same way as the OEMs. Exhibit 20.2 omits the detailed explanations of each company's trend. Instead, the listing contains just each company's leanness grade and the ranking itself. Most of these suppliers are sizeable. Fifty-two of them are on the Mergent list of the 1,000 World's Largest Companies.[15] A few merit special mention. Our discussion begins with comments about the top- and bottom-ranked companies, then a segment on Dana, and finally some special remarks about some of the other 91.

Dorbyl, a South-African maker of metallic vehicle components, is top-ranked for having raised its inventory turns at a 3.1 percent annual rate for 26 years (the entire span for which we have its data). SKF, the Swedish bearing manufacturer, improved at a 2.5 percent rate for 29 years, and its upward trend line is nearly arrow-straight. Bottommost of the 91 is Gamma Holding (Netherlands), producer of textiles for household as well as automotive applications. Gamma, also with a line of conveyor belting, mainly for food processors, had an inventory turnover of 5.2 in 1985. Its turns have slid steadily since then, to 4.4 in 2006.

DANA

Even though it has been hard times for U.S.-based auto parts makers in the past few years, I was surprised to find Dana following others into Chapter 11 bankruptcy.[16] Dana's 4th-best rank in Exhibit 20.2 is based on improved inventory turns at a yearly rate of 2.7% for 26 years; its trend is marred a bit by a slump from 1999 to 2002, before a surge in 2003 through 2006. This producer of drive-train and other auto components has been an avid student and implementer of JIT/lean since the mid-1980s. Actually, before that; according to Roger Harnishfeger, long-time dean of Dana University, the

Exhibit 20.2   Motor-Vehicle Suppliers Ranked Best to Worst by Long-Term Trend in Inventory Turnover

Rank	Grade	Company
1	A	Dorbyl (S. Africa)
2	A	SKF AB (Sweden)
3	A	Eaton Corp.
4	A	Dana Corp.
5	A	Valeo (France)
6	A	Carclo Engineering Gr. (U.K.)
7	A	Magna International (Canada)
8	A	Borg Warner
9	A	Johnson Matthey (U.K.)
10	A	Continental (Germany)
11	B	TRW Automotive
12	A	Pilkington plc
13	A	Alpine Group
14	A	Modine Manufacturing Co.
15	A	Eagle Picher
16	A	Federal Mogul
17	A	GKN plc (U.K.)
18	A	Freudenberg (Germany)
19	A	Rieter Holdings (Swiss)
20	A	Minebea Co. (Japan)
21	A	Collins & Aikman
22	A	Kenwood Corp. (Japan)
23	A	Kolbenschmidt (Germany)
24	A	Mahle Gmbh (Germany)
25	A	Standard Motor Products
26	A	Coventry Group (Australia)
27	A	Nisshin Steel (Japan)
28	A	Grupo Industrial Saltillo (Mexico)
29	A	Tenneco Automotive
30	B	Johnson Controls
31	B+	ArvinMeritor
32	B	Avon Rubber (U.K.)
33	B	Superior Industries International
34	B	Teleflex
35	C+	Stanley Electric (Japan)
36	C+	Clarion Co. (Japan)
37	C+	NSK (Japan)
38	C+	NTN Corp. (Japan)
39	C	George Fisher (Swiss)
40	C	Hayes Lemmerz Int'l.
41	C	Donaldson Inc.
42	C	G.U.D. Holdings (Australia)
43	C	Sumitomo Rubber Industries (Japan)
44	C	Panasonic Mobile Communications (Japan)
45	C	Sanden (Japan)

(continued)

Exhibit 20.2   (Continued)

Rank	Grade	Company
46	C	Trelleborg (Sweden)
47	C	Pirelli (Italy)
48	C	CEAT (India)
49	C+	Sumitomo Electric (Japan)
50	C+	Goodyear
51	C	Plastic Omnium (France)
52	C	Renold (U.K.-on sales)
53	C	Victor Company of Japan (Japan)
54	C	Tsubakimoto Chain (Japan)
55	C	Gentex
56	C	Lear Corp.
57	C	Timken
58	C	Grupo Desc (Mexico)
59	C	Nisshinbo (Japan)
60	C	Sika (Switzerland)
61	C	Vredestein (Netherlands)
62	C	Vallourec Group (France)
63	C	Apogee Enterprises
64	C	Japan Storage Battery Co. (Japan)
65	C	Vitro (Mexico)
66	C	PPG Industries
67	C	Cooper Tire & Rubber
68	C	Futuris (Australia)
69	C	Nippon Sheet Glass (Japan)
70	C	Champion Parts
71	C	Tomkins plc (U.K.)
72	C	Denso (Japan)
73	C	American Standard
74	D+	Rockwell International
75	D	Kayaba Industry Co. (Japan)
76	D	Cummins
77	D	Textron
78	D	Federal Signal
79	D	Danaher
80	D	Asahi Glass (Japan)
81	D	GenCorp, Inc.
82	D	Aisin Seiki (Japan)
83	D	Autoliv (Sweden)
84	D	Rheinmetall (Germany)
85	D	Toyota Industries Corp. (Japan)
86	D	Carlisle Cos.
87	F	NGK Spark Plug (Japan)
88	F	Yokohama Rubber (Japan)
89	F	Bridgestone Australia (Australia)
90	F	Bridgestone Tire (Japan)
91	F	Gamma Holding (Netherlands)

company had begun applying group technology (GT)—a cousin of cellular layout—in 1975 in its clutch business. Among GT-inspired activities were conveyor removal and, to a limited degree, inventory reduction.[17] In 1980, Dana embraced quality circles. In 1985, Dana began sending study missions to Japan. Some 500 company people participated in 25 such missions, the early ones organized by Norman Bodek, then of Productivity, Inc.

All that activity began to express itself positively on the balance sheet after Dana's inventory turns hit bottom in 1980, at 3.3, and began to climb. Spurring the improvement effort, Dana has excelled in employee involvement. Twenty or more per-employee suggestions per year are commonplace among Dana's many plants. And, as with a few other companies, suggestions are not counted until implemented. A few years ago, the 500-employee Cape Girardeau (Missouri) light-axle plant hit 11 suggestions per person per month, which is equivalent to 132 per year, before falling back to a still-impressive 6 per month. Several Dana plants have received national awards: *Industry Week*'s Best Plants, Shingo Prizes, and Baldrige Prizes.[18]

Yet this company is losing money and restructuring under bankruptcy protection. Why? A financial analyst for automotive says Dana was slow to outsource. It stayed too long with a costly vertical-integration strategy, rather than becoming a true tier-1 system integrator. They didn't learn "how to manage suppliers that well."[19] Supporting that view are Dana's component inventory numbers. From 1997 through 2004, Dana greatly improved its turnover of work-in-process/finished goods (Dana reports WIP and finished goods as one number rather than two separate ones). Over the same period, its raw-materials turns did not improve. About 40 percent of its total inventory consists of raw materials.

Dana is not alone in its sector. A check on 17 other tier-1 automotive suppliers finds that in the past few years 15 of them have either had unchanging or worsening raw-material turns. The mostly unchanging are Borg Warner, Delphi, Hayes Lemmerz, Johnson Controls, and SKF (Sweden). Those with worsening numbers are Aisin Seiki (Japan), Avon Rubber (U.K.), Eaton, Gentex, Goodyear, Lear, Magna (Canada), Modine, NTN (Japan—bearings), and Timken. The exceptions, with improving raw-material turns, are Federal Mogul and Superior Industries.

These have been difficult years for western motor-vehicle suppliers. Their customers demand annual price cuts even as they cut their own production and ordering from suppliers. And commodity prices—steel, copper, others—keep rising. Yet, Dana's example suggests that some of the tier-1 suppliers' own supply-chain practices have contributed to their difficulties. When times are tough, companies tend to want to pull work back from their suppliers—to keep their own capacity busy. These days call for a sharper pencil. The lesson from electronics is: Let it go. Let the ownership of parts move to the most capable entity. In auto parts, this means turning over much of fabrication to low-cost suppliers, domestic ones where it makes sense. In that regard, Sweden's industrial-equipment maker, Atlas Copco, serves as a good model (please see discussion in Chapter 17). The tier-1s become true system integrators, with a core competence in supplier development and tight synchronization with low-cost fabricators. Telltale evidence of success in this too-long-delayed endeavor would be, for each tier-1, years of rising raw-material turnover—better yet, reduced *joint inventory* (discussed in Chapter 17).

OTHER SUPPLIERS

In sharp contrast to Dana, with its backward-integration preference, is the Global Engine Manufacturing Alliance (GEMA), a Dundee, Michigan, joint venture of Daimler-Chrysler, Hyundai, and Mitsubishi Motors. GEMA was formed to develop and produce powerful, fuel-efficient four-cylinder engines in large numbers for its three partner companies worldwide. GEMA's first plant began operations in October 2005 and a second plant a year later. In cooperation with the United Auto Workers union, the plants have only one job description. The resulting labor flexibility is referred to as the *4A* concept: *Anyone, Anytime, Anywhere, Anything*. Four *A*'s could also fit with its approach to who will produce the engine components, except it would be any company instead of anyone. Bruce Coventry, GEMA president, says all the main components were subjected to a make-or-buy analysis. "We're only producing three parts of the more than 215 part numbers that go into the engine—the cylinder block, the cylinder head, and the crankshaft."[20]

Because it is visible, staring you in the face every day, the WIP side of lean gets the attention. But for 20 tier-1 automotive supplier companies studied, WIP generally amounts to only about 20 percent of total inventory value, whereas raw materials range from 25 percent to 75 percent. (Federal Mogul, producing chassis and engine components, and Modine, air and heating systems, are the exceptions. Each carries about the same small percentages of raw and WIP inventories: in the low 20s.) As stated in other chapters, today the biggest opportunities for lean gains are in the pipelines, not in the factories. Outsized inventories in the external value chains mean long lead times with accompanying slacks and gluts and slow response to problem resolution and model-mix swings.

Thirteen of the suppliers in Exhibit 20.2 produce rubber items (tires, belts, hoses) for motor vehicles. Just three of them are U.S. based. The rest span the globe. Overall, the rubber-products makers have poor leanness trends. Ten of the 13 fall below the median rank, which is 46th. They are Trelleborg (Sweden—tires for lumber vehicles), Pirelli (Italy), Ceat (India), Carlisle, Goodyear, Cooper Tire & Rubber, Tomkins (U.K.), Yokohama Rubber (Japan), Bridgestone Australia, and Bridgestone Japan. But leanness is not a lost cause for this industry subsector. Germany's Continental, graded *A* and 10th ranked, has improved its inventory turns at an annual rate of 2.9 percent for 19 years. Also on the high side of the median are Avon Rubber (U.K.), graded *B* and ranked 32nd, and Sumitomo Rubber (Japan), graded *C* and ranked 43rd.

The exhibit includes three major suppliers to Toyota, each with low grades and rankings. One of them, Toyota Industries, graded *D* and ranked 85th, is wholly owned by Toyota itself, and is both a supplier of parts and an assembler of Toyota vehicles. The other two are Denso (*C* and 72nd) and Aisin Seiki (*D* and 82nd). One reason for those two companies' low grades may be related to their membership in the Toyota *keiretsu*, which protects companies from outside influences. Such protection seems likely to retard exposure to new and evolving best practices—DFMA (design for manufacture and assembly), for example. (DFMA, in automotive, has two sides to it. One is commonizing from model to model, which paves the way for running more than one model on the same production line; this is a strength among Japanese automakers. The other is minimizing parts within a model while avoiding excessive parts changes from one model year to another. This is not a Japanese strength. It has proven difficult to rein in engineers' tendencies to keep changing ("improving") designs, which proliferates numbers of parts in the system.[21])

Even within a *keiretsu,* there will not necessarily be a high degree of collaboration. Toughness is lacking within a happy family. According to *Business Week,* as part of a company effort to upgrade its quality, Toyota's quality chief is, finally, "asking suppliers to share information and use common parts. Denso, Aisin Seiki, and others have just started using one design for voltage stabilizers for electronics in Toyota's cars."[22]

Suppliers notable for their absence from Exhibit 20.2 include U.S.-based Delphi, Littlefuse, Metaldyne, and Visteon, and also Burelle (France), Grupo Imsa (Mexico), Pacifica (Australia), and Showa Corp. (Japan). These companies have not been publicly traded for the required 15 years for proper grading and trend assessment. For the reduced years of so-far available data, only one of the companies' inventory trends has a clear pattern: Australia's Pacifica (13 years of data) had a spectacular rate of improvement going from 7.0 in 1994 to 18.5 in 2003; but its inventory turns have slipped since then, down to 14.2 in 2006.

AWARDS

Many supplier plants have applied for and won best-plant and other awards that recognize leanness and quality. A quick count comes up with at least 100 winners—of just the Shingo Prize and *Industry Week* Best Plant honors. (Shingo Prize eligibility is limited to the United States, Canada, and Mexico. *Industry Week's* awards have branched out to include, so far, a few plants in Europe.) Many of the automotive winners have received both awards. The dominance of automotive suppliers as winners of these awards should not be presumed to mean that this industry has distinguished itself more than others on the lean/TQ scales. Rather, it would seem, these prizes emerged in the industry as a de facto standard, something like the ISO-9000 series is for quality management. Each plant has been saying to itself, or is being told by corporate, or being advised by GM or Nissan: "We had better get the award, or we'll look bad." Or, "We need to get the award before our competitors do." Or, "Pressure's on, because our competitors have won several already."

NOTES

1. Richard J. Schonberger, *World Class Manufacturing Casebook: Implementing JIT and TQC* (Free Press/Simon & Schuster, 1987), pp. 152–164.

2. Ibid., pp. 120–123. See, also, Robert Hall, "Case Study: Kawasaki U.S.A.: Transferring Japanese Production Methods to the United States," American Production and Inventory Control Society, 1982.

Best Practices in Lean Six Sigma Process Improvement

3. Jill Jusko, "America's Best Plants, Tenth Annual Salute: JLG," *Industry Week* (October 18, 1999), pp. 66–68.

4. Sources: Annual reports for JLG and Gradall.

5. Neal E. Boudette, "Big Deal to Detroit: Fix How You Make Cars," *Wall Street Journal* (February 9, 2007), pp. A1, A8.

6. H. Thomas Johnson and Anders Bröms, *Profit Beyond Measure: Extraordinary Results through Attention to Work and People* (New York: Free Press, 2000), Chapter 9, pp. 115–140.

7. Scania's annual report for 1997, p. 7.

8. Scania's annual report for 2005, p. 20.

9. Ibid., p. 11.

10. Lea A.P. Tonkin, "Then and Now . . . Cultural Change at John Deere's Harvester Works, Moline, IL," *Target* (November–December 1994), pp . 22–25.

11. David Maloney, "Billion Dollar Baby," *DC Velocity* (April 2006), pp. 43–46.

12. Plant-with-a-future, brainchild of Frenchman Pierre Guerindon, a group president, began in 1985, with a focus on flexibility via small batches, quick inventory turns, close links with suppliers, a multi-skilled work force, and continuous small improvements: Jeremy Main, "Manufacturing the Right Way," *Fortune* (May 21, 1990), pp. 54–60.

13. Michael Arndt, "Cat Sinks Its Claws into Services," *Business Week* (December 5, 2005), pp. 56–59; and Ilan Brat, "Caterpillar Gets Bugs Out of Old Equipment, *Wall Street Journal* (July 5, 2006), p. A16.

14. U.S. suppliers in Chapter 11 bankruptcy include Delphi, Dana, Collins & Aikman, Federal-Mogul, Tower Automotive, and Dura Automotive: Jeffrey McCracken and Paul Glader, "New Detroit Woe: Makers of Parts Won't Cut Prices," *Wall Street Journal* (March 20, 2007), pp. A1, A16.

15. The 1,000 World's Largest may be found on www.industryweek.com.

16. Jeffrey McCracken, "Dana Follows Auto-Parts Peers into Chapter 11," *Wall Street Journal* (March 4, 2006), pp. A1, A7.

17. Phone interview with Roger Harnishfeger, dean (at the time) of the Dana University Technical School (October 10, 2003).

18. For more on Dana's aggressive employee suggestions system, see Alan G. Robinson & Dean M. Schroeder, *Ideas Are Free: How the Idea Revolution Is Liberating People and Transforming Organizations* (San Francisco: Berett-Koehler, 2004).

19. Brett Hoselton, analyst at KeyBanc Capital Markets, quoted by Terry Kosdrosky, "Analysts Worry Dana Is Sputtering," *Wall Street Journal* (January 23, 2006), p. B3.

20. Patrick Waurzyniak, "Lean and Flexible Manufacturing," *Manufacturing Engineering* (September 2006), pp. 65–73.

21. This impression is based on interviews with executives at four motor-vehicle parts remanufacturers, as reported in Richard J. Schonberger, "Japanese Production Management: An Evolution—with Mixed Success," *Journal of Operations Management*, vol. 25 (2007), pp. 403–419.

22. Ian Rowley, "Even Toyota Isn't Perfect," *Business Week* (January 22, 2007), p. 54.

Chapter 21

Aerospace-Defense: OEMS Are Soaring; Suppliers Are Not

Aerospace-defense (A-D) ranks below average on long-term leanness: 17th out of 33 industries (Chapter 18). Closer study shows, however, that the giants of the industry— 12 end-product producers of aircraft, missiles, ships, tanks, and the like—are mostly doing well on the inventory-turnover scale. The rest, 40 components suppliers that make up our 53-company A-D database, include some stellar performers. Many more weak ones drag down the A-D sector's overall ranking. If treated as two separate industries the OEMs would rank in the top 8 of 33 industries, and the suppliers in the bottom 7.

This is opposite to automotive, where the component suppliers' 12th rank is far better than that of makers of light-vehicles (29th) and heavy-vehicles (31st). Reasons why A-D and motor vehicles are opposite in this respect is a topic for later discussion.

In probing the industry, this chapter examines three kinds of data: One is the inventory-turnover trends for the 53 A-D companies. The second is the World Class by Principles Benchmarking database, which ranks the A-D industry not low, but third best of 26 industries. The third is published reports on lean successes at various A-D plants. Aerospace-defense, though, is a complex industry full of confusing claims and counterclaims. Later in the chapter, we demonstrate that typical performance metrics from individual A-D plants and programs—flow times, cost reductions, yield improvements, and so on—can stem, in part, from factors other than excellence in the lean core and external pipelines.

OEMS ARE IMPRESSIVE, SUPPLIERS LESS SO

Prior to the 1990s, lean was largely missing on the radar screens of aerospace-defense as a whole. But that was then. Since the mid-1990s, several giants of A-D have achieved strong multi-year improvement trends in inventory turnover. In their book on lean in the A-D industry, Ruffa and Perozziello include their calculation of the costs of just work-in-process inventory. "We found that by the time a product reaches the latter stages of assembly, these carrying costs can make up *over 70 percent of the total cost of assembling the product.*"[1]

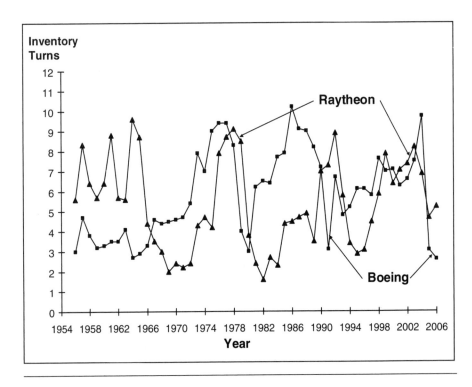

Exhibit 21.1   Trends for Two Major A-D Companies

PLANES, MISSILES, SHIPS

Exhibits 21.1 and 21.2 show sharply improving trends for three of the "big-five" in A-D. The improvements began in the early 1990s, which is when that industry first became infected by the lean bug. Before that, aerospace-defense was mostly disinterested in lean—in denial as to its applicability in the A-D industry.

Boeing's performance is the weakest of the five, but nevertheless is a turnaround story—with two primary catalysts. One is Airbus, the other Toyota Company. Airbus, with better designs and helpful governmental loans and grants, had been chewing off large bites of Boeing's market share. That roused Boeing, as tough competition will do. But what could Boeing do about it? A large part of the answer follows.

In the late 1980s, various Boeing groups had been studying and attending seminars on just-in-time, world-class manufacturing, and related manifestations of lean, and paying benchmarking visits to plants with worthy lean attainments.[2] These efforts failed to trigger meaningful action to alter the company's entrenched batch-and-queue mode of operating. That changed in 1990, when a group of the company's most-senior executives went on a study mission to Japan. If they left as doubters, they returned converted, initiating lean-based competitiveness training for more than 100,000 employees.[3] Lean implementations followed, and within a few years showed up

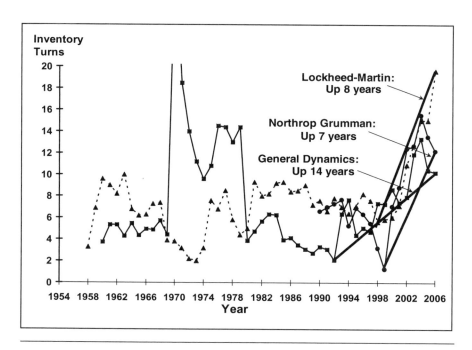

Exhibit 21.2   Up-Trends for Three Major A-D Companies

as a strong upward trend in total corporate inventory turnover. From a low point of 2.9 in 1995, Boeing's turns rose to 8.2 in 2003 (Exhibit 21.1). On the heels of its lean campaign, Boeing also has avidly adopted design for manufacture and assembly (DFMA) and modular deliveries from integrated suppliers. Boeing's inventory turns have fallen back since 2003. When the turmoil of global sourcing and selling off multiple production units to suppliers matures, inventories should be expected to take off again.

Raytheon's story is much like Boeing's, and both companies have similar highly erratic long-term inventory turnovers. Raytheon actually had a strong 12-year, *A*-graded upward trend, but in 2005 and 2006 lost all those gains and a bit more.

Trends for three other A-D companies, Exhibit 21.2, are much better. *A*-graded General Dynamics has upped its turns at a 1.5 percent annual rate for 14 years. Northrop Grumman and Lockheed Martin have steeply inclined trends for 7 and 8 years, respectively. All three had prior long-term worsening trends.

Three other major OEMs in the industry have impressive trends. BAE Systems (U.K.) and Thales (France) are *A*-graded for their sharply upward trends. Bombardier (Canada) exhibits a slight improvement trend over 8 years. Just 4 of the 12 OEMs have not improved. Both Loral and Alvis (U.K.) show no clear trend at all; and Dassault (France) has a 14-year slightly worsening trend, and Textron a 10-year fade.

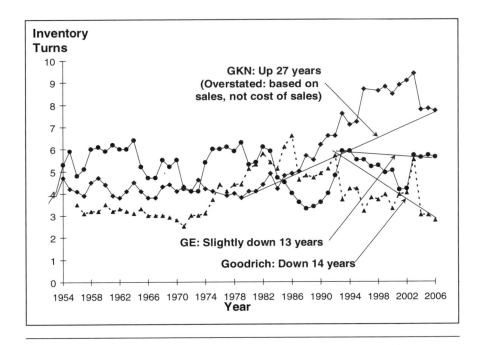

Exhibit 21.3   Trends for Three Major A-D Suppliers

A-D SUPPLIERS

The 40 suppliers provide anything from engines, to avionics, to hoses, to fasteners. Those with superior inventory trends include Honeywell, GKN (U.K.), and Ishikawajima Harima Heavy Industries (Japan). Among the down-trending lean laggards are General Electric (slightly down), Goodrich, Teledyne, Rheinmetall (Germany), and Fuji Heavy Industries (Japan). Graphs for three of these A-D suppliers are shown in Exhibit 21.3

Why should the OEMs show up so much better than their suppliers? A possible explanation is that most of the OEMs are nearly 100 percent dedicated to aerospace, whereas many of the suppliers are conglomerates. Steering a diversified company—toward lean or any other target—should be more difficult than in a one-industry company. Many suppliers in the automotive industry are exclusively automotive, possibly a structural advantage for managing a lean transformation.

A-D SCORES HIGH ON QUALITY, RELIABILITY, AND TRAINING

In contrast to A-D's relatively low ranking on leanness is its third-best ranking in the World Class by Principles (WCP) Benchmarking. In that benchmarking, discussed in two earlier books,[4] about 500 companies, business units, or plants have self-scored on 16 principles of customer-focused excellence. The likely reasons A-D scores high on the WCP but not on inventory turnover are these: The WCP's 16 principles strongly assess the lean side of process improvement, but give just as much weight to quality and value in the eyes of the customer. The aerospace-defense industry has long had some of the most stringent quality and reliability requirements of any industry. Because of very tight tolerances, the industry has tended to spend heavily on the best and most advanced production and testing equipment. It devotes equal attention to training aimed at prevention of defects, nonconformities, and equipment malfunctions. Criteria for earning points in the WCP benchmarking include quality and training in nearly every one of the 16 principles. Thus, even with no commitment to lean, a typical A-D facility may score fairly well on world-class excellence. The industry may have scored creditable points even back in the 1960s and 1970s. In that era, most companies practiced and trained people in primitive (by today's standards) quality methods, favoring defect correction rather than prevention.

How important is training? The late Peter Drucker credited training in the U.S. defense industry as a key reason why the Allies were victorious in World War II. Drucker explained that war making was highly dependent on optics for precision targeting. He compared Germany's plentiful highly skilled optical technicians with America's lack of them. It didn't take long to close the gap. Mass training in optical technology generated the expertise and triggered an outpouring of high-precision optical weaponry, greatly raising the potency of Allied bombers, fighters, warships, and cannonry.[5]

In those war years, a highly structured methodology called Training Within Industry emerged in the U.S. Department of Defense. The TWI effort was assigned in 1940 to a new agency called the Training Within Industry Service. In recent years, there have been efforts to resurrect TWI and attach it to training for lean and related initiatives.[6] Whether TWI or not, it seems clear that process improvement requires a high commitment to training. A-D generally does this well; in other industries, as discussed in other chapters, training is all too superficial and inadequate.

COMPLEX INDUSTRY, COMPLEX METRICS

The mostly strong trends shown in Exhibit 21.1 for the big-five A-D companies are evidence that those companies' lean efforts are paying off. Is there more? We turn to published reports detailing how some of those companies' various business units have excelled. Examples follow.

In 1998, Boeing's (at that time McDonald-Douglas's) C17 Globemaster Airlifter cargo plane complex in Long Beach, California, was recipient of the Malcolm Baldrige Award, the U.S. national award for quality. The same plant was designated as an *Industry Week* "Best Plant" in 2002 for production of an advanced version of the plane, the Globemaster III. Winners of these awards are obliged to publicize what they did and how they did it. Following are summarizations of key reported achievements from three separate sources.

1. Many self-directed work teams; many improvement teams grouped under eight interconnected process families. Job classifications reduced to 10. From 1994 to 1998, rejection rates from suppliers cut from 0.9 percent to 0.08 percent, key quality measures improved by 50 percent, and [flow] times reduced more than 80 percent. Since 1992, rework cut 54 percent. Since 1993, mean time between corrective maintenance on C-17's increased 8-fold. (Source: Baldrige web site.[7])
2. Redesigned horizontal stabilizer has 90 percent fewer parts, is 20 percent lighter, requires 70 percent fewer tools, costs 50 percent less to produce. Main landing gear has 45 percent fewer parts, can be installed 80 percent quicker than original, with 90 percent fewer defects. Cargo door redesign eliminated 600 assembly hours, 4 crane moves, and 5 critical-path days. (Source: A Boeing web site.[8])
3. Reduced defects 53 percent, rework and repair 48 percent, costs of rework, repair, and scrap 44 percent. High employee involvement with gain-sharing. U.S. Air Force paid $438 million for first plane, only $175 million "now." (Source: *Industry Week* "Best Plant" report.[9])

Among the three reports of creditable improvements, one item stands out: the price reduction to the U.S. Air Force customer of from $438 million to $175 million per plane. Those quality, flow time, and design improvements, *and a 60 percent price reduction, too?*

But wait. In the murky world of defense contracting things are sometimes not as they seem. The original contract was for 210 planes. Then in 1990, restructuring of the contract chopped the planned buy to 120 aircraft. Later, for various reasons including serious test-flight mishaps, Congress capped the buy at 40 airplanes. By 1993, the total program cost divided by 40 pushed the price to more than $500 million per aircraft. Such a cost could not be allowed to stand. To "wipe the slate clean" and provide relief to the contractor and the government, there was a "highly guarded effort" to rewrite the specifications. "It was one of the better-kept secrets in the infamously leaky halls of the Pentagon," and by summer of 1995, the flyaway cost per plane had been brought down to $172 million.[10]

We see that if the terrific price reduction was what led the "Best Plant" examiners to bestow their award on the C-17 complex, the honor would not have been deserved. Such is the hazard of using cost as a primary tool for assessing an improvement effort. Cost accounting is notoriously unreliable—and manipulable—and not only in government contracting. And cost can go up through the roof for uncontrollable reasons (e.g., general increases in the price of steel or energy) even as lean, six sigma, and total quality are doing magnificent work.

While the cost/price reductions for the C-17 must be discounted, the product design simplifications should not be. There is no more effective way to help neutralize the complexity of major A-D programs than through design for manufacturing and assembly: standardizing parts, slashing numbers of components, and so on. Design simplicity, because it occurs in an early stage before any production, has beneficial effects on almost everything: on quality, reliability, throughput times, inventories, training, and most direct and overhead costs.

LEARNING CURVE

The A-D industry has long been proficient not only in training, but also in learning. They are not the same thing. As far back as the 1920s, studies in the manufacture of airplanes suggested that direct labor per unit would improve at some rate as successive units were produced.[11] That rate came to be called the *learning curve*, or *experience curve* (see the box). A common pattern turned out to be 80 percent. At that learning rate, the second aircraft requires 80 percent as much direct labor as the first; the fourth requires 80 percent as much as the second; and so forth. The learning rate, in other words, is 20 percent between doubled quantities. Though 80 percent was common, each manufacturer was obliged to find its own characteristic learning rate.

> The learning-curve formula employs exponents and logarithms.[12] However, for any unit that is a power of 2, logarithms may be avoided. For example, in a 90 percent learning-curve, if the first unit's labor hours are 100, the second's are 90, obtained by (100)(.9); the fourth's are 81, from (100)(.9)(.9); the eighth's are 72.9, from (100)(.9)(.9)(.9), and so on.

Later studies showed the learning phenomenon applies not only to labor but also to overhead and to total cost per unit; by extension it should apply to manufacturing throughput time. The explanation for the learning curve is that big, unique endeavors are full of bugs to begin with. Bugs are worked out quickly in production of early units—the low-hanging fruit idea—and progressively more slowly for later units.

Getting back to the Globemaster's $438 million to $175 million price cut, if contract rewrites were not involved (which they were), maybe the learning-curve would explain it. We might wonder the same thing about other award-winning A-D programs.

Consider, for example, two Shingo Prize winners: Lockheed-Martin's F-16 fighter operation in Fort Worth, Texas (Shingo winner in 2000), and Boeing's AH-64 Apache Longbow helicopter, Mesa, Arizona (Shingo Prize in 2005). Among the reported improvements in Fort Worth was reduction of build time for the F-16 from 48 to 24 months;[13] and for Boeing's Apache there was a 40 percent reduction of manufacturing flow time.[14] Would the learning curve explain some or all of these reductions? We won't attempt an answer, because the Apache has been in production though various upgrades for many years, and current production includes both new and remanufactured Apaches. So the learning-curve calculations would be difficult. A hypothetical calculation using some actual data, though, is instructive.

Say that the first Apache was delivered in 2003 with a flow time of 60 days. If the learning rate were 90 percent, the second unit would take 54 days (60 times 0.9), the fourth unit would take 48.6 days (60 times 0.9 times 0.9), and so on. The actual delivery quantities were 73 in 2003, 83 in 2004, and 90 in 2005, totaling 194 for the three years. Presumably, by some date in early 2006, total deliveries would have reached 256, which is the number obtained by doubling the quantity eight times (X^8). For the 256th unit, the 90 percent rate would have cut the flow time from 60 days to 23 days. That is a 62 percent improvement, which is better than the 40 percent published figure.

These calculations are not accurate (e.g., production of Apaches had started many years earlier than 2003). The intent here is to show that even an improved flow time—the metric that best sums up the main benefit and goal of lean—might arise from normal learning rather than lean practices. Still, flow time is a far more reliable metric than cost, especially in defense contracting, for reasons already noted.

Putting aside the metrics issue, other published information about the Apache program indicates an impressive lean achievement.[15] The traditional method of helicopter assembly is like house construction: Build them in separate bays, which requires helter-skelter methods of bringing materials, tooling, fixtures, test equipment, job information, and human resources to multiple build positions. Apache was that way in 1999. By the end of the year, assembly had been converted to a pulsed U-shaped assembly line of 15 stations with aircraft lined up nose to tail along the line. Various models of both new and remanufactured Apaches run mixed down the line. The stability and regularity of this mode of manufacturing makes delays and problems more apparent to people on the line, which allows an accelerated pace of process improvement.

CRITICAL CHAIN

Question: What will go down in history as Eli Goldratt's most important contribution? Theory of constraints, you say? Here is an alternative answer: critical-chain project management.[16]

The primary basis for this viewpoint is a single case study: use of critical chain in aircraft repair and overhaul at Warner Robins Air Logistics Center (WR-ALC). This application of critical chain, along with plenty of the lean core, was successful in getting C-5 aircraft in and out of repair and overhaul more quickly. In FY2000, when turnaround time was 360 days, 16 C-5s were in process at any given time. The new system, in force in FY2005, reduced the time to 240 days and the number of planes in process to 12 or 13—and later 11. That freed up 5 C-5s, worth $2.37 billion replacement value, for mission duty. Because the air force is very short of C-5 capacity, the savings are genuine. Does the learning curve play a part in these achievements? The authors of the case study say it does, but in a small way.[17]

PIPELINING

The new practices make up a large, integrated set. A main feature is what the WR-ALC people call *pipelining*. In a sense it is opposite to what this book has said repeatedly: that the main job of industry must be to shrink the pipelines. Here, the key to gaining quicker turnaround is allowing some aircraft to sit idle in the in-process (not external) pipeline! The former, conventional practice assigns mechanics (as the assemblers are called) to a first-in-line plane. It then continually shifts them around. They go to an area where parts are in need of removal, repair, or installation. They work for a while until they become stalled for lack of parts. Then they move to another area where the same thing happens again. This sounds a bit like scenes out of the Keystone Kops. It is ineffective in three ways. It moves mechanics to jobs that are often not within their best skill category. It is highly reactive, requiring continual rescheduling and switching people and other resources. Too many planes are always on the floor in a state of partial completion.

Pipelining halts production on a given plane if key parts are missing. Critical chain restarts production after some days when all the parts are available. Then mechanics swarm the plane and get it done. They do so with most mechanics assigned to their best skill and with little time wasted in moving, job-shifting, and waiting. Mechanics are said to have higher levels of satisfaction. It is frustrating to be jerked around. ("Frustration Relief" is a main section of Chapter 6.)

Conceptually, critical chain is in tune with the view that improvement must be in the eyes of the customer, in this case getting work done swiftly, predictably, and with cost avoidance. Aside from critical chain, other aspects of theory of constraints focus on increased throughput, which is not a customer priority. Throughput *time* is, and that is the main purpose and outcome of critical-chain project management.

CRITICAL CHAIN AND PARALLEL PROCESSING

Reducing the number of units in process is a central aim of critical chain. On a micro-manufacturing basis, it is also the central aim of kanban. It is a universal best practice, one that pays off big in the manufacture of large, complex products. The straightforward way to trim end products in process, and therefore total throughput time, is through parallel rather than serial final assembly: produce modules and subassemblies in spurs on the main line, while the main line is doing final assembly. It is a concept that seems poorly understood by engineers who design production lines. They tend to want to line up everything into one long, serial-processing line.

At Warner Robins, parallel processing is applicable but in limited ways. Some of what is in need of repair may be processed as modules, but much of it is unpredictable mixes of piece parts. Critical chain becomes all the more attractive in such a highly complex, unpredictable kind of manufacture.

Critical chain is still new to A-D manufacturers. The entire lean core is relatively new as well. In applying the full set of best practices, along with its traditional high emphasis on training and reliability, A-D should be expected to vault upward from its present below-average lean ranking among industries.

SUMMARY

The main points in this chapter are the following: The aerospace-defense sector is still in an early stage of lean implementation. Most end-product companies have impressive lean trends, but that is not true of their suppliers. Judging from their mostly poor trends in inventory turnover, the suppliers have not yet made lean a high priority. In part that may be because their hands are full coping with diversified product lines. A-D end-product companies, seeing that their own internal lean efforts are doing well, may see fit to refocus on lean in their supply chains. That would press the suppliers to upgrade their lean initiatives.

Lean got a late start in A-D. Nevertheless, the industry shows up well on excellence measures other than lean. Contributing to that is the necessity for ultra-high reliability and quality, which has led the industry to outspend others on best equipment and training.

Some of the usual metrics that define lean excellence can be flawed. Cost as a metric is problematic in any industry because cost accounting is notoriously unreliable. All the more so in government/defense contracting in which contract quantities and specifications are commonly rewritten in ways that radically change unit costs.

Moreover, cost—and also flow times, scrap, rework, and downtime—may improve with no help from lean. The learning-curve phenomenon, which originated in the airframe industry, provides its own pathways to improvement. That does nothing to invalidate a sound lean/total-quality initiative, which employs an array of new practices capable of accelerating rates of improvement. Improvement in aerospace-defense must be driven by these practices, not by metrics.

NOTES

1. Stephen F. Ruffa and Michael J. Perozziello, *Breaking the Cost Barrier: A Proven Approach to Managing and Implementing Lean Manufacturing* (New York: Wiley, 2000), pp. 16–17.

2. Example: Davis R. Steelquist, Jr., "Just-in-Time Manufacturing: Applications for the Boeing Commercial Airplane Group," Seattle, WA: Boeing Commercial Airplane Group; 64-page monograph, dated July 1989 through 1990 (foreword by Richard J. Schonberger). Topical coverage included uniform plant load, flow and cellular manufacturing vs. traditional functional manufacturing, kanban containers, and push and pull systems; several examples of applications at Boeing were included, along with a 76-item bibliography. An 11-page Executive Summary of the monograph was released at the same time.

3. Boeing web site: www.boeing.com/commercial/initiatives/lean/history.html.

4. Richard J. Schonberger, *Let's Fix It! How the World's Leading Manufacturers Were Seduced by Prosperity and Lost Their Way* (New York: Free Press/Simon & Schuster, 2001); Schonberger, *World Class Manufacturing: The Next Decade* (Free Press, 1996).

5. Peter F. Drucker, *Post-Capitalist Society* (New York: HarperCollins, 1993), pp. 36–39.

6. Jim Huntzinger, "The Roots of Lean: Training Within Industry: The Origin of Kaizen," *Target* (2nd qtr 2002), pp. 9–22; Donald Dinero, *Training Within Industry: The Foundation of Lean* (Portland, OR: Productivity Press, 2005). It seems likely that TWI in Japan was widely employed in the cause of total quality control. Some companies also may have used the TWI methodology in teaching about just-in-time.

7. Baldrige Award web site, www.nist.gov.

8. No author, "Integrated Defense Systems Key Contributor to Boeing Lean Enterprise," www.boeing.com/ids/ids-back/lean-bh.html.

9. John Teresko, "A Partnership in Excellence," *Industry Week* (October 2002), pp. 36–40.

10. www.globalsecurity.org/military/systems/aircraft/c-17-history.htm.

11. The commander of Wright-Patterson Air Force Base was reported to have observed it in 1925; Winfred B. Hirshmann, "Profit from the Learning Curve," *Harvard Business Review* (January–February 1964), p. 125. See also Chapter 8, "The Experience Curve," in Robert H. Hayes and Steven C. Wheelwright, *Restoring Our Competitive Edge: Competing Through Manufacturing* (New York: Wiley, 1984), pp. 229–274.

12. Mathematically, the general learning-curve formula is: $Y = aX^b$, where Y is cost or labor-hours per unit, X is unit number, a is cost or labor-hours for the first unit, and b = logarithm of learning-curve rate divided by logarithm of 2.

13. Ross Olexa, "Flying Lean," *Manufacturing Engineering* (March 2003), pp. 71–79.

14. www.shingoprize.com.

15. Lisa Dunbar, "Lean Fever: Mesa Site Evolves into Top Performer," *Journal of Boeing Integrated Defense Systems*, 2, no. 3 (December 2004).

16. Eliyahu M. Goldratt, *Critical Chain* (Great Barrington, MA: North River Press, 1997).

17. Mandyam M. Srinivasan, William D. Best, and Sridhar Chandrasekaran, "Warner Robins Air Logistics Center Streamlines Aircraft Repair and Overhaul," *Interfaces* (January–February 2007), pp. 7–21. For a condensed version, see Mandyam M. Srinivasan and William D. Best, "Back on the Runway," *APICS* (March 2006), pp. 20–24.

Chapter 22

Other Industries

Every industry has its own unique features. This chapter looks for a few of them. Main targets are the biggest among the 33 sectors in the leanness database, not counting electronics, which has its own chapter. The three other largest are liquids/gases/powders/grains, metal-working/machining, and plastic/rubber/glass/ceramic.

LIQUIDS/GASES/POWDERS/GRAINS: 21ST RANKED

Three hundred sixteen companies are included in the liquids/gases/powders/grains category (*LGP*, for short), which is the natural home of the "process industries." Most of the 316 get counted in one or more additional industry groups. For example, most of the food/beverage/tobacco producers are co-members of LGP. So are companies in chemicals, pharmaceuticals, petroleum, and most of personal-care products. (Basic metal processing and paper making are not counted within the LGP category, although their manufacturing does involve early stages as fluids.)

Exhibit 18.1 quickly shows why LGP ranks low, in 21st place. The 43 producers of petroleum, first-ranked, are not nearly enough to offset the downward pull of 135 in 24th-ranked food/beverage/tobacco, 106 in 30th-ranked chemicals, and 66 in 33rd-ranked pharmaceuticals. Petroleum, lonely at the top, turns out to be an industry that may portend much for the manufacturing industry in general.

PETROLEUM: 1ST RANKED

Soaring inventory turnovers characterize the petroleum group: 19 A's, only 2 D's, and 1 F.

Larry Goldstein, president of the Petroleum Industry Research Foundation, offers this opinion: Cheap gas prices of the 1990s made the industry cost-conscious. They began implementing systems "to reduce their stockpiles of oil and gasoline, mirroring the just-in-time technology that Dell Inc. and others used to cut costs."[1]

A spokesperson at Imperial Oil (Canada) adds insights pertaining to crude-oil pipelines,[2] which are the ultimate transport device (discounting Scotty's dematerialization transporter in *Star Trek*). In the past 20 years, the North American crude-oil pipeline system has been expanded and modified. It allows transport of a wider variety of crude sources, such as Canadian heavy crudes, as well as of both refined and midstream products. Related to that, refineries in the northeast and Gulf coast have increased their capacity and capability to process a wider variety of crudes. Pipeline

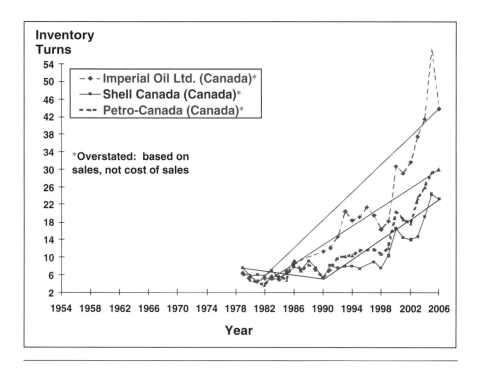

Exhibit 22.1   Three Oil Companies: Trending Together

and refinery versatility mean less product waiting in storage or moving to refineries by slower means.

An overriding explanation of the oil and gas industry's long lean trend may center on supply-and-demand factors. For many years, global demands have grown faster than supply. That drives oil companies to adopt every lead-time and delivery-shortening scheme they can think of. Except they try to avoid building new refineries, which are enormously expensive, unwelcome in countries that are the greatest users, and take many years to develop. Because it is a global industry, most petro companies should be affected by the supply–demand imbalance in much the same ways. The surprise finding is that the inventory graphs for some of them are even much alike in shape, except for height. Exhibit 22.1 is for three Canadian petro companies in the database, one of them the aforementioned Imperial Oil. An uncanny similarity showed itself first for these three companies because their graphs happened to be together in the same PowerPoint display. Give or take a year or two, the 10-year pattern starts with up in 1996; then it heads down in 1998, up in 2000, down in 2002, and way up in 2005.

A look through the rest of the petro-company graphs, and overlaying them onto Exhibit 22.1, turned up several more with about the same pattern: Amerada Hess, Exxon Mobil, Giant Industries, Holly Corp., Marathon Oil, Murphy Oil, Santos Ltd.

(Australia), and Tonen General (Japan). Further inspection revealed four more that fit the pattern, though a bit less perfectly. The ups and downs for Ashland, Inc. (which became a part of Marathon in 2005) are like those in Exhibit 22.1, but with much less amplitude. Woodside Petroleum (Australia) is the opposite—extremely large ups and downs. Woodside actually had been removed to an inactive file. Some of its inventory-turnover numbers had gotten so large—89 turns in 2000 and 147 in 2003—that we assumed, wrongly, that Woodside had become exclusively an extractor and no longer an inventory-intensive processor. Its graph, though, had been retained, and visual inspection showed that its turns were well matched with 7 years of the 10-year pattern: high in 1996, down in 1998, way up in 2000, and way down in 2002; then, way up, but in 2003 rather than 2005. Total SA (France) is like Woodside, with the same ups and downs to 2003. Both Woodside and Total trended down in 2004, 2005, and 2006, contrary to that part of the pattern.

That makes 14 of 43 companies much alike in ups and downs in inventory turnover. What all this suggests, tentatively, is the following:

- It's not coincidence. The commonality can be explained only by an external force—the market.
- These 14 are not sheep following the leader. All have positive long-term leanness trends, which means progressive tightening of their links with global demands. That suggests a succession of process improvements, internally and with suppliers and customers.
- Most of the other 29 petro companies, by not following the same tighten-with-demand pattern, would seem to be losing ground competitively. Some may compensate with superior technology, timing, or financial expertise. Others, especially those operating under protectionist governments—such as Mexico's PEMEX—seem destined to fall further behind.
- As petroleum goes, so will go other industries, because petroleum is among the most globally sensitive on the planet (except where protected). The scenario is that global demand becomes chronically in excess of supply. This forces companies, the most astute anyway, to step up their improvement activities. They generate innovative practices for tightening linkages all along their value chains. Before long, because of lockstep reactions to factors that change demand and supply, the companies with improving trends will come to look alike in their inventory-turnover ups and downs.

From the upside of liquids/gases/grains/powders we go to the downside. Chemicals and pharmaceuticals are alike in that both are ranked very low on long-range leanness: pharmaceuticals 33rd of the 33 industries and chemicals 30th. They are a pair in that pharmaceuticals come from chemical processes. They differ in other respects. Pharma produces high-margin, highly regulated, highly marketed, specialized products requiring long development times. Chemicals are lower-margin, capital-intensive products with mostly commodity-like marketing.

CHEMICALS: 30TH RANKED

The 106 chemical companies in the research are not all weak on inventory performance. Five of them look outstanding not only within chemicals but among all 1,200-plus companies studied. Already featured, in Chapter 17, was Rohm & Haas, up 1.2 percent yearly for 31 years. The others are Sterling Chemicals, 2.4 percent, 33 years; Clorox, 2.8 percent, 26 years; AECI (South Africa), 2.9 percent, 21 years; and Kemira (Finland), 3.2 percent, 22 years. Besides those five, 12 other chemical companies meet the criteria for an *A* grade.

At the other extreme are 26 *D*- and *F*-graded chemical manufacturers, 13 of them Japanese. Overall, the 106 chemical manufacturers include 30 Japanese companies compared with 26 U.S. and 13 German. For Japan, all that in-country competition might be expected to drive high levels of improvement. It has not. Likely obstacles are the common ones: Japanese industry being late to restructure, and disinclination to look for best practices originating elsewhere.

Chapter 2 noted, though, that things are looking up for Japan, which has improved its leanness score somewhat in the twenty-first century. A close look shows the same in chemicals. Twenty of the 30 Japanese companies have improved their inventory turns in the past 3 to 5 years.

For its size, the Germany/Austria region is a far more concentrated center for chemical manufacturing than the United States. Leanness grades are evenly distributed for these companies: two *A*'s, one *B*, seven *C*'s, one *D*, and two *F*'s. The United States contingent is similarly distributed: three *A*'s, four *B*'s, 14 *C*'s, four *D*'s, and one *F*. Most of the German 13 are in chemicals secondarily. Their primary sectors tend to be pharmaceuticals (e.g., Bayer, Boehringer Ingelheim, and Degussa) and petroleum (e.g., Erdoelchemie and OMV AG). Most in the U.S. 26 are just chemical companies. A probe of the entire list of 106 chemical companies shows that single-industry companies and multiple-industry companies have about the same long-term leanness scores.

To sum up these findings in the chemicals sector, Japan's insularity stands out as a strong negative influence on process improvement. Localism tends to have a stultifying effect. No other factor emerges as making much difference.

PHARMACEUTICALS: 33RD RANKED

Of 66 pharmaceutical companies in the leanness database, just two merit a grade of *A*. One is Johnson & Johnson, with a 1.3 percent annual rate of improvement for 19 years. The other, getting an *A* by a slim margin, is Japan-based Taisho, which raised its inventory turns from a low of 3.21 in 1993 to 3.67 in 2006. One company qualifies for a *B*: Johnson Matthey (U.K.). *D*'s (14), and *F*'s (7) are so much more numerous than the *A*'s and *B*'s that the average score for the pharma group is a mere 0.01. That is nearly a negative score, and it would be if just one of the two *A*'s were missing. The average score for pharmaceuticals has been going down since 2002, when it was 0.30—then, as now, by far the lowest score of the 33 sectors.

The average score, however, may have hit bottom. The small sign of that is that nine companies are graded *C+* (Asahi Kasei, Bayer, Boehringer Ingelheim, Chiron, Elan, Kyowa Hakko Kogyo, Novartis, Numico, and Roche Holdings). The plus sign, worth ½ point, is for steady (not jumpy) improvement in the most recent 5 to 7 years in a 10-year span with no clear trend otherwise. Perhaps the nine companies are the vanguard: pharmas that are finally reversing the dominant, dubious mode of the industry. Among the elements of that mode is a sales and market-share strategy of pushing more and more inventory into the pipelines. (For a very small number of drugs, though, it is prudent and necessary to build huge stocks. For example, there needs to be plenty of vaccine or serum in the unlikely but possible and unpredictable event of a disease pandemic.) Another is paying little heed to operational efficiency and costs of production, because profit margins have been so high. What attention operations does get is mostly on compliance, not process improvement.[3] It is possible, as well, that the operations end of the business is money- and talent-starved. Science gets the big money and support.

For all that, governmental and social pressures on healthcare to rein in costs and improve quality may be having their effects. The main factor may have something to do with RFID (radio-frequency identification). The healthcare industry has stood by and watched for many years as other industries have parlayed bar-coding into some semblance of synchronization along the pipelines. The main, new impetus for the industry to take the electronic-tagging plunge is probably not cost so much as global counterfeiting of drugs.[4] The industry cannot stand still if people die by the thousands because of tainted medicines. Nor will governments stand for it. Tagging right down to pill delivery at the hospital bed can save lives one at a time by preventing wrong meds being delivered to the wrong patient at the wrong time.[5]

Now RFID is overtaking plain old bar-coding. Pharmaceuticals, with plenty of profit margin to play with, see good reason to get involved. For example, Cardinal Health is interested in an advanced, high-frequency version called *UHF RFID*. In early 2006, it inaugurated a nine-month feasibility study of using UHF RFID for keeping tabs on products at the unit, case, and pallet level. Cardinal's interest is twofold. Besides its manufacturing arm, it has a large 3PL drug-distribution business.[6] If electronic tagging's day has come to pharma and healthcare, it is owing to four combined forces: cost, quality, market synchronization, and effectiveness. Of these, quality—mostly meaning product integrity—is number one. Market synchronization, which collapses lead times and slashes inventories while keeping pipelines full and fresh, may be seen merely as an afterthought or by-product.

HIGH-SCORING LGP SUBSECTORS: CEMENT AND CLEANING/ SKIN-CARE PRODUCTS

Within LGP are two sub-industries with good trends in long-term inventory turnover. One is cement and aggregates. That subsector is made up of 24 companies that average a high 0.80, mainly because 9 of them are graded *A*. They are: Associated Cement (India), which has the most impressive rate (2.2 percent) and time span (25 years) of the cement companies; Boral (Australia); Buzzi Unicem and Italcementi (Italy); Cemex (Mexico); Cimenteries CBR (Belgium); Eerste Nederlandse Cement Industries (Netherlands); St. Lawrence Cement (Canada); and Titan Cement (Greece). (Cimenteries and Eerste have not been publicly traded for a few years. They have not yet been retired from the database because of its prime focus on long-term trend, not on the latest level of leanness.)

What, no U.S. companies in the group? The leanness research includes only one U.S.-based cement manufacturer. *C*-graded Lone Star Industries is still in the database although it was bought a few years ago by Dyckerhoff of Germany, which in 2005 was bought by Buzzi Unicem of Italy. In 1980, 22 percent of U.S. cement capacity was foreign owned. By 2003, that figure had gone up to 81 percent.[7] (The other 19 percent may be privately held or do not meet the required 15 years of being publicly held.) Global consolidation has created giant companies with the financial wherewithal to invest heavily in newer, more efficient cement-making technologies. At least some of these companies are well versed on lean manufacturing. Italcementi, for one, was involved in JIT and TPM training in the 1980s.[8]

The second high-scoring subsector is companies specializing in cleaning and skin-care products—mainly soaps and cosmetics—11 of them. Their mean score on long-term inventory trend is a very high 1.14. That score is bulwarked by 6 *A*-graded companies: Colgate-Palmolive, Rev Holdings, Godrej Industries (India), Henkel (Germany), L'Oreal (France), and Unilever (U.K. and Netherlands). L'Oreal's 1.6 percent rate of improvement for 26 years is best of the 11, though its turns fell a bit in 2004 and 2005. (Several other producers of soaps and cosmetics are not counted in this tally because they are primarily in the chemical or pharmaceutical sector.) That this subsector should score well makes sense. These are packaged consumer goods manufacturers. They either get their operations into the close synchronization of the Wal-Marts of the world, or wither.

FOOD/BEVERAGE/TOBACCO: 24TH RANKED

"Food Banks Go Hungry." So said a headline in the business press.[9] Why? Because "many food manufacturers began producing food in quantities more closely tailored to individual retail customers' needs." In addition, improved quality "eliminates production errors such as producing canned food without labels or producing an entire order of cereal boxes using upside-down text." The improved processes reduce overstocks, over-age goods, mislabeled items, dented cans, and so forth that formerly would find their way to food banks. The odd, unfortunate food-bank effect, notwithstanding lean/supply-chain management/TQ, is alive and well in food/beverage/tobacco.

But that observation is selective. Atria (nee, Philip Morris), Campbell Soup, and Pepsico, had 30-year (more-or-less) upward trends that stalled or reversed direction in the 1990s and 2000s. The same pattern applies to Nestle (Switzerland) and Uniq (U.K.), except for a reduced number of years of upward trend. (The database goes back fewer years for non-U.S. companies). Campbell's low year was 1957 when its inventory turns were 2.6, and its peak was in 1995 at 6.3 turns. To its credit, after a slump Campbell has improved for five years for a current grade of C+.

Five others of the 134 companies in the food/beverage/tobacco sector are a better fit with contemporary expectations. Skandinavisk Tobakskompagni (Denmark), tobacco and also convenience stores, has raised its inventory turnover at an annual rate of 3.9 percent for 23 years. The rate is 2.9 percent for 25 years at Fraser & Neave (Singapore), producer of soft drinks, milk and dairy products, and beer. Just as impressive are Dole Foods, 2.3 percent for 34 years; H.J. Heinz, 1.9 percent for 32 years; and Lancaster Colony (sauces, unbaked pies, frozen breads and noodles), 1.8 percent for 33 years.

But eight companies, four based in the U.S. and four in Japan, are quite the opposite. Hormel (meats) has a negative trend of 3.0 percent for 37 years; Bridgford Foods (meats, frozen foods processor, and wholesaler), negative 2.2 percent for 34 years; Smithfield Foods (meats), negative 3.3 percent for 26 years; and Conagra Foods, negative 2.6 percent for 21 years. The other four with severely worsening trends are: Nissin Food (ramens, soups, frozen foods), minus 3.0 percent for 23 years; Nisshin Seifun (flour, bakery mixes, ready-to-eat foods), minus 2.2 percent for 23 years; Meiji Seika Kaisha (confections), minus 2.1 percent for 20 years; and Nippon Meat Packers, minus 2.7 percent for 19 years. Exhibit 22.2 provides examples: the down-trend for Hormel (meats), the up–down trend for PepsiCo (soft drinks and snack foods), and the uptrend for Skandinavisk Tobakskompagni (tobacco).

Since Hormel's bad-looking graph was to be included, I invited the company to comment. Fred Halvin in Hormel's investor relations office pointed out that Hormel's product mix has changed steadily since the 1970s. Something like 80 percent of its output had been in the form of commodity-like products such as bulk-boxed fresh pork and bone-in hams, which had to move quickly from processing to markets. Today such products are more like 20 percent. Dominant today are a value-added mix of products requiring capital-intensive processing and more steps, such as smoking, precooking, slicing, high-pressure, and infusion with flavorings. Advanced packaging technologies provide films that preserve freshness, flavors, and shelf life. Hormel still makes lots of Spam, but profit margins are much better today on the newer mix of products.

Another source, however, indicates that Hormel clings to an outmoded method of operational control: time standards for labor efficiency reporting.[10] Chapter 10 explained that that heavy-handed control system is contrary to today's thinking about the management of human resources. It is a poor alternative to cross-training and work-force empowerment. More to the point, the focus on labor efficiency encourages over-production, which is opposite to the JIT/lean mandate to synchronize production to demand.

The situation at Hormel may apply somewhat to Bridgford, Conagra, and Nippon Meat. Perhaps it applies in general to other food processors as well. Whether it does or not, wrong-way trends in inventory turnover should be seen for what they represent: increasing remoteness from the market and the undesirable mode of producing to inaccurate forecasts.

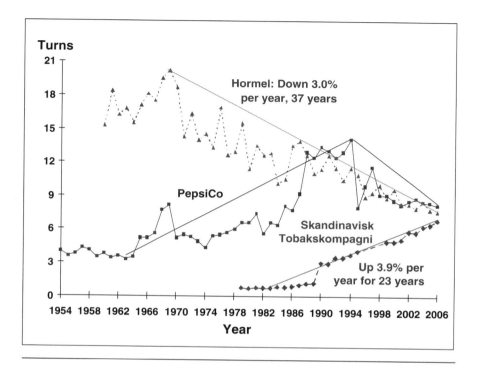

Exhibit 22.2   Contrasting Trends in Inventory Turnover, Three Food/Beverage/Tobacco Companies

   In most food processing, work-in-process is nearly nil. The live chicken, ear of corn, truckload of grain, or milk in the cow are raw materials. Their arrival at the manufacturer opens them to the elements. For the sake of freshness and sterility, they must be processed and packaged in quick time. Thus, the inventory breakdown of most food processors is mostly finished goods, a modest percentage of purchased materials, and hardly any WIP. Getting lean, therefore, does not have much to do with the factory. It is a matter of getting close to real demand by shrinking the pipelines, chiefly those at the finished-goods end of the value chain.

   Detailed data are available for several of the above-named companies with worsening leanness. The data show that finished goods account for not only large, but growing percentages of total inventory. Thus, these down-trending companies are pushing greater amounts of product into the finished-goods pipelines. If they are also trying to adopt Wal-Mart-like practices and technologies for shrinking the pipelines, that makes two strategies at cross purposes—which is good for no one but competitors (and maybe food banks).

METAL-WORKING/MACHINING (MM): 8TH RANKED

For metal-working/machining, being 8th ranked on leanness means that many of the sector's 241 companies have long records of improvement in inventory turnover. That means reducing supply, production, and delivery lead times with customers. The top-ranked Nordic global region includes—no surprise—several of the notable achievers: for example, Sweden's SKF (bearings), up 2.5 percent yearly for 29 years; and Denmark's NKT (cables, vehicular sweepers), up 1.8 percent for 27 years.

Others in the MM sector worth mentioning are three long hitters, to use a golf analogy. Their improvement trends exceed 30 years. That means they were shedding lead time, flow time, and inventory 10 to 15 years before the dawning of the JIT/lean age in western industry. And they still are doing so. They are U.S.-based L.S. Starrett and Mine Safety Appliances (MSA), and Schlumberger, headquartered in Netherlands Antilles. One other with a 30-plus-year trend, but going the wrong way, is Tecumseh Products (pumps, compressors, gasoline engines for yard care, etc.), down 1.6 percent per year for 31 years. Exhibit 22.3 displays the graphs for those four manufacturers.

MSA, producing respirators, gas detectors, and other safety equipment, has the longest span, 38 years. It is also nearly a straight line, but with a bit of an upward

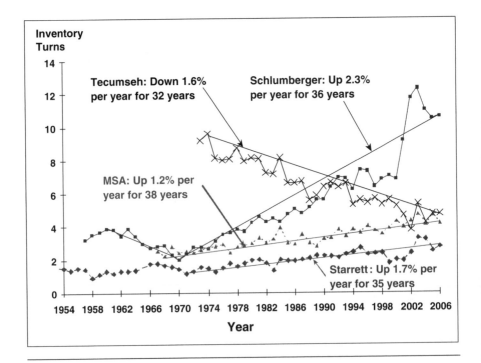

Exhibit 22.3 Long Up- or Down-Trends, for Four in Metal-working/Machining

slant—a better rate of improvement—from 1989 to 2006. Schlumberger's excellent 36-year rise was at an average yearly rate even better than its current 2.3 percent before its past three down years. As an oil-field equipment maker, Schlumberger's story matches up well with that of its petroleum-industry customers. L.S. Starrett's 35-year, 1.7 percent improvement is as a producer of coordinate measurement equipment, and also tools.

For many companies, especially non-U.S. based, the database does not go back far enough to reveal trends as long as 30 years. If we had the additional data, no doubt other companies would look as good. Usually (not always) very long upward trends indicate consistency, continual learning of best practices, and continual improvement of processes.

The entire metal-working/machining sector, including the 241 publicly held companies in the database, is too vast and diverse for detailed sorting out. Rather we limit further discussion to two subsectors—machine tools and specialized end-use equipment. Final remarks about the many small shops not included in our research follow.

The database includes just 11 purely machine-tool manufacturers, though a few other diversified companies are machine-tool producers secondarily. Of the 11, Milacron gets the lone A, and three Japanese companies get F's: Amada, Okuma, and Toshiba Machine. What can we make of these overall low grades?

Based on my own plant visits, machine tools looks something like aerospace-defense a decade ago. Performance and advanced technology are everything. Of low concern are throughput times, inventories, and flow distances. Lack of concern applies as well to excesses in some of the machine-tool makers' factories. Examples are: (1) large numbers of machines in a state of assembly, (2) serial processing in final assembly rather than parallel production of modules in nearby subassembly cells, and (3) demonstrator systems with elaborate ways to store and move parts and tools. Emphasis is on dazzling the customer. Some customers will be wrongly influenced, emulating weaker practices of the machine-tool makers.

Another smaller MM subsector specializes in end-use machines for gambling, banking, ticketing, point-of-sale transactions, and the like. Most impressive of the group is A-graded NCR (ATMs and POS equipment) with a 26-year, 2.6-percent-per-year uptrend in inventory turnover (although sharply down in the past 4 years). Companies producing similar kinds of equipment have some good lean history behind them. In the mid-1980s, Control Data's Lottery Division in Arden Hills, Minnesota, was engaged in bidding wars. One of its larger bids was for providing all lottery machines for the state of Florida. Contracting people from Florida paid the Minnesota plant a visit and found it devoid of finished machines, whereas other bidders had finished units in stock. The Control Data people had to talk fast. They explained that their JIT manufacturing was so quick and flexible that they produced to order rather than holding finished-goods inventory. They would deliver all machines on time as the contract specified. Control Data won the five-year contract, ramped up a second shift, and began churning out 320 big lottery terminals a week.[11]

International Game Technology, a leading supplier of gambling machines today, may owe something to Control Data's early implementation of the lean core. IGT is *A*-graded with an upward trend in inventory turns at a 2.9 percent average over the 23 years since 1983—which is around the same year that Control Data Lotteries began implementing JIT production. The two companies may have competed on the same lean terms. Two other current lottery/casino gambling machine makers have not followed suit. GTech Holdings and WMS Industries have been stuck at very low levels of inventory turnover—around 2.0—for 10 or more years.

Large numbers of machining job shops do not get their due here, because they usually are small, privately owned, and not in the leanness database. There is plenty going on among these firms, though. Many are joining the upward movement into assembly. They do so as a valued service to their customers, who are interested in reducing their numbers of component parts, simplifying their production, and shortening their own throughput times. Also, thanks to flexible CNC (computer numerical-controlled) equipment and high-speed machining, the job machining shops have floor space available.[12]

PLASTIC/RUBBER/GLASS/CERAMICS: 9TH RANKED

There are 210 manufacturers in the plastic/rubber/glass/ceramics (abbreviated *PRG*) sector. Just a few of them are identifiable with ceramics. Of the rest, we have isolated 79 companies for which PRG products are a fairly dominant or critical line of business. That excludes many that produce PRG items secondarily, and also others that specialize in basic raw materials but very little in end products made from them. (Petrochemical companies produce the resins and powders that are raw materials for plastics. They are among the 79 if they produce both the raw materials and the products; otherwise not.) The PRG group includes 18 producers identified with rubber, 20 glass, and 41 plastic.

The rubber products companies have unimpressive leanness scores: one *A*, one *B*, but three *F*'s. Germany's Continental was already noted in Chapter 20 for its grade-*A* improvement trend. Avon Rubber (U.K.) gets the *B*. The other rubber tires/belts/hoses makers are a drag on overall scores and ranking for both PRG and the automotive components sector.

Grades are better for the glass-makers: five *A*'s and two *B*'s, countered by just one *D* and one *F*. Pilkington (U.K.) had one of the two best-looking trends, but its last year was 2004, when Nippon Sheet Glass bought the company. Executives at the Japanese company may or may not have appreciated the lean expertise that came with the purchase. The difference shows up in Exhibit 22.4. Pilkington had a strong uptrend of 1.7 percent per year for 29 years, whereas Nippon Sheet was on the borderline between *C* and *D* grades. (It actually gets a *C*, because the upward spike in 1995 interferes positively with the downward trend.) Bausch & Lomb, also in the exhibit, has an improvement trend that curls upward somewhat. That shape, signifying improvement in the rate of improvement, is the subject of Chapter 4, in which Bausch & Lomb was listed in an "honorable-mention" group.

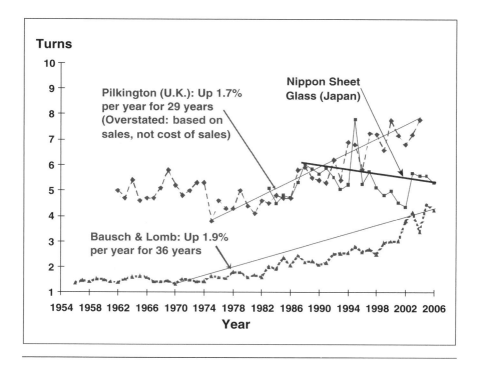

Turns

Exhibit 22.4   Inventory Turnover Trends for Three Glass Manufacturers

The 41 companies producing plastics products have strong lean credentials overall. Fifteen get *A* grades and five get *B*'s, as compared with just three *D*'s and two *F*'s. The high average grades are indicative of a competitive industry, which puts the pressure on those lacking in lean and quality credentials. The vast majority of molders and extruders are privately held (e.g., Webster Plastics and Phillips Plastics, discussed in Chapter 13), and thus not included in the leanness database.

A strong example is Milton Plastics in Pune, India, producing insulated containers, thermo ware, and special-purpose containers for drugs and vaccines. An early step in Milton's lean journey was to break up the plant into five product-focused plants-in-a-plant, each with its own dedicated molding machines, materials area, and assembly and pack stations. Conveyors and walls were torn out, and a full complement of lean-core practices came in: color-coding, quick-change molding equipment, empowered improvement teams, and job rotation. Also, the facility practiced "management by process" rather than "management by results." With kanban linkage to molding machines, storage was reduced 60 percent. Within storage the emphasis was on "search-free, count-free, air-free, and climb-free" practices. Reported results include reduction of throughput time from 12 days to five hours, WIP inventory by 97 percent, and floor space by 50 percent.[13]

As in metal-working/machining, plastics include large numbers of small privately held shops excluded from the leanness database. They, too, are moving up the food chain into assembly. Aside from the usual reasons, here is one more, pointed out by Len Czuba, whose molding firm specializes in plastic medical devices: "The industry realized that at the time of molding, the part is oriented."[14] It is natural, then, to run the part down a conveyor directly into an assembly station for joining with another part.

DISTRIBUTION: 2ND RANKED; RETAIL: 23RD RANKED

Nonmanufacturers in the research database—47 distributors and 131 retailers—are even more inventory dependent than the manufacturers. Judging by their high rank—2nd out of the 33 industries—the distributors/wholesalers seem to have figured this out. More than half have good grades (19 *A*'s, 2 *B*'s) or improving grades (5 with *C*+). For example, Avnet, a global distributor of electronic parts, has improved its turns at an annual rate of 3.7 percent for 18 years.

Genuine Parts, distributor for the automotive replacement market and also of industrial parts and office products, does not fare so well. The record of *F*-graded Genuine Parts had been 39 years of steadily worsening inventory turns before turning up a bit in 2003 through 2006. Sid Jones, VP of Investor Relations at Genuine, did not attempt to explain the first 30 years of the downside. He did offer comments on more recent years. First, cars are more durable, so Genuine must maintain more parts for more car models longer. Second, he spoke of parts proliferation. Genuine stocks some 320,000 different automotive parts. Just for new vehicles in 2006, it added 34,000 new parts, while retiring just 18,000.[15] Parts proliferation? The auto industry keeps telling us that it is bent on parts standardization via DFMA. As for Genuine's performance, its suppliers in the motor vehicle industry may deserve much of the blame. Still, overall—given the high rank of the distribution/wholesale sector—Genuine's performance looks genuinely weak.

Retail, however, ranks low, 23rd of the 33 sectors. That may change. Retailers (134 companies) that have been improving their inventory turns in recent years outnumber those getting worse. In between are 71 that are graded *C*. One of the latter, is Lowe's the U.S. building-materials retailer. Seemingly way off the lean mark, Lowe's' 2006 annual report states, as a supply-chain objective, running more goods through its distribution centers. No wonder its grade is *C*. One best practice in pipeline management is getting more goods to go direct from producers to stores, *by-passing* the retailers' DCs. (Home Depot, Lowe's' chief competitor also grades *C*.)

Though the retail rank is low, chain stores that sell groceries, exclusively or partly, are strong and maybe getting stronger in leanness. Of 32 *A*-graded retailers, 11 are in groceries. They include 7-Eleven, Wal-Mart, and South Africa's Pick 'N Pay—all innovators in practices that elevate inventory turns while keeping shelves filled with what customers are buying.

7-Eleven has come a long way since 1991, when it was losing money and market share. Since then, the company has abandoned its preference for vertical integration. ("It even owned the cows that produced the milk it sold.") In moving to outsourcing of

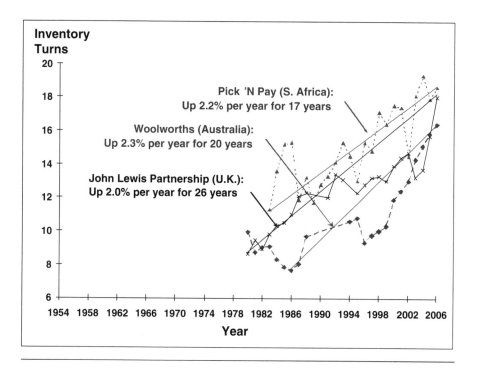

Exhibit 22.5 Inventory Turnovers for Two Grocery Chains and an Apparel Chain

whatever was not in its strategic core, 7-Eleven retained ownership of customer data. Some of its supplier-partners deliver right to the stores and fill shelves, but 7-Eleven specifies lot sizes and frequencies of delivery. By keeping close tabs on buying patterns, different from one store to the next, 7-Eleven typically gets deliveries at least daily for many fresh items. Formerly, deliveries were only a couple of times per week.[16]

Exhibit 22.5 shows three examples of companies in groceries that have strong upward trends. The Pick 'N Pay chain has a 2.2 percent annual rate extending for 17 years; that of the Woolworths supermarket chain in Australia is slightly better, 2.3 percent for 20 years. The uptrend is at a rate of 2.0 percent for an even longer stretch, 26 years, for the U.K.-based John Lewis Partnership, a chain of grocery and department stores.

Other grocers are pressed to learn and apply lessons from the leaders. Slim profit margins, along with global expansion of leading chains, do not allow much competitive wiggle room. The following companies in the supermarket business have been improving their inventory turns in recent years, which should raise some of their scores and grades within a year or two: Albertson's, Ingles Markets, Marsh Supermarkets, and Weis Markets in the United States; and Ahold (Netherlands), Delhaize (Belgium) and Sainsbury (U.K.). Also with uptrends are two department-store chains

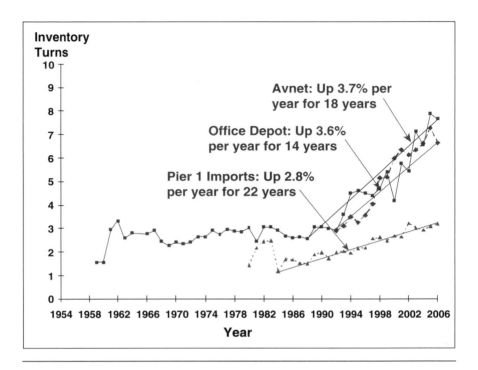

Exhibit 22.6   Inventory Turnover Trends for Avnet, Office Depot, and Pier 1 Imports

that include food markets in most of their stores: Carrefour (France) and Karstadt Quelle (Germany). If the trend continues, foods may pull the whole retail sector up some notches in the leanness rankings. In turn, their expertise should press some of the food/beverage/tobacco producers to improve as well.

Besides the grocers, a variety of other kinds of retailers have enough leanness to be *A*-graded. A few are petroleum companies that have their own gas stations with convenience stores. Others are furniture makers that have their own furniture stores. Two large office supply retailers, Home Depot and Staples, have almost identical 14-year upward trends. Exhibit 22.6 shows that of Staples, along with the nearly arrow-straight 22-year improvement trend of furniture retailer Pier 1 Imports. The third company in the exhibit is Avnet, the electronics distributor discussed earlier in this section. Avnet's turns had hovered around 3 for some 25 years until the late 1980s. Perhaps Avnet's awakening was related to its JIT-inspired customers in electronics.

FINAL REMARKS

This chapter, and all of Part VI, uses long-term inventory-turnover data for ranking industries, and for scoring and grading companies within those industries. That is because almost any sort of process improvement has inventory reduction as a by-product. Improving product design or administration and accounting, upgrading the labor force and facilities, or tightening supply and customer pipelines reduces the need for inventory. The more vital benefits go to the customer, namely quicker, more flexible response, better quality, and greater value.

The advantage can be lost, though, if there is too little inventory. There is always a happy medium between too little inventory protection and too much. But progress is in the direction of less. Finally, it must be said again: Inventory reduction is not a proper goal. Inventory is but a symptom, and its reduction must come from fixing processes, not the other way around.

NOTES

1. Chip Cummins, Bhushan Bahree, and Jeffrey Ball, *Wall Street Journal* (September 24–25, 2005), pp. A1–A2.

2. Phone interview and e-mail correspondence (April 2007).

3. A quote from an anonymous engineer at Aventis-Pasteur: Monica Elliot, "Strong Medicine: Can Lean Manufacturing Help the Pharmaceutical Industry Get Better?" *Industrial Engineer* (February 2006), pp. 39–43.

4. Purdue Pharmaceuticals, maker of OxyContin, preferred by addicts, conceals RFID tags behind the bottles' existing labels: "Vertical Focus," *DC Velocity* (April 2005), pp. 28–29. Counterfeiting has the attention of the technology providers as well. Cardinal Health and GlaxoSmithKline have contracted with IBM's RFID system, which is mainly targeted as an anticounterfeiting technology: "IBM Rolls Out RFID Systems," *DC Velocity* (September 2006), p. 37.

5. St. Alexius Medical Center in Bismarck, North Dakota, on its own, began applying barcodes to incoming items in 1985, and before long was scanning every supply item or pill in patients' rooms, thus stamping out the wrong-medication problem: Richard J. Schonberger, *Let's Fix It! How the World's Leading Manufacturers Were Seduced by Prosperity and Lost Their Way* (New York: Free Press/Simon & Schuster, 2001), pp. 211–212.

6. John R. Johnson, "Pharmaceutical Market Tunes in to UHF," *DC Velocity* (January 2007), p. 33.

7. "Economics of the U.S. Cement Industry," Portland Cement Association, November 2006 update, found at www.cement.org/econ/industry.asp (March 21, 2007). Also, "Overview of the Cement Industry," Portland Cement Association, May 2003 update, found at www.cement.org/basics/cementindustry.asp (March 21, 2007).

8. Italcementi had engaged Milan-based Efeso Consulting on JIT and TPM matters. Richard Schonberger conducted training at Italcementi in October 1987.

9. Lauren Etter, "Food Banks Go Hungry," *Wall Street Journal*, May 22, 2007, pp. B1, B12.

10. Rob R. Kekkonen, "Hormel Gets Technical," *Industrial Engineer* (July 2007), pp. 38–43.

11. Dave Peters, "CDC Wagers Big on Lottery Division," *St. Paul Pioneer Press Dispatch* (February 22, 1988), pp. 1, 9. Richard Schonberger visited the Lottery Division in about that time period.

12. Malcolm Mason, business director at the Association for Manufacturing Technology, makes this point as a contributor to: Austin Weber, "Upstream Assembly," *Assembly* (March 2007), pp. 26–32.

13. Yogesh Vaghani, "Milton Plastics Ltd., Pune, India: A Kaizen Dream Unfolds," *Target* 4th issue (2005), pp. 21–30.

14. Austin Weber, "Upstream Assembly," *Assembly* (March 2007), pp. 26–32.

15. Phone interview with Sid Jones (April 24, 2007).

16. Mark Gottfredson, Rudy Puryear, and Stephen Phillips, "Strategic Sourcing: From Periphery to the Core," *Harvard Business Review* (February 2005), pp. 132–139.

Epilogue

Everyone wants to be slim and trim, but few achieve that aim. Or they achieve it but are unable to maintain it. And so it is with lean in industry. In either case, it is because there are too many diversions and too little perseverance. That may explain why so many companies are losing ground in the lean quest. The research shows that, both in the long run and over the past few years, most companies, industries, and regions are getting worse on the main leanness metric, *inventory*. Lead times are lengthening, and companies are losing connectivity with customers and suppliers.

Most of the inventory and the lead-time growth, and the many problems they cover up, are in the pipelines. One reason seems obvious: elevated global risks. Friedman's *The World Is Flat*, though, gets you thinking. If there is validity to the Theory of Conflict Prevention, the world is less scary than we thought. That means risk is less of a reason for all that inventory in global pipelines.

That brings us to the second obvious reason for long, bulging pipelines: Ever-more goods move to and from distant, developing countries. The truism that all that off-shoring is raising global inventories is amply supported by the leanness data. Yet one industry, electronics, bucks the trend. The strategy of sending production to whoever can do it best spawned the huge electronics manufacturing services sector. In so doing, it made the electronics industry by far the most geographically dispersed. For all that dispersal, electronics scores high on long-term leanness.

MULTIPLE RESPONSES

Some companies, and not just in electronics, have been able to keep reducing inventories as they expand globally. Best practices for doing so are known and in use. Collaboration, logistics, and IT are direct means. Standardization, modularity, and flexible capacity are among the less direct factors. A many-faceted, continuous effort to improve quality, response time, flexibility, and value—the golden goals of customers—gets results.

A few companies grow, and grow leaner, by astute acquisitions, mergers, and divestures. They mine acquired companies for talent. They assign best people to the new business units as turnaround experts and specialists in process improvement. In providing them with challenges, they retain their best people.

The most potent process improvers do not use known concepts and tools so much as they develop new ones. These innovators are driven to do so by their own special business models, two of which have been presented: Dell-direct and Wal-Mart's EDLP (everyday low prices).

Yet, the problem remains—that of weak, weakened, and lost expertise in wide-angle process improvement. Part of the deficiency is that most companies take an approach that is overly narrow and limited—necessary but insufficient. The lean core is one example. The project form of process improvement is another.

OUTCOMES, INPUTS, AND BEST PRACTICES

The desired outcomes of lean/total quality are well known. They trip off the tongue like *amen*s at the ends of prayers. Many of them use a form of the verb, *to reduce*, as in reduce response times, throughput times, lot sizes, setup times, scrap, rework, defectives, and variation.

Desirable inputs do not come to mind quite so readily. By inputs, we mean the *means*—the resources and processes required to bring about the desired outcomes of lean/TQ. Historically, the means have not received their fair share of emphasis—in the form of clear-cut best practices. Tom Johnson and Anders Bröms's much-quoted book, which is all about *management by means*, helps correct that deficiency.[1] So does a newish academic subfield of management and economics called the *resource-based view of the firm* (RBV). As applied to means of achieving big-*L* lean, here are a few prominent areas of best practice, each receiving a fair amount of discussion in the chapters of this book:

Less: inventory, accounting, inspection, material handling, kitting, and stock-picking; also, a process: management goal-setting.
More: cells, machines, load/unload docks, and fabrication capacity; also, processes: training, cross-training, cross-careering, job rotation, and process data.
Fewer: conveyors, fork trucks, stockrooms, transactions, job classifications, component parts, and suppliers.
Smaller: machines, containers, and factories.
Shorter: production lines and assembly lines.
Longer: value streams and linked supply/customer chains.

Best Practices, as a whole, is about responding to the customer quickly, dependably, and well. Process improvement is not a short-term pursuit, nor a narrow one. It is never-ending. And its reach is broad enough to take in the many interrelated effects of a process change. Until you've seen the broad effects, you don't know if you really are using a best practice.

NOTE

1. H. Thomas Johnson and Anders Bröms, *Profit Beyond Measure: Extraordinary Results through Attention to Work and People* (New York: Free Press/Simon & Schuster, 2000).

Index

D

Daihatsu, x, 233, 236, 238

Daimler-Chrysler, 52, 148, 162, 184, 187, 232, 242

Dana, x, 238–239, 241–242, 244n

Danaher, x, 119, 121–125, 134, 171, 240

Dashboards, 45, 58, 77–79

Dassault, x, 248

Data collection (see also, Process data), 53
  on job-related fears, 61, 207
  on job-related frustrations, 61, 63–65

Data General, 221

Davies, Christopher, 70n

Day, Joseph, 174, 181n

Dealerships, motor-vehicle, 166, 234–235

Deere & Co., 233, 236–237, 244n

Degusa, 259

Delhaize, 269

Dell Theory of Conflict Prevention, 195

Dell, Michael, 42n

Dell, x, 27–30, 83, 93, 100, 116, 130, 131n, 155, 157–161, 187, 194n, 195, 209n, 219, 224–226, 229, 256

Dell-direct, 111–112, 159

Delphi, x, 52, 238, 241, 243, 244n

Delta Airlines, 52

Delta Point, 172

DeLuzio, Mark C., 69n

Demand shaping at Dell, 112

Demand-flow technology (DFT), 138–139

Demand-leveling; see Load-leveling

Deming Prize, 133–134

Deming, W. Edwards, vii, 51, 61–62, 66–67, 69n, 75, 81n, 132

Denso, 240, 242–243

Design for manufacture and assembly (DFMA), 103, 177–179, 198, 203, 243

Design for robotics, 223

Designed [design of] experiments, 50, 103

Deutsche Telecom, 52

Dewhurst, Peter, 43n, 223, 229n

DHL, 201, 205

Diebold, 99

Digital Equipment Corp. (DEC), 221

Dinero, Donald, 254n

Dionics, 196

Direct shipment, 103, 158, 199

Discontinuity, executive, 132, 134

DJO, Inc., x, 104, 109n

DMAIC, 62

Dole Foods, 262

Donaldson, 239

Dong, Jocellyn, 93n

Dorbyl, x, 238–239

Dover Corp., 143

Drew, Dick, 86

Drucker, Peter, 147, 153n, 249, 254n

Duba, John, 140–1241

Duin, Spencer, 136

Dunbar, Lisa, 255n

DuPont, 52, 87, 92n

Dura Automotive, 244n

Dyckerhoff, 261

Dynamit Nobel, 185

E

Eagle Picher, 239

Eastman Kodak, x, 27, 35–37, 43n, 52, 87, 107, 110n, 158

Eaton, x, 134, 136–137, 152n, 188, 239, 241

Echikson, William, 220n

Economic value added (EVA), 40

Economy-of-control principle, 57, 68n

Economy-of-scale, discredited, 150, 182

EDS, 52

Eerste Nederlandse Cement Industries, 261

Ehlers, Edward, 43n

Einhorn, Bruck, 118n

Elan, 260

Elcoteq, 224

Electrolux, 196

Electronic manufacturing services (EMS), ix, 39, 221–224

Elliot, Monica, 271n

Ellison, Sarah, 168n

EMC, 221

Emerson Electric, x, 1, 94–95, 97–99, 101n, 171

Employee involvement, 122, 140, 241, 250

Employee ownership, 4

Empowerment, 4, 7, 53, 59, 104, 140, 221

Engineering changes, 176

Enterprise requirements planning (ERP), 40, 198

Epic Technologies, 72, 81n

Equipment:

Jones, Sid, 268, 272n
Jusko, Jill, 244n
Just-do-its, 134
Just-in-time (JIT):
　as renamed *lean*, 1, 98
　definition of and as philosophy, viii
　deliveries, shipping, 204–205
　fatigue of, 17
　manufacturing/production, 98, 133–135
　purchasing, supply, 133, 197, 205
　with TQC (JIT/TQC), 1, 12

K
Kaizen:
　blitz, 50
　events, 47
　trap, 50
Kampouris, Emmanuel, 138
Kanban:
　as element of visual management, 76
　role and importance of, ix, 23, 28, 107, 253
　quantities set by work force, 73–74
Kanter, Rosabeth Moss, 92n
Kao, John, 92n
Kaplan, Robert S., 68n
Kapoor, Vinod, 136, 151–152n
Karstadt Quelle, 270
Katz, Jonathan, 110n
Kawasaki Heavy Industries, xi, 50, 232–234, 243n
Kayaba Industry Co. 240
Keiretsu, 160–161, 166, 168n, 242–243
Kekkonen, Rob R., 271n
Kemira, 259
Kenwood Corp. 239
Kenworth, xi, 235
Khermouch, Gerry, 167n
Khintchine, Alexander, 142
Kiley, David, 169n, 181n
Kimberley, William, 194n
Kinnevik, xi
Kitting, wasteful practice of, 49, 107–108, 164, 203–204
Kmart, 52
Knight, Charles, 97–99, 101n
Knowledge management, 150
　through sharing rallies, 80–81, 148
　through study missions, 241

Knowledge mis-management, 119, 147
Knowledge transfer, 62, 80
Kolbenschmidt, 239
Komatsu, 232–233, 236
Krafcik, John F., ix
Kubota, xi, 232–234, 238
Kulwiec, Ray, 118n, 167n
Kumar, Ashok, 42n
Kyocera, 52
Kyowa Hakko Kogyo, 260

L
L'Oreal, 158, 261
Labor classifications, reduction of, 136
Lam Research, xi, 27, 37–39, 43n
Lancaster Colony, 262
Latour, A., 230n
Lawler, Edward E. III, 8n, 49, 54n
Laws of Reduction, 199–200
Lawton, Christopher, 42n, 118n
Layout, re-layout, 73, 183, 185
Lazalier, Mike, 72–73, 81n
La-Z-Boy, 196
Lead time; see Flow time
Lean:
　core, ix
　external mode of, 195–196
　fatigue, 17
　origin of, ix
　with total quality (TQ), viii–ix
Lean accounting, 7, 24, 45, 56–57, 68f
Lean machines, 7, 182
Lean manufacturing, 23, 98–99, 174
　as philosophy, 47
Leanness:
　gained through acquisition, 39, 143, 170–171
　grading system for, 26
　long-term, sustained, 12–13
　rankings of, by global regions, 18–19
　scoring, reliability of, 215–218
　scoring system for, 13
Lear, xi, 187, 194n, 240–241
Learmouth, Mark, vii
Learning curve, 251–252, 254, 255n
Learning organization, 27
Lee, Hau L., 42n
Lee, Louise, 118n